D1252811

THE SPIRIT OF ANGLICANISM

THE HALE LECTURES OF
SEABURY-WESTERN THEOLOGICAL SEMINARY

THE HALE LECTURES were established in 1900 under the terms of the will of the Right Reverend Charles Reuben Hale, D.D., LL.D., Bishop Coadjutor of Springfield, Illinois. Born 1837; consecrated July 26, 1892; died December 25, 1900.

It was Bishop Hale's intention that the Lectures should promote 'the Catholic Faith, in its purity and integrity, as taught in Holy Scripture, held by the Primitive Church, summed up in the Creeds, and affirmed by the undisputed General Councils'.

TITLES OF PREVIOUS HALE LECTURES

CHURCH MUSIC IN HISTORY AND PRACTICE. Winfred Douglas. Revised edition, enlarged by Leonard Ellinwood.

AN ERA IN ANGLICAN THEOLOGY. Arthur Michael Ramsey. (In England: FROM GORE TO TEMPLE.)

JOHN WHITGIFT AND THE REFORMATION. P. M. Dawley.

SACRIFICE IN GREEK AND ROMAN RELIGIONS AND EARLY JUDAISM. Royden Keith Yerkes.

THE DOCTRINE OF THE ATONEMENT. Leonard Hodgson.

WITNESS TO THE LIGHT. Alec R. Vidler. (In England: THE THEOLOGY OF F. D. MAURICE.)

THE PERMANENT ELEMENT IN OLD TESTAMENT PROPHECY. Frank Arthur McElwain.

MEN AND MOVEMENTS IN THE AMERICAN EPISCOPAL CHURCH. E. Clowes Chorley.

PERSONALITIES OF THE OLD TESTAMENT. Fleming James.

THE CHURCH IN JAPAN. Henry St. George Tucker. (Published as: THE HISTORY OF THE EPISCOPAL CHURCH IN JAPAN.)

THE PRAISE OF GOD. Winfred Douglas. Published as: CHURCH MUSIC IN HISTORY AND PRACTICE.

THE SOCIAL IMPLICATIONS OF THE OXFORD MOVEMENT. William George Peck.

PASTORAL PSYCHIATRY AND MENTAL HEALTH. John Rathbone Oliver.
(Published as: PSYCHIATRY AND MENTAL HEALTH.)

CHRIST IN THE GOSPELS. Burton Scott Easton.

NEW HORIZONS OF THE CHRISTIAN FAITH. Frederick C. Grant.

SOME ASPECTS OF CONTEMPORARY GREEK ORTHODOX THOUGHT. Frank Gavin.

THE ETHIOPIC LITURGY. Samuel A. B. Mercer.

BIOGRAPHICAL STUDIES IN SCOTTISH CHURCH HISTORY. Anthony Mitchell.

THE NATIONAL CHURCH OF SWEDEN. John Wordsworth.

CHURCH HYMNS AND CHURCH MUSIC. Peter C. Lutkin.

THE SPIRIT
OF ANGLICANISM

✣ ✣ ✣

*A Survey of Anglican Theological Method
in the Seventeenth Century*

HENRY R. McADOO

Bishop of Ossory

Charles Scribner's Sons
New York

Theology, doctrinal

PREFACE

ANGLICANISM is not a theological system and there is no writer whose work is an essential part of it either in respect of content or with regard to the form of its self-expression. Richard Hooker has some claim to be the greatest Anglican writer, but his work was to state a method in theology rather than to outline a system. The concern of the *Ecclesiastical Polity* was with interpretation and application and not with formulation. The absence of an official theology in Anglicanism is something deliberate which belongs to it essential nature, for it has always regarded the teaching and practice of the undivided Church of the first five centuries as a criterion. This appeal to antiquity was closely involved with the distinction between fundamentals and matters of secondary importance. Part of its function was to show that the Church of the first five centuries regarded the credal summaries as the rule of faith, and the whole tenor of seventeenth-century writing indicates that this undifferentiated Catholicism was the pivotal point for Anglican thinking. This was seen within the context of continuity, and both aspects of the appeal to antiquity are brought out, for example, by Bramhall, when he writes that the 'ground for unity of faith is the creed; and for unity of government, the same form of discipline, which was used in the Primitive Church, and is derived from them to us'.[1] Equally consistent in the works of the writers of the period is liberality of outlook on secondary questions. Gore called this a liberal Catholicism but it was in fact simply Anglicanism, and the subject matter of this book is an attempt to show a conscious agreement in this view-point, with varying emphases according to circumstances, on the part of seventeenth-century writers. This chosen image was not only projected explicitly but was implicit in the writing of the period, and the distinctiveness of Anglicanism proceeds not from a systematic theology but from the spirit in which theological questions are handled. This explains in part the title 'The Spirit of Anglicanism'.

It does not follow from the use of the word 'spirit' that what is implied is something indeterminate, an attitude loosely-defined, for the spirit of Anglicanism is something real and ponderable expressing itself by a specific theological method. This theological

1. *Works* (1676), p. 407.

v

method, varying its stress according to the demands of different situations, consists in the appeal to Scripture, to antiquity and to reason, and it is not confined to any individuals or groups during the century. As Paget wrote in his *Introduction to the Fifth Book of Hooker's Ecclesiastical Polity*: 'The distinctive strength of Anglicanism rests on equal loyalty to the unconflicting rights of reason, Scripture and tradition'.

If the distinctiveness of Anglicanism lies not in a theology but in a theological method, the distinctiveness of the method lies in the conjunction of these elements in one theological instrument. The impression of basic unity in the writers of the seventeenth century is accounted for by concurrence in the use of this common theological method. Party theology in the later sense did not exist until the latter part of the century but there were differing emphases in theology. These were minimised by means of a shared method, so that, on occasion, Hammond will take a characteristically Latitudinarian line while Stillingfleet will make use of ideas usually associated with the Laudian point of view.

No attempt is made here to write history, partly from inability to do so, and partly because what is envisaged is the endeavour to examine the elements constituting that theological method by which the spirit of Anglicanism is expressed. But inevitably there lie behind this the stuff and substance of history, the glory and the callousness, the literary sensitivity and the painstaking and often uninspired use of sources, the loyalty and the bigotry, the devotion and the self-seeking, the splendid certainty and the uneasy beginnings of questioning which are the seventeenth century. It was a century which saw the departure of the *Mayflower* and an Archbishop of Canterbury on Tower Hill, the golden era of the Church at work in the country parishes of England and the parochial disruption of the Civil War, the Church appearing to better advantage in persecution than in restored preeminence, the Clarendon code and the deprivations, the sharp beginnings of denominationalism and the hesitating growth of tolerance, the initial rapprochement of scientists and theologians, and the quest of ordinary people for stability amid the unfolding wonders of a world suddenly seen to be complex where it had been assumed to be simple. It is a century which none but an expert historian would venture to assess as it bridges the gap between the medieval and the modern. What is attempted here is an examination of theolo-

gical method as it evolved in this setting, taking account of the
effect on its constituent elements of the confrontation with other
ways of thinking, of changes in basic outlook consequent upon the
emergence of new studies and fresh discoveries, as well as of the
turn of events as these influenced the thinking of the times. The
spirit of Anglicanism is not a seventeenth-century phenomenon but
something perennial answering the dual need for freedom and for
certainty.

The aim throughout has been to proceed by way of a detailed
examination of sources. This tends to uncover some of the foundations on which the writers' work rests, and, of course, the preference of a theologian for a particular author is often illuminating
in respect of his own view of the purpose and method of theology.
At the same time, it does something to underline the inner
unanimity of the period with regard to theological method by
bringing to light cases of interdependence and of the close connection of ideas. By noting instances of the influence of one
individual on another it helps to clarify the way in which a particular line of thought has developed, often more or less out of
sight, before it finally breaks surface.

My gratitude is due to the Trustees and to the Faculty of
Seabury-Western Theological Seminary for the invitation to give
the Hale Lectures. The hospitality of the Dean, the Very Rev.
C. U. Harris, and Mrs. Harris, is something to be remembered
and appreciated with sincere thanks for their kindness.

CONTENTS

CHAPTER I

HOOKER AND LIBERAL METHOD:
THE TEW CIRCLE

THE TERM theological method needs some comment. There is a distinctively Anglican theological ethos, and the distinctiveness lies in method rather than in content, for Anglicanism, as Chillingworth put it, has declined to call any man master in theology. There is no specifically Anglican corpus of doctrine and no king-pin in Anglican theology such as Calvin, nor is there any tendency to stress specific doctrines such as predestination, or specific philosophies, such as Thomism or nominalism or any other one of the several medieval brands of philosophy.

Richard Montague's assertion that he was neither a Calvinist nor a Lutheran but a Christian, illustrates the point that Anglicanism is not committed to believing anything because it is Anglican but only because it is true. Perhaps the most important thing about Hooker is that he wrote no *Summa* and composed no *Institutes*, for what he did was to outline method. What is distinctively Anglican is then not a theology but a theological method.

The phrase implies more than fashions in theology, although there is something of that in it too. It means not only the approach of any given period to theological problems, but the presuppositions which determine the approach. These are in turn influenced by the climate of thought in which the theologian finds himself, by the movements of thought in his day, by the progressive uncovering of the mechanics of the physical universe as these impinge upon his particular generation and by the clash of events which forces to the surface new factors or insights. From this interplay of shifting emphasis there emerge certain permanent elements, and from the various historical situations of the seventeenth century there passed into Anglicanism certain clearly-marked elements without which, as many believe, theology would be impoverished.

Such situations are those centring on the Anglican-Puritan tension, the rise of the Laudians and of the Moderates, the work of the Cambridge Platonists and of the Latitudinarians, and the appearance of what the period called 'the new philosophy,' that is to say, the arrival of a genuine scientific outlook. All these situations are composed of the work of individuals as well as of the movement of events.

In order to see their implications, it is important to recall the kind of theological method which held undisputed sway up to and during the Reformation period.

The Middle Ages began to give new vigour to 'faith seeking understanding', and in his own way, Anselm aimed at this in the *Proslogion*. But from the patristic period, with certain exceptions, until the seventeenth century, it is in general true to say that the authoritative method in theology reigned supreme. Obviously, there were variations and degrees, but the problem of fusing faith and reason was always with theology in some form or other. Although the general tendency of medieval thought is ultimately towards theological agreement, this was compatible with considerable philosophical disagreement.

Against the background of the rationalism of the Averroists, and of the Platonism and Neo-Platonism which influenced the thinking of the Middle Ages, Aquinas can be seen as the fore-runner of an approach to reason and to the synthesis of faith and reason which left its mark on Hooker and others. The rationalism of the Latin Averroists like Sigur of Brabant was the direct progenitor of the rationalism of the Encyclopaedists and of Marxism. With this rationalism which rejected all that was not self-evident, Aquinas had to contend,[1] just as he had to resist the obscurantism which effected his own condemnation in 1277 and which would have baulked all his efforts to achieve a synthesis, a view of reality as a whole. His refusal 'to do violence to the autonomy of reason in its own sphere',[2] and his independence of authorities had an effect on the evolution of theological method. In him, Anselm's *fides quaerens intellectum* is brought a step forward.

Further, against these advances must be set the situation in which they were made, when, as C. E. Raven put it, minds like Roger Bacon were always in danger. Under late medieval nominalism there was a strange combination of rigorous logical analysis and criticism in philosophy with blind obedience to authority and fideism in theology.

1. *Saint Thomas Aquinas*, G. Vann, Introduction and Chap. II.
2. *Ib.* p. 91.

The reaction from the attempt to set reason and faith in an integrated view of life which implied some sort of unified idea of experience, was typified by Continental solifidianism with its distrust of reason, but the same method of appeal to authorities and of categorical assertions persisted. It would be some time before fresh influences could be brought to bear on the situation. Oxford was in many ways medieval until 1670 in which year the University distinguished itself as the home of lost causes by welcoming Cosimo dei Medici with a dissertation against the Copernican astronomy.

The danger of over-simplifying situations seen in retrospect is an obvious one and cannot altogether be avoided. Yet it is in the main true to say that the mediaeval method of proceeding by authorities and the mediaeval cosmology and general background of ideas constituted the dominant outlook of theologians at the end of the sixteenth and the beginning of the seventeenth centuries.

The Anglican-Puritan tension lasted from before 1572, the date of the Puritan *Admonition to the Parliament* and through the ecclesiastical controversies of the post-Reformation period, but by the end of the seventeenth century Calvinism was theologically a spent force in England and it was Puritanism considered as a religious attitude and as an ecclesiastical polity which survived. The non-conformists of the eighteenth and nineteenth centuries were the heirs of Puritan church-order and of Puritan piety, but the Calvinism, which for much of the seventeenth century walked together with Puritanism, had by this time gone its own way. Furthermore, during the early part at any rate of the seventeenth century, Calvinism was a far from negligible force within the Church of England itself. From the beginning, the controversy between Anglican and Puritan made a notable contribution to theological method, and with the *Admonition* as a starting point, the manner and extent of this contribution can be seen.

This was the first public manifesto of the Puritan party and it was written by Field and Wilcox. Its declared purpose was to establish a Presbyterian order in the English Church, for the effect of the exile during the Marian persecutions was that many of the ideas transplanted to England by the returning exiles were those of the Continental reform.

The *Admonitions* are more than an airing of certain grievances or an expression of dissatisfaction with various features of the

Elizabethan Church. They constitute a comprehensive plan of change which included the abolition of episcopacy and the three-fold ministry, the Prayer Book and many common practices involved in its use: 'Instead of an Archbishop or Lord bishop, you must make equalitie of ministers,' and 'to the ministers, seniors and deacons is the whole regiment of the church to be committed'.[1] The second *Admonition*, the work of Cartwright, is not so trenchant in style and repeats the arguments of the first, but taken together, they form a comment on the temper of the times and on the aim of the Puritan movement. The primary interest is theological, for there is accepted in these manifestoes a type of authoritative view-point which was identified with Puritanism from then onwards, and which it was the main purpose of Hooker's writings to confute. The second *Admonition* points out that the defect of the English Reformation lies in its incomplete acceptance of what it describes as a clearly laid down platform in Scripture, a platform which is also seen in 'the examples of the best Churches beyond the seas'.[2] The method is that of attempting the justification from Scripture of a system in all its details.

Throughout the subsequent century the whole of Puritan controversy was managed in this fashion. Instead of the teaching of the Articles concerning the sufficiency of Scripture in fundamentals, there grew up a doctrine which required this authority for non-essentials. It was at this point that the impact of historical and theological factors upon each other caused to emerge a principle of importance for theological method. Three elements in the outlook of the time need however to be considered.

Firstly, all branches of opinion up to the close of the seventeenth century regarded the authority of Scripture as unquestioned. More might make tentative suggestions about the early chapters of Genesis, or Hales might stress the sense rather than the literal aspect, the scientists might use in conjunction with it the book of nature, but the acceptance was general. It is in this connection, however, that much of the significance of the writings of Hooker, Chillingworth and the Cambridge Platonists appears.

In the second place, everyone, down to the last couple of decades of the century, held a pre-scientific cosmology. The improbable was accounted for by reference to magic, and to query the

1. *Puritan Manifestoes*, ed. W. H. Frere and C. E. Douglas, p. 16.
2. *Ib.* pp. 94-5.

existence of witches and spirits was regarded by Cudworth or Sir Thomas Browne as evidence of a tendency to materialism, an attitude shared by More who was a correspondent of Descartes, and by Isaac Barrow, the mathematician. This background in which the arbitrary always seemed present, and in which there was no accumulated or tested knowledge of natural phenomena in themselves, had its effect on thinking generally, so that the establishment of a reasonable ground for experience, with the consequences for theology which this implies, was only gradual.

The third factor was Calvinism which was in the ascendant in England until the middle of the century. The disagreement between Anglican and Puritan began with questions of church order and not of teaching, and it has been said that there was hardly one of the Elizabethan bishops who was not a Calvinist. The returned Marian exiles had brought Calvinism with them, its appeal strengthened for them by the events in which they had taken part. The fall of Laud and the convening of Westminster Assembly mark the summit of its development in England, although from the beginning the system had its opponents who, like John Hales at the Synod of Dort, bid John Calvin goodnight.

It was however the new movements of thought after the Restoration, the rise of the new philosophy, which contributed most to the eventual decline of English Calvinism, for its authoritative character had not the flexibility associated with the idea of reason and law as an implanted directive in the universe which was Hooker's theme. It was this which predisposed Anglican theological method to accept and to assimilate the work of the scientists and naturalists.

These three factors are behind Hooker's work which is in one sense a defence of reason, an attempt to establish a liberal method which holds reason to be competent to deal with questions of ecclesiastical polity, and to be in itself an ultimate factor in theology. F. J. Shirley describes his influence: 'He ruled no city, like Calvin, nor did he appear defiant before an Emperor, like Luther, much less perish in battle, like Zwingli. Half of the twenty years of his active ministry were spent in the shelter of a University Fellowship or the tranquil retreat of a country living', but he produced a work which stands out, as has been well said, in a magnificent isolation among the lesser writings of the day, which, belonging to no school, influences all, and is an abiding possession, for it has 'given to Anglican theology a tone and a direction which it has never lost'.[1]

P. E. More summed it up when he wrote, 'What we have to look for in the ecclesiastical literature of England is not so much finality as direction'.[2] Hooker goes back to the beginning by maintaining that the first question to be answered is 'what is the source of authority?'. His answer is law, and his writings show the contrast between this and the solution offered by others. The key to Hooker's thought is to be found in the idea that law is an implanted directive, that it is reason, inherent, governing the universe, an inner principle expressing itself by the fulfilment of proper ends. He defines a law as 'a directive rule unto goodness of operation',[3] and as being 'properly that which reason in such sort defineth to be good that it must be done'.[4]

In his preface, Hooker considers that the defect of the authoritative method of using Scripture as the only source of authentication in questions of polity and liturgy, and in matters that are not essential, lies in the way in which individual interpretations become in fact the authority. Hooker held that Calvin saw this and set up a model which he claimed to be the only legitimate authority, but that this was to beg the question. Because the authors of the *Admonitions* chose this 'platform of Geneva' instead of 'the orders and laws' of the Church, he sets himself to explain upon what ecclesiastical polity depends.[5]

His aim therefore is to describe, first of all, 'how different kinds of law there are, and what force they are according unto each kind',[6] with a view to disproving the supposition that 'the laws for which ye strive are found in Scripture, but those not against which ye strive'.[7] It is from this surmise that there is drawn what Hooker terms 'the very main pillar' of this position, namely 'that Scripture ought to be the only rule of all our actions', and his second book deals with this and with the contention that the polity he defended was not acceptable because it was not commanded in Scripture.[8] He then discusses the view that there must of necessity be found therein an unalterable ecclesiastical polity.[9]

---

1. *Richard Hooker and Contemporary Political Ideas*, pp. 35–6, by F. J. Shirley.

2. *Anglicanism*, ed. More and Cross, p. xx.

3. *The Laws of Ecclesiastical Polity*, I.VIII.4.

4. *Ib.* 9.

5. *Ib.* Preface, II, 7–10.

6. *Ib.* VII.3.

7. Preface, VII. 3.

8. *Ib.*

9. *Ib.* 4.

He begins by indicating the extent of the matter: 'All things that are, have some operation not violent or casual. .... That which doth assign unto each thing the kind, that which doth moderate the force and power, that which doth appoint the form and measure, of working, the same we term a law ... all things therefore do work after a sort according to law'.[1] Law is not so much a series of promulgations as a pattern of characteristic behaviour whereby all things are directed 'in the means whereby they tend to their own perfection'.[2] It is a living chain of connecting links in the universe beginning with 'that order which God before all ages hath set down with himself, for himself to do all things by'.[3] This is the first eternal law and it informs the whole created order and con-stitutes 'that which he himself hath set down as expedient to be kept by all his creatures, according to the several conditions where-with he hath endued them'.[4] Not only is the universe a hierarchic system of law or laws, but 'those laws are investigable by reason, without the help of revelation'.[5] As far as voluntary agents are concerned, this law appears as natural law, and the general con-sequence of this is clear, since for Aquinas man partakes in the eternal law by means of reason, and this participation constitutes the law of nature for voluntary agents. As a law has been defined as something pertaining to reason, the natural law is the law of reason: 'The natural measure whereby to judge our doings is the sentence of reason'.[6] A similar view of reason is taken in the writings of Chillingworth and Hales, in those of the Cambridge Platonists and in the work of naturalists such as Ray and scientists such as Boyle.

In the first book, Hooker develops this, that 'the rule of volun-tary agents on earth is the sentence that reason giveth concerning the goodness of those things which they are to do',[7] and that the natural law, 'meaning thereby the law which human nature knoweth itself in reason universally bound unto ... compre-hendeth all those things which men by the light of their natural understanding evidently know'.[8] The purpose of Scripture is 'to deliver the laws of duties supernatural,' but in it is included much of natural law. It includes all necessary things, but these must be

1. *Ecclesiastical Polity*, I.II.1.
2. *Ib*. I.III.5.
3. *Ib*. I.II.6.
4. *Ib*. I.III.1.

5. *Ib*. I.VIII.9.
6. *Ib*. I.VIII.8.
7. *Ib*. I.III.4.
8. *Ib*. I.VIII.9.

distinguished from those things which are being 'urged upon this church under the name of reformed church discipline' for they have not been shown to be contained in, nor to be deduced 'out of Scripture to be necessary'.[1] 'It sufficeth therefore' he writes, 'that nature and Scripture do serve in such full sort, that they both jointly and not severally either of them be so complete that unto everlasting felicity we need not the knowledge of anything more than these two may easily furnish our minds with on all sides'.[2]

This is the basis of the method which Hooker develops, setting the question of ecclesiastical laws within the wider context apart from which he considers that it can have no solution: 'Lest therefore any man should marvel whereunto all these things tend, the drift and purpose of all is this ... to teach man a reason why just and reasonable laws are of so great force, of so great use in the world: and to inform their minds with some method of reducing the laws whereof there is present controversy unto their first original causes, that so it may be in every particular ordinance thereby the better discerned, whether the same be reasonable, just and righteous or no'.[3]

In the second book, Hooker makes some comments on enlarging the necessary use of Scripture: 'For whereas God hath left sundry kinds of law unto men, and by all those laws the actions of men are in some sort directed; they hold that one only law, the Scripture, must be the rule to direct in all things'.[4] Such actions need only to be framed according to the law of reason,[5] for 'there are other kinds of laws which notify the will of God ... nor is there any law of God, whereunto he doth not account our obedience his glory'.[6] If the argument were carried to its conclusion there would be no such thing as an indifferent action,[7] and it is difficult to see why there should be required some external sanction for following 'the judgment of natural discretion', when 'the nature which himself hath given to work by he cannot but be delighted with, when we exercise the same any way without commandment of his to the contrary'.[8] Nor is it clear on what basis it is assumed that revelation cancels natural law. Hooker's writings on law and reason stem from the *Summa Theologica*, which together with the emphasis on

1. *Ib*. I.XIV.1.   4. *Ib*. II.I.2.   7. *Ib*. II.IV.5, 6.
2. *Ib*. 5.   5. *Ib*.   8. *Ib*. 7.
3. *Ib*. I.XVI.1.   6. *Ib*. II.II.2.

practical divinity also found in the *Ecclesiastical Polity*, play a recurring role in the development of theological method as the century progresses.

Hooker is at pains to point out that to deny to human authority any validity save a qualified one in 'human sciences',[1] which was all that Cartwright would allow, is to undermine all ecclesiastical order and polity[2] and would eventually leave not even the 'memory' of a Church in the world.[3] It was at variance with all analogy from temporal matters in which 'the sentences of wise and expert men were never but highly esteemed,'[4] and would be a cause of confusion. Many things cannot and need not be known with demonstrable certainty, and therefore weight should be given to the opinions of duly qualified authority, since 'in defect of proof infallible, the mind doth rather follow probable persuasions'.[5] In a memorable phrase Hooker wrote 'such as the evidence is . . . such is the heart's assent thereunto',[6] and from the way in which he approached the problems of his times there passed something of substance into the developing theological method of the day. He saw clearly that the ignoring of the existence of other kinds of law, the attempt to bring everything 'under the determination' of revealed authority and the 'abating of the credit of man',[7] were varying aspects of the one trend. Here the stress was on a transcendent authority working on the human situation from without, as against an implanted directive expressing itself as and through reason within a situation in which freedom was real and grace not irresistible. Yet he is aware of the limitations of reason: 'nature is no sufficient teacher what we should do that we may attain unto life everlasting'.[8] There is no insufficiency in this respect in Scripture, for 'the absolute perfection of Scripture is seen by relation unto that end whereto it tendeth'.[9]

The opinions which Hooker sought to confute were no academic matter but a living issue, and there is a foreboding note in the preface to his book, for as has been observed, 'Elizabethan England, as mirrored in the House of Commons, was overwhelmingly Puritan in its sympathies'.[10] Yet from Hooker's writing something emerged which had about it a vitality and a perennial quality

1. *Ib*. II.VII.4.
2. *Ib*. 1.
3. *Ib*. 2.
4. *Ib*. 5.
5. *Ib*.
6. *Ib*.
7. *Ib*. II.VII.1.
8. *Ib*. II.VIII.3.
9. *Ib*. 5.
10. J. E. Neale, *Elizabeth I and Her Parliaments*, 1559–81, p. 418.

which became a lasting factor in the thought of the period. Significantly, it was Hooker's work which later showed to Robert Sanderson an alternative to Calvinism.

During the period stretching from the latter part of the reign of Elizabeth I, when Calvinism had its supporters within the Church of England, to the Restoration, when the need for a settlement seemed to be more important, and when the new philosophy was turning to a different kind of question, varying aspects of the problem came to the fore. In 1593, just as the subject of ecclesiastical order and polity was discussed by Bilson in the *Perpetual Government of Christ's Church* and by Bancroft's *Survey of the Holy Discipline* published in the same year, in both of which the traditional position was maintained, so, two years later, Barrett and Baro actually incurred charges of heresy for their dissent from the predestinarian tenets of the decrees, so firmly was the system entrenched at Cambridge. The case gave rise to the Lambeth Articles which attributed man's salvation to the action of arbitrary will upon which alone, and not upon any merit or condition, depended acceptance or rejection. There were inevitably many like Andrewes who opposed the Articles and they were eventually withdrawn, but that Archbishop Whitgift should have accepted them is a measure of how strong Calvinism was then in England. For while Whitgift insisted that they were not to be regarded as 'laws and decrees', he still described them as 'certain propositions which we are persuaded to be true'. Although he was careful to note that they must 'be taken . . . as our private judgment', he nevertheless considered them to be 'correspondent' to the teaching of the Church.[1]

When the wisest fool in Christendom came to the throne, his taste for theological disputations and his natural propensity for meddling made it almost inevitable that the Millenary Petition should result in the Hampton Court Conference of 1604. Sir John Harington records that its consequences and the way in which it was managed gave little satisfaction to those who sought it, for James had already learnt that presbytery and monarchy consorted ill together.[2] The importance of what was involved is to be seen in the fact that the Puritan party wished to have the Lambeth Articles inserted in the Book of Common Prayer, and to remove

1. J. Strype, *Whitgift* (1822), II, p. 282.
2. *Anglicanism*, ed. More and Cross, p. xlviii.

the existing sixteenth Article which rejected the idea that the elect cannot fall away. A determined attempt to force the issue was being made, which, if it had succeeded, could have retarded indefinitely the effects of Hooker's work, and which, in any case, offered a sustained opposition to the growth of that method, widespread though the support for it may have been.

During Bancroft's primacy the Church grew in popularity, and had he been followed by Andrewes, as some expected, the progress of Calvinism might have been less striking in view of the position he had taken. As it was, Abbot, the last primate to favour these views, was appointed, but despite this and for various reasons, some of them political, there were setbacks, including an order from the king that preachers were to refrain from discussing its more distinctive tenets. This was the reverse of the policy inaugurated by him when he had sent a group of theologians to the Synod of Dort, where their terms of reference as a commission clearly committed them to upholding Calvinism. This interference might have had more noticeable results were it not for the restraining pressure of other factors, such as the growth of Arminianism and the appearance during Abbot's primacy of books like those of Richard Montague which testified to the increasing number of those who could not accept the system.

It was clear where Laud's sympathy lay, and as the Civil War drew on, an alignment was taking shape which was formed partly by these less tangible considerations and partly by the pressure of the divisive situation then developing. The compulsion of seemingly more urgent loyalties and the effect on others of the affiliations of those who became prominent in the ensuing struggle combined to score more sharply the lines of difference between the parties. These lines were drawn in an atmosphere of theological debate which, if not calm, was at any rate unclouded by the bitter conflict of interests which resulted when the terms in which both sides saw the future government of the nation were irreconcilable.

Calvinism reached the zenith of its influence with the Westminster Assembly, and for the next quarter of a century it was a major factor to be reckoned with in the theological situation. It possessed the powerful appeal of a close-knit system and there was about it an austere impressiveness which could not fail to carry weight with many. At the time of the Restoration, its decline in England was already under way, and not only because of the event, but also by reason of the steadily growing theological opposition to it and because of the fact that its uncompromising formulations had become synonymous with obscurantism in the minds of many thinking people. It is symptomatic of this that the decline of Calvinism coincided with the rise of the Royal Society and a steadily growing interest in natural history and scientific developments. The earlier debates on the quinquarticular controversy no longer seemed to have the same importance. Among those five points, none had excited more interest than absolute predestination, and perhaps none did more to harden theological opposition as the century advanced.

During the first sixty years of the century, this opposition was found in various quarters, and one of the noticeable results was to reveal the existence of a common ground on which met individuals of differing ecclesiastical outlook, such as Chillingworth, Taylor, Hammond and Sanderson. Before the Civil War, a group had gathered around Lucius Cary, Lord Falkland, whose house at Great Tew, near Oxford, became their centre. It included Gilbert Sheldon, later to be Archbishop of Canterbury, George Morley, William Chillingworth, John Hales, Henry Hammond, John Earle, Edmund Waller, Sydney Godolphin, Francis Wenman, and Hyde, who as Lord Clarendon was to become one of the political architects of Restoration England. These were the men who, in Hyde's words, made the house resemble the University. Cary was born in 1610, and came to Ireland as a youth during his father's term of office as Lord Deputy from 1622 to 1629. In 1632 he settled on his estate, and began to gather a group of men who shared his desire to study and who benefited by being made free of his extensive library. In their writings, as in those of the Cambridge Platonists a little later, is to be seen a development of the method indicated by Hooker. For they asked similar questions, though from a different angle, and in the answers they gave is to be discerned the shape of things to come, for in some important respects they developed away from Hooker. The Civil War dispersed them as a group and events carried Falkland into the army, the House of Commons, the Secretaryship of State, finally to lose his life at the battle of Newbury in 1643. But the tenor of his writings and of those of his associates is of significance in considering the changes in theological method, for they attempted to liberate their thinking by means of rational enquiry from the systematised statements of the Reformation and Counter-Reformation. It is not possible at this distance of time to say how far, if at all, they were influenced by Socinian ideas. The charge had been levelled at Falkland, Hales and Chillingworth, with little or no basis to it, but doubtless their writings, reacting from what they regarded as dogmatism, must have appeared to many of their contemporaries as verging on a disquieting type of sceptical rationalism. At any rate, their attitude in such an age must have seemed to many to be too near Rakow for comfort.

Ultimately, it was the basis of authority which Hooker had regarded as of central importance, that concerned them most. B. H. G. Wormald wrote of them that they 'were determined to separate saving truth from correct theology',[1] and it is in their almost exaggerated reaction in this direction, in their spirit of free investigation, and in their view of Biblical authority, that they may be seen to be the first wave of that tide of thought which, by the end of the century, had swept past the breakwaters of traditional orthodoxy. H. J. McLachlan, in his *Socinianism in Seventeenth Century England*, refers to them as the Oxford school of rational theologians and in describing them he notes that they 'were unmoved by Socinian teaching on the Trinity and the Atonement'.[2] It is of interest for the discerning of the development of theological method that the members of a group so diverse in outlook as Hales and Chillingworth on the one hand and the Laudian Hammond on the other, should have in common something which, in varied degrees, is to be seen in Andrewes, Hooker, Sanderson, the Cambridge Platonists and the Latitudinarians. Falkland himself, in his *Discourse*, indicates that to attempt to answer the question as to the basis of authority by appealing to a system or to the writings of the Fathers, is to move in a circle. There is no need for such definitive pronouncements, since for those 'who follow their reason in the interpretation of the Scriptures',[3] there will be either assistance in finding the truth or pardon for missing it. In so far as this is an over-simplification it is inadequate, but the common ground is clear.

William Chillingworth was indebted to Tew and its library but above all to the learning and hospitality of Falkland himself. It is

1. *Clarendon*, p. 255.   2. p. 89.
3. Quoted in H. J. McLachlan, *Socinianism in Seventeenth-Century England*, p. 66. cp. Chillingworth, *The Religion of Protestants a Safe Way to Salvation*, Chap. II, Pt. I. (119).

not without significance that he was a mathematician and inventor as well as a theologian. In his *The Religion of Protestants a Safe Way to Salvation* which appeared in 1637, there can be seen the same emphasis on the place of reason and the same demarcation between what is fundamental and what is not, as is found in the *Ecclesiastical Polity*. There is no difference between the theme of Hooker's first book and Chillingworth's 'right reason, grounded on divine revelation and common notions written by God in the hearts of all men'. The Bible is the criterion, but he emphasises also the individual's interpretation of it in the light of reason, and in his third chapter he distinguishes between fundamentals and non-fundamentals, stating that only that which is clear to the understanding and commonly accepted by all Christians is necessary: 'Who doth not see that seeing (as we suppose here and shall prove hereafter) all necessary truths are plainly and evidently set down in Scripture, there would of necessity be among all men, in all things necessary, unity of opinion'.[1] Falkland makes the same point when he writes of believing 'what is there plain to be only necessary'.[2] Chillingworth observes that when Scripture is affirmed to be a perfect rule of faith, this does not mean 'that by Scripture all things absolutely may be proved, which are to be believed', for the fact that a thing is written will not necessarily convince one who does not accept it. What is really meant is that 'to them which presuppose it divine, and a rule of faith', Scripture, since it contains all necessary things, 'is a compleat and total, and not only an imperfect and a partial rule'.[3] There is also a continued stress on what he calls liberty of judgment, so that in one sense, his book is a defence of this principle. In the same book he explicitly denies any feeling for Socinianism, and accepts as basic all things that are plainly deduced from Scripture.

Chillingworth's was for a considerable period a mind *in via*, as the chequered history of his opinions testifies, a mind that was sensitive and seeking. His sincerity in refusing preferment until he was able to satisfy himself about the Articles is altogether in keeping with his courage, for he espoused the royalist cause, as befitted Laud's godson, and was taken prisoner by Waller to Chichester where he died in 1644.

1. *Ib.* Chap. III, Pt. I (81).
2. B. H. G. Wormald, *Clarendon*, p. 259. cp. Chillingworth, 'nothing is necessary to be believed, but what is plainly revealed', loc. cit. Chap. II, Pt. 1 (104).
3. Loc. cit. Chap. II, Pt. I (8).

Pearson's *Golden Remains of the Ever Memorable Mr. John Hales*, published in 1659, three years after the death of Hales, gives an insight into the temperament and thinking of one who was also connected with Laud, but as his chaplain, and who shared much of the outlook of Chillingworth. A tolerant man, he was linked by his office with one whose name was not conspicuous for tolerance, and he was himself a victim of intolerance, being deprived of his Oxford Fellowship during the Commonwealth period.

There is a phrase in one of his sermons where he is attacking the practice of 'keeping up the conceits and authorities of other men,' which reveals clearly the temper of his mind: 'For many of the learned themselves are fallen upon this preposterous conceit, that learning consisteth rather in variety of turning and quoting of sundry authors, than in soundly discovering and laying down the truth of things'.[1] This desire to understand experience and to enquire into the ideas that men hold concerning it is a noticeable element in the writings of Hales, to be paralleled more and more in others as time went on.

His method and outlook are fairly indicated by his view of the use of Scripture which was in sharp contrast with that which was the norm in his time. 'The sense is Scripture,' he writes, 'rather than the words', and all efforts to deal with it 'as chemists deal with natural bodies, torturing them to extract out of them that which God and nature never put in them' are pointless, for Scripture interprets the interpreter.[2] He warns against being anxious when there may not be an obvious answer to every trivial objection made against scripture, for to do so 'is a certain argument of great defect of inward furniture and worth, which should as it were balance the mind'.[3] There are many apparent contradictions but doubts about such things ought to be put 'to some day of hearing afar off'.[4] The essentials are clear, and as to non-essentials, Hales recommends a modest scepticism: 'It shall well befit our Christian modesty to participate somewhat of the sceptic . . . till . . . the remainder of our knowledge be supplied by Christ', for that which is plain and generally understood in Scripture is the only ground of faith: 'For it is not depth of knowledge, nor knowledge of antiquity, or sharpness of wit, nor authority of councils,

1. *The Golden Remains of the Ever Memorable Mr John Hales*, (Third Impression), p. 18.

2. *Ib.* p. 3.

3. *Ib.* p. 17.

4. *Ib.* p. 28.

nor the name of the Church, (that) can settle the restless conceits, that possess the minds of many doubtful Christians'.[1] Elsewhere, he instances the various views about predestination and remarks that there is value to be found in them all, but that the thing 'which keeps the Churches this day so far asunder' is 'this peremptory manner of setting down our conclusions, under this high commanding form of necessary truths',[2] where there is in fact ambiguity. 'Where Scripture is ambiguous', he writes, there is no better way 'than we would be willing to think, that these things, which with some show of probability we deduce from Scripture, are at the best but our opinions.'[3]

Pearson describes him as 'a man never to be truly expressed but by himself',[4] a sentence which goes a long way towards explaining the adjective 'memorable', and he makes it clear that it was not only his industry and learning that impressed his contemporaries, but his kindness, affability and approachableness.[5] He was too self-effacing to allow his friends to prevail on him to write, but in private intercourse he was notably 'communicative',[6] his view being that there were already writers enough and that teaching was more important.[7] In consequence, as Pearson pointed out, there were collected only 'such as he could not but write, and such as when written, were out of his power to destroy'.[8] His gentle and courteous nature was reflected in his tolerance, but in this matter, he and those who thought like him were in a minority. Up to the close of the period, Anglican and Puritan were not contending for or against the principle of toleration, but for supremacy, as the varying fortunes of both demonstrated. The tolerance of Hales and his fellows was to be echoed shortly in the writings of the Cambridge Platonists, as were also his emphasis on reason and his sensitivity to 'the truth of things', a phrase they shared. Like them, as his friend Anthony Farindon observed, 'in his younger days he was a Calvinist', but when he was at the Synod of Dort and heard Episcopius, one of the Remonstrant spokesmen, 'well pressing St John iii, 16. . . . There I bid John Calvin good night, as he has often told me'.[9]

It is significant that this same emphasis on love rather than on power and justice is a recurrent theme with the Cambridge Platonists, for they regarded it as that which united the human

1. *Ib.* p. 31.   3. *Ib.* p. 66.   5. *Ib.*   7. *Ib.* p. 45.   9. *Ib.* Letter.
2. *Ib.* p. 65.   4. *Ib.* Preface.   6. *Ib.*   8. *Ib.* Preface.

with the divine, and for them faith was 'caritate formata'. It was this very point which Anthony Tuckney had raised when, in a letter to Whichcote, he criticised them as appearing to attach greater importance to 'an estate of love, in this life, above a life of faith'.[1] The dissatisfaction with current fiduciary ideas which More and Smith were to express later is to be seen also in Hales, and his letters from Dort in 1618, although an impartial piece of reporting, support Farindon's comment on the change in his outlook. Elsewhere, Hales shows how far he had moved from the new Continental orthodoxy, for he cannot see how faith can be considered apart from 'an honest conversation,' and he writes, 'the first, though it seem the worthier . . . yet the second in the end will prove the surer'. He takes the same line as that later adopted by Whichcote and his colleagues, affirming that obedience is 'required as a part of faith', and that things done 'by the light of nature' are obedience to a law which gives men 'title and interest' in faith. He quotes Salvianus to the effect that faith is 'to be faithful . . . which is nothing else but faithfully to keep the commandments of God'.[2] 'Not therefore only a bare belief, but fidelity' must be taken into account, and it is 'a gross mistaking of our age'[3] that men should tie their judgment 'to this outward profession', separating 'the acts of the second table' from 'the acts and observations of the first'.[4] There is the same refusal, so noticeable in the later writers, to cry down the potentialities of human nature; 'In some things we agree, as we are men, and thus far the very heathen themselves are to be received'.[5] There is the same capaciousness of outlook and reaction from exclusiveness: 'Let it not offend any that I have made Christianity rather an inn to receive all than a private house to receive some few'.[6]

It is impossible not to discern here the effects of what he had seen and heard during his stay abroad. He had learnt 'that we be not too peremptory in our position, where express texts of Scripture fail us',[7] and there is an echo of Hooker in the words 'for unto all causes, be they never so good, weakness of proof, when it is discovered, brings great prejudice'.[8]

1. *Eight Letters of Dr Anthony Tuckney to Dr Benjamin Whichcote, Moral and Religious Aphorisms of Whichcote*, Letter II, ed. Salter, 1753).
2. *Golden Remains of the Ever Memorable Mr John Hales*, p. 48.
3. *Ib.* p. 49.
4. *Ib.* p. 49.
5. *Ib.* p. 42.
6. *Ib.* p. 44.
7. *Ib.* p. 24.
8. *Ib.* p. 22.

On the subject of the decrees he writes that they 'lay not upon things any violent necessity, they exempt not from the use of ordinary means, they infringe not our liberty, they stand very well with common casualty; yea, these things are the very means by which his decrees are brought about'.[1] He agrees that original sin is 'an infection' of human nature, but it may not be used as a 'stalking-horse':[2] 'So may we speak of the fall of our first parents, it hurts not us that Adam fell; nay, our strength and glory is much improved, that by Christ we are redeemed'.[3]

His sermons were penetrating, vividly illustrated and phrased— 'all our pleasures, all our honours, all the May-games of our life'.[4] In temperament, as in the retired circumstances of his life, Hales resembles Whichcote, Cudworth, More and Smith, but most of all in the liberal and candid approach which he made to the questions of his day. Listening to Episcopius speaking had the same releasing effect on him as reading Ficino had on More, in that it helped him finally to rid himself of the feeling that the logical dilemma apparently implied in the decrees was a real one. From this time onwards, it is this outgoing, creative love and the human response of fidelity and obedience which seemed most important to Hales.

The year after the Synod of Dort he retired to Eton, and it is putting no strain on probability to suggest that More, who went there as a boy some years afterwards, was influenced by the sermons and perhaps by the conversation of Hales. Certainly, one of the dozen or so surviving sermons was preached at Eton and contains a reference to others having been preached there,[5] and as Pearson tells us, he was 'so communicative' and 'affable' that he was always ready for discussion. It would be fairly surprising if More had not heard any of the sermons or joined in any discussions or had not had the subject-matter related to him. Particularly would this have been unlikely since from his own account his mind was then much occupied with these questions and his time at Eton was a critical and formative one for his opinions.

He had, before going to Eton at the age of fourteen, a teacher who, like his parents, was a Calvinist, and for him as for them he had respect and affection. A change in his ideas was however approaching, and he records that 'I immediately went to Eton

1. *Ib.* p. 132.   3. *Ib.* p. 148.   5. *Ib.* p. 73.
2. *Ib.* p. 158.   4. *Ib.* p. 80.

school . . . but neither there, nor yet anywhere else, could I ever swallow down that hard doctrine concerning fate'.[1] It looks as if this was the turning-point, and this is borne out by the fact that, at the time of his entering the University, this change in his views was the reason for an estrangement, happily only of a temporary nature, between him and his father. We do not know how far, if at all, in those days, a clever and enquiring boy like More would have come into actual contact with one occupying Hales's position. We do know that these ideas were gaining ground and that Hales held them, that he spoke of them both in sermons and conversation. Whether therefore More met them there for the first time, or whether encountering them there served but to give form and direction to an instinctive reaction against Calvinism, is not clear. What is clear is that during those years at Eton there was a progressive formulation of More's ideas. That either directly or indirectly Hales had no part in this seems improbable.

Hales and the Cambridge Platonists share the same optimistic view of humanity, the same practicality and belief in reason, the same quiet determination to use more 'maybes and peradventures', more 'old men's modesty',[2] the same devout, generous and constructive outlook, the same modest spirit of withdrawal. They convey the same impression of having no particular axe to grind, yet every point they make is an implicit criticism of the systematic theology of Calvinism, or rather of those aspects of it that had bearing on the questions arising out of the decrees, for in other contexts Calvin's position was respected. But this criticism of a systematic theology came not only from Hooker, and from the Oxford group of rational theologians, from the Cambridge Platonists and later from the Latitudinarians, but from Andrewes and from Laudians like Heylyn and Hammond, and from moderate writers like Sanderson. It is a striking demonstration of the self-awareness of Anglicanism, and it testifies to the widespread nature of the conviction that what was required was not theological systematisation but theological interpretation.

The letters of Hales to Sir Dudley Carlton are an effort to give an accurate and impartial account of what took place at Dort, but

1. Introduction to the Latin edition of his *Collected Works*, translated by Richard Ward.
2. *Golden Remains*, p. 7.

they are far from being just a reporter's record, and his observation is not of the surface only. He comments with humour that 'our synod goes on like a watch, the main wheels upon which the whole business turns are least in sight. For all things of moment are acted in private sessions; what is done in public is only for show and entertainment'.[1] While he is aware of what goes on, there is no facile criticism, but rather a fair endeavour to give a sympathetic account of the proceedings. There are personal comments and opinions, news of individuals and substance of speeches, and he mentions among other things a request by a party from Utrecht for a simpler catechism which would not contain 'any man's glosses',[2] a point Sanderson was to make years later for the same reason. Censorship of books such as those of David Georgius and Nicolaus Socinus was discussed,[3] but the chief matter was of course the question of the decrees. Hales reports a speech by Episcopius 'that they descried many conceits passing in our Churches which could not stand with the goodness and justice of God', and not only so, but these views seemed to make sacraments and duties to be unnecessary and caused 'many strange imputations' to be laid upon them. Episcopius claimed that 'their endeavour had been none other but to remove these imputations, and to provide as much as in them lay, that the conceits of some few might not pass for the general doctrine of our Churches'.[4]

He suggested 'mutual toleration, of the possibility of which alone they had hope',[5] saying that they were 'unjustly charged with the bringing in of a sceptic theology', when all they sought for was reasonable liberty to discuss 'only such a matter, which for a long time had been without danger, both pro and contra disputed of'. He maintained 'that all fundamental points of divinity they had preserved untouched', and that it had always been held that 'sundry opinions even amongst the Fathers themselves' were allowable on these matters. They agreed with Paraeus that treating 'the Schoolmen's conclusions as . . . articles of faith' was the greatest cause of contention.[6] He said 'that they profess they oppose themselves, first against those conclusions concerning predestination, which the authors themselves called horrida decreta. Secondly, against those who for the Five Articles so called have made a separation. . . . Thirdly, against those who cast from them all those

1. *Ib.* p. 463.   3. *Ib.* p. 401.   5. *Ib.* p. 422.
2. *Ib.* p. 385.   4. *Ib.* p. 421.   6. *Ib.* p. 423.

who in some things dissent from them', and they accepted 'the Scriptures and solid reason'.[1]

Hales records how another speaker requested that they might not 'be dealt withal by authority, but by reason'.[2] It is along similar lines that his own thinking developed, and it is clear that, as he himself noted, this was for him the end of a period. He returned to Eton in 1619, and was appointed chaplain to Laud in 1639, but within ten years the deaths of Laud and then of Charles I also marked the end of a period, and during the Commonwealth, Calvinism and Puritanism would appear to be supreme. Yet there were solvents acting on both. As far as Calvinism was concerned, Arminianism and the growth of a method which took account of reason had to be reckoned with, and even Socinianism had filtered in through the Amsterdam bridgehead in spite of Laud's censorship, and if its impact was slight yet it inclined others to question the presuppositions of the system. Also other interests were arising with the formation just before the Restoration of what was to become the Royal Society. Considerations of the relevance of the created order to questions of theology, of an alternative discipline of observation and deduction, in which direction the work of Hales and the Cambridge Platonists had unmistakably pointed, came to the fore, so that by the end of the century a climate of thought had arrived in which the great questions of the Five Articles no longer seemed to have the same vitality.

With regard to the general religious situation, sufficient attention has not been paid to the implications of the facts noted by R. S. Bosher, that many complaints recorded in the State Papers of 1658–60 witness to the growing popularity of Anglican worship and that during the Commonwealth there was 'a steady demand for episcopal ordination'.[3] The evidence indicates that very many ordinary people longed for the return of the religion they had loved with its ordered and familiar liturgy, and that this longing increased as time went on: 'To some who had once fretted under the Laudian discipline, the days of prelacy now suggested a newly valued uniformity and order in religion'.[4]

This tendency cooperated with the trend of theology and worked towards the same end, but it is in itself the but partly conscious

---

1. *Ib.* p. 424.
2. *Ib.* p. 439.

3. R. S. Bosher, *The Making of the Restoration Settlement*, pp. 38, 48.
4. *Ib.* p. 48.

expression of a theological conviction which was at that very time being lavishly and fully expressed in learned and also in popular books by Anglican writers in exile or at home. This conviction, an active belief in the visible Church, sustained the exile in France and the Low Countries when the ambassadors' chapels were its only apparent token. It sustained the dispossessed at home, and it is something that may not be discounted in the development of theological method. It was inevitable that it should come to the fore during the Commonwealth when the Church was proscribed, for this forced upon people's notice the contrast between it and the sects which had arisen side by side with a solid and constructive Puritanism. This type of Puritanism did not approve of such men as Nayler or sympathise with the many sects then flourishing any more than the Church of England did. But, as an anonymous writer put it, the point was that 'once allow that private persons by their own instinct and impulse, a power to erect Churches',[1] and confusion follows, and he maintains that what he calls the experiment of 1641–60 very nearly extinguished religion in England by proceeding on those lines. Once grant this, and there is neither argument nor complaint to be made against Messianists such as William Franklin, whose story he relates, or against the existence of the different groups of which he gives an account.[2]

Another anonymous book written somewhat earlier holds that the fissiparous tendency observable in the Netherlands and in Scotland is the result of the policy adopted.[3] Both books give some interesting accounts of little-known incidents in confirmation of what the writers are endeavouring to prove. Their chief significance, however, is that they both assume what might be called a Laudian view of the Church, and that they are not the work of well-known partisans but may be fairly taken to represent rank-and-file opinion.

It may seem to be part of the perennial paradox of Anglicanism that its theological method should be involved not only with the freedom of reason, but with the inevitability of the visible Church. It was so with Hooker and it was so during the seventeenth century and the situation was in all important respects the same at the

---

1. *The Unity of the Church of England Asserted* (1710), p. 88.
2. *Ib.* pp. 259–263.
3. *A Vindication of the Primitive Church and Diocesan Episcopacy*, (1682), pp. 383–406.

time of the *Lux Mundi* debate, for Gore and his colleagues believed in the Church and they also believed in the freedom of
reason.

Looked at more closely, the paradox may seem less of a paradox
when it is noted that this theological approach takes account of a
reason which is living because it is free, of a concept of law as a
living directive implanted in all things, and of a living society
whose form is in some way part of its life since the society is for
its members the continuation and the living embodiment of
primitive antiquity. Is there here a logic, the terms of which are
less easily defined but more readily apprehended than those of the
logic of that system which, with all its light and shade, magni-
ficently dominated thought for more than a century?

An understanding of the impact made by the system in England
and of the nature of the reaction to it is of the first importance as far
as the development of theological method is concerned. It is one
of the signal differences between the situation in the seventeenth
and in the nineteenth century that the Continental influence
which was so marked in the earlier period was almost non-existent
in the later.

CHAPTER II

CALVINISM AND THEOLOGICAL SYSTEM: ANDREWES, SANDERSON AND TAYLOR

THE extent of Calvinist influence in England has already been referred to. Its immediate source was those who had returned from exile on the Continent.[1] Its ultimate source was a whole climate of thought and opinion which had been making itself felt in England before Mary's policy obliged those to whom such ideas were congenial to take refuge in places where they were not proscribed.

The returned Marian exiles played an increasingly important part in the opening years of Elizabeth's reign, and it is significant that, of the nine Protestants who took part in the disputation held before the passing of the Uniformity Bill in 1559, eight had been exiles and eight were to become bishops.[2] For although the refugees numbered only about five hundred persons in all they were largely gentry and clergy from whose ranks leaders were naturally and chiefly recruited. Neale suggests that they learned more than theology during their sojourn abroad. They learned the art of combining and of preparing a position. He refers to 'the general pattern of the Puritan revolutionary conspiracy'[3] in the introduction of a bill in the summer of 1571 just before the first *Admonition to the Parliament* made its appearance, 'with its Calvinistic features'. The *Admonition* had made an immediate stir and it was widely circulated in spite of press censorship, being in fact printed by a secret press. 'Planning came from the Marian émigrés, an art learnt in exile and prolonged and refined by the organizing genius of Calvinism: a "conspiracy" as the Bishop of London so aptly described it in 1573. The Puritan divines who operated through their gentlemen friends and patrons in the Lower House taught their generation, and through them their Stuart successors, the rudiments of parliamentary politics'.[4]

That is the ecclesiastical and political aspect of events. A new

1. J. E. Neale, *Elizabeth I and her Parliaments* 1559–81, p. 72.
2. Including Jewel.
3. Loc. cit. p. 298.
4. *Ib*. p. 421.

view of ecclesiastical polity had arrived, 'a true platforme',[1] from abroad. 'And out of this realme, they have all the best reformed churches thorouwte Christendome againste them'[2] was the criticism of the second *Admonition* in which the newly-acquired accents of the returned travellers are clearly heard. But with the polity, and informing it, came the theological method which Hooker opposed. It is relevant that the *Admonition* was reprinted in 1617 and again in 1644.

It is fatally easy to criticise Calvinism, for of all systems it suffers from the faults of its qualities, to miss the grandeur of it and thus to fail to recognise the strength of its appeal for many in that period, for as G. R. Cragg wrote, 'the leaders of the Elizabethan Church were Calvinists to a man'.[3] Vastly impressive in the sweep of its transcendental thinking, cohesive and logical, its sturdiness and the aura surrounding the names of Calvin and Geneva, made it almost irresistibly attractive in the circumstances of the time. In other words, contemporaries succumbed to the undoubted attractions of a system. Nor could it be denied that the times required a systematiser if the gains of the Continental Reformation were not to be dissipated by the theological anarchy which had begun to appear in many quarters. In one sense, a very important sense from the point of view of theological method, Calvin is medieval where Hooker shows the beginnings of something different. For Calvin performed for the Continental Reform the office of a Schoolman when he produced his *Institutes*. His background as a lawyer and a classicist helped to make him ideally suited for the task and the magnificence of his achievement cannot be in question. While he is not an initiator, a begetter of thought, his learning, insight and clarity created a system and a polity which gave shape and coherence to all that had gone before. His work is architectonic.

Calvin constructed a system, and because as a systematiser he felt the compulsion to reduce reality to dependence on one central and easily-stated factor, the focal point of that system was the transcendent, 'soli Deo gloria'. While there is here an element of permanent and lasting value, it is when it is followed up that the system falls a victim to its own inexorable logic, seeming to place the reality of human freedom at a discount and ending with those

1. First *Admonition*.
2. Preface.
3. G. R. Cragg, *From Puritanism to the Age of Reason*, p. 14.

conclusions which ultimately brought about its eclipse, for they are as irrational as they are logical. Calvinism is scholastic in that its approach is syllogistic. Nowhere is this more clear than in the question of the decrees, of election and rejection, which constituted a point of no return for so many during the seventeenth century. The fatal clarity which maintained that predestination to election implied predestination to rejection is the negative side of the Pauline assertion that election is not of merit. The conclusion was drawn by the inner logic of the system's own presuppositions, and it was not recognised that in spite of the existence of paradox within the biblical evidence, the evidence as a whole was not consistent with the conclusion.

Calvin was doubtless conditioned here not only by the logic of the situation as he saw it but by his own view of the complete sufficiency of Scripture as the only authoritative source and by the necessity of having its warrant. Hooker's achievement was to see the created order whole in terms of law, of which the biblical was one component. Calvin's achievement was to construct a system in terms of the transcendent, of which the Scripture was the sole authoritative declaration. The contrast is between the liberal and the doctrinaire, between awareness of the implications of the visible world and a pure metaphysic.

The whole subject, however, was under review from a point in time closer to it, in Peter Heylyn's *Historia Quinquarticularis*, the preface of which is dated 1659. Heylyn was not only the biographer of Laud, but he was a Laudian who remained opposed to the new order during the Commonwealth, and who by his presence and his pen had made an active contribution to the defence of the Church during that period. He was one of a group whose writings were of material and proven advantage to the cause of the Church of England.

But the importance of his book in this connection is not so much the story or the manner of its telling as the fact that he perceives the ultimate issue to be a question of theology. What he terms 'the Genevian rigors in the points before us'[1] imply a method and approach in theology and his book is concerned with an analysis of this and of its history and consequences, particularly in England. The sub-title of the work, *A Declaration of the Judgment of the Western Churches, and more particularly the*

1. *Historia Quinquarticularis*, Preface.

Church of England; in the Five Controverted Points, reproached in
these last times by the name of Arminianism, sketches the outline of
his plan. His theme is to show how and when this manner of
thinking on these subjects appeared and to demonstrate that its
upholders were not what he terms 'old English Protestants'[1]
and that it does not represent the teaching of the English Church.

Beginning in true Laudian fashion with the Fathers, he passes
in review the debates on predestination in the Council of Trent
and at the Synod of Dort, and coming to Calvin, he asserts that
the horrible decretum could find no support in Scripture or in
ancient writers: 'and in this point he was so resolutely bent, that
nothing but an absolute decree for Adam's fall, seconded by the
like, for the involving of all his race in the same prediction, would
either serve his turn, or preserve his credit'.[2] Heylyn comments on
the way, noted by Hooker, in which Calvin has acquired in
Reformed circles the position of the Master of the Sentences.[3]
Summarising the conclusions of the Synod of Dort[4] on the absolute decree, on redemption for the elect only, on the loss of free-
will and the consequent unavoidable necessity controlling human
actions, his criticisms are trenchant, especially in the latter article,
when he hits out at this seventeenth-century determinism which
undermined all endeavour and effort, since nothing done or left
undone can influence the outcome. He records that a gleam of
sanity appeared in the members of the British delegation who
insisted that redemption was universal.

In the second part of his book, he acutely observes that the
whole weight of the Prayer Book is against the idea of an absolute
decree of reprobation, nor is it to be found in the Articles or in
the works of Hooper and Latimer, who maintained that the cause
of reprobation was not in a decree but in the individual.[5] The
sixteenth Article clearly opposes the Calvinist view of the certainty of grace nor do the Homilies, with their emphasis on the
co-operation of the human will, lend it any support.[6]

Even at this stage of the debate a critic like Heylyn could put
his finger on the syllogistic nature of the system. Of a certain
pamphlet he wrote 'Now this man goes to work like a logician,

---

1. *Ib.* C.XXII, VII.   2. *Ib.* C.V, IV.   3. *Ib.* C.V, V.
4. Which represented all the Calvinist Churches except that of France, 'some
   few divines of England being added to them'. *Ib.* C.V, VI.
5. *Ib.* Pt. II. C.IX, C.X.   6. *Ib.* Pt. II, C.XIII, C.XIV.

and frames his syllogism in this manner, viz. that whatsoever was in Adam, was in him by God's will and ordinance. But sin was in Adam, ergo, sin was in him by God's will and ordinance'.[1]

The subject of the third section is to explain how these views gained not only currency but ascendancy in England. He dates what he terms the first alteration in doctrine from the return of the Marian exiles, who 'though otherwise men of good abilities in most parts of learning, returned so altered in their principles, as to points of doctrine, so disaffected to the government, forms of worship here by law established, that they seem'd not to be the same men at their coming home, as they had been at their going hence'. Because of the necessity of the times they were taken 'without relation to their private opinions in doctrine or discipline'.[2]

Fox's views on predestination in his Acts and Monuments were 'the first great battery which was made on the bulwarks of this Church, in point of doctrine, by any member of her own, after the settling of the Articles by the Queen's authority, Ann. 1562'.[3] It was the well-known Perkins who opened the breach wider with his *Armilla Aurea* (1592) against which Arminius wrote. Heylyn returns to one of his basic criticisms of the system as undermining the sense of responsibility, when he records the opinion of a contemporary that Perkins's views 'cut off the sinews of man's endeavours'.

Although Calvinism spread rapidly there were those like Baro and Barrett who opposed it. When the latter was charged with maintaining certain propositions contrary to Calvinist teaching, he agreed that he did so but denied that they were contrary to the teaching of the Church of England and therefore he would continue to maintain them.[4] 'There must be many more Barretts' was Heylyn's comment 'though their names through the envy of the times are not come to us'.[5] Referring to the case of Baro and the Lambeth Articles, he says of the latter that their authority 'was plainly none at all',[6] and as evidence for this he asserts that Whitgift defended them to Elizabeth as a purely *ad hoc* formulation designed to deal with a local dispute: 'They were not made to be a standing rule'.[7]

---

1. *Ib*. Pt. III. C.XVI, VI.
2. *Ib*. Pt. III. C.XIX, I.
3. *Ib*. Pt. III. C.XIX, VI.
4. *Ib*. Pt. III. C.XX, IX.

5. *Ib*. Pt. III, C.XX, XI.
6. *Ib*. Pt. III. C.XXI, III.
7. *Ib*. Pt. III. C.XXII, II.

Heylyn notes that another reason for the prevalence of Calvinism was the fact that 'his book of Institutes being for the most part the foundation on which the young divines of those times did build their studies' the system spread. As time passed however, opposition became increasingly vocal, and when at the Hampton Court Conference in 1604, Reynolds petitioned King James 'that the nine assertions orthodoxal as he termed them concluded upon at Lambeth might be inserted into the Book of Articles', this suggestion was turned down, and they were left to be discussed in the Schools 'as more proper for them'.[1]

An effort to change the sense of Article XVI was also resisted, and Bancroft maintained that 'laying all religion on predestination, if I shall be saved, I shall be saved', was 'a desperate doctrine'. He perceived that it was to put the theological cart before the horse. A logic more true to life would hold, says Bancroft in effect, that a man observes the duties and therefore trusts in his election. It does not hold that he is elected and that nothing can effect the issue.[2]

Heylyn notes the preferment of men like Bancroft, Barlow, Buckeridge, Cary, Houson, Laud, Mountain and Neill: 'By which encouragements the anti-Calvinians or old English Protestants took heart again and more openly delivered themselves than they had done formerly'. Anti-Calvinism was also helped by 'the differences betwixt the Remonstrants and the Contra-Remonstrants in the Belgick Provinces . . . who published their discourses one against the other, (and) sharpened the appetite of many students'.[3]

Lastly, he recounts the order of 1622 that these subjects were no longer to be handled 'in any popular auditory' but reserved for learned discussion 'rather than by way of positive doctrine',[4] and he refers to the approval given to Richard Montague's book 'in which he asserted the Church to her primitive and genuine doctrines and disclaimed all the Calvinian tenets as disowned by her'.[5]

Andrewes and Sanderson have already been mentioned in this connection, and their views are worth looking at in more detail. In the case of Andrewes, there is in his treatment of the current thinking in the Cambridge of his time, in addition to the emphasis on antiquity and continuity, a wise and balanced determination

1. Bancroft, Bilson, Andrewes and Richard Field were present.
2. Ib. Pt. III, C.XXII, IV.
3. Ib. Pt. III, C.XXII, VII.
4. Ib. Pt. III, C.XXII, X.
5. Ib. Pt. III, C.XXII, XI.

not to go beyond the evidence. Marginal matters may not be put at the centre and he resists the attempt to limit the freedom to maintain reserve on such questions. The Church may not be committed to opinions which make a dogma of an opinion.

This charateristic reticence on non-fundamentals gathers strength with the passage of time and remains a part of theological method. It outlasted all tendency to erect a system on what is essentially speculative, because it allows for the free exercise of discernment, and, doubtless for the most part unconsciously, for the unfolding state of thought during the period.

The strong position reached however by Calvinism in England is best gauged by the fact that public censure should be passed by the University in 1595 on men like Baro and Barrett who held that its tenets were not in accord with the formularies of the Church of England. What is significant about the resulting Lambeth Articles is not their authority, for they had none and they were in fact suppressed by order of Elizabeth. Nor is their true significance to be sought in the documents themselves, for they were drawn up to deal with a local matter, and were interpreted as such.[1] Their importance stems from the fact that Whitgift and others should hold them not only to be consistent with the teaching of the Church of England, but that they should regard the views which they set out as a criterion.

In his *Judgment of the Lambeth Articles*,[2] Andrewes reveals his approach to the whole question. So much does he regard these problems as ultimately insoluble that his practice has always been to avoid public or private discussion concerning them. Few are capable of handling them or of profiting by them, and people would be better advised to occupy themselves with what is plain and obligatory than with what is hidden and obscure.[3] This vein of what may be called pragmatism is always present to some degree or another in Anglican theological method in the seventeenth century. Relevance to the conditions of reality is highly rated from Andrewes to the Latitudinarians.

Andrewes's emendations or additions are all in a liberalising direction, as in his view of man, and in his assertion that the question of reprobation so much discussed by all at this time was being approached from the wrong angle. It should be seen in

1. J. Strype, *Life and Acts of Whitgift*, II, p. 282.

2. *Minor Works*. L.A.C.T. ed.
3. *Ib*. pp. 294–5.

terms of men's own actions and not in terms of an absolute decree.[1] In the eighth article, while the Lambeth commission had not accepted the word 'tractum' which referred to human nature being drawn to sin as implying an irresistible determinism, but as meaning an operation which did not take away the freedom of the will,[2] Andrewes added further 'that the cause of their not being so drawn was not an absolute decree, but a perverted human will'.[3] In this whole context, he recommends that the use of the word 'necessity' be discontinued as it is ambiguous and begs the question.[4] Both here and elsewhere he submits terms to a careful and exact scrutiny.[5] Discussing the fifth and sixth articles, he does not agree that there is any evidence to support the view of the indefectibility of grace, and as to assurance about man's future state, he maintains that this is more a matter of hope than of faith as the article asserts.[6] If, as has been said, Andrewes's emendations are in a liberal direction, his position is clear. He is not only dissenting from a system, but he is affirming that the system is based on what is speculative, on what cannot certainly be known and for which the evidence is not available. At an early stage there emerges from the situation the outline of a characteristic method which draws a clear distinction between what is revealed and what is a matter of opinion, and which is not prepared to treat any formulation on this basis as authoritative.[7]

In the year before Andrewes died, Sanderson, who had previously held sublapsarian views on the grounds that they were more moderate and reasonable, found that a change had come about in his opinions.[8]

Walton records that 'In the first parliament of this good king, which was in 1625, he was chosen to be a clerk of the Convocation

1. *Ib.* p. 295. 3. *Ib.* p. 300. 5. *Ib.* pp. 290, 300.
2. *Ib.* p. 293. 4. *Ib.* p. 298. 6. *Ib.* p. 299.
7. This had been a marked element in the thinking of John Donne whose sermons have been described in a recent work by W. R. Mueller, *John Donne: Preacher* (Oxford, 1962), pp. 149, 152, as 'the most compelling presentation of that Summa of Anglicanism, Richard Hooker's *Of the Laws of Ecclesiastical Polity'*. Mueller regards them as doing for Hooker's theology an office somewhat similar to that performed for Thomism by Dante or for Puritanism by Bunyan. On this significant distinction he writes 'It would be difficult to overemphasise the importance which Donne places on the Church's responsibility to distinguish between the fundamentals and the non-fundamentals of belief, and he finds one of the great triumphs of the Anglican Church to lie in its ability to make such an all-important distinction'.
8. Sanderson, L.A.C.T. ed. V, pp. 297–9.

for the diocese of Lincoln; which I here mention, because about that time did arise many disputes about predestination, and the many critical points that depend upon or are interwoven in it, occasioned, as was said, by a disquisition of new principles of Mr Calvin's, though others say they were long before his time. But of these Dr Sanderson then drew up for his own satisfaction such a scheme (he called it Pax Ecclesiae) . . . and here the reader may note, that in letters writ to the said Dean, Dr Sanderson seems to have altered his judgment in some points since he writ his scheme called Pax Ecclesiae'.[1]

The letter referred to is quoted in a reply from Pierce to Walton in which the former states that it contains an account of the development of Sanderson's thinking and that while part of it was published by Hammond, the extracts which he now gives have not been printed heretofore.[2] He recalls that the part used by Hammond recounts how Sanderson, reading Hooker, found that he was mistaken 'whilst he took things upon trust, in the sublapsarian way'. The phrase itself, and the source of the change in his ideas, are both indicative of the development of Sanderson's thought.

Sublapsarianism differs from supralapsarianism in that the former regards the decrees of election and rejection as having reference to mankind as already fallen, while the latter looks on mankind simply as creatures, and regards the decrees as antecedent to the means appointed to achieve them. In other words, before the creation, a part of mankind was chosen and a part rejected, and creation, fall and redemption were simply the means appointed to give effect to this. It is the logician's approach disapproved of by Heylyn, and it depends on the proposition that the end precedes the means and it evacuates freedom of any reality. It can hardly be said that this is Calvin's view, although Sanderson was unable to make up his mind on the point.

It is small wonder that Sanderson, as quoted in the letter to Walton, should characterise this as being 'like a spider's web' when he encountered it, with individual variations, in the book published by Twiss in 1632.[3] The author was an old Oxford acquaintance, whose ability Sanderson respected, but whose position he regarded as untenable. The book subordinated all to what it conceived to be the chief end of all the decrees,[4] 'soli Deo gloria', and

1. *Ib.* VI, pp. 297–8.
2. *Ib.* VI, pp. 351–2.
3. *Ib.* VI, p. 354.
4. *Ib.*

Sanderson criticises it as being based on what his correspondent calls an untrue 'logic maxim',[1] 'that whatsoever is first in the intention is last in execution'.[2] Sanderson had read the book by de Arriba on the subject which had been published in 1623, and while he evidently had not formed a high opinion of the work, it had served to convince him that free will and 'the contingency of inferior causes and effects' were not to be ignored.[3]

Before his appointment in 1625, he had been loth, like Andrewes, to concern himself with the question,[4] but as it was anticipated that there might be a discussion of the matter in Convocation, he resolved to turn his attention to it and the result was that he could no longer accept the views he had previously held.[5]

Sanderson's earlier standpoint came very close at times to the language of the Lambeth Articles, and his editor instances a passage in a sermon which approximates to the fifth and seventh of those articles.[6] The date of the sermon was 1627, although not so specified in the first edition, and Hammond had remarked on the confusion resulting from Sanderson not having made the appropriate alterations in his published work, seeing that his views were not the same as they had been before.[7] In the 1657 edition the word Pelagian had been substituted for Arminian, but the fact is that Sanderson's thinking was, like that of many writers of the time, in reaction against any suspicion of Pelagianism. In various passages the ideas of Pelagianism and *meritum congrui* are rejected, although there is a balancing stress on the aspect of response.[8] While his conclusions on reason and natural law, which show the use made of Aquinas, are such as preclude extremism, he writes 'nature is all naught'.[9] Elsewhere, in a sermon delivered in 1621, having defended the election of some 'without any motives in or from themselves', he qualifies this by adding that these things must be rightly understood, and he explicitly denies that such teaching implies that rejection is 'by a stoical fatal necessity . . . whether they deserve it or no', or that people may act as they like, 'as if we cried down good works'.[10]

Frequent references to humanity as being 'in Adam' point in

1. *Ib.* V, p. 300.
2. *Ib.* VI, p. 354.
3. *De Concordia Gratiae et Liberi Arbitrii. Ib.* V, pp. 352–3.
4. *Ib.* V, pp. 297–9.
5. *Ib.*

6. *Ib.* III, p. 267.
7. *Ib.* I, p.v.
8. *Ib.* III, pp. 30, 41.
9. *Ib.* III, p. 254.
10. *Ib.* II, pp. 46–7.

the same direction, although Sanderson hedges at 'splendida peccata' when unbelievers 'follow the direction and guidance of right reason' according to the light that they have. This might be called 'rectus usus naturalium' if Pelagians and others had not spoilt the term.[1] Reason has for them 'the strength of a law',[2] and Sanderson adds elsewhere that 'without all doubt the law of nature and the light of reason was the rule whereby they were guided'.[3]

It is this stress on reason and its function which, running through all his work, finally brings Sanderson to his new position. 'Scripture we acknowledge to be a perfect rule ... yet not as excluding the use of reason but supposing it', he writes, adding 'He left us as he found us, reasonable creatures still, without any purpose, by the gift of that greater and sublimer light, to put out the light he had formerly given us, that of reason, or to render it useless or unserviceable'.[4]

Given this, it was only a matter of time until the basic incompatibility with what he had hitherto taken on trust became apparent. Ultimately, his agreement with Hooker and Aquinas on law conceived of in terms of reason would have made it impossible for him to take any other direction.

The *Pax Ecclesiae* was a posthumous publication, not appearing until 1678, but as Walton made clear, it was the result of Sanderson's thinking on the subject at an earlier date. Its most distinctive note is the conviction that in these matters so much is speculative that a wide latitude ought to be given to individuals since conclusions can only be tentative. The very nature of the question makes differences of opinion inevitable,[5] and there must be a sensitivity to the complex nature of the discussion,[6] a refusal to treat tenets as formularies[7] or to stress terms rather than their general meaning.[8] He suggests 'that particular Churches would be as tender as may be in giving their definitions and determinations in such points as these, not astricting those that live therein determinately to the affirmative or negative'.[9] He maintains that if Churches should find it necessary 'synodically to determine something in these points', they ought not to require individual subscription, but allow people 'their own private opinions'.[10] For this reason,

1. *Ib*. III, p. 236.
2. *Ib*. III, p. 237.
3. *Ib*. II, p. 113.
4. *Ib*. II, p. xlvii (1657 Preface). Cp.
　　Prae. I, 25, IV, 24, IX, 3.
5. *Ib*. V, p. 256.

6. *Ib*. V, p. 260.
7. *Ib*. V, p. 259.
8. *Ib*. V, p. 259.
9. *Ib*. V, p. 257.
10. *Ib*. p. 258.

catechisms should not contain such private tenets but only fundamentals.[1]

As to his own conclusions, the most Sanderson will say on the subject is that they have 'hitherto given me better satisfaction than any other' and are not 'subject to so great difficulties' as those of either extreme.[2] Because of the nature of the question some difficulties will still remain and those who will not accept the fact that a logical system cannot be imposed have become immersed in further difficulties and have been obliged to 'maintain strange opinions'.[3] He is content to wait patiently for new insights, 'not intending hereby to prescribe unto other men, nor yet to tie myself to mine own present judgment, if I shall see cause to alter it'.[4] This is in line with Hooker, the study of whose works had, in Sanderson's own words, been a preparative for a cautious reading of the *Institutes*.[5]

The essentially tentative nature of any enquiry or discussion is clear in the penetrating assessment, 'For considering often with myself, that the abettors of either extreme are confirmed in their own opinions, not so much from the assurance of their own grounds as from the inconveniences that attend the opposite extreme, I have ever thought that a middle way between both might be fairer and safer to pitch upon, than either extreme'.[6]   Sanderson's merit, and his contribution to the development of theological method, is to be found in his readiness to suspend judgment, in his recognition of the existence of paradox in this connection and in his insistence that paradox is turned into an artificial dilemma if there is an attempt to systematise: 'sundry passages in the Scriptures . . . which have in them some appearance of contradiction, may, by following this way, be easily reconciled'.[7] But he claims no more than that this may give some light on the matters involved, and will not settle the question.[8] His *Series* aims at avoiding the extremes of those who concentrate on 'soli Deo gloria' or on free-will, and is in accord with the general tenor of the Scriptures, the Articles and the Book of Common Prayer and the Fathers, 'especially St Augustine and those that followed him'.[9]

There are some signs of reaction from any kind of Pelagianism, as in the tendency to view the situation almost exclusively in terms

1. *Ib.* p. 258.   4. *Ib.* p. 266.   7. *Ib.* p. 273.
2. *Ib.* p. 266.   5. *Ib.* p. 297.   8. *Ib.* p. 277.
3. *Ib.* p. 256.   6. *Ib.* p. 266.   9. *Ib.* p. 271.

of a justice whose primary form of self-expression is through sovereignty which cannot be questioned. He explains that it is not possible to make any imputation against the justice which elects some and rejects others since both were 'equal in the sinful mass of corrupt nature', and it is through mercy that all were not rejected 'for their sin in Adam'.[1] He adds that, while in his view, the will is 'freed from all coactive necessity,' it is not itself 'the prime cause' or 'determinating' power.[2]

The design is to show that the situation in 'which either extreme presseth sore upon the opposite extreme'[3] is unreal, where one regards the other as holding an inadequate concept of justice 'for placing the decree of reprobation before that of Adam's fall', and being criticised in turn for making everything 'to depend upon man's free will'.[4] In the order of the decrees, Sanderson puts first the creation of the rational creature, followed by the covenant of works, and 'after this covenant made', the allowing of freedom to choose. The permitting of man 'thus left to himself' to fall is followed by a new covenant 'that the whole species of so noble a creature might not perish' and in case this covenant 'should yet be ineffectual . . . to elect a certain number . . . passing by the rest'.[5]

Hammond, who was in many ways the most considerable figure among those who were regarded as promoters of Anglican apologetic during the Commonwealth, published the *Pacific Discourse* in 1660. As Bosher remarks, the extensive output of Anglican books at a time when the Church was suppressed was due in large measure to his efforts and his encouragement of others.[6] Although Baxter regarded him as the leader of those he called 'the new prelatical divines', he went so far as to say that had Hammond lived the course of things might have been very different.[7] The book takes the form of a discussion of a letter from Sanderson. In it, Hammond concurs that the ground of their agreement on such matters as freedom and contingency is an approach based on 'Scripture, reason and experience'.[8] A recurring feature of seventeenth-century theological method appears in his disinclination to attach too much importance to terms.[9] This is not a refusal to define but a determination not to substitute definition for reason.

1. *Ib.* p. 272.
2. *Ib.* p. 273.
3. *Ib.* p. 271.
4. *Ib.* p. 271.
5. *Ib.* pp. 266–70.
6. R. S. Bosher, *The Making of the Restoration Settlement*, p. 36.
7. *Ib.* p. 29.
8. *Ib.* p. 293.
9. *Ib.* p. 291.

Hooker, Hales, Andrewes, Heylyn and others are at one in their mistrust of a system which depends on closely-knit logic rather than on reason autonomous and illuminative, the human characteristic as Whichcote called it.

Sanderson had suggested that the whole difficulty was 'how to reconcile the certain futurition of what God foreseeth with the liberty of the rational creature, and the contingency of casual effects, as they proceed from inferior causes'.[1] Hammond agreed, indicating that such prescience could only mean 'seeing every thing that ever exists, as it is, contingents as contingents, necessary, as necessary', and that it 'can neither work any change in the object, by thus seeing it, (convert a contingent into a necessary)',[2] for, in Sanderson's words, this was 'a necessity infinitely distant from that which predetermination importeth'.[3] Here and elsewhere, Sanderson is resisting the idea of physical predetermination which he saw as inconsistent with the natural liberty of the will.[4]

Hammond reacts against the logical approach,[5] and on two or three occasions refers with approval to Sanderson's determination to maintain scepticism on conjectural matters.[6] Hammond regards what he describes as absolute election and unconditional rejection as invention,[7] and Sanderson observes on this point that condemnation on the grounds of Adam's disobedience ('and they being yet unborn, could not help it') might be consistent with power but not with love.[8] There is something of a change here as compared with Sanderson's earlier views, and the letter represents a further modification of what Hammond called inconditionate election by regarding the object of the decrees as 'the generality of men preached unto'.[9] Election is then conditional on the response of the individual, and men are 'left in the hand of their own counsel'.[10] It is at this point that Sanderson's emphasis on the order of the decrees carries weight, for the logical dilemma upon which sublapsarianism and supralapsarianism impaled themselves ceases to exist when the decree of election is no longer placed first as the end to which all that follows is the means.

There is a candour in Sanderson's writing, and a determination neither to overestimate nor to underestimate the place of reason.

1. *Ib.* p. 294.   5. *Ib.* p. 300.   8. *Ib.* p. 301.
2. *Ib.* p. 295.   6. *Ib.* pp. 303, 306.   9. *Ib.* p. 312.
3. *Ib.* p. 294.   7. *Ib.* pp. 302, 307.   10. *Ib.* p. 313.
4. *Ib.* p. 323.

It is to be used to infer, deduce and weigh, but reason must also 'learn to know her distance', for the understanding is not the measure of all things.[1] At some cost, he has freed himself from the impasse and from the entanglement of words, so that reason and experience can be taken into account.

Sanderson's awareness of the claims of reason in connection with these questions takes the form of a liberality of outlook, and, like Hooker, he brings this to a theological method in which the appeal to Scripture and to antiquity have their part. It appears also however in his concern with practical reason and with the constant assertion of the involvement and relevance of theology. For it is as a moral theologian that Sanderson is chiefly remembered, and in view of his statement about 'giving myself mostly to the study of moral divinity',[2] it is probably the way in which he would have preferred to be remembered. This strain of 'practical divinity' is a permanent feature in seventeenth-century writing, being by no means confined to those who, like Taylor and Sanderson, made a formal study of the subject, and it had a formative influence on theological method. From Hooker to the Latitudinarians there are very few major writers who do not concern themselves, frequently to a considerable degree, with some aspect of the subject. It is one of the positive forms of expression of a general trend in Anglican theology at the time, which was the turning away from speculative systems and a reaching out for relevance and realism. In one form or another this trend may be observed in the Cambridge Platonists and the Latitudinarians, in Taylor and in Barrow, and one of the most widely diffused aspects of it was the preoccupation of the period with what it significantly called 'practical divinity'. This was notably so in the case of Sanderson for whom it was applied theology, something of practical relevance to the individual in society where the corporate and the personal were constantly impinging on one another. In this sense of applying theology to existing contemporary situations, Sanderson had a social gospel or was a sociologist, whichever way one prefers to put it, and this is his distinctiveness as compared with the majority of writers in this field during the seventeenth century.

As Sanderson's contribution to the subject of moral theology has been considered elsewhere in some detail,[3] it is enough for the

1. *Ib.* I, p. 235.
2. *Works*, (L.A.C.T. ed.), Vol. V, p. 298.
3. See my *The Structure of Caroline Moral Theology*.

present purpose of relating it to the general development of theological method to emphasise two matters in this connection. The first is that the interest in practical divinity was sufficiently widespread in the seventeenth century to impart a distinctive quality to the general theological approach, and Sanderson's work was a factor in this. It could even be maintained that it was more influential than Taylor's as far as contemporaries were concerned. The latter had set himself to accomplish his task on a grand scale and in a specialised form, that of 'a general instrument of moral theology',[1] but many found Sanderson's lucidity and directness of application something which answered to the situation, as did Jean La Placete, sometime minister of the French Church at Copenhagen, who regarded his work as exceptional.[2] The second matter to be stressed is the use which Sanderson made of Aquinas, for this is something which reappears throughout the century, often in unexpected ways, and which was a not insignificant influence on the form of theological method during the period. Frequently handling the *Summa* with independence, he draws on its illustrations as well as on its content in respect of law, conscience and acts, and although he presents his material with originality, often taking a different line, the *Summa* plays an acknowledged part as the background to much of his writing on practical divinity.

Both these matters, namely, the effect of practical divinity on theology generally, and the effect of the *Summa* on Anglican practical divinity, and also the application and involvement of theology on the day-to-day level, find fresh illustration in Sanderson's treatment of the subject of justice. Preaching at Lincoln Assizes in 1624, he describes justice as being, next to religion, the security and adornment of the State, an essential element through which all things cohere: 'as the cement in a building, that holdeth all together, so is justice to the public body'.[3] In the *Summa*, the one follows the other, and its exposition of justice lies behind or informs a great deal of what Sanderson has to say on the subject in general, but when he comes to application his treatment is direct and contemporary. He discusses general principles in his lectures on conscience and in *The Case of a Military Life*, one of a number

1. Preface to *Ductor Dubitantium* (Jeremy Taylor, *Works*, ed. R. Heber, Vol. XI, p. 363.)
2. See his *The Christian Casuist* (Tr. B. Kennett), Preface.
3. Robert Sanderson, *Works* (L.A.C.T. ed.), Vol. II, p. 217.

of cases posthumously published, and his outline coincides with
the general outline of the *Summa*. He distinguishes general, or
legal, justice and particular justice, the latter being divided into
distributive justice which has as its function the administering of
law, and commutative justice, the sphere of which is the regulation
of contracts, chiefly those affecting commerce and trade. For
Aquinas, general or legal justice 'directs the acts of all the virtues
to the common good,' and Sanderson also describes it as 'em-
bracing all virtues within its compass'.[1]

Similarly, dealing with the promulgation of positive law as it is
regulated by justice, his discussion of how laws may be unjust
shows the influence of the treatise on law in the *Summa*. Aquinas
says that a law may be unjust 'in respect of the end, as when an
authority imposes on his subjects burdensome laws, conducive,
not to the common good . . . or in respect of the author, as when a
man makes a law that goes beyond the power committed to him;
or in respect of form, as when burdens are imposed unequally on
the community, although with a view to the common good'. These
are instances of laws being unjust because they are opposed to
human good, and laws may also be unjust through being 'opposed
to the Divine good . . . or to anything else contrary to the Divine
law'.[2] In his sixth lecture, Sanderson follows this closely, maintaining that a law may be unjust in respect of its efficient cause, 'if
it be imposed by one not having legitimate authority', or in respect of its final cause, 'if it does not tend to the common good', or in
respect of the formal cause, 'if it apportions awards and punish-
ments unfairly', or in respect of the material cause, 'when it orders
something that is wrong in itself'. While he has his own method
of presentation, and never hesitates to follow his own line, the
form of Sanderson's thought owes much, here and elsewhere, to
the *Summa*.[3]

In the *Case of a Military Life*, where he is drawing a distinction
between what he calls political and private justice, Sanderson's
treatment of international relations is an interesting individual
contribution.[4] The problem is, by what rules of justice are the
mutual relations of princes and states to be measured? As far as

1. Sanderson, *Praelectiones Decem, De Obligatione Conscientiae*, Prae. V, 19, Prae. VI, 10, 14, 15. *Summa Theologica*, IIa IIae, Q.58, AA, 5, 6, 7, and Q.61, A1, and Q.79, A.1.
2. S.T. Ia, IIae, Q.96, A.4.
3. Prae. VI, 14, 15.
4. Sect, III, 4, 5, and Sect. IV, 5–7.

individuals are concerned, justice has as its rule the law of nature, the divine law and positive law, and the cases are parallel to this extent that governments, as well as individuals, 'are obliged to keep faith, both with friends and enemies, every whit as exactly and punctually, without equivocation, reservation, or other eluding devices'. It is neither necessary nor possible, however, in Sanderson's view, that the rules of justice determining international relations should be precisely the same as those governing individuals. The chief obstacle is that there is no body of positive law common to all states, and no sovereign legislative authority. (The history of the attempts to provide such an effective authority during the last thirty-five years is a sufficient comment on the point.) A law of larger extent must be looked for, and this is the 'jus gentium' which 'the great necessity of human affairs hath . . . introduced, by the common consent of nations'. Under this law 'sundry things are by the rules of politic justice allowed as lawful and just between princes, which between private men would, by the rules of mere moral justice, be condemned, and that deservedly too, as unjust and unlawful', and he instances the deviousness of diplomacy, espionage, plots and certain military practices. Sanderson's phrase 'the rules of politic justice' may be roughly the equivalent of such modern concepts as international law or agreed international conventions. The content of the idea of 'jus gentium' has never really been clear, and some have simply equated it with the natural law, while for others it is synonymous with international law. Neither is completely true, for, as R. C. Mortimer put it, 'parts of the "jus gentium" are embodied in international law. International law is the body of agreed rules governing the mutual conduct of sovereign states; in so far as it is unwritten, it is simply the natural law or the "jus gentium".'[1] Sanderson certainly saw that there was a distinction, and he endeavoured to show that here too theology had something to say.

The just administration of laws can, in certain circumstances, only be effected by equity, which, says Hooker, is necessary 'in very truth to practise general laws according to their right meaning'. It is not against but above, law, because it is of the essence of law to be the voice of right reason.[2] The principle of equity is not a side-exit but a way of obtaining justice for an individual whose

1. R. C. Mortimer, *The Elements of Moral Theology*, p. 16.
2. *Ecclesiastical Polity*, Bk. V, C.IX, 3.

particular case would result in the defeat of the purpose of the law
if its letter were strictly applied. Its aim is to interpret the mind
of the legislator in circumstances which he had not foreseen when
framing the law. According to the *Summa*, 'legislators in framing
laws attend to what commonly happens: although if the law be
applied to certain cases it will frustrate the equality of justice and
be injurious to the common good, which the law has in view', and
Aquinas adds, 'epikeia (epieikeia) does not set aside that which is
just in itself but that which is just as by law established'. It is not
the law which is being judged but some particular contingency, so
that the underlying principle is that of interpreting the law-
maker's intention with regard to a special set of circumstances.[1]

Sanderson, who repeatedly stresses the importance of circumstances in cases, expands this as he reminds the magistrates in an
Assize sermon of its practical importance: 'When, taking advantage of the law, we prosecute the extremity thereof against our
brother, who perhaps hath done something contrary to the letter
of the laws but not violated the intent of the law-giver, or offended
either against common equity, which ought to be the measure of
just laws, or against the common good, which is in some sort the
measure of equity. In that multitude of laws, which for the re-
pressing of disorders and for the maintenance of peace and tranquillity among men, must needs be in every well governed commonwealth, it cannot be avoided, but that honest men, especially
if they have much dealing in the world, may have sometimes just
and necessary cause to do that, which, in regard of the thing done,
may bring them within the compass of some statute or branch of a
statute, yet such as, circumstances duly considered, no wise and
indifferent man but would well approve of. Now, if in such cases
always rigour should be used, laws intended for the benefit,
should by such hard construction become the bane of society'.

'Secondly, since laws cannot be so conceived, but that, through
the infinite variety of human occurrences, they may sometimes
fall heavy upon particular men; and yet, for the preventing of more
general inconveniences, it is necessary there should be laws . . .
there hath been left, for any thing I find to the contrary, in all well
governed policies, a kind of latitude more or less, and power in the
magistrates, even in those courts that were "strictissimi juris",
upon fit occasion to qualify and to mitigate something the rigour

1. S.T. IIa, IIae, Q.120, A.1.

of the laws by the rules of equity'.[1] The phrases 'circumstances duly considered' and 'the infinite variety of human occurrences' are a thought never far from Sanderson's mind.

In one of his lectures he observes that reason itself insists that necessity may require legal justice to yield to equity, and he defines the latter as a corrective of legal justice.[2] In more than one place, he remarks that the golden rule is the essence of equity. The same rule—he calls it 'the grand rule'—lies behind the question of restitution, one of the least equivocal 'in the whole body of moral divinity'.[3] Restitution is an act of commutative justice, and Sanderson summarises it: 'Whosoever shall have wronged his neighbour, in anything committed to his custody, or in fellowship, or in any thing taken away by violence or by fraud, or in detaining any found thing, or the like, is bound to restore it, and that "in integrum", to the utmost farthing of what he hath taken, if he be able'.[4] The casuists, he notes, have written whole volumes on the subject but all are clear on the essentials of the matter. He refers to 'Samuel's equity' in offering restitution voluntarily in case he may have wronged anyone, and he also instances Zacchaeus, as does Aquinas, but Sanderson cites him as an example of the principle of restoring more than he took.[5] Aquinas holds that to give back more than one is bound to restore is not necessary to 'equality',[6] while Sanderson maintains that the restorer ought 'beside the principal, to offer some little overplus also, by way of compensation for the damage, if at least the wronged party have sustained any damage thereby, and unless he shall be willing freely to remit it'.[7]

Such is the outline of Sanderson's treatment of justice, a subject to which he frequently returns because of its wide and practical implications. It is when he comes to distributive and commutative justice, to questions of application, that the import of practical divinity for his theology is seen, for it creates an atmosphere of reality and confrontation. For Sanderson, it is through practical divinity that the contact between religion and life is best brought out, so that his theology conveys a notable impression of being in touch with everyday problems.

Since the chief concern of distributive justice is with the work

1. *Works*, Vol. II, pp. 217, 231.
2. *De Obligatione Conscientiae*, X, 16.
3. *Works*, Vol. II, pp. 360-2, and cp. *Ib.* pp. 282, 345. and Vol. III, p. 313.
4. *Ib.* Vol. II, p. 362, and cp. Vol. 1, p. 20.
5. *Ib.* Vol. II, p. 361.
6. S. T. IIa IIae, Q.62, A.3.
7. *Ib.* Vol. II, p. 362.

of the law-courts and such matters as appointments to offices, it is to be expected that Sanderson's sermons before the magistrate will have much to say on this subject. He writes, 'where commutative justice is by private persons violated, through fraud, oppression or bribery, there it behoveth the magistrate to set in, and do his part in the administration of distributive justice, for the rectifying and redressing thereof. It is the very end for which, principally, laws and courts and magistrates were ordained'.[1]

His description is as realistic as it is penetrating and it is clear that he is speaking out of the midst of a society that he understood and was not afraid to criticise. There is no tossing down of abstracts into the pews, for Sanderson knows where the shoe pinches and says so. Principles are stated but always with reference to real situations. He sees the magistrate's office as fourfold.[2] He must do justice with zeal and not discharge his office casually or as a formality. He must help the oppressed and those in distress, but such help must 'stand with equity and justice'. In another place, he cautions the magistrate in this connection against the extremes of 'incompassion' and 'foolish pity'. But while he cannot allow a sentimental sympathy to lead him into injustice, the rule is that 'in doubtful cases, it is doubtlessly better and safer to incline to mercy than to severity: better ten offenders should escape, than one innocent person suffer. But that is to be conceived only when things are doubtful'.[3] A sense of proportion, for instance, is needed in connection with the problems arising out of vagrancy, and in Sanderson's view people ought first to satisfy themselves as to 'who is a poor man'.[4] On another occasion he observes that justice requires that professional beggars should be prevented from robbing 'the truly poor, to whom properly all the fruits of our alms are due'.[5]

The magistrate's third duty is to be diligent in searching out the facts of each case and not to be content until, humanly speaking, he is sure that he has all the evidence before him.[6] Lastly, he must be courageous in the execution of his office, for courage, is often needed when dealing with the great and the wealthy.[7]

Considering the personnel of his hearers, Sanderson has some

1. *Ib.* Vol. II, p. 347.
2. *Ib.* Vol. II, pp. 173–203.
3. *Ib.* Vol. II, p. 288.
4. *Ib.* p. 185.

5. *Ib.* Vol. III, p. 110.
6. *Ib.* Vol. II, p. 187.
7. *Ib.* p. 192.

extremely pointed things to say about the venality of courts in his day and on such matters as the racking of rents by landlords and the depopulating of districts by enclosure. He indicts various economic practices and laments the powerlessness of the law to control them: 'the unconscionable racking of rents, the selling of cattle to poor husbandmen that have not their money ready to buy in the markets, upon a year's day for double the price, the under-buying of commodities far below the worth for disbursing a little money beforehand to supply the present necessity of such an one as might very ill afford such a penny-worth and the like which are all very grievous oppressions in themselves, and by the magistrate known so to be. Yet what can he do to help it, so long as the laws have provided no remedy thereagainst'.[1] These practices are wide-spread and he couples them with the contemporary disregard for practical religion and the preoccupation with 'wranglings in matters of religion',[2] and this reaction on the part of Anglicans recurs in a variety of forms throughout the period. John Evelyn could complain in 1656 that 'nothing practical' was heard in the pulpits but only 'high speculative points and strains'.[3] Sanderson's sense of realism and relevance compelled him to point out that these offences against commutative justice bore heavily on those who could least support it, and he refers to sub-orning of witnesses, packing of juries, depredations of lawyers and bribes offered to magistrates. One of the social evils of the time was the practice by landlords of enclosing commons and waste land, chiefly as pasturage for sheep. The result of this was almost always to depopulate the area and, as Sanderson pointed out, to increase vagrancy. Over a period of twenty years he advised the magistrates to resist this anti-social practice which had always had outspoken opponents such as Laud and Hall. E. C. E. Bourne has drawn attention to Laud's attitude to what was in effect virtually a system of evictions, claiming to have as its object the improve-ment of holdings but which mainly resulted in the betterment of the few rather than in higher national agricultural prosperity.[4] Sanderson recognised the resulting social abuse, referring to the 'carcases of depopulated towns',[5] meaning farms and hamlets, and

1. *Ib.* Vol. II, p. 314, and cp. *Ib.* p. 263 p. 353.
2. *Ib.* p. 264.
3. *Diary of John Evelyn*, Vol. III, p. 184 (ed. E. S. de Beer).

4. E. C. E. Bourne, *The Anglicanism of William Laud*, pp. 119–120.
5. *Ib.* Vol. II, p. 204.

commenting on 'these hard and depopulating times'.[1] He accuses
great men of 'pulling down houses and setting up hedges, in
unpeopling towns and creating beggars'.[2] He indicts the land-
owner that 'Ahab-like wringest thy poor neighbour's vineyard
from him, (and) drivest him by continual molestations to this
strait, that either he must forsake the town, if thou hast a mind to
enclose it, or else consent to his own and most of his neighbour's
undoing'.[3] If the sole intention were to improve on wasteful
medieval methods all would have been well, but Sanderson did
not see how a man's farming could be improved by taking away
his farm, and he said so.

His concern for the rights of the individual and for the magistrate's defence of them is constantly reflected as in his condemnation of the practice of cornering the market, known in his day as
'ingrossing', by which large quantities of corn or other goods were
bought up and then sold later at an unreasonable profit.[4] Monopolies, too, and the letters patent granting them, were a great
grievance in the seventeenth century, being looked upon as a
convenient method of raising money by the court and government: 'but as in all monopolies there is a pretension of some
common good held forth to make them passable, when as in most
of them it may be there is no good at all intended to the public,
but private lucre only, or at the best, together with some little
good to the public, such an appearance withal of private interest
over-balancing it, as that wise men justly fear they will prove
rather mischievous than beneficial'.[5] This stripping away of com-
forting secondary or pretended motives was not the arm-chair
criticism of a theologian, but was said at Court, and again, at St
Paul's in 1621, he observes that such practices may have some
small pretension of 'benefit to the commonwealth, but certainly
not without sensible and grievous pressures of those that are a
great part of the commonwealth'.[6]

Because he saw and applied the importance of the subject of
justice in all its practical and far-reaching implications, Sanderson
was able to discern the features of contemporary society and fear-
lessly to confront it with a mirror. The hucksters, the regraters, the

1. *Ib.* p. 186, and cp. *Ib.* p. 191, and
Vol. 1, p. 159.
2. *Ib.* Vol. II, p. 204.
3. *Ib.* Vol. II, p. 344, and cp. Vol. I,
p. 122.

4. *Ib.* Vol. I, p. 386, and cp. Vol. III,
p. 120.
5. *Ib.* Vol. I, p. 338.
6. *Ib.* Vol. III, p. 120, and cp. Vol. I,
p. 131 and Vol. II, p. 55.

forestallers, whose activities meant that the purchaser paid more for grain and cattle offended against every canon of fair bargaining.[1] Moderate gain is not only allowable but, as Hall pointed out, is essential to the carrying on of 'all trade of merchandise',[2] but a just price is fair to both parties. Sanderson attacks unfair raising of rents, which he classes as a national sin[3] and an oppression of the poor,[4] regretting that the law allows the magistrate to do little or nothing to prevent it.[5] It simply creates bankrupts, he tells the Court at Greenwich in 1637[6], and on another occasion, preaching to a similar congregation on the subject of contentment, he says that the first mark of contentment is to despise an unjust gain, and 'racking of rents to an unreasonable proportion'[7] is such an unjust gain.

Sanderson did not hesitate to recall the times to a realisation of the fact that religion was for life and that there was no sphere of human affairs which was alien to theology or a neutral area as far as its application was concerned. More than any other in a period which occupied itself with many aspects of practical divinity, Sanderson was alive to the corporate and social aspect, and he spoke to the times with a mixture of the judicious and the prophetic, the directness of his preaching combining with his knowledge of practical divinity.

Like Gore, he had a zeal for social justice which was entirely theological in context and practical in content. Gore came to it primarily because a theology of the Incarnation demanded it, and Sanderson because of the nature of his special study, and both had the forth-telling quality in their approach to society. Yet it is obvious from his writings that for Sanderson a concern with social problems was not a substitution for a genuinely theological stand-point, but rather a consequence of the conviction that theology had to be relevant not only to the intellectual but also to the corporate setting. Whenever theology loses this sense of the need for communication and contact it slips away into a rarefied atmosphere which devitalises it and makes it appear irrelevant to the existing situation. Because of his chosen subject, Sanderson did not have to manufacture this contact between theology and the daily concerns of society. It was already there in the composition

1. *Ib.* Vol. III, p. 120.
2. Hall, *Resolutions and Decisions of Divers Practical Cases of Conscience,* Dec. I, Case IV.
3. *Ib.* Vol. II, p. 263.
4. *Ib.* Vol. II, p. 352 and cp. *Ib.* p. 55.
5. *Ib.* Vol. II, p. 314.
6. *Ib.* Vol. I, p. 131.
7. *Ib.* Vol. I, p. 156.

and function of theology as he saw them, for as he put it, 'the whole body of divinity' has been rightly reduced by some to 'God and ourselves'.[1] Nor for that matter was his study a special one in the sense of being an adjunct or an extra, but it developed naturally out of the balance of theological method and the inter-relationship of its elements. Scripture is the rule of faith,[2] 'a per-perfect and constant rule',[3] but with Hooker he maintains that it cannot be regarded as 'the sole rule of all human activities what-soever'.[4] Referring to peoples and societies 'before the Scriptures were written', he comments that 'if we must grant they had a rule . . . then we must also of necessity grant that there is some other rule for human actions besides the written Word . . . which rule, what other could it be than the law of nature and of right reason imprinted in their hearts? Which is as truly the law and Word of God, as is that which is printed in our Bibles'.[5] Law and reason are therefore the connecting link and they constitute the frame-work of moral theology which is theology at work in one part of the sphere of application. Combining the three elements of theo-logical method, Sanderson asserts that no convincing argument can be brought against this position 'either from reason or from authority of Holy Writ, or from the testimony either of the ancient Fathers or of other classical divines of later times'.[6]

For Sanderson, the three elements are integrated into a com-plementary relationship, as when he writes of Scripture; 'using withal all good subsidiary helps for the better understanding there-of, especially those two as the principal, the rule of right reason, and the known constant judgment and practice of the universal Church'.[7] Scripture is acknowledged as the rule of faith, 'yet not as excluding the use of reason but supposing it',[8] and while Scripture is the criterion of the truth of any teaching, it is conducive to sound judgment in this connection, particularly if the meaning is obscure, 'to inform ourselves as well as we can . . . what the received sense, and . . . what the constant usage and practice of the Church, espe-cially in the ancient times, hath been concerning these matters'.[9]

The liberality of approach already referred to and which is com-mon to the great majority of seventeenth-century writers from

1. *Ib*. Vol. p. 82.
2. *Ib*. Vol. IV, p. 74.
3. *Ib*. Vol. II, p. 253.
4. *Ib*. Vol. II, p. 114.
5. *Ib*. Vol. II, p. 113.

6. *Ib*. Vol. II, p. 114.
7. *Ib*. Vol. II, p. 166, and cp. Vol. IV, p. 90.
8. *Ib*. Vol. II, Preface, 1657, p. xlvii.
9. *Ib*. Vol. I, p. 243.

Hooker and Andrewes to Wilkins and the Latitudinarians, is a natural result of this combination. Remarking on the objection of many ancient philosophers to the way in which his followers treated the work of Pythagoras as oracular, a procedure 'prejudicial to . . . that freedom of judgment which was behoveful for the study of philosophy', Sanderson indicates the parallel in theological matters. Like Chillingworth, he holds that, apart from Scripture, no formulations and no particular individual's writings can have the status of authority: "There is . . . much reverence to be given to the writings of the godly ancient Fathers, more to the canons and decrees of general and provincial councils, and not a little to the judgment of learned, sober, and godly divines of later and present times, both in our own and other reformed Churches. But we may not "jurare in verba", build our faith upon them as upon a sure foundation, nor pin our belief upon their sleeves, so as to receive for an undoubted truth whatsoever they hold, and to reject as a gross error whatsoever they disallow, without further examination'.[1] The last phrase catches something that is part of the spirit of Anglicanism, and something which is even more inextricably part of it appears in the statement that it is 'blameworthy' to wish 'to be accounted rigid Lutherans, or perfect Calvinists'.[2] Sanderson strikes the authentic note of Anglicanism which consistently rejected the idea that it had any specific doctrines of its own in that it demanded subscription to no confession other than the creeds, its aim being one of interpretation by means of a theological method which combined the use of Scripture, antiquity and reason. A confirmed exponent of this method, Sanderson's contribution was not to moral theology alone, for his emphasis on this subject succeeded in underlining part of the general function of theology in respect of the human situation by maintaining a relationship of meaning between theology and man in society. This he did with a prophetic directness and a simple practicality born of long experience.

Sanderson is linked with Jeremy Taylor because each left his mark on the same subject, and certainly his prelections had an influence on Taylor's work. They differed however in circumstances, temperament and in the nature of their achievements. While Sanderson passed the greater part of his active life in a country parish and concentrated, within the wide limits already

1. *Ib*. Vol. III, p. 288.   2. *Ib*. Vol. III, p. 289.

indicated, on a subject which was as extensive as the range of its practical implications, Taylor's course was marked by greater variety of output and event. He had been recommended by Laud for a Fellowship at All Souls, Oxford, the only dissentient being Gilbert Sheldon, on the grounds that Laud had been misled as to his right of presentation.[1] After an interval the matter was put in order by Laud exercising his authority as Visitor since no appointment had been made in the intervening period. Taylor became chaplain to Laud, and, in 1638 he went to Uppingham as rector, and he joined the royal forces at Oxford four years later. From then until the Restoration his fortunes varied, and he lived for a time in Wales and also worked in London. During the years of the Commonwealth he wrote most of his works, nor was his life without vicissitudes as he was captured by the Parliament's forces and twice imprisoned. A couple of years before the Restoration Taylor went to Ireland with Lord Conway, where he was at work on the *Ductor Dubitantium*, and where he was again arrested but the charge came to nothing as political changes were fast approaching. In 1660 he was nominated to the diocese of Down and Connor, and there is no doubt that the controversy occasioned by his views in *The Liberty of Prophesying* and in *Unum Necessarium* was not without effect in determining where his future work would lie.* To do more than suggest the biographical outline is unnecessary in view of the work that has been done in recent years, particularly in C. J. Stranks's *The Life and Writings of Jeremy Taylor*.†

1. C. J. Stranks, *The Life and Writings of Jeremy Taylor* (1952), p. 43, refers to a letter from Laud to the Warden of All Souls, in which Laud makes mention of a visit from a Mr Osborn who was resigning his Fellowship and who offered the nomination of his successor to the Archbishop; 'Mr Osborn had done something he had no right to do. The nomination to the Fellowship was not his to offer, but Laud who seems also to have been ignorant of other provisions in the statutes of All Souls, took Osborn at his word and expected his nominee to be elected without question. The Archbishop was not disappointed so far as the majority of the Fellows were concerned, they were willing to elect Taylor; but one of their number, Gilbert Sheldon, himself to become Primate later, was against the whole proceeding and opposed the election. There the matter rested, for time was on the side of Laud so long as the majority refused to change their minds. The Archbishop was the Visitor of the College and, if no valid election was made, the right of appointment accrued to him by virtue of his office. Sheldon does not seem to have been in any way bitter about the matter, but this was the first of one or two unfortunate disagreements between the two men which were to have a deeper influence than Taylor himself was aware'.

Taylor's mind was discursive and his interests widely diffused and something of this is reflected in the vividness of his style with its profusion of images. His prose often has an essentially poetic quality which was missing when he attempted verse. Taylor is exuberant yet contriving to be rich and delicate by turns, where Sanderson is lucid and frequently pungent, conforming in advance to the style which would become the model in the years following the Restoration. Taylor is observant and appreciative of the visible, by temperament a natural Laudian in churchmanship, although this was strengthened by his patristic and scholastic studies and by his association with Laud. During the Commonwealth he was in touch with the Laudian party and although Sanderson shared this connection it is of interest that his more moderate approach kept him on the margin of the group. Bosher writes that 'friendship linked Robert Sanderson to the circle, but his deviations from party orthodoxy were a constant source of anxiety'.[1] Taylor's friendships however included William Chillingworth and Henry More, the Cambridge Platonist. These contacts are reflected in the general impression that, while Sanderson is nearer to Hooker and the *Summa*, Taylor is closer to the ideas of Chillingworth and of the Cambridge Platonists. For Sanderson, reason is right reason, in the sense in which Hooker employs the term, but for Taylor it is not quite so simple. When he described it as 'a transcendent that runs through all topics'[2] he was attempting to show that the sharp outlines of the older definition made insufficient allowance for the fact that more was involved in reason than reasoning. Reason was not only resistant to definition because the personality was involved but also because the range of personality and the variety of

1. R. S. Bosher, *The Making of the Restoration Settlement*, p. 30.
2. *Works* (ed. R. Heber), Vol. V, p. 498.

---

* Loc. cit. pp. 216–7, 'After the shocks administered to orthodoxy, first by *The Liberty of Prophesying* and then by *Unum Necessarium*, those in authority considered him unsafe. Sheldon, writing in August 1667, when the news of Taylor's death had just reached him, referred to him as "a man of dangerous temper, apt to break out into extravagancies", and no doubt this was what he thought of him in 1660'. Stranks goes on to point out however that it was no dishonour to be sent to join Ussher and Bramhall, and in addition, Taylor knew the district and the conditions prevailing there.

† See also, H. T. Hughes, *The Piety of Jeremy Taylor* (1960); T. Wood, *English Casuistical Divinity During the Seventeenth Century, with Special Reference to Jeremy Taylor* (1952), and F. R. Bolton, *The Caroline Tradition of the Church of Ireland, with Special Reference to Jeremy Taylor* (1952).

capacity were to be reckoned with: 'reason is such a box of quick-silver that it abides nowhere; it dwells in no settled mansion; it is like a dove's neck, or a changeable taffata; it looks to me otherwise than to you who do not stand in the same light that I do; and if we enquire after the law of nature by the rules of our reason, we shall be as uncertain as the discourse of the people, or the dreams of disturbed fancies'.[1] Commenting on the same point, he writes that 'that which will demonstrate a truth to one person, possibly will never move another. Because our reason does not consist in a mathematical point: and the heart of reason, that vital and most sensible part, in which only it can be conquered fairly, is an ambulatory essence, and not fixed; it wanders up and down like a floating island, or like that which we call the life-blood'.[2]

Taylor of course was much younger than Sanderson, and had been in contact with this line of thought at Cambridge, at Oxford through his friendship with Chillingworth, and also through his close and lasting association with More. Like More, he knew both Plato and Descartes, and by that preference alone a fresh element found a place in his outlook. But because of his Laudian affilia-tions, his sense of the continuity of the Church in history, and his liturgical feeling, neither of which was shared to any marked degree by the Cambridge Platonists although Chillingworth had something of both, Taylor remains, more typically than they did, an example of theological method in its wholeness.

Yet to say this is not enough, for he remains also and indisput-ably himself, revealing inevitably the influences that helped to shape him, but still distinctive with that indefinable original quality which is individuality where it is not something more. That there has always been an awareness over the years of Taylor's excep-tional quality, has been shown by Paul Elmen in an article assessing the changing fortunes of Taylor's reputation as a theologian and as a prose stylist. The number of editions through which several of his works had passed before the close of the seventeenth century indicated the appreciation of contemporaries, while the eighteenth century on the whole, as was to be expected, found his style and the form of his thought uncongenial. The early nineteenth century saw a great revival of interest with Heber's edition, although the latter part of the century was less in sympathy with Taylor's

1. *Ductor Dubitantium*, Bk. II, C.I,R.I.
2. *Works*, Vol. XI, p. 485.

exuberant style.[1] Since then there has been a slow but steady growth in interest, and in 1952, C. J. Stranks published a full historical and theological appraisal, using some new material, and while this is the first life to appear since Gosse's *Jeremy Taylor* at the beginning of the century, there are signs that the interest is being maintained.

Taylor's adherence to seventeenth-century theological method is evident when he declares that 'I affirm nothing but upon grounds of Scripture, or universal tradition, or right reason discernible by every disinterested person'.[2] This was the form through which the content of his erudition and originality expressed itself in a remarkable succession of writings, some of which caused controversy, while some made definite contributions valued by theologians and others became handbooks used by the many. This many-sidedness is perhaps the main reason why Taylor's work was never quite forgotten because there was always someone to whom he made an appeal. His theological method has the same context of liberality which was to be found in Hooker, Andrewes, Sanderson, Hales, Chillingworth, Hammond and Bramhall, as well as in the Cambridge Platonists and the Latitudinarians. In fact, he anticipates the latter in his insistence on plainness and simplicity instead of intricacy of method, using their favourite phrase 'Fear God and keep his commandments; for this is the whole duty of man'.[3] Like Hammond and Bramhall, fellow-Laudians, he valued Grotius, and like Hales, he read Episcopius. This unity of theological method is a major factor in the understanding of the period. The method constituted the means by which the spirit of Anglicanism expressed itself in one direction, just as the use of the liturgy expressed it in another. Furthermore, there were strong connecting links between the two forms of expression. Not only did the original preface of 1549 visualise the Book of Common Prayer as 'an order for prayer, and for the reading of the holy Scripture, much agreeable to the mind and purpose of the old Fathers', but another link was continually being strengthened by use. The constant recitation of creeds and the large amount of Scriptural material in the structure of the services linked the theological and the liturgical in an intimate way. If this process

1. *The Fame of Jeremy Taylor, Anglican Theological Review*, Vol. XLIV, Number 4, p. 389.
2. *Works* (ed. Heber, 1828), Vol. XI, p. 356.
3. *Ib.* Vol. XI, p. 355.

of interaction was largely by way of unconscious absorption, its cumulative effect was still considerable. Moreover, the number of catechetical and devotional works appearing during the seventeenth century, and the popularity of many of them, constituted a positive reinforcement in that they too combined the theological, the devotional and the practical. Taylor himself produced one of the best known of the latter, and in addition to *Holy Living* he wrote the first life of Christ in English, *The Great Exemplar*. Both books have the sustained emphasis on the practical and devotional to be expected from a writer who regarded practical divinity as one of the mainstays of 'the life of religion'. They relate in a positive way the inward aspects of membership in the Church to the outward aspects of relationships in society. As well as a narrative which is neither critical nor chronological, *The Great Exemplar* contains discourses, meditations and prayers, in which the devotional blends with the practical. Under the chapter headings of sobriety, justice and religion, *Holy Living* includes humility, pride, content, obedience, the several duties comprised in justice, business transactions, the question of restitution, faith, hope, charity, and the external and internal acts of religion. But such a summary, while it shows how Taylor fits into the seventeenth-century pattern, gives no indication of his originality or depth. For Taylor infuses into his writing a warmth of feeling, a practicality of understanding and insight, and a beauty of expression, which are the real individuality of his work.

The general estimate of Taylor is more often based on his authorship of *Holy Living* than on the *Ductor Dubitantium* or his other theological works, for, as Paul Elmen has noted, it went through eighteen editions before the turn of the century. That there was a need and that Taylor was felt by many to answer it is evident from this and from the fact that his other devotional writings, *Golden Grove* and *The Great Exemplar*, had nineteen and nine editions respectively published in the same period.[1] This was by no means exceptional for works like these at such a time, but it indicated that not the least important facet of Taylor's output was that which dealt with the development of personality 'in relationship with God and his fellows', which is how H. T. Hughes summarises this aspect of Taylor in his book, *The Piety of Jeremy*

---

1. *Anglican Theological Review*, Vol. XLIV, Number 4, p. 390.

Taylor.[1] In the same book, which is mainly concerned with this side of Taylor's writings, he makes the point already referred to here from the angle of theological method, that Taylor's 'conception of piety had a marked and increasing influence on his whole theological outlook'.[2] This is important from the point of view of theological method for it emphasises a distinctive quality, a wholeness of outlook in which his concern with the development of personality in its devotional and practical aspects is integrated into the general theological approach. Taylor's style is so much his own and his range is so wide that the true distinctiveness of his work tends to be overshadowed. He embraced the full extent of the Anglican appeal to Scripture and to antiquity, expressing this with a liberality of view-point and a sensitive understanding of the nature and function of reason. To this he added a wide reading in later writers, poets and philosophers, part of his distinctiveness being the way in which he kept this theological and intellectual element in contact with the emphasis on the development of personality through the means of grace and the experiences of the individual in relation to the corporate. Moreover, he saw all this as within the continuing life of the Church which, with its sacraments and observances, provides not only the setting but the means of implementation. In this connection, the effect of Taylor's study of practical divinity and the importance he attached to it can be seen in his practicality and also in the form of his work, as for example, in the arrangement of material. He writes of distributive and commutative justice, the duties of different individuals, business transactions, and restitution, the internal actions of religion, faith, hope and charity, the external actions of religion, reading Scripture, fasting, and church-going, and the mixed actions of religion, prayer, alms, repentance, and communicating.[3] On all these subjects, his instructions share that blend of insight and practicality which is as much his own as his style of writing. Each subject is related to practice by detailed rules followed by prayers. Some have seen in him occasional resemblances to Francis de Sales, but he can be as matter-of-fact as *The Whole Duty of Man* while at times there is a suggestion of à Kempis. The fact is, however, that

1. H. Trevor Hughes, *The Piety of Jeremy Taylor*, p. x.
2. *Ib*. p. 153.
3. The references are to the chapter headings and divisions of material in *The Rule and Exercises of Holy Living*, the title of which is in itself significant.

there is a certain unique quality in Taylor stemming from a particular combination of an imaginative style and a sensitive, widely-ranging mind at once devout and enquiring, which is peculiarly his own. Two words have been applied to his works by those who wrote about them over the years, 'sweetness' and 'warmth', and they touch on something of the individuality of Taylor so long as his practicality is not forgotten for it had its origin not in the happy accidents of style and temperament but in his theological position. To this his study of practical divinity gave a distinct orientation in the direction of relevance, as was the case with Sanderson in whose writings this emerged as a concern for relationships in society. As a moral theologian Taylor was alive to this side of things, but because he wrote devotional books his relevance had a context of inwardness also for something common to St Bernard's sermons on the Song of Songs, to George Herbert's poems, and to à Kempis is in him too.

His theological method, seen, as it were, in a cross-section taken through his various works, reveals the combination of these different constituents. There is in the *Ductor Dubitantium* a lengthy discussion of the use and place of reason in religion and of its relationship to faith which is basic to the understanding of Taylor's approach to theological matters. It arises out of the explanation of something else, but because he sees that fundamental questions are involved, he is content to devote thirty pages to the subject. It is the experience of some, writes Taylor, that reason is a guide and they conclude that, since it is 'concreated with us' and in that sense precedes religion, the latter cannot take away from it or abolish its function, for it is the 'noblest part of this reaction'. The difficulty arises when the claims of both do not appear to be reconcilable: 'but then, because some articles which are said to be of faith, cannot be made to appear consonant to their reason, they stick to this, and let that go'. For others, 'reason is a good guide in things reasonable and human, but our reason is blind in things divine, and therefore is of little or no use in religion. Here we are to believe, not to dispute'. Each side has some support for its contention and therefore merits examination in order to find 'what part of truth each aims at, and join them both in practice'.[1]

The basis of the argument against this partnership is that while in ordinary activities reason is the eye, this cannot hold good in

1. *Works*, Vol. XI, p. 434.

matters of religion where there are needed 'new eyes and a new light': 'faith is the eye, and the Holy Spirit gives the light, and the word of God is the lantern'.[1] Some questions in religion are so mysterious that they transcend reason and natural reason is power-less to handle them, 'so that our biggest reason in religion is to submit our reason'.[2] In this context, understanding does not come by the exercise of reason, 'if ye will obey, then shall ye understand'.[3] The concluding argument then is 'this is in Scrip-ture, therefore it is true: and this is against Scripture, therefore it is absurd, and unreasonable'.[4] This line is generally taken by those who rely on the magisterial authority of the Church, and by those who rely on and claim individual guidance as the source and authentication of their views.[5] Somewhere between the two is a third that accepts neither of these stand-points, 'but offers to prove what he says, but desires not his arguments to be examined by reason, upon pretence that he urges Scripture . . . thus . . . the systems of divinity rely upon a certain number of propositions from generation to generation, and the scholar shall be no wiser than his master for ever; because he is taught to examine the doc-trines of his master by his master's arguments, and by no other'. Taylor makes it clear that he shares the view maintained by all Anglican writers of the seventeenth century. He cannot adhere to a concept which deprives authority of the possibility of being freely accepted, nor will he agree that everyone is his own authority. His reaction against the trammels of a systematic theology is the same as that of Andrewes or of the Cambridge Platonists. His criti-cism of all three points of view is that basically they are agreed on allowing people 'to be Christians' only if they 'will lay aside . . . reason',[6] leaving the individual with no protection against the imposition of opinions which are either purely subjective or which will not stand the impact of questions.

Taylor then turns to look more closely at the objections, and he begins by setting out his own position and the reasons for it, declaring that in fact faith and reason are not opposed to each other, 'for faith is but one way by which our reason is instructed, and acquires the proper notices of things'. There are three ways in which reason apprehends things; 'the first is called "nœsis", or the "first notices" of things abstract . . . the second is called "dianoesis", or "discourse", that is, such consequents and emanations which the understanding draws from her first principles. And the third is "pistis", that is, such things which the understanding assents to upon the report, testimony, and affirmation, of others, viz. by arguments extrinsical to the nature of the thing, and by collateral and indirect principles'.[1] These three ways of knowing are not confined to any one subject or sphere, but in all branches of knowledge reason has these ways of informing itself. Taylor works this out in some detail with illustrations, and his conclusion is that 'now in all this, here is no difference in my reason, save that as it does not prove a geometrical proposition by moral philosophy, so neither does it prove a revelation by a natural argument, but into one and the other it enters by principles proper to the inquisition; and faith and reason are not opposed at all. Faith and natural reason are several things, and arithmetical and moral reasons are as differing, but it is reason that carries me to objects of faith, and faith is my reason so disposed, so used, so instructed'.[2]

The result of this is to show that men enter into the most mysterious parts of religion, 'the deepest articles of faith', by reason. It does not mean that all such articles can be proved by reason, but it means that 'he hath causes and reasons why he believes'. If those reasons are insufficient, he may not believe wisely, 'but for some reason or other he does it'. But if a person has no reasons at all he cannot be said to believe in any real sense because the act of the understanding is an act of reason, 'and faith, which is an act or habit of the understanding consenting to certain propositions for the authority of the speaker, is also as much an act of reason, as to discourse in a proposition of Aristotle'. When faith assents to something for a reason 'à testimonio' it is just as much an act of the reason as to assent to something on the basis of 'the nature of things'. All this, writes Taylor, is sufficiently clear 'when we discourse of faith formally in its proper and natural capacity, that is, as it is a reception of propositions "à testimonio" '. This however is not all that can be said about faith, and it is precisely here that the centre of the problem of the relationship of faith and reason is situated. Considered formally faith can be shown not to be the antithesis of reason, but what of faith considered materially?: 'indeed if we consider faith as it is a habit infused by God, and by God's Holy Spirit, so there is something more in it than this: for so, faith is a vital principle, a magazine of secret truths, which we could never have found out by natural reason, that is, by all that reason which is born with us, and by all that reason that grows with us, and by all secular experiences and conversations with the world; but ... now here is the close and secret of the question, whether or no faith, in this sense, and materially taken, be contrary to our worldly or natural reason, or whether is any or all the propositions of faith to be exacted, interpreted, and understood, according to this reason materially taken?'[1] Put another way, is not the reason which is rightly followed in philosophy and science sometimes contrary to faith? Or conversely, can anything be said to be an article of faith which is contrary to right reason?[2]

Taylor maintains that a distinction is involved here, in that 'although right reason is not the positive and affirmative measure of any article, yet it is the negative measure of every one'.[3] As to right reason not being the positive measure in such questions, Taylor considers that 'the reasons are plain: 1. Because many of them depend upon the free will of God',[4] and because '2. The reason of man is a right judge always when she is truly informed; but in many things she knows nothing but the face of the article'.[5]

While this problem's solution (if there be a solution in terms of the understanding) is not something demonstrable so much as something sensed or experienced, it cannot be said that Taylor either solved the problem or evaded the issue. He has safeguarded reason 'truly informed', but he has too much affinity with the Cambridge Platonists to have any sympathy with the idea of an omnipotent, self-illuminating reason. He has a sense of the mysteriousness of things, but he does not take refuge unfairly in this as an explanation, for mystery means for him something more in the nature of unexplained reality than something essentially inexplicable. This is apparent when he says of someone 'that will inquire and pry into the reason of the mystery, and because he cannot perceive it, will disbelieve the thing, or undervalue it, and say it is not at all, because he does not understand the reason of it'. There is a humility here, an awareness of human limitations even when reason is being carefully guarded, which has no point of contact with a self-sufficient idea of the function and capacity of

1. *Ib.*
2. *Ib.* p. 443.
3. *Ib.* p. 448.
4. *Ib.* p. 443.
5. *Ib.* p. 446.

reason. In fact, Taylor says so in so many words, when he writes
that 'there is a "ragione di stato", and a "ragione di regno", and
a "ragione di cielo", after which none but fools will inquire, and
none but the humble shall ever find'.[1] Reason for Taylor is contained in a view of reality which includes the spiritual as well as the
intellectual, so that his Laudian churchmanship with its emphasis
on sacraments and devotional practices keeps company quite
naturally with that aspect of his thinking which he shares with the
members of the Tew circle. Like Hales who advocated a modesty
which was prepared to wait until the remainder of our knowledge
is supplied, Taylor agrees that in some of these matters, until the
reasons are given, men can 'be still and silent, admiring the
secret . . . and expecting till the curtain be drawn'.[2] The real
check on reason, in Taylor's view, is not something imposed from
without, but its own inner experience of its unaided inadequacy.
This is not the evasion of the issue as between faith and reason,
but a preliminary statement of what reason is and is not. It is a
declaration not of the bankruptcy of reason but of its inherent
limitations. In support of this position, Taylor points to the paradox at the centre of things which he maintains to be a paradox
simply because human reason has not a standard of reference in
the matter. How is it, for example, in view of all that is known that
grace is not irresistible, or how can the divine foreknowledge be
reconciled with human freedom? How to explain the manner in
which sacraments, using ordinary material means, produce real
effects, seemingly 'disproportionable instruments to such effects'?
He instances the Incarnation, and his comment on Socinian ideas
in this connection emphasises the point already made, that reason
cannot go beyond its instruction or information: 'But the Socinians, who conclude that this was not thus, because they know not
how it can be thus, are rightly to be reproved for their excess in
the inquiries of reason, not where she is a competent judge, but
where she is not competently instructed'.[3]

It follows then that reason whenever it is truly informed is competent to judge, but frequently reason is incapable of penetrating
beneath the surface, with the result that 'we can see what, but not
why; and what we do see, is the least part of that which does not
appear; but in these cases our understanding is to submit, and
wholly to be obedient, but not to inquire further'.[4] (Later, he

1. *Ib.* p. 443.   2. *Ib.* p. 443.   3. *Ib.* pp. 443–6.   4. *Ib.* p. 446.

discusses the particulars in which this obedience of understanding consists).[1] In one of those similes which are so much a part of his writing, Taylor tries to imprison in a few sentences something of the fleeting truth of the matter: 'the reason of man is a right judge always when she is truly informed; but in many things she knows nothing but the face of the article; the mysteries of faith are oftentimes like cherubims' heads placed over the propitiatory, where you may see a clear and a bright face and golden wings, but there is no body to be handled; there is light and splendour upon the brow, but you may not grasp it; and though you see the revelation clear, and the article plain, yet the reason of it we cannot see at all; that is, the whole knowledge which we can have here, is dark and obscure'.[2] Frequently, the lavish use of simile and metaphor obscures rather than clarifies, and often Taylor himself is no exception to this, but here he has managed to convey an inkling of something which eludes definition but is yet experienced. In the same section he produces another of these illuminating similes which seems to sum up in picture form a good deal that is at the root of his theological thinking. Reason and religion, he writes, are like Leah and Rachel: 'reason is fruitful indeed, and brings forth the first-born, but she is blear-eyed, and oftentimes knows not the secrets of her Lord; but Rachel produced two children, faith and piety, and obedience is midwife to them both, and modesty is the nurse'.[3] This is more than a clever parallel, for he has managed to convey the importance of reason yet within the whole complex of faith and devotion, of religious observance and practicality, which is not only the judgment of a theologian and writer on moral theology and devotional subjects, but which catches something of the essence of the spirit of Anglicanism.

Certain things emerge at this point, Taylor maintains, such as that it is unsafe to conclude that because a thing is agreeable to right reason it is necessarily so in Scripture. It is true that one reason cannot be against another (this is the stress on the unity of truth, recurring from the Cambridge Platonists to Gore) when 'all things are equal'. But they so seldom are, and what is right reason in one 'constitution of affairs . . . is not so in others'. An instance of this is the repelling of force by force, which is right reason and a natural right, but which is forbidden in Scripture.[4] It also appears at this stage of the discussion that a thing ought not to be

1. *Ib.* pp. 461–5.   2. *Ib.* p. 446.   3. *Ib.*   4. *Ib.* p. 447.

suspect because it is above the understanding.[1] Taylor then turns to his second consideration, which is that right reason is the negative measure of every article of faith, or in other words, that whatever contradicts right reason 'is at no hand to be admitted as a mystery of faith'. This is so primarily because truth is one, and a thing cannot be true and untrue at the same time. The bearing of this on the question is that by believing one truth 'no man can be tied to disbelieve another'. If a thing be against right reason it cannot be true, and 'if therefore any proposition be said to be the doctrine of Scripture, and confessed to be against right reason, it is certainly not the doctrine of Scripture, because it cannot be true, and yet be against what is true'. Because truth in all its forms is at the centre of things, Taylor regards the miracles and fulfilment of prophecy in the New Testament as a proving of religion 'that our faith might enter into us by discourse, and dwell by love, and be nursed by reason'.[2] This is supported by the proving of right reason, that is, 'by discourses merely like ours', for 'God . . . exposes his proceedings to be argued by the same measures and propositions by which he judges us, and we judge one another'.[3]

Taylor is referring to certain theological opinions, such as the Calvinist doctrine of absolute reprobation which he instances,[4] which predicate what is contradictory of justice. He is at one with the reaction against these ideas, already discerned in Hooker, Andrewes and Sanderson, and which, with the Cambridge Platonists in his own lifetime, gathered force increasingly as the century progressed. 'It follows demonstratively', he writes, 'that what is unjust in men, and what is falsehood in our intercourses, is therefore false or unjust, because it is contrary to the eternal pattern'.[5] Theological propositions which maintain the contrary are therefore inadmissible since they contradict that reason planted in human nature as the means of apprehending the law of nature and 'the eternal pattern'. In such matters there can be no doubt as to what is right reason, since no mystery is evolved, but the rule holds good also in every context where reason is right, or can be right.[6] In all discussions of the relationship of faith and reason a distinction must be made between what is against and what is beyond reason: 'whatsoever right reason says cannot be done, we cannot pretend from Scripture, that it belongs to God's almightiness

1. *Ib.*
2. *Ib.* p. 448.
3. *Ib.* p. 449.
4. *Ib.* p. 452.
5. *Ib.* p. 451.
6. *Ib.*

to do it; it is no part of the divine omnipotency to do things contradictory'. It is no defence of an article or opinion which contains such a contradiction to say that, although it may appear to human reason to be contradictory, this in fact is due to a defect of reason.[1] On the other hand, it is by no means implied that 'God could do nothing but what we can with our reason comprehend or know how'. Emphatically it may not be held that omnipotency means performing things that reason says cannot be, 'but it must be said and believed that God can do those things, to which our understanding cannot, by all its powers ministered here below, attain'.[2] It is a sufficient presumption against any proposition being treated as an article of faith if it contain anything 'really absurd, or unreasonable', by which Taylor means anything opposed to a truth in which reason is instructed.[3] In this connection however care is to be exercised, 'for every man's reason is not right, and every man's reason is not to be trusted: and therefore, as absurd foolish things are not to be obtruded under the pretence of being mysteries, so neither must mistaken philosophy and false notices of things be pretended for reason'. He observes how all the central doctrinal questions, the Incarnation, the Trinity, the eucharistic presence, have been confused throughout history by those who have added explanations of what they do not understand. In this way, that 'which in its own simplicity was indeed mysterious, and not to be comprehended by our dark and less instructed reason, but yet was not impossible to be believed, is made impossible to be understood by the appendages'.[4]

Summarising his position at this stage of the discussion, he writes, 'now the measure and the limit of this, is that very thing which is the reason of this and all the preceding discourse—one truth cannot be against another—if therefore your opinion or interpretation be against a truth, it is false, and no part of faith. A commandment cannot be against a revelation, a privilege cannot be against a promise, a threatening cannot mean against an article, a right cannot be against a duty; for all reason, and all right, and all truth, and all faith, and all commandments, are from God, and therefore partake of his unity and his simplicity'.[5]

Taylor closes his examination of the subject with some comments on the arguments advanced against the use of reason. He observes

1. *Ib.* p. 451.   3. *Ib.* p. 454.   5. *Ib.* p. 455.
2. *Ib.* p. 452.   4. *Ib.* p. 456.

that it is not true to say that reason has no place in matters of religion, and the distinction he draws implies the concept of reason as 'res illuminata illuminans' as used by the Cambridge Platonists: 'but though natural reason cannot, yet it is false to say that reason cannot; for reason illuminated can perceive the things of God'. He agrees that 'humility and piety' are the best dispositions because they 'remove those prejudices and obstructions which are bars and fetters to reason'. He is alive to the fact that this only holds good within the household of faith, and he adds 'if you are to dispute against a heathen, a good reason will sooner convince him than a humble thought'.[1] To the objection that what is required is the obedience of the understanding, he replies that this is so, but 'yet we must judge and discern the sayings of God from the pretences of men; and how that can be done without using our reason in the inquiries of religion, is not yet discovered'. Such obedience is certainly required, but certain safeguards are essential if it is not to be misplaced. We must be sure that it is not in fact to human opinions that we are submitting, unless these have 'authority from reason or religion to command conformity'. Many things, claiming to be based on reason, have acquired a 'usurped authority', and he uses the same phrase as Chillingworth—'we must call no man master upon earth'—referring to the acceptance of such opinions.[2] Again, a situation may arise 'when reason and revelation seem to disagree', and then, so long as we believe it to be a revelation, no reason ought to be allowed to change that belief. If right reason can convince us that it is not a relevation, the way is clear, 'but if reason leaves us in the actual persuasion that it is so, we must force our reason to comply with this'. 'If we cannot quit our reason or satisfy it, let us carry ourselves with modesty', acknowledging the revelation and our inability to reconcile 'the two litigants'.[3] Taylor's reply to the argument based on the fallibility of reason indicates something of his own position, and while there is a hint of the atmosphere of Hales's writings, and of Chillingworth's, there is also a suggestion of Hooker in the last sentence. It is a question of kinship rather than of derivation: 'it is true, reason is fallible; or rather to speak properly, ratiocination, or the using of reason, is subject to abuse and deception; for reason itself is not fallible; but if reason, that is, reasonings, be fallible, so are the pretences of revelation subject to abuse; and what are we

1. *Ib.* p. 460.　　　2. *Ib.* p. 461.　　　3. *Ib.* p. 462.

now the nearer? Some reasons are but probable, and some are certain and confessed, and so it is in the sense of scriptures, some are plain and need no interpreter, no discourse, no art, no reasonings, to draw out their sense; but many are intricate and obscure, secret and mysterious; and to use a fallible reasoning to draw out an obscure and uncertain sense of Scripture, is some-times the best way we have, and then we must make the best of it we can: but the use of reasoning is not only to find out truth the best we can, but sometimes we are sure of it, as of light; but then and always our reason (such as it is) must lead us into such proportions of faith as they can: according as our reason or motives are, so ordinarily is the degree of our faith'.[1]

It will be seen that Taylor has adhered faithfully to his plan of taking the truths aimed at by both sides in the debate and bring-ing them together in some sort of dialogue. While it cannot be claimed that his findings are definitive or that he has produced something startlingly original, his treatment disposes to a large extent of the feeling that there is a necessary opposition between faith and reason. His very refusal to seek a solution on paper which purports to cover all points, and his implicit assumption that the nature of the problem requires that there must always be an element of the paradox, of something in the last resort insoluble, is of value in itself. More perhaps than any passage in his writings, this lengthy digression in *Ductor Dubitantium* gives an insight into Taylor's theological method. It is a full discussion of what is in effect the conclusion of *The Liberty of Prophesying*, that reason is 'the best way we have', but reason 'not guided only by natural arguments, but by divine revelation, and all other good means'.[2] For Taylor, as has been seen, has no sympathy with what he calls the excess of enquiries in reason,[3] the exaggerated claims as to its unaided capacity which, as he puts it, would only have a foundation if reason were omniscient.[4]

The Liberty of Prophesying is an expression of that liberality which Taylor found in Hales and Chillingworth, and in many ways the book is as Chillingworthian in manner as it is in concep-tion, being written with a plainness of style quite uncharacteristic of Taylor. Being written specifically on the topical subject of

1. *Ib.* p. 462.
2. *The Liberty of Prophesying*, Sect. X, (1650 ed. p. 165.)
3. *Works*, Vol. XI, p. 446.
4. *Ib.* p. 453.

toleration in 1647, part of his theme is to show that while essentials
are clear, only enlightened reason can be relied upon in other
questions. It was no academic matter for Taylor and he pressed
his arguments as far as they would go. Remarking that 'Taylor's
subjects always carried him away',[1] C. J. Stranks writes that 'most
of the arguments in favour of that toleration for which he pleads he
had borrowed from others, notably from Chillingworth, Hales,
and Daillé, and it has been objected that to some extent he spoiled
the arguments he borrowed by carrying them far beyond the
limits to which their originators intended them to go'. Stranks
points out that the existence of different versions does not materially affect the authority of Scripture to the extent Taylor suggested, nor in spite of textual and other difficulties is it impossible
to obtain the views of the Fathers. He adds: 'If all the guides whom
Taylor examines one after another are as untrustworthy as he pretends, then we have no real grounds for the principles upon which
all Christians are agreed. It depends only upon a consensus of
opinion which might any day be broken'.[2] It seems likely that
Taylor was to some extent at any rate carried away by his subject,
and he certainly was influenced by Daillé's book, to which he
refers his readers, so that he tends to concentrate on the negative
aspect of the question. He was himself conscious of this, particularly in respect of the differing weight of emphasis on the appeal
to antiquity in his first book, *Episcopacy Asserted*, and in *The
Liberty of Prophesying*. Stranks comments on this that 'in an
effort to explain the discrepancy he included a lengthy defence of
his apparent inconsistency in the 1657 dedication to Lord Hatton.
He had been accused, he said, of seeming "to pull down with one
hand what I build up with another". His defence takes the form of
asserting that the Fathers and the councils may afford an excellent
corroborative to arguments which can be proved true on other
grounds, but have no absolute authority in themselves. He had
appealed to them in *Episcopacy Asserted* because some who read
that book might value their testimony. "But episcopacy relies not
upon the authority of the Fathers and councils, but upon Scripture,
upon the institution of Christ, upon an universal tradition and an
universal practice not upon the words and opinions of doctors".
This type of argument does very little to mend the situation.
Taylor had attacked the final authority of Scripture as strongly as

1. Loc. cit. p. 85.		2. *Ib.* p. 84.

he had that of the Fathers and the councils, and if the testimony of the Fathers was actually ignored it would be a harder task to prove that universal tradition and practice upon which Taylor now professed to rely. Possibly, though he does not admit it, some of the difference in treatment was due to the fact that in the interval he had been reading Daillé'.[1]

The influence of Daillé was strong on the members of the Tew circle, especially on Falkland, and his book unquestionably left its mark on the development of the subject in *The Liberty of Prophesying*. But it ought to be added that in so far as Taylor is correct in asserting that he considered patristic evidence as corroborative and complementary, he was running true to type as far as the use of the appeal to antiquity in the seventeenth century was concerned. This will be examined in more detail later, but it would appear to be accurate to say that the appeal to antiquity was never made as to an independent authority. Rather was it used to confirm that the Church of the first centuries accorded a central place to Scripture in matters of doctrine and treated the creed as the rule of faith. It was used to establish continuity of teaching and practice as between the Primitive Church and the contemporary Church. In so far as Taylor is in accord with this he is in line with the attitude generally taken during the period to the appeal to antiquity. In *The Liberty of Prophesying* he maintains that 'we are secured in fundamental points from involuntary error, by the plain, express, and dogmatical places of Scripture, yet in other things we are not'[2] because of the fact that those parts of Scripture about which controversy arises are uncertain of interpretation. In such cases neither tradition nor councils give unequivocal leading. It is in such matters that he considers the Fathers unable 'to determine our questions', and elaborates this.[3]

On the other hand, he points out, as Simon Patrick was to do later, that the only tradition which could command universal assent was 'in the canon of Scripture itself', adding 'and therefore there is wholly a mistake in this business; for when the Fathers appeal to tradition ... it is such a tradition as delivers the fundamental points of Christianity, which were also recorded in Scripture'.[4] Taylor concludes that 'we are acquitted by the testimony of

1. Loc. cit. p. 86.
2. *The Liberty of Prohesying*, Sect. VII, (1650 ed. p. 150).
3. *Ib*. Sect. VIII, (*ib*. p. 151).
4. *Ib*. Sect. V, (*ib*. p. 91).

the primitive Fathers, from any other necessity of believing than of such articles as are recorded in Scripture'.[1] It would appear as if Taylor was right in assuming that confusion existed as to the scope and function of the appeal to antiquity. 'There are some', he writes, 'that think they can determine all questions in the world by two or three sayings of the Fathers, or by the consent of so many as they will please to call a concurrent testimony'.[2] Others, like Falkland, dismissed the appeal, while some, like Chillingworth, allowed it in a modified form as being of corroborative value. Daillé's book had done a great deal to lessen the credit of the Fathers as a court of appeal, but it can be maintained that the general tendency among Anglican writers of the seventeenth century was not to regard them in this light but to connect them with the unchangeableness of fundamentals and the centrality of the rule of faith. To establish their agreement with the Church of the first centuries on these matters was the main purpose of the appeal to antiquity from Andrewes onwards. Taylor fits into this pattern, although in *The Liberty of Prophesying* the negative approach, partly dictated by the subject-matter, shows very clearly the effect of his contacts and his reading.

The book was evoked by Taylor's view of the need for tolera-tion in the existing situation, and the case is well presented, the line taken showing the influence of Chillingworth. The book is a defence of toleration but it is by no means a plea in vague terms for a general liberality of outlook. Rather is it an attempt to show that the basis of such an outlook is a theological one. The chief interest of *The Liberty of Prophesying* from the point of view of the present subject is that it is an application of the three-fold theological method to the situation then obtaining. The application naturally reflects Taylor's affiliations and preferences, but the wholeness of the use of Scripture, reason and tradition expresses itself through these and through the medium of his own individuality. 'I have writ this', he notes in the dedication, 'because I thought it was necessary and seasonable, and charitable, and agreeable to the great precepts and design of Christianity, and consonant to the practice of the apostles, and of the best ages of the Church, most agreeable to Scripture and reason, to revelation and the nature of the thing'.[3]

Taylor's theme is that, since men can only 'know in part, and prophesy in part', charity is to be observed to all who differ on

1. *Ib.* p. 97.   2. *Ib.* Sect. VIII, (*ib.* p. 151).   3. *Ib.* Dedication, p. 45.

non-fundamental questions. A distinction is to be drawn between 'things necessary, in matters of creed, and articles fundamental' and unnecessary things which are speculative, or in their nature not capable of being determined either way. In these latter, people should have liberty because the things were left 'by the Scripture indeterminately'. The marked tendency to treat superimposed opinions as fundamentals, and 'fancies' as faith, should be resisted, and he gives evidence from patristic sources in support of this position.[1] Having shown from history the wisdom of toleration and discussed the rise of intolerance, he concludes that the solution is 'to be united in that common term, which as it does constitute the Church in its being such, so it is the medium of the communion of saints, and that is the creed of the apostles, and in all other things an honest endeavour to find out what truths we can, and a charitable and mutual permission to others that disagree from us and our opinions'.[2]

This insistence on the unchanging character of fundamentals accompanied by reticence on questions which do not come under this heading is a continuing expression of the Anglican spirit in theology during the seventeenth century, and is to be discerned in writers as dissimilar in approach and background as Andrewes and Hales. Taylor voices the conviction that 'a foundation of faith cannot alter, unless a new building be to be made, the foundation is the same still'.[3] That foundation is the creed 'composed . . . to be a rule of faith,' and this is witnessed to by the Fathers and by its use as a baptismal interrogation. 'This symbol is the one sufficient unmovable, unalterable and unchangeable rule of faith, that admits no increment or decrement',[4] and writing of faith considered formally he holds that 'its duty is completed in believing the articles of the apostles' creed'. This was the purpose for which the four gospels were written, and Taylor points out the comprehensive nature of that purpose by underlining the fact that the act of believing certain propositions is not an end in itself but derives its significance from the purpose. 'Now God's great purpose being to bring us to him by Jesus Christ, Christ is our medium to God, obedience is the medium to Christ, and faith the medium to obedience, and therefore is to have its estimate in proportion to its proper end, and those things are necessary which necessarily

1. *Ib.* pp. 6–20.
2. *Ib.* p. 33.
3. *Ib.* Sect. I (*ib.* p. 16).
4. *Ib.* Sect. I (p. 18, *ib.*).

promote the end . . . so that those articles are necessary, that is those are fundamental points, upon which we build our obedience'.[1]

This practicality and emphasis on the inseparability of faith and obedience is also part and parcel of the Anglican approach to theology. It was inherent in the reaction against the Lambeth Articles and the idea of faith presupposed in them, and it was to remain prominent throughout the century. Taylor was not just expressing his own views when he remarked that preoccupation with speculative opinions often cools interest in 'practical duties'.[2]

Taylor then considers 'the difficulty and uncertainty of arguments from Scripture, in questions not simply necessary, not literally determined'.[3] Because Taylor may be misrepresented as rejecting Scripture authority, it is necessary to stress the fact that it is not the ultimate authority and clarity of Scripture in fundamentals which Taylor is questioning, for he writes that 'all the articles of faith are clearly and plainly set down in Scripture'. There can be no doubt as to credal essentials or as to their being stated in a way which makes it possible for everyone to understand them, and he gives a number of references to the Fathers and to Aquinas in support. The emphasis on the plain places he shares with Chillingworth. Taylor is far from taking up an agnostic position concerning these central affirmations, for not only does he insist that they are plainly stated, but that 'many things which are only profitable are also set down so plainly'.[4] He does assert however that many of the questions so widely discussed, and so divisive in their effect, cannot find positive authentication in Scripture. In this area of secondary and speculative matters, the appeal to Scripture can afford no decisive answers, and perhaps it was meant to be so, and obscurities left to be treated as occasions of charity and humility rather than as material for formularies.[5] When he deals with the difficulties arising in this connection out of textual variations, different versions and readings, Taylor overstates the case by exaggerating the effect of the difficulties. As to what he terms the internal means of expounding Scripture, comparing the context, comparing different places, using the analogy of reason or of faith, his criticism of them all is not only of the uncertainty of the procedure in each case, but of its essentially

1. *Ib*. Sect. I (*ib*. pp. 7–8).   4. *Ib*. Sect. III (*ib*. p. 59).
2. *Ib*. Dedication (*ib*. p. 37).   5. *Ib*. Sect. III (*ib*. p. 60).
3. *Ib*. Sect. III (*ib*. p. 59).

subjective nature.[1] The first of the extrinsical means of interpretation is tradition, 'which is pretended not only to expound
Scripture . . . but also to propound articles upon a distinct stock'.[2]
As he treats of this subject, it is clear that he has two things in
mind, namely, to show that because the Fathers frequently dis-
agreed on the enumerating of traditions therefore they cannot be
used now to verify what they did not then clearly agree upon. In
the second place, he wishes to show that tradition was not the
independent source of any received doctrine, and that the Fathers
were agreed that the only universal tradition was 'the testimony of
the Churches apostolical'.[3] Many early writers refer to this as
tradition, but in fact, says Taylor, 'these doctrines which they called
tradition, were nothing but such fundamental truths which were
in Scripture',[4] and his conclusion is that 'no doctrines or speculative mysteries are so transmitted to us by so clear a current, that
we may see a visible channel, and trace it to the primitive fountains'.[5]

From this it appears that the negative aspect of Taylor's handling of the appeal to antiquity is confined solely to demonstrating
that, as Scripture provides no guaranteed interpretation of
matters of speculative theology, so it is idle to seek a similar
authentication from the writings of the patristic period. Here, the
influence of Daillé is noticeable, and in fact Taylor refers the
reader to his book, as he lists in a later section instances of varying
and opposed ideas among the Fathers, or of opinions held by some
and later questioned generally.[6] Commenting on the additional
hazards to certainty arising from the inevitable corruption of texts
or of works wrongly attributed, Taylor writes, 'but I will rather
choose to show the uncertainty of this topic by such an argument
which was not in the Fathers' power to help, such as makes no
invasion upon their great reputation, which I desire should be
preserved as sacred as it ought. For other things, let who please
read Mr Daillé, *Du vrai usage des Pères*'.[7] In fact, Taylor's admiration for the Fathers, freely expressed here and elsewhere, was
genuine, and his criticism is directed against the attempt to use
them as guarantors in respect of non-fundamentals when it
could be shown that they were never unanimous on questions of

1. *Ib*. Sect. IV.
2. *Ib*. Sect. V (*ib*. p. 83).
3. *Ib*. Sect. V (*ib*. p. 91).
4. *Ib*. Sect. V (*ib*. p. 91).
5. *Ib*. Sect. V (*ib*. p. 92).
6. *Ib*. Sect. VIII (*ib*. pp. 151–161).
7. *Ib*. Sect. VIII (*ib*. p. 157).

'secret theology'.[1] In such matters the writings of the first centuries could never be used 'as a concluding argument in matters of dispute',[2] but this was not to impugn in any way the appeal to antiquity as he, together with most Anglican theologians of the seventeenth century, saw it, for to them it was confirmatory of their own attitude on fundamentals. 'We are acquitted by the testimony of the primitive Fathers from any other necessity of believing than of such articles as are recorded in Scripture'.[3]

His conclusions on the rôle of councils resemble Chillingworth's view in that Taylor regards them as 'excellent intruments of peace' and as 'the greatest probability from human authority'.[4] He holds that if a general council has determined a question, its decree should be accepted,[5] but 'there was never any council so general, but it might have been more general'. This, in conjunction with the fact that it has never been suggested that councils cannot err,[6] means that disagreement is possible if the matter is necessary and the reason strong enough.[7] Here again Taylor reiterates the distinction implied in the appeal to antiquity, for he considers that the work of councils is concerned with essentials and not with the sort of questions which occupy those who are interested in controversy or who are given to discussing obscure matters. It follows from this that the magisterial authority of the Church— 'the Church in its diffusive capacity'[8]—is not applicable to such debated subjects. Nor is the argument based on claims to the guidance of the Spirit anything but irrevelant in this case for it must first be proved to others if they are to accept it as a certain way of resolving difficulties.[9]

The consequence is that in the interpretation of difficult places of Scripture none of these methods is free from uncertainty. Since therefore there is 'nothing certain but the divine authority of Scripture, in which all that is necessary is plain, and much of that that is not necessary is very obscure, either we must set up our rest only on articles of faith and plain places, and be incurious of other obscurer revelations, (which is a duty for persons of private understandings, and of no public function) or if we will search further

1. *Ib*. Sect. VIII (*ib*. p. 151).
2. *Ib*. Sect. VIII (*ib*. p. 154).
3. *Ib*. Sect. V (*ib*. p. 97).
4. *Ib*. Sect. VI (*ib*. p. 124).
5. *Ib*. Sect. VI (*ib*. p. 101).
6. *Ib*. Sect. VI (*ib*. pp. 107, 113, 115.)
7. *Ib*. Sect. VI (*ib*. p. 124).
8. *Ib*. Sect. IX (*ib*. p. 161).
9. *Ib*. Sect. IX (*ib*. p. 164).

(to which in some measure the guides of others are obliged), it remains we enquire how men may determine themselves'.[1]

Accordingly, in all debated questions which are outside the scope of the certainty referred to, the best judge is reason, 'not guided only by natural arguments, but by divine revelation and all other good means'. Taylor points out that 'there is an obedience of understanding' also, and that it is therefore essential to make sure of the reasonable basis of whatever is commended to us. 'Even our acts of understanding are acts of choice' and it is a duty to prove all things.[2] This in fact is universally true whether it be admitted by all or not, 'and this very thing (though men will not understand it) is the perpetual practice of all men in the world that can give a reasonable account of their faith. The very Catholic Church itself is "rationabilis et ubique diffusa", saith Optatus, reasonable as well as diffused everywhere'.[3]

There is an echo of Whichcote in Taylor's phrase to the effect that nothing is more unreasonable than to exclude the use of reason from religion, and he refers to what he calls the common prejudice that reason and authority are necessarily opposed to each other. It is the most reasonable action, he says, to believe a supreme authority, and it is equally reasonable to ensure that the 'authority that pretends to be such, is so indeed'. Human dictates do not carry such weight with them, 'and yet reason and human authority are not enemies'. It is often a good argument, 'and the best reason we have in a question', to follow such an opinion 'because it is made sacred by the authority of councils and ecclesiastical tradition'. If a better reason presents itself, then it is to be followed. Taylor then maintains that this alleged opposition is basically, and in the light of experience, a comparison of reasons, and the idea of reason which appears as he discusses this has affinity with the Cambridge Platonists: 'but then the difference is not between reason and authority, but between this reason and that, which is greater: for authority is a very good reason, and is to prevail, unless a stronger comes and disarms it, but then it must give place. So that in this question, by (reason) I do not mean a distinct topic, but a transcendent that runs through all topics; for reason, like logic, is instrument of all things else, and when revelation, and philosophy, and public experience, and all

1. *Ib.*   3. *Ib.* Sect. X (*ib.* p. 168).
2. *Ib.* Sect. X (*ib.* pp. 165, 168).

other grounds of probability or demonstration have supplied us with matter, then reason does but make use of them'.[1]

Not only are the influences which helped to fashion Taylor's thought here hinted at, but the foundations of his theological method are revealed. This is brought out, with the same stress on the instrumental quality of reason, as he continues: 'and all these disputes concerning tradition, councils, Fathers are not arguments against or besides reason, but contestations and pretences to the best arguments, and the most certain satisfaction of our reason. But then all these coming into question, submit themselves to reason, that is, to be judged by human understanding, upon the best grounds and information it can receive. So that Scripture, tradition, councils and Fathers, are the evidence in a question, but reason is the judge'. In matters therefore which are not necessary, and in which we are 'left to our liberty', the best way is 'right reason proceeding upon the best grounds it can, viz. of divine revelation and human authority, and probability is our guide, (stando in humanis) and supposing the assistance of God's Spirit'.[2]

What Taylor is here endeavouring to express is something which constantly breaks surface during the seventeenth century, and indeed later too, for it was Butler in the *Analogy* who described probability, humanly speaking, as 'the very guide of life'.[3] The basis of the *Analogy* had been provided by Ray's work, and Ray, like Taylor, was influenced by the Cambridge Platonists, and if these are nothing more than coincidences they still hint at a prevailing current of ideas beneath the surface.

The close of Taylor's book in which he applies the results obtained to the question of toleration is less important in respect of theological method except in so far as it indicates the relevance of this to the contemporary scene. It may serve to place his method in perspective, however, to note that he regarded it as holding good in the first centuries also, a point made later from a slightly different angle by Stillingfleet. Referring to councils, he says that 'there is no question but that they are obliged to proceed according to some rule', and he states that he knows of no instance of a general council offering a decree 'which they did not think sufficiently proved by Scripture, reason, or tradition,

1. *Ib*. Sect. X (*ib*. p. 169).
2. *Ib*. Sect. X (*ib*. p. 170).

3. Joseph Butler, *The Analogy*, Introduction.

as appears in the acts of the councils'.[1] The conclusion that 'Scripture is the rule they are to follow'[2] places the appeal to antiquity in its meaningful setting for Taylor.

Taylor's first book, *Episcopacy Asserted*, was produced when the entire political and ecclesiastical situation was in the melting pot of civil war. Its publication at such a juncture of affairs did not make for its author's security, and that he himself was aware of this is clear from the epistle dedicatory. The full title of the work indicates the procedure followed, in that Taylor claims for episcopacy 'Divine Institution, Apostolical Tradition, and Catholic Practice'. Along these three lines he proposes to substantiate the case for episcopacy, and he holds that Christ instituted a government for the Church which was first committed to the apostles who had the power of appointing successors. These successors were bishops, and were distinguished from presbyters by the separate commissioning of the seventy (from whom Taylor maintains them to be derived) and by the fact that the functions of ordination and confirmation were confined to the apostles and their successors. So far, Taylor's arguments are drawn from Scripture, but now the appeal to antiquity is called into service with a wide range of support from early writers. 'Hitherto', he observes, 'the discourse hath been of the immediate divine institution of episcopacy, by arguments derived from Scripture; I shall only add two more from antiquity, and so pass on to the tradition apostolical'.[3] These arguments which he documents very fully are that the Primitive Church held 'that bishops are the ordinary successors of the apostles, and presbyters of the seventy-two', and that there is 'direct testimony of the Fathers for a divine institution'.[4] He then returns to the Acts and the Epistles to show that 'the second basis of episcopacy is apostolical tradition'.[5] The appeal to antiquity then furnishes material to show 'how the Church hath followed the apostles' for 'Catholic practice is the next basis',[6] and the remainder of the book deals with distinction of order, function and jurisdiction. Such a summary can give no indication of the extent of patristic reading involved, for Taylor shared to the full in the seventeenth-century acquaintance with the Fathers, and if he

1. *Ib*. Sect. VI (*ib*. p. 102).
2. *Ib*. Sect. VI (*ib*. p. 104).
3. *Episcopacy Asserted*, par. 9. (1650 ed. bound with *Liberty of Prophesying*, p.49)
4. *Ib*. par. 10 (*ib*. p. 49).
5. *Ib*. par. 13 (*ib*. p. 68).
6. *Ib*. par. 22 (*ib*. p. 125).

necessarily shared also the uncritical approach to the period, his knowledge was extensive enough to enable him to assemble a wide selection of material. Like Bull's *Defence*, the book is historical theology in the sense that the appeal to antiquity is applied to a subject in which the content is immediately historical as well as theological. Taylor's aim is to establish the existence of a pattern in Scripture, and the appeal to antiquity serves to support the continuance of this in the following centuries, and its use is supplementary. The main function of the appeal to antiquity is in respect of 'fundamentals and the rule of faith', but it was also applied within the context of continuity and, from Andrewes onwards, the norm obtaining in early centuries was an integral part of the appeal to antiquity during the period.

Unum Necessarium, the book which brought Taylor into controversy, was written with a practical aim as the complete title indicates, and the chapter which gave rise to a conflict of views was only incidental to the development of the subject, although he was aware that what he had written on original sin could not escape criticism from the dominant Augustinianism of the day. The book, dealing with 'the doctrine and practice of repentance' from the personal and practical point of view, appeared in 1655, but the general purpose of the book was speedily lost sight of in the controversy which ensued about the sections 'of original sin', especially the seventh chapter. Into the details of the controversy it is not necessary to enter here. It involved Taylor in much correspondence, obliged him to write two further contributions on the subject, *Deus Justificatus* and *A Further Explication of the Doctrine of Original Sin*, and disturbed those who knew him, particularly Sanderson. It will be recalled that Sanderson was especially sensitive to anything which he felt to be approaching Pelagianism, but the truth is that the hand of Augustinianism lay heavily on the whole theological scene in the seventeenth century, and neither the *Summa Theologica* nor the Reformers had done anything to loosen its hold. In his treatment of the subject, Taylor would have the support of many today, doubtless the majority, but in his own time he had the majority against him and in particular those who treated the Thirty-nine Articles as confessional. For Taylor, as for many in his own time, they were an 'instrument of peace', although he by no means granted that his views were opposed to or excluded by them. 'It is pretended and talked of' he writes, that his views on original sin are contrary to the ninth Article, and that his attempt 'to reconcile them was ineffective'. He considers that, although 'this be nothing to the truth or falsehood' of what he writes, 'yet it is much concerning the reputation of it'. To clear himself of the charge of being contrary to the Article he expounds the Article and shows that 'not only the words of it are capable of a fair construction, but also that it is reasonable they should be expounded so as to agree with Scripture and reason'.[1] This he does, and as he has already devoted a lengthy section to the 'doctrine of antiquity in this whole matter',[2] the nature of Taylor's reaction against current ideas on the subject becomes evident. It is the reaction against the doctrinaire, the remnants of an authoritative approach which allowed a disproportionate weight to a single authority or to a nexus of ideas which it declined to submit to further testing from Scripture, reason or the records of the first centuries. Taylor reacted from within the liberality which he shared with Chillingworth, Grotius and the Cambridge Platonists, and he also reacted from within the attitude to Scripture which distinguished clear fundamentals from obscure non-essentials and which sought for support and confirmation in the patristic writings. It is this which is of special interest for theological method, for Taylor's views do not arise from any preconceived attitude or from the respect accorded to any particular authority such as that of St Augustine. They arise from the undifferentiated position that what cannot be reconciled to Scripture, antiquity and reason, cannot be imposed or treated as essential.

He will not assert that those who framed the article meant exactly what he means. They may have done or they may not, but one thing is certain 'that they framed the words with much caution and prudence, and so as might abstain from grieving the contrary minds of differing men'.[3] He adds that 'it is not unusual for churches, in matters of difficulty, to frame their articles so as to serve the ends of peace, and yet not to endanger truth, or to destroy liberty of improving truth, or a further reformation'.[4] In the letter to the Bishop of Rochester, prefixed to the seventh chapter, he again expresses his anxiety 'to prevent apprehensions that some have of this doctrine, that it is of a sense differing from the usual expressions of the Church of England'. His misgivings

1. *Works*, Vol. IX, p. 107. 3. *Ib.* p. 108.
2. *Ib.* pp. 93–107. 4. *Ib.* p. 108.

that a whole-hearted Augustinianism may be regarded by many as the official view of the Church is surely well founded when it is recalled that Baro and Barrett had been condemned in Andrewes's lifetime·for dissenting from the ideas which lay behind the Lambeth Articles. To understand the contemporary mistrust of anything that hinted at Pelagianism is hardly to condone a reaction which had swung far in the other direction, and in this, circumstances were hard on Taylor for his alleged unorthodoxy was largely a refusal to accept as a standard views which, far from being those of Scripture and primitive antiquity, could not be found in the writings of the first three centuries. A more serious objection is also mentioned in the letter, where Taylor expresses his surprise 'that any man should desire to believe God to be more severe and less gentle: that men should be greedy to find out inevitable ways of being damned', and that they should try to 'invent reasons to make it seem just'.

All are agreed as to the Article, he points out, but not as to explaining it, and he indicates how he has approached the question: 'having therefore turned to all the ways of reason and Scripture, I at last apply myself to examine how it was affirmed by the first and best antiquity'. In order that 'there may be no impertinent allegations of antiquity for both sides', he clears the ground by stating that 'it is not therefore intended, nor affirmed, that there is no such thing as original sin; for it is certain, and affirmed by all antiquity, upon many grounds of Scripture'.[1] It is the later additions to and deductions from this that are in question: for example, it can be shown 'that the Fathers before St Austin generally maintained the doctrine of man's liberty remaining after the fall',[2] or in other words the determinism alleged by many has no basis and freedom of choice is real.[3] Nor is there any proof that Adam's sin was imputed to men for their condemnation. Having referred to the implications of this in connection with baptism and having pointed out the absence of these views in writings of the first four centuries, Taylor considers that 'all of which to my sense seems to declare, that if men would give themselves freedom of judgment, and speak what they think most reasonable ... they would speak honour of God's mercy and not impose such fierce and unintelligible things concerning his justice and goodness'.[4]

He summarises his conclusions in the matter and then assembles

1. *Ib.* p. 73.   2. *Ib.* p. 85.   3. *Ib.* p. 88.   4. *Ib.* p. 91.

a large selection of extracts from the Fathers to endorse them. 'All that I desire of the usual propositions which are variously taught now-a-days', he writes, can be summed up by saying that original sin is not 'an inherent evil; not a sin properly' but rather that it should be regarded as 'the effect of one sin, and the cause of many; a stain, but no sin'. It neither destroys liberty nor introduces 'a natural necessity of sinning'. Taylor then gives patristic writers' views, commenting, 'and now how consonant my explication of the article is to the first and best antiquity, besides the testimonies I have already brought here concerning some parts of it, will appear by the following authorities, speaking to the other parts of it and to the whole question'.[1]

Taylor's liberality of outlook and his use of antiquity concur in his assessment of his own position: 'thus everyone talks of original sin, and agree that there is such a thing, but what it is, they agree not ... for my own part, now that I have shown what the doctrine of the purest ages was, what uncertainty there is of late in the question, what great consent there is in some of the main parts of what I affirm, and that in the contrary particulars men cannot agree, I shall not be ashamed to profess what company I now keep in my opinion of the article; no worse men than Zwinglius, Stapulensis, the great Erasmus, and the incomparable Hugo Grotius, who also says there are ... "many in France, which with great argument defend the same sentence"; that is, who explicate the article entirely as I do; and as St Chrysostom and Theodoret did of old, in compliance with those holy fathers that went before them: with whom although I do not desire to err, yet suppose their great names are guard against prejudices'.[2]

In a final apologia, he draws attention to certain unfortunate practical and theological consequences of what he refers to as 'the usual doctrines about original sin'. Apart from the fact that no competent proof can be alleged for them, they undermine effort, 'they are no friends to piety', and they are 'dishonourable to the reputation of God's goodness and justice'.[3] To make people question what they have for so long accepted has therefore practical relevance. From the point of view of theology 'there is in Holy Scripture no sign of it' and it was 'unknown to the primitive church', and yet its consequences have been made the basis of much systematic theology. 'It is not easy to give a reasonable

1. *Ib.* p. 93.   2. *Ib.* p. 106.   3. *Ib.* p. 117.

account', Taylor comments, 'why such tragedies should be made of it, and other places of Scripture drawn by violence to give countenance to it, and all the systems of divinity of late made to lean upon this article, which yet was never thought to be fundamental, or belonging to the foundation, was never put into the creed of any church, but is made the great support of new and strange propositions, even of the fearful decree of absolute reprobation, and yet was never consented in, or agreed upon what it was, or how it can be conveyed, and was (in the late and modern sense of it) as unknown to the primitive church, as it was to the doctors of the Jews, that is, wholly unknown to them both'.[1] Taylor's position briefly appears at the close of the discussion: 'I hope I have done my duty, having produced scriptures, and reasons, and the best authority, against it'.[2] It was the method he always used,[3] for his theological method is the natural expression of the wholeness of his Anglicanism. With all his contradictions and the lavish variety of his subject matter and the richness of his style, his thought moves outward from a steady centre. His devoutness and practicality, his liturgical feeling and his sense of the continuity of the Church, his concern for the truth of things and his desire for a relevant theology, all combine with that theological method which is woven into the substance of all his writings, a three-fold cord not easily broken.

Taylor died in 1667, and Sanderson three years after the Restoration, but in those intervening years Sanderson, in addition to his work in the diocese of Lincoln, took part in the Savoy Conference and contributed the preface to the revised Book of Common Prayer, and Taylor, facing many difficulties of administration in his work in Ireland, produced two further books. The outstanding figures of the period are doubtless such for a multiplicity of reasons, but not the least striking feature common to so many of them was their industry and application which neither pressure of affairs nor adverse circumstances seemed to affect.

1. *Ib.* p. 118.   2. *Ib.* p. 119.   3. Cp. *The Real Presence and Spiritual* (1654).

CHAPTER III

THE CAMBRIDGE PLATONISTS

SANDERSON died three years after the Restoration, and Hammond in the very year of the event which brought back from enforced obscurity the Laudian party, ideologically hardened and intellectually tempered by the pressures of a strenuous exile.

During their lifetime there had been coming to maturity a group of younger men, the Cambridge Platonists, whose work during the Protectorate was to be of considerable importance for theological method. Not only did they lay emphasis on the place of reason, as did Laudians such as Hammond and Heylyn, moderates like Sanderson, or members of the Oxford circle such as Hales and Chillingworth; not only did they oppose Calvinism despite the fact that they were nearly all products of Emmanuel; but their criticism was a new criticism in depth, and their picture of reason seemed to be three-dimensional too, having about it both warmth and colour. It seemed to be at home in the visible world as compared with the rather cold intellectualism of Tew which appeared to belong more in the study. Not unaffected by Hooker, Hales and Chillingworth, the emphasis in their writings has shifted and the debate is concerned with fundamentals.

Despite a certain aloofness still perceptible after the passage of time, subsequent development owed much to their influence, which in the case of the scientists and the Latitudinarians was subtle and penetrating. The fact that their dates overlap and their interests tended to be complementary, each group being related to the others by contacts of varying degrees of closeness, makes dividing lines to be in a sense arbitrary. Most of the Latitudinarians had heard More and Cudworth and Whichcote, and the naturalist Ray had learnt much from them. The Cambridge Platonists were the older generation, but it may be recalled that Whichcote died after Glanvill, and Cudworth predeceased Tillotson by only six years, while More was only thirteen years older than Ray or Boyle.

The significance of this is that the Cambridge Platonists, the scientists and the Latitudinarians, spanning by their works the latter part of the century, were moving in the same direction, and while this was not a co-ordinated movement, it arose from a common situation. The naturalists and scientists were seeking an alternative to Aristotelianism, and thinkers like the Cambridge Platonists were reacting against Augustinianism. It was the problem of authority in a new form, made pressing through the accumulation of facts by the scientists and through the writings of such as Descartes, and by the implications of these for theological method. Describing their position, G. R. Cragg writes 'With a single voice the Cambridge Platonists declare the unity of faith and reason'.[1] But Ernst Cassirer adds something further when he notes that the language of Whichcote, Smith and Cudworth does not differ from that of the humanistic thinkers of the English Renaissance, Colet, Erasmus and Thomas More.[2] The direction in which they were moving was clear. At a critical and creative changing-point, men were being confronted by an ever-growing new range of observable data concerning the physical universe, the implications of which obliged them to revise their way of thinking. How did this fit in with a view of man in which freedom was regarded as unreal and natural reason as in some way tainted, or was empiricism the answer?

The Cambridge Platonists considered that theology had become preoccupied with word-spinning, and that contemporary dogmatic formulations and the tendency to regard reason as being somehow or other suspect would cut religion off from life and make contact with the new world and its problems difficult to establish. They were apprehensive lest the Church should be isolated in an intellectual ghetto by an undue emphasis on what could not be accepted as certainly valid or true. They held that reason and faith were not in antithesis, but supplemented each other. Whichcote wrote that 'a man's reason is nowhere so much satisfied as in matters of faith' and 'that is not revealed, which is not made intelligible'.[3]

They were misunderstood by many of their contemporaries, but Simon Patrick in his *Brief Account of the New Sect of Latitudinarians, together with some Reflections on the New Philosophy*, observes 'that they are so far from being dangerous to the Church that they seem to be the very chariot and horsemen thereof'. Their

1. G. R. Cragg, *From Puritanism to the Age of Reason*, p. 44.
2. Ernst Cassirer, *The Platonic Renaissance in England*, p. 34.
3. *Whichcote's Aphorisms*, ed. W. R. Inge, 943, 1168.

method depends on 'letting (the Church's) old loving nurse, the Platonic philosophy, be admitted again into her family in place of Aristotle and the School-men'. Baxter refers to them as Platonists and Burnet says that 'men of narrower thoughts and fiercer tempers fastened upon them the name of Latitudinarians'. Their latitude was not a vagueness about fundamentals but was directed, as Overton remarked, against the prevailing contemporary trend in theological thought.[1]

Their predecessor in point of time was the learned Joseph Mead of Christ's College, Cambridge, whose works had been edited by Ray's friend John Worthington. Mead, 'an accurate philosopher, a skilful mathematician, an excellent anatomist', according to Worthington, appears to have had early contact with More whose work had in turn influenced Ray.[2]

Benjamin Whichcote was an outstanding member of the group, although Cassirer regards Ralph Cudworth as the real theoretical founder of the school.[3] And while there is some doubt as to whether the Cambridge men wished to found a school, or considered themselves as such, the virtual unanimity of their opinions clearly proceeds from shared convictions. Whichcote was Provost of King's College, Cambridge, where he remained until the Restoration, and Cudworth was Master of Christ's College. Henry More, a Fellow of the same College, was alone in not being, like the others, an alumnus of Emmanuel, and John Smith, a pupil of Whichcote at Emmanuel, had transferred to Queen's College in 1644, where he later died at the age of thirty-four. The association was close and their political sympathies coincided, for they were not royalists. Most of their works, however, did not appear in print until the Restoration, those of Smith being published posthumously in that year. The publication of Whichcote's writings was also posthumous.

Brought up in the tradition of which they became opponents, they found themselves in basic disagreement with the idea of a system, and with the almost exclusive emphasis on the transcendent. Smith wrote that 'the knowledge of divinity that appears in systems and models is but a poor wan light' and he describes as 'thin' the knowledge that is 'ushered in by syllogisms and demon-

1. J. H. Overton, *Life in the English Church*, 1660–1714, p. 50.
2. C. E. Raven, *John Ray*, p. 461.
3. Ernst Cassirer, *The Platonic Renaissance in England*, p. 42.

strations'.[1] He criticises the assertion that arbitrary will is the absolute governor of all things.[2] His belief that 'It's a fond imagination that religion should extinguish reason'[3] is paralleled by Whichcote's statement that 'nothing without reason is to be proposed; nothing against reason is to be believed'.[4] But there is more in this than a tenuous and negative rationalism. What the Cambridge Platonists meant by reason is not to be simply defined. It can be partly understood within the context of a view of man which is sharply distinguished from that of contemporary Calvinism: 'For, there is in man, a secret genius to humanity; a bias that inclines him to a regard of all of his own kind. For, whatsoever some have said; man's nature is not such an untoward thing, unless it be abused, but that there is a secret sympathy in human nature, with vertue and honesty'.[5] There is a descent from Erasmus, Colet, and the Florentine school, in one who could write of 'keeping up the grandeur of our being'.[6]

The writer of the preface to the selection of Whichcote's sermons notes that if more stress had been laid previously on this aspect, 'it should not have grown customary to explode goodnature, and detract from that good which is ascrib'd to natural temper, and is accounted natural affection, as having ground and foundation in meer nature'. He continues that for some, 'revelation was to owe its establishment to the depression and lowering of such principles as these, in the nature of man', but it would have been of more use 'to have shewn, how deep a root and foundation they had in human nature; and not, just contrary-wise, to have built on the ruine of these'. He adds 'But, certainly, it may be said of the Church of England, if of any Church in the world, that this is not her spirit', and he concludes with his opinion that 'to make this evident, is, in a manner, the scope of all his discourses'.

There was something living, flexible and close to reality in their concept of reason, which for them, was not something self-contained, but as W. R. Inge wrote, an 'appeal to the inner experience of the whole man acting in harmony'.[7] It appeared to depend to a considerable extent on what might be described as an optimistic attitude to the human situation, a humanism having as its

---

1. *Select Discourses* (1673 ed.), p. 3.
2. *Ib* p. 385.
3. *Ib.* p. 377.
4. *Whichcote's Aphorisms*, ed. W. R. Inge, 880.
5. Whichcote, *Select Sermons* (1698), p. 381.
6. *Ib.* p. 429
7. W. R. Inge, *The Platonic Tradition in English Religious Thought*, p. 52.

characteristic a spirit of enquiry rather than a note of finality, and which welcomed Terence's phrase 'Homo sum; humani a me nil alienum puto'. Overton observes that by reason they understood not merely the ratiocinative faculty but 'the breath of a higher, diviner reason'.[1] Whichcote's frequent descriptions of it as 'the candle of the Lord', 'the candle of God's lighting within men', '*res illuminata illuminans*', or Smith's phrase 'a beam of divine light' illustrate how, for the Cambridge Platonists, the authority of reason is mediated not self-authenticating. They agreed that 'if there be anything like infinite in the creation . . . it is in invention, and the power of thinking',[2] but they also held that 'reason is not a shallow thing: it is the first participation from God'.[3] It illuminates but its light is not self-generated.

Whichcote regards reason not only as the 'efficient', natural knowledge of religion being the effect or product of reason, but as the 'recipient', in that it receives what is declared.[4] It is instrumental rather than originative, 'the reason of our mind is the best instrument we have to work withal',[5] and, in consequence, it is devoid of over-confidence. 'We must not think we have then attained to the right knowledge of truth', declares Smith, 'when we have broke through the outward shell of words and phrases that house it up; or when by a logical analysis we have found out the dependencies and coherencies of them one with another'.[6] Whichcote adds, 'Because I may be mistaken, I must not be dogmatical and confident'.[7]

This 'not imposing one upon the other',[8] being 'tender-spirited, out of the sense of our own fallibility',[9] is characteristic of the theological method of the Cambridge Platonists.

Their view of reason was moreover in contrast with that of the prevalent philosophy: 'For English empiricism was scrupulously intent on separating the province of knowledge from that of faith and allowing to the latter full validity within its own spere'.[10] For Whichcote, Cudworth and More, the two fertilised each other.

1. J. H. Overton, *Life in the English Church*, 1660–1714, p. 50.
2. Whichcote, *Select Sermons*, p. 68.
3. *Whichcote's Aphorisms*, 460.
4. *Select Sermons*, p. 112.
5. *Whichcote's Aphorisms*, 459.
6. Smith, *Select Discourses* (1673), p. 8.
7. *Whichcote's Aphorisms*, 114.
8. Whichcote, *Select Sermons*, p. 100.
9. Whichcote, *Several Discourses* (1702), p. 31.
10. Ernst Cassirer, *The Platonic Renaissance in England*, p. 52.

This is not a facile ignoring of the difficulties involved, but the result of their conviction that truth is one, and that in whatever manner it appears, it is reason that accepts it. Whichcote, for instance, considers that truth is 'of first inscription or after revelation', and the first kind 'flows from the principles, of which man doth consist, in his very first make'.[1] These principles are based, not on a law promulgated, but on the fact that 'God made man to them, and wrought his law upon men's hearts; and as it were, interwove it into the principles of man's reason'.[2] Similarly, Smith writes of 'the truth of natural inscription and the truth of revelation',[3] and both agree that the second kind is required because nature is impaired and reason imperfect.[4]

For the Cambridge Platonists, reason is the human characteristic and its activity cannot be excluded from or limited in any aspect of human experience. It is, says Smith, 'the formal difference of man',[5] and Whichcote defines it as that which is 'proper and peculiar to man'.[6]

What they mean then by reason is something considerably wider and deeper than ratiocination. It is Jeremy Taylor, whose friendship with Henry More led him to the same sources, who comes somewhere near to a description: 'It is a transcendent that runs through all topics'.[7] W. R. Inge referred to the work of the Cambridge Platonists as an 'intellectual and philosophical movement to vindicate for the Church a greater liberty of thought, and a frank recognition of the place of reason in belief'.[8] This was the basis of Whichcote's reaction against the predominant thinking of the day with its stress on 'sovereignty . . . to show power'.[9] In his view, reward and retribution were consequential[10] and arose not from the action of arbitrary will but out of the nature of things.[11] 'It is greatly hazardous, for a finite and fallible creature', he writes, 'to be limited and confined by will and pleasure, where there is no reason that the mind of man can discern, why he should be restrained'.[12] There is an implicit rejection of the contemporary

1. *Select Sermons*, p. 6.
2. *Ib.* p. 7.
3. *Select Discourses*, p. 16.
4. Whichcote, *Select Sermons*, p. 6; Smith, *Select Discourses*, p. 371.
5. *Select Discourses*, p. 377.
6. *Whichcote's Aphorisms*, 71.
7. Quoted in *The Life and Writings of Jeremy Taylor*, C. J. Stranks, p. 307.
8. *Whichcote's Aphorisms*, ed. W. R. Inge, p.v.
9. *Select Sermons*, p. 122.
10. *Ib.* p. 164.
11. *Ib.* pp. 166–7.
12. *Ib.* p. 345.

dogmatic system and an implied acceptance of a view of man which
is alien to it in the phrase 'That which is not of a man's self, it may
be his burden, but never his fault',[1] and in the refusal to accept
as valid any approach which is inconsistent with wisdom and
reason—'what hath not reason in it is superstition'.[2]

Because of their nature men are bound to think and enquire.
'Men are wanting to themselves, if they do not see with their own
eyes', says Whichcote, contrasting this with 'received dictates'.[3]
But this enquiry is not academic, for if the first thing is 'to teach
a man's own mind; to satisfy a man's self, in the reason of things;
to look to the grounds and assurance that a man hath for his
thoughts, apprehensions and persuasions',[4] a practical rule of
life will result. It is found by experience, he says, that the best way
for a man to do himself good 'in intellectuals' is to be concerned
with others. 'No man so improves in intellectuals, as by communication'.[5] If it is pragmatism to turn aside from what is speculative
to what is of practical bearing on human interests, then there is a
strong element of pragmatism in Whichcote's advice 'Be communicative',[6] and in his emphasis on 'good nature', kindness,
friendliness, patience and candour, which he denies to be 'low
things' as compared with the more exalted subjects which some
persist in discussing.[7] He stresses 'making fair allowance, and
candid construction',[8] and 'making allowance for ignorance, for
necessity, for harder circumstances'.[9] They are not to be blamed as
neglecting or undervaluing the idea of grace, Whichcote writes,
who remind men that they should use reason and the principles of
creation, and those who 'take offence to hear reason spoken of' are
mistaken, for these things have a more than human foundation.[10]

Whichcote does not seem to have concerned himself directly
with the new philosophy, but the fundamental contact between his
outlook and that of the naturalists and scientists appears in his
recognition of the fact that, as Glanvill wrote, there are 'immutable
respects in things'.[11] 'The truth of things lies in this', says Whichcote, 'that things do exist of their own principles', and 'our
apprehensions are then true when they agree with the truth and

1. *Ib.* p. 175.
2. *Ib.* p. 117.
3. *Ib.* p. 4.
4. *Select Sermons*, p. 58.
5. *Ib.* p. 57.
6. *Ib.* p. 58.

7. *Ib.* p. 414.
8. *Ib.* p. 364.
9. *Whichcote's Aphorisms*, 1122.
10. *Several Discourses*, No. XXIII.
11. Introduction to Rust's *Discourses*,
    (1682).

existence of things; when we conceive of things as they are'.[1]
When Ray wrote 'Let us ourselves examine things as we have
opportunity, and converse with nature as well as with books',[2]
he was applying one aspect of Whichcote's wider assertion that
'the reason of things is the only rule in matters of natural knowledge',[3] and that 'the reason of the mind must be the same with the
reason of things'.[4]

This acceptance of the reason of things, that 'things do exist of
their own principles', is an acceptance, as Ray agreed, of the fact
that the variety of created things is evidence of wisdom, and of
Glanvill's contention that things are not so simply because they
are willed, but because they are in themselves 'settled . . . immutable and independent'.[5] If this is not so, says Rust, then 'anything may be the cause of any effect', and then how can infinite wisdom be inferred 'from the dependence of things and their relations unto one another'.[6] There is something of Hooker—'all
things that are have an operation not violent or casual'—but with
an added awareness of the natural creation and of the implications
for theological method of the growing range of information about it.
For Whichcote's 'Believe things, rather than men',[7] seems to lead
on to Sprat's 'unanswerable arguments of real productions',[8]
which he describes as the means by which the Royal Society endeavoured to establish certain reforms in scientific studies. It was
in fact the deliberate reply of the new philosophy to the entrenched
scholasticism which had controlled by its deductive system the
realm of scientific enquiry, and there is an underlying connection
between the Cambridge Platonists and those who, by means of
what Sprat calls 'this affection to sensible knowledge',[9] were fur-
nishing people 'with the materials for a wholly new understanding
of the world'.[10]

Whichcote considers that 'there is nothing in religion necessary,

1. *Select Sermons*, p. 226.
2. Ray, *The Wisdom of God, manifested in the Works of the Creation*, Pt. I.
3. *Whichcote's Aphorisms*, 728.
4. *Select Sermons*, p. 117.
5. Introduction to Rust's *Discourses*.
6. *Discourse*, IX.
7. *Whichcote's Aphorisms*, 39.
8. T. Sprat, *History of the Royal Society*, V.
9. *Ib.* XXIII.
10.Cp. G. R. Cragg, *From Puritanism to the Age of Reason*, p. 88.

which is uncertain',[1] and that in all important questions Scripture is 'clear, full and perspicuous',[2] and must be taken as a whole, for it 'is not one single text, which may be short, and intend another thing, but the fulness of Scripture'.[3] He holds that 'the Scripture way . . . is always by evidence of reason and argument',[4] and that 'nothing without reason is to be proposed; nothing against reason is to be believed; Scripture is to be taken in a rational sense'.[5] This is not a minimising view, because he gives due weight to revelation: 'The revelation in Scripture is the only rule, in all matters of faith'.[6] There can be no opposition between truth of natural inscription and revealed truth. Reason is always the means of apprehension, and 'that is not revealed, which is not made intelligible'.[7] Such a view is saved from any triteness or complacency by the conviction that reason is not self-authenticating, but is *res illuminata illuminans*, and by the constant awareness of the transitory and fragmentary quality of human capacities: 'for fallible to fail, is no more than for frail to be broken; and for mortal to die'.[8]

It is within the context of such ideas that what reason meant for the Cambridge Platonists begins to take shape, and while in the last resort it may elude definition, it has recognisable features of harmony, pervasiveness and intermediate agency. A full desscription of what they meant by the term may remain outside the reach of words, possibly because one ingredient in it is a quality of mysticism, if such an idea be allowable in the context of reason. At any rate, if a mysticism of reason is to be a meaningful expression, it can only be so when, as in the case of the Cambridge Platonists, it is based not on the inexplicability of things, but on a sense of wonder at the progressive uncovering of the workings of wisdom in an infinite variety of forms.

It is noticeable that Whichcote never attempts fully to define or describe reason, almost as if he finds it beyond his powers, and he who is so trenchant when writing of the place and function of reason, is allusive when writing of the thing itself: 'Any man that hath obtain'd any degree of the perfection of reason; that doth follow the divine governour of man's life, reason; he doth find

1. *Whichcote's Aphorisms*, 869.
2. *Select Sermons*. p. 369.
3. *Ib.* p. 53.
4. *Ib.* p. 117.
5. *Whichcote's Aphorisms*, 880.
6. *Ib.* 778.
7. *Ib.* 1168.
8. *Select Sermons*, p. 323.

that there are suggestions and inspirations; and that, many times, when he was resolv'd another way, there comes a light into his mind, a still voice'.[1] It is clear from such passages that reason for the Cambridge Platonists includes the action of conscience and what might be called mystical insights as well as ratiocination.

Whether such an idea of reason can be compassed by definition or not, it remains as something distinctive, an idea difficult to transmit in its completeness, but which had its effect on the Latitudinarians and on the scientists and naturalists. The former laid constant stress on reason, but for them the outline tended to sharpen and the picture as a whole to lose depth. The closer kinship in this connection between the Cambridge Platonists and the scientists and naturalists may perhaps be traced to the element of wonder in the works of the latter as they uncover what Boyle calls the delicate and slender lineaments and traces of a wisdom which expresses itself in organic design: 'It is not for themselves that the rubies flame, other jewels sparkle, the bezoar-stone is antidotal, nor is it for their own advantage that fruitful trees spend and exhaust themselves in annual profusions'.[2]

Possibly because reason is regarded unconsciously as being in some way abstract or self-existent, much that is written on the subject has an air of remoteness. Part of the distinctiveness of the Cambridge Platonists' treatment derives from the emphasis on reason as within the fragile and fallible personal setting. It is a view conditioned not only by a passive acceptance of the common limitations of men, but by an active acceptance of the implications of individuality: 'Men must think as they find cause'.[3]

This distinctive quality owes something also to the insistence on the operation of reason as being incomplete until it issues in a practical application to life. Far from being concerned simply with abstracts, reason is inextricably involved in the totality of experience. The accent on life is characteristic of John Smith, Whichcote's pupil at Emmanuel College, whose writings occasionally convey an impression of anticipating later ways of thinking and phrasing.

The tree of knowledge must be planted by the tree of life, he writes,[4] and 'the labour and sweat of the brain' are useless without

1. *Select Sermons*, p. 111.
2. Robert Boyle, *The Usefulness of Experimental Natural Philosophy*.
3. *Select Sermons*, p. 111.
4. *Select Discourses*, p. 3.

the 'warmth' of life'.[1] 'It is but a thin airy knowledge that is got by mere speculation, which is ushered in by syllogisms and demonstrations'.[2] Knowledge cannot be separated from goodness for then it brings its own illumination, 'more clear and convincing than any demonstration'.[3] Truth 'is not so much enshrined as entombed' in theological systems, and to look for it there 'is to seek the living among the dead'.[4] Wisdom and truth do not come solely by the exercise of speculation: 'It is only life that can feelingly converse with life. All the thin speculations and subtilest discourses of philosophy cannot so well unfold or define any sensible object, nor tell anyone so well what it is, as his own naked sense will do'.[5] He appears to be more aware of the work of the scientists than is Whichcote.[6] He criticises Aristotle 'whom so many take for the great intelligencer of nature',[7] and he is alive to the implications for theology of the gradual unfolding of natural causes: 'As the events in nature begin sometimes to be found out better by a discovery of their immediate natural causes',[8] old ideas undergo change, and 'a lawful acquaintance with all the events and phenomena that shew themselves upon this mundane stage'[9] would have a liberating effect on men's thinking and will give a truer picture of the divine origin of created things.

There is here a further stage in the development of a method which is beginning to take account of what Glanvill called sensible knowledge, and a moving away from a system based on a principle which is in itself not so much an explanation as a *ne plus ultra*. Viewed from any angle, the system showed a definite antagonism to reason, and in so far as it dealt in concepts which it could not or would not submit to reason, and defined faith in terms which opposed it to reason, it was in contrast to all that the Cambridge Platonists held. For them, reason is not only the formal difference of man but an active expression of life. The antithesis is between 'the knowledge that is got by mere speculation and which is ushered in by syllogisms and demonstrations',[10] and a 'new law' which is 'an efflux of life' and which 'produceth life'.[11] What is involved is 'a vital form and principle',[12] 'a vital and quickening

1. *Ib.*
2. *Ib.* p. 4.
3. *Ib.*
4. *Ib.* p. 3.
5. *Ib.* p. 278.
6. *Ib.* cp. *Discourses* II, III, IV.
7. *Ib.* p. 101.
8. *Ib.* p. 31.
9. *Ib.* p. 44.
10. *Ib.* p. 4.
11. *Ib.* p. 307.
12. *Ib.* p. 303.

thing',[1] 'something which is more than a piece of book-learning, or an historical narration'.[2] 'It is not so properly a doctrine that is wrapt up in ink and paper, as it is vitalis scientia'.[3]

As compared with the old covenant, the new covenant 'is not so much a system and body of saving divinity' as 'a living impression' made upon man.[4] 'We may in a true sense be as legal as ever the Jews were, if we converse with the Gospel as a thing only without us; and be as far short of the righteousness of God as they were, if we make the righteousness which is of Christ by faith to serve us only as an outward covering, and endeavour not after an internal transformation of our minds and souls into it'.[5] There is here no pietism or withdrawal into an ingrowing individualism, but a feeling for the proportion of inward to outward which is strengthened by a clear perception of what research into natural causes implies for theology. It is further strengthened by practicality of outlook, by insight and by the conviction that reason requires more than the truth of natural inscription. It may be *lumen de lumine*, or 'as Tully phraseth it, *participata similitudo rationis aeternae*', but, because of man's fall, its 'virtue and vigour' are impaired.[6]

Smith is critical of the fiduciary ideas of the statements on justification which were common in his day, regarding them as diminishing the stress on conformity and obedience, for this latter is contained in any comprehensive view of justification as 'a necessary reference'.[7] He attempts to reformulate by examining the meaning of the terms involved, because the effect of 'some of our dogmata and notions about justification' may be to give men 'higher and goodlier conceits'[8] of themselves. While he does not doubt that there is a changed relationship, yet in this respect, 'I think we may sometimes be too lavish and wanton in our imaginations'.[9] So, to clarify the position, he turns to a discussion of acceptance and faith: what it is that makes men to be acceptable, and how faith and its function in this connection are to be defined.

There are, he writes, two propositions necessary for the understanding of the matter. In the first place, 'the Divine judgment and estimation of every thing is according to the truth of the thing',[10] and it follows that the Divine acceptance is proportionable

1. *Ib.* p. 305.
2. *Ib.* p. 305.
3. *Ib.* p. 315.
4. *Ib.* p. 315.
5. *Ib.* pp. 315-16.
6. *Ib.* p. 371.
7. *Ib.* p. 321.
8. *Ib.* p. 316.
9. *Ib.* p. 317.
10. *Ib.*

to the judgment. In other words there can be no partiality, but 'wheresoever God finds any stamps and impressions of goodness, He likes and approves them'.[1] It is on this account, he continues, 'that St. James attributes a kind of justification to good works, which unquestionably are things that God approves and accepts, and all those in whom he finds them',[2] adding that the same writer disparages a 'barren, sluggish and drowsy belief'[3] which holds that the believer is accepted simply on the fact of his believing. Smith considers it fair comment to say that this means that it is not a strong conviction or 'a pertinacious imagination' of being accepted that makes men accepted,[4] for 'a mere conceit or opinion... makes us never the better in reality within ourselves', and the Divine judgment is 'of all things as they are'.[5] It is in fact 'compliance with the Divine will' which makes men accepted, and it is this and not 'any other external privilege' which is 'that which God justifies ... and in whomsoever he finds this, both it and they are accepted of him'.[6]

In the second place, justification 'carries in it a necessary reference to the sanctifying' of human nature, otherwise it would be only a name or a device.[7] It is not 'an abstract justification',[8] but 'Christ having made peace through the blood of His cross, the Heavens shall be no more as iron above us: but we shall receive freely the vital dew from them'.[9] Justification therefore has a dual aspect, for the creating of a new relationship implies the 'reconciliation' of human nature and begets a 'reciprocity' of love: 'Divine love to us, as it were by a natural emanation, begetting a reflex love in us'.[10] Faith is a response,[11] and it looks for 'an internal participation of the Divine nature'.[12] It is *caritate formata*, and it unites men 'more and more to the Centre of life and love',[13] and it is based on dependence[14] and conformity.[15]

It is not possible that 'religion should extinguish reason'[16] when the former is 'a living form',[17] when it produces 'a generous spirit', 'an amplitude',[18] and when the latter from being a dis-

1. *Ib.* p. 318.
2. *Ib.* p. 319.
3. *Ib.*
4. *Ib.* p. 320.
5. *Ib.*
6. *Ib.* pp. 320-1.
7. *Ib.* p. 321.
8. *Ib.* p. 322.
9. *Ib.* p. 323.
10. *Ib.* p. 324.
11. *Ib.* p. 325.
12. *Ib.* pp. 330, 369.
13. *Ib.* p. 325.
14. *Ib.* p. 325.
15. *Ib.* p. 332.
16. *Ib.* p. 377.
17. *Ib.* p. 384.
18. *Ib.* pp. 382-3.

cursive faculty becomes 'a serene understanding', 'an intellectual calmness'.[1] The quality of attractiveness which Worthington and Simon Patrick[2] recognised in him is felt also in his writings, in an imaginative feeling for words and in an individual way of looking at things and describing them. Patrick observes that his words were 'pregnant and significant, joined with such an active fancy, as is very rarely found in the company of such a deep understanding and judgment'.[3]

Sharing in Whichcote's outlook, he adds to its expression a feeling of contact with life, for there are in his work a descriptive warmth and a visual quality which are as much a matter of age as of temperament.

Whichcote's individuality lay not only in his ideas but in his ability to condense and in his original and cogent presentation. Smith had the same clarity and capacity for choosing words, but there is an element of colour as well. Where Whichcote analyses, Smith, as often as not, depicts, yet without any loss of accuracy, for he never loses himself in words, but has a linguist's feeling for them (Patrick comments on his interest in languages).[4] He inherited from Whichcote a certain precision which was doubtless fostered by his own mathematical studies. He had, as Patrick noted, an ability to get quickly to the centre of a question,[5] and a facility 'in expressing his mind'.[6] But the dominant impression is of what Patrick refers to as his 'capacious',[7] 'universalised',[8] outlook for he was interested in people and things, approachable[9] and business-like.[10] The feeling of modernity in his writing owes as much to this interest in life and personality as it does to his method of expression. This interest arises in part from a vitalistic element in his thinking, the conviction that life originates in a vital principle apart from the concurrence of any physical forces: 'and therefore it becomes us whom he hath endued with vital power of action, and in some sense a self-moving life, to stir up his good gifts within ourselves . . . to prepare our own souls more and more to receive his liberality . . . that that stock which he is pleased to impart to us

1. *Ib*. pp. 16–17.
2. *Select Discourses* (1673), Preface by J. Worthington: Short account by Simon Patrick.
3. *Ib*. p. 499.
4. *Ib*. p. 501.
5. *Ib*. p. 492.
6. *Ib*. p. 494.
7. *Ib*. p. 492.
8. *Ib*. p. 497.
9. *Ib*. pp. 493–4.
10. *Ib*. p. 495.

may not lie dead within us'.[1] It is involved also with his constant use, already referred to, of the terms life and love as being ultimate terms in the understanding of religion and of the relationship of man with his Creator. There is a certain kinship between Smith's ideas and those of Ficino, whose work influenced More. 'Ficino's aim, both before and after he was installed at Florence (1459) by Cosimo de Medici as translator and editor of Platonic works, was to seek in Greek thought a rational basis for Christian theology'.[2] His originality lay in his attempt to interpet the speculative and ethical philosophy of Plato as a theory of practical religion[3] and in this practicality of approach Smith shared, as Worthington indicated.[4] The emphasis on love as 'the creative energy of the divine'[5] increases the similarity: 'Ficino's theory of love united the human with the divine by means of an immanent grace which was not the arbitrary gift of God to a few chosen, but the light of the world, the force of intellect and faith, the very life of all men'.[6] The opening pages of a section in one of the discourses resembles this in substance.[7] It is one of those passages where Smith writes prose almost as if it were poetry, and its theme is that the promises are made effectual to men through active dependence on the love of God, 'all whose dispensations to the sons of men are but the dispreadings and distended radiations of his love, as freely flowing forth from it through the whole orb and sphere of its creation as the bright light from the sun in the firmament'.[8] 'Divine love and bounty' he writes 'are the supreme rulers in heaven and earth',[9] and faith in it 'would make us melt and dissolve out of all self-consistency, and by a free and noble sympathy with the Divine love to yield up ourselves to it, and dilate and spread ourselves more fully in it . . . it would lead us into the true liberty of the sons of God, filling our hearts once enlarged with the sense of it with a more generous and universal love'.[10] Men should maintain what he calls 'converse . . with God's unconfined love',[11] and he writes 'Could we once be thoroughly possessed and mastered with a full confidence of the Divine love'

1. *Ib.* p. 139.
2. *Philosophical Poems of Henry More*, ed. Geoffrey Bullough.
3. *Ib.*
4. *Select Discourses*, Preface, p. xxx.
5. *Philosophical Poems of Henry More*, ed. Geoffrey Bullough, p. xxix.
6. *Ib.* p. xxx.
7. *Select Discourses*, pp. 326–30.
8. *Ib.* p. 326.
9. *Ib.*
10. *Ib.* p. 328.
11. *Ib.* p. 330.

we would find ourselves 'borne up' and enabled 'to walk on strongly', and 'beholding his glory shining thus out upon us in the face of Christ, we should be deriving a copy of that eternal beauty upon our own souls'.[1]

Whether or not Smith had studied Ficino as had More who had read him before he had read Plotinus, the ideas are the same and they stem from the same source, for the most frequently quoted name in Smith's works is that of Plotinus. Taken together with references to such as Porphyry and pseudo-Dionysius, this is significant with regard to the basis of thought of the Cambridge Platonists, for theirs was a filtered Platonism, passing through Plotinus and other writers and acquiring various elements as it passed. But as far as the development of theological method is concerned, Smith inherited from his tutor Whichcote the synthesis of faith and reason which the latter derived from Platonist and Neo-Platonist sources. Sharing not only his ideas but that 'sweetness of temper' that contemporaries observed in Whichcote, he added to their formulation a quality of his own. The 'ingenuity, courtesy, gentleness and sweetness'[2] which Simon Patrick saw in him belong to one who was an uncomplicated person and who was singularly successful in transmitting the same quality to his work.

It would help to give perspective if it could be seen how a fair-minded and perceptive Calvinist viewed this line of thought. Such a reaction may be seen in a letter to Whichcote from Anthony Tuckney who criticised what he regarded as a new and unjustifiable departure in theology: 'And hence in part hath run a vein of doctrine, which divers very able and worthy men, whom from my heart I much honour, are, I fear, too much known by. The power of nature in morals too much advanced—reason hath too much given to it in the mysteries of faith—a recta ratio much talked of: which I cannot tell where to find—mind and understanding is all; heart and will little spoken of . . . those our philosophers and other heathens, made fair candidates for heaven; than the Scriptures seem to allow of; and they, in their virtues preferred before Christians overtaken with weaknesses; a kind of moral divinity minted; only with a little tincture of Christ added: nay, a Platonique faith unites to God—inherent righteousness so preached as if not with the prejudice of imputed righteousness,

1. *Ib.* pp. 328–9.   2. *Ib.* p. 502.

which hath sometimes very unseemly language given it; yet much said of the one, and very little or nothing of the other. This is not Paul's manner of preaching—this inherent righteousness may be perfect in this life—an estate of love, in this life, above a life of faith—and some broad expressions, as though in this life we may be above ordinances: with divers other principles of religion, by some very doubtfully spoken of'.[1]

This is unquestionably an able summary, and considering the difficulties attendant on assessing a situation from within, a fair one. At many points he has rightly discerned the drift of the new movement, although it is to be questioned whether he really read the signs of the times and recognised the existence of the situation which Whichcote and his colleagues sought to meet.

He refers to their use of Platonist material, and his comment on the preference given to the heathen philosophers is supported by Whichcote himself who tartly observes that Tully is 'a better divine than some who . . . seem to deny reason'.[2] He discerns the emphasis on 'the power of nature' as being an important element in a general appraisal which has nothing in common with a trans-cendentalist outlook. As the writer of the preface to Whichcote's sermons noted, it was on a favourable view of the human situation that the unity of faith and reason ultimately depended.

Tuckney is correct also in detecting that there is a change-over from a nexus of ideas in which that of sovereignty is decisive: 'the excellency of these men's divinity is sovereignty to ruin a great part of His creation to show His power'.[3] He fails to see that any acceptance of the unity of things forces the querying of affirmations which do not match the observed facts of reflective experi-ence. Nor is he successful in understanding that what was meant by reason was something more than *recta ratio*. Also the opposition alleged between the Cambridge Platonists and the Pauline epistles is dubious, and is restricted in fact to the questionable identifica-tion of one element in them with the position which the Cambridge Platonists opposed. The quality of his observation appears in the sentence 'an estate of love, in this life, above a life of faith', but the contrast drawn depends for its meaning on delimiting faith

1. Eight Letters of Dr Anthony Tuckney to Dr Benjamin Whichcote, *Moral and Religious Aphorisms of Whichcote*, Letter II, ed. Salter, (1753).
2. Whichcote, *Select Sermons*, p. 105.
3. *Ib*. p. 122.

rather than on recognising the interconnection indicated in the epistles, 'faith working through love'.[1]

Again, no candid appreciation of the writings of Whichcote and Smith could possibly regard them as amounting to a vague and approximately Christian moralising. Here, as often, it is doubtless that part which is found least congenial which forms the basis for a judgment on the whole. The remarkable thing, however, is not that Whichcote's correspondent failed to appreciate their meaning, but that, from the opposite point of view, he was able to go so far in understanding them. It is clear, too, from Tuckney's comments that the members of the group had by and large a common approach to the questions referrred to in his letter. The main elements in this are shared by Henry More, who had nevertheless an individual contribution to make because of the extent of his interests, so that Tulloch could describe him as 'at once the most typical and the most vital and interesting'[2] of the Cambridge Platonists. The note not only of variety, but of interests rarely combined, lends an almost paradoxical air to one whose contacts with the contemporary scene included such seeming contradictions as philosophy and the study of psychic phenomena, poetry and science, as well as theology.

Sharing the disinterestedness of his associates, he neither desired nor accepted preferment, living and working in the university. Yet, although the marks of detachment were easily discernible, More was sociable and his company was sought after. He enjoyed a game of bowls, was an amateur of music, and kept up various friendships with such as Lord and Lady Conway, at whose house he used to stay. He maintained a large correspondence, including his well-known exchange of letters with Descartes. A reference to the reading of the latter's work in company with Lord Conway, to whom he dedicated one of his books, gives a glimpse of the association: 'I recollect with myself the first occasion of busying my thoughts upon this subject, which was then when I had the honour and pleasure of reading Descartes his "Passions" with your lordship in the garden of Luxenburg to pass away the time, (in which treatise though there be nothing but what is handsome and witty), yet all did not seem so perfectly solid and satisfactory to me

1. Smith, *Select Discourses*, pp. 325, 328.
2. J. Tulloch, *Rational Theology and Christian Philosophy in England in the Seventeenth Century*, Vol. II, p. 303.

but that I was forced in some principal things to seek satisfaction for myself'.[1] The last sentence tells also something of his method, and in this connection More's prefaces are of service for the understanding of his thought, for he saw his various books as one connected work, having certain linking themes. He reflects very clearly the transitional nature of the age in which he lived, for there is in his interest in scientific facts, in natural and psychic phenomena, a mixture of observation and credulity. This is rather the paradox of the times than of the man, but More's writings have a colourful diversity of content as well, ranging as they do from a series of philosophical poems to the interpretation of prophecy and the reading of the cabbala. Rationalist and mystic, scientist and poet, recluse and sociable member of his circle, he combined this with a study of philosophy, so that while his outlook was generous, it was not one which readily gave a lodging to every opinion.

Born in 1614, he outlived by twenty-seven years the Restoration which, with pardonable optimism, he regarded as 'the recovery of the Church to her ancient apostolic purity' and the occasion for the return of a liberal orthodoxy, 'that doctrine that depends not upon the fallible deduction of men, but is plainly set down in the Scripture; other things being left to the free recommendation of the Church'.[2]

His father was a Calvinist, who read Spenser to his children, and from whom his son was temporarily estranged at the time of his entering College. Significantly, the cause of their disagreement was Henry More's refusal of Calvinism: 'I being bred up, to the almost fourteenth year of my age, under parents and a master that were great Calvinists, (but withal, very pious and good ones): at which time, by the order of my parents, persuaded to it by my uncle, I immediately went to Eton school . . . but neither there, nor yet anywhere else, could I ever swallow down that hard doctrine concerning fate. On the contrary, I remember . . . that I had such a deep aversion in my temper to this opinion'.[3]

He went to Cambridge, to Christ's College, of which he became a Fellow in 1639, and which he never left, being buried in the College Chapel. With his older contemporary Milton, he shared

1. *Immortality of the Soul* (1662), Dedication.
2. *Explanation of the Grand Mystery of Godliness* (1660), Introduction, p. xiii.
3. Introduction to the Latin edition of his *Collected Works*, translated by Richard Ward.

as tutor William Chappell, afterwards Provost of Trinity College, Dublin, and later Bishop of Cork and Ross, whom Fuller looked on as an outstanding tutor.[1] It is not without relevance to the development of More's opinions that during the time which Chappell spent at Cambridge his views were regarded as having changed in the direction of Arminianism. That this was so is almost certain, as Laud and Wentworth would hardly have chosen as the agent of their policy one who held the same opinions as Chappell was known to have favoured previously.[2] His influence in this direction on his pupil must not therefore be discounted.

More is remembered as having written a poem on the death of Edward King, Milton's Lycidas. He was a lover of the out-of-doors and of the things of nature, and it is to be recalled that his *Antidote* was the starting-point, as Raven indicates, of the naturalist Ray's book *The Wisdom of God, Manifested in the Works of the Creation*.[3]

He was an interested man, whose diverse interests, ranging from his efforts to prove the dependence of ancient philosophers on the Mosaic code, through witchcraft to the literature of mysticism, neither muddled him fundamentally nor made him a crank, for his outlook was balanced and wise. The truth is that he was too learned to allow himself to become immersed in any one aspect of learning to the detriment of the rest, and too concerned with the place of reason to adopt any position which was not consistent with it.

In the introduction to the collected works, More gives some details concerning the development of his ideas, recounting how during the commencement of his time at the university, he experienced a 'mighty and almost immoderate thirst after knowledge, especially for that which was natural: and above all others, that which was said to dive into the deepest cause of things, and Aristotle calls the first and highest philosophy or wisdom . . . Thus then persuaded and esteeming it what was highly fit, I immerse myself over head and ears in the study of philosophy; promising a most wonderful happiness to myself in it. Aristotle therefore, Cardan, Julius Scaliger, and other philosophers of the greatest note I diligently peruse. In which, the truth is, though I

1. *History of the Worthies of England* (1840), Vol. II, p. 571.
2. *An Epoch in Irish History*, J. P. Mahaffy, p. 232.
3. *John Ray*, C. E. Raven, p. 458.

met here and there with some things wittily and acutely and sometimes solidly spoken; yet the most seemed to me either so false or
so uncertain, or else so obvious and trivial, that I looked upon myself as having plainly lost my time in the reading of such authors
... Those almost four years which I spent in studies of this kind,
as to what concerned those matters which I chiefly desired to be
satisfied about ... ended in nothing, in a manner, but mere
scepticism'.

His studies, however, began to take a different direction, that
of the mystic and Platonist writers: 'Especially having begun to
read now the Platonic writers, Marsilius Ficinus, Plotinus himself,
Mercurius Trismegistus; and the mystical divines, among whom
there was frequent mention made of the purification of the soul,
and of the purgative course that is previous to the illuminative'.
This, and particularly the expression of it in the *Theologia Germanica* appealed to More as the way to 'simplicity of mind', so
that after a few years he found himself tranquil and content, enjoying 'a lucid state of mind' and 'a greater assurance then ever I
could have expected, even of those things which before I had the
greatest desire to know'.

Drawn to the same sources as were Whichcote and Smith, his
greater interest in their physical aspect is the response of a temperament which is not only poetical and meditative, but which sees
in the underlying presuppositions of immanence and harmony
a basis for bringing philosophy and theology closer together. The
assumption that the two should be kept in water-tight compartments had been challenged by Whichcote and Cudworth.
Whichcote, who had influenced More, had outlined a synthesis of
reason and faith in which he followed Plotinus and Ficino whose
works More had studied. 'The age we live in is ... a searching,
inquisitive, rational and philosophical age',[1] wrote More, and he
asserts that truths of religion ought to be stated 'in such a way as
would be most gaining upon men of a more rational and philosophical genius'.[2] He concludes 'that there is no real clashing at all
betwixt any genuine point of Christianity and what true philosophy and right reason does not determine and allow, but that, as
Aristotle somewhere speaks ... there is a perpetual peace and
agreement betwixt truth and truth, be they of what nature or kind

1. *Apology* (1664), Chap. I, 2.   2. *Ib.* Chap. I, 3.

so ever'.[1] It was this conviction that provided the disciplinary factor for More's diverse interests, preserving his thinking from disequilibrium, since he regarded all facts and experience as being ultimately illustrative of the unity of reality and consciousness. This fusion of matter and spirit in a unified reality he maintained against Hobbes on the one hand and Descartes on the other. Temperamentally more inclined to pietism than were the other members of the group, this is counter-balanced by the stress on practicality and obedience, and he approximates in ideas and phrasing to Smith when he writes of mysticism in terms of 'union of life' rather than 'imagination'.[2]

'The influence of Plotinus on More's mind was greater than that of any other single writer', wrote the editor of his philosophical poems, and in an able study he indicates how the *Enneads* satisfied More's requirements of a philosophy of immanence, an inner harmony of life, and 'gave him an orderly cosmos, the contemplation of which kindled him for a short time into poetry filled with wonder at a picturesque, vitalistic universe'.[3] Plotinus's rejection of materialism constituted, of course, a major link, but because, for More, 'God was a Person and His relation to man must be a personal relationship',[4] he found Neo-Platonism inadequate and supplemented its deficiences from such as the Renaissance Platonist Ficino. More was influenced not only by his attempt to achieve a synthesis, but also by his interpretation of the Platonic philosophy as a theory of practical religion.[5] It was inevitable, too, that one of More's temperament who had refused the picture of a world sharply divided by the current transcendentalism, should have accepted Ficino's picture of a world united in terms of inherent life and immanence. For the Cambridge Platonists, the words 'the spirit in man is the candle of the Lord' seemed to express this immanence which is one of the chief elements in their thinking.

Possibly the most important part of their contribution to the development of theological method, and one which ran counter to the general assumption of the time, was their determination to end the separation between philosophy and theology, holding that

1. *Ib.*
2. Quoted in *Philosophical Poems of Henry More*, ed. Geoffrey Bullough p. xxxvii.
3. *Ib.* pp. xxvii–xxviii.
4. *Ib.* p. xxvii.
5. *Ib.* p. xxix.

there was required, as Cudworth said, 'a philosophy of religion confirmed and established by philosophical reasons in an age so philosophical'.[1]

'To take away reason', wrote More, 'is to rob Christianity of that special prerogative it has above all other religions in the world, namely, that it dares appeal unto reason'.[2] He describes his purpose 'to search to the very bottom of things', indicating the usefulness of the Platonist and Cartesian hypotheses,[3] and adding, 'for being persuaded in my own judgment that what I have applied is very consonant to the faculties of human understanding, and considering also how far that philosophy has already got foot in Christendom . . . as also how hugely disadvantageous it would be to religion and theology to seem to be left so far behind, or to appear to be so opposite to that, which I foresaw might probably become the common philosophy of the learned'.[4]

It was against this background of Neo-Platonism and of mingled agreement and disagreement with Descartes that More's position evolved. It would probably be fair to say that the division of matter and spirit implied in varying degrees in philosophy up to the time of Descartes was by the latter so stated that a considerable part of philosophical writing after him was given over to the confuting of the concept of a divided reality. The significance of More's writings appears in his insistence on the unity of reality: 'in the main line of English philosophy of the seventeenth and eighteenth centuries, this opposition to dualism appeared on the one hand in the materialism of Hobbes, and on the other in various forms of subjective idealism. In each case, the demand for unity was met by the sacrifice of one of the factors of traditional dualism. In the same time of transition there were other attempts to overcome this opposition of matter and spirit. Though inadequate, often, and incomplete, these show the same groping after a unified conception of reality. Among them is the work of Henry More. In partly conscious antagonism to the prevailing method of analysis and division, More emphasises the concrete unity of life and spirit'.[5] F. I. Mackinnon also notes that it is with the development of vitalistic speculation rather than with the

1. *The True Intellectual System of the Universe* (1678). Preface.
2. *Collection of Several Philosophical Writings* (1662), Preface General, p. vi.
3. *Ib.*
4. *Ib.* p. xix.
5. *Philosophical Writings of Henry More*, ed. Flora Isabel Mackinnon, p. xix.

materialism or the idealism of the period that More and Cudworth, and it might be added, Smith, are connected: 'The sense of the pervading life and activity of the universe, which goes back for its earliest expression to the animism of primitive belief, had been strongly felt by the nature-philosophers of the Renaissance. Their reaction against the barren categories of the peripatetic philosophy led them at once backward to the mystical thought of Alexandrian Platonism and forward into the new science of observation and experiment.'[1]

This latter discipline, dependent as it was on fact and on experience, doubtless contributed its share to More's rejection of a dualism which on these grounds he could not regard as substantiated. Nevertheless, despite the vitalistic and personalist quality of his thinking, his debt to Descartes is neither inconsiderable nor unacknowledged: 'The more I read, the more I admired his wit, but at last grew the more confirmed that it was utterly impossible that matter should be the only essential principle of things'.[2] References are frequent, and the four letters to Descartes underline the connection.

Two sentences in his general preface seem fairly to indicate More's basic outlook, in one of which he remarks that, for him, Christianity is 'rational throughout'. The second is a quotation from Clement of Alexandria, in whose succession the Cambridge Platonists stood, to the effect that, while the Divine image is the Logos, 'the image of this image is the human intellect'.[3] Yet of none of the Cambridge Platonists could it be less truly said that his attitude was that of a self-contained intellectualism, for his outlook on religion is as personal and realistic as his appreciation of the visible world is keen. One of his prefaces shows that the admirer of Plato—'whose philosophy to this very day I look upon to be more than human in the chief strokes thereof'[4]—was one who held that obedience was 'the entrance into divine knowledge.'[5] The indispensable duty is the conformity of the Christian life,[6] the root of which is obediential faith and trust, its branches being

1. *Ib.*
2. *An Explanation of the Grand Mystery of Godliness* (1660), Preface, p. vii.
3. *A Collection of Several Philosophical Writings* (2nd ed. 1662), Preface General, p. iv.
4. *An Explanation of the Grand Mystery of Godliness*, Preface, p. vi.
5. *Ib.* p. v.
6. *Ib.* p. xxviii.

charity, humility and purity, justice, temperance, fortitude and
prudence being comprehended in it.[1] Even in so volatile and ver-
satile a writer as More, with his interest in mysticism, in science
and in psychic matters, this element acts as a ballast, keeping him
on the level of everyday contacts. In fact, it is a major constituent
in his make-up just as it is a persistent element in one form or
another in the theological method of the period. But whatever
form it takes, whether as with Sanderson it appears more clear-cut
and close to the definitions of the *Summa Theologica*, or whether
as with More it merges into a wider background constituted by
his philosophical reading and by his study of Ficino and the
Theologia Germanica, it retains its basic realism and practicality
and remains a common denominator from Hooker to the Latitudinarians.

More writes of confidence and joy, as in the account of how
one of his books was written after 'a dangerous sickness',[2] and he
comments at the close of his preface on 'faith working by love'.[3]
Various passages give indication of a sensitive and mystical
simplicity, but 'the light within' must be reason,[4] for to More, as to
his fellow-Platonists, man's 'very nature is reason'.[5] 'The spirit
of man is said to be the lamp of the Lord', he writes, and there are
'sealed upon it' certain 'common characters and ingenuous senti-
ments of indispensable truth . . . which are hardly obliterated
quite in any', and it 'judges according to . . . the common notions
of reason in all men'.[6] More divides life into the divine and the
natural, but there is also what he calls a middle life which is
neither one nor the other 'but is really . . . such as that with which
it is conjoined'.[7] Of this, reason is 'the general principle or common root', and he defines reason as 'a power or faculty of the soul,
whereby either from her innate ideas or common notions, or else
from the assurance of her own senses, or upon the relation or
tradition of another, she unravels a further clue of knowledge,
enlarging her share of intellectual light, by laying open to herself
the close connexion and cohesion of the conceptions she has of
things, whereby inferring one thing from another she is able to

1. *Ib.* Bk. VIII, Chap. XII, 2, 9.
2. *Ib.* p. vii.
3. *Ib.* p. xxx.
4. *Ib.* Bk. VIII, Chap. XII, 2.
5. *Ib.* Bk. I, Chap. II, 4.

6. *A Modest Enquiry* (1664), Pt. I,
   Bk. II, Chap. II, 9.
7. *Explanation* (1660), Bk. II, Chap.
   XI, 3.

deduce multifarious conclusions as well for the pleasure of speculation as the necessity of practice'.[1] This stress on the practical aspect of reason is a recurring one, particularly with the Latitudinarians who make considerable use of the idea, found in the *Summa Theologica* and in the Wisdom books, of prudence as practical reason.

Referring to those who are critical of giving reasons for things— 'religion seeming to them in the best dress when it appears most unreasonable'—he is unable to understand why 'freedom, ingenuity, reason and philosophy' should be regarded in this light,[2] since to exclude reason is to ignore what is distinctively human.[3] Reason is a 'settled and cautious composure of mind' which tests things by agreed notions or by evidence, 'or else a clear and distinct deduction from these'.[4]

While More uses 'solid and unresistible reason in a perspicuous method',[5] he emphasises with Plotinus 'divine sagacity' or intuition, quoting from Scaliger 'that there is something before and better than reason, whence reason itself has its rise'.[6] It is something unitive, arising not only from 'firmness of ratiocination' but from 'integrity of the will and affections, as well as the light of understanding'.[7] This intuition he describes as 'a certain principle more noble and inward than reason itself, and without which reason will falter, or at least reach but to mean and frivolous things. I have a sense of something in me while I thus speak, which I must confess is of so retruse a nature that I want a name for it, unless I should adventure to term it divine sagacity, which is the first rise of successful reason, especially in matters of great comprehension and moment, and without which a man is as it were in a thick wood, and may make infinite promising attempts, but can find no outlet into the open champain, where one may freely look about him every way without the safe conduct of this good genius'.[8] More considers that this divine sagacity does not come by the mind only, but by the 'purity and integrity of the will and affections' lso, by the whole personality acting in harmony.[9] The human

1. *Ib.* i.
2. *Explanation*, Preface, p. xxii.
3. *Conjectura Cabbalistica* (1662), Preface, p. 2.
4. *Enthusiasmus Triumphatus* (1662), p. liv.
5. *Antidote* (3rd ed. 1662), preface, p. i.
6. *Collection of Several Philosophical Writings*, Preface General, p. ix.
7. *Ib.* p. viii.
8. *Ib.* p. vii.
9. *Ib.* p. viii.

spirit, sincerely endeavouring to this end, is 'Divinely indued' with this quality 'which is a more inward, compendious, and comprehensive presentation of truth, ever antecedaneous to that reason which in theories of greatest importance approves itself afterwards, upon the exactest examination, to be most solid and perfect every way'.[1] In More's work it is not difficult to see the application of W. R. Inge's phrase 'mysticism based on a foundation of reason',[2] as a description of the view-point of the Cambridge Platonists.

More holds also that the mind has actual knowledge of its own,[3] in other words, that it helps to form its own object, 'that we have some ideas that we are not beholding to our senses for, but are the mere exertions of the mind occasionally awakened by the appulses of the outward objects'.[4] These innate ideas he calls 'active sagacity'.[5] 'But the mind of man more free, and better exercised in the close observation of its own operations and nature, cannot but discover that there is an active and actual knowledge in man, of which these outward objects are rather the reminders than the first begetters or implanters. And when I say actual knowledge, I do not mean that there is a certain number of ideas flaring and shining to the animadversive faculty, like so many torches or stars in the firmament to our outward sight ... but I understand thereby an active sagacity of the soul, or quick recollection, as it were, whereby some small business being hinted unto her, she runs out presently into a more clear and large conception'.[6] The mind is seen as related to experience and to the impressions of the senses, but arranging and co-ordinating them by an activity which is its own.

More's main theme is then that of the unity of reality, and instead of minimising either element, his aim is to show the interdependence and connections of spirit and matter. The created order, the nature of consciousness, the work of naturalists and physicists and psychic research, are brought together to demonstrate 'that it was utterly impossible that matter should be the only essential principle of things'.[7] Since 'matter shows itself to us in abundance of varieties of appearance, therefore there must be another principle

1. *Ib*. p. ix.
2. W. R. Inge, *Vale*, p. 34.
3. *Antidote*, Chap. V.
4. *Ib*. Bk. I, Chap. VI, p. 19.
5. *Ib*. Bk. I, Chap. V, p. 17.
6. *Ib*. Bk. I, Chap. V, p. 17.
7. *Explanation*, Preface, p. vii.

besides the matter, to order the motion of it so as may make these
varieties to appear'.[1] It is towards this insistence on the spiritual-
significance of reality that the several lines of More's thought con-
verge. His acceptance of the Platonic idea of immanence, his
tendency to vitalistic and to mystical thinking, his interest in facts,
draw him to this central conclusion, as does his assertion of the
unity of consciousness. He is opposed to 'talking of faculties and
operations . . . as separate and distinct from the essence they
belong to'. He disapproves of such expressions as 'the will being
the cause of willing, and of its being the necessary cause of voluntary actions, . . . whenas, if a man would speak properly, and
desired to be understood, he would say, that the subject in which
is this power or act of willing, (call it man or the soul of man) is the
cause of this or that voluntary action'.[2] This early protest against
any kind of faculty psychology derives from More's awareness of
the importance of the idea of unity in interpreting experience.
More's work, dealing with this central theme from different
aspects, moves in an atmosphere quite unlike that of the systematic
theology of his day. There is an emphasis on experience as well as
on reason, a consideration of the implications of known facts, a
refusal to abandon the opening world of unified reality for areas
reserved to mutually exclusive departments of knowledge. While
this point of view has the defects of its qualities, it has the advantage of acknowledging the best of human achievements and of
handling with candour new discoveries instead of ignoring them.
The work of the Cambridge Platonists gives the impression of a
determined effort to face the complexity of experience, and to
make sense of it. Nor do they seem to relax their hold on fundamentals. It would be true to say that they appeared to be more
aware than their contemporaries of the universe around them, of
an element of mystery in it as well as of its evidences of design, and
that this awareness arose in part from their immanentist and
creationist outlook.

More has not received credit for having, in two of his books,[3]
anticipated by forty years the method adopted by Richard Bentley
in 1692, when, in the first series of the lectures founded under the
will of Robert Boyle, he sought to prove the central affirmations of
belief from reason, and from the nature of the creation. Bentley

1. *Antidote*, Bk. II, Chap. I, p. 38.   3. The *Antidote* (1652), and the
2. *Immortality*, Bk. II, Chap. III, 8.   *Immortality*.

held that these affirmations were supported by the discoveries of scientists and naturalists. G. R. Cragg writes, 'His whole method is significant. He made no appeal to Scripture; its authority was not admitted by his opponents and he did not even postulate that it must be included as part of the relevant material'. 'But however their are other books extant which they must needs allow of as proper evidence; even the mighty volumes of visible nature, and the everlasting tables of right reason'.[1] In the eight lectures, Bentley endeavours to prove the existence of God from three sets of observable facts, the human faculties, such as reason and intelligence, the structure and origin of human bodies, and the origin and frame of the world, making full use of the discoveries of physics.

It is noteworthy that the sub-title of the first of More's books is *An appeal to the natural faculties of the mind of man, whether there be not a God*, and of the second, *So far forth as it is demonstrable from the knowledge of nature and the light of reason*. Furthermore, his method is the same, in that his arguments are borrowed 'not from books . . . but from the very nature of the thing itself, and indelible ideas of the soul of man',[2] and he continues, 'But I did not insist upon any sacred history, partly because it is so well and so ordinarily known, that it seemed less needful; but mainly, because I know the atheist will boggle more at whatever is fetched from established religion, and fly away from it . . . but that he might not be shy of me, I have conformed myself as near his own garb as I might . . . and have appeared in the plain shape of a mere naturalist myself'.[3] The second book 'pretends to handle the matter only within the bounds of natural light, unassisted and unguided by any miraculous revelation'.[4]

There is a close parallel between the theme of Bentley's second lecture, that 'matter and motion cannot think', in which he advances arguments from the human faculties, and that of the first book of *The Antidote*, in which More develops as the main hypothesis that 'our faculties are true'.[5] In the final chapter of that book he argues 'that the brain has no sense, and therefore cannot impress spontaneously any motion', but that there is in man 'a

1. G. R. Cragg, *From Puritanism to the Age of Reason*, p. 107.
2. *Antidote*, Preface, p. 3.
3. *Ib.* pp. 6, 7.
4. *Immortality*, Preface, p. 2.
5. *Antidote*, Preface, p. 3.

spiritual substance' in which reside the properties 'of understanding and of moving corporeal matter', and in the world a similar substance 'that is able to move and actuate all matter'.[1] The last three Boyle lectures base their deductions on the origin and frame of the world, and the second book of *The Antidote* examines 'the external phenomena of universal nature', beginning with day and night and the seasons which 'naturally imply a principle of wisdom and counsel in the Author of them'.[2] More observes that since matter shows itself 'in abundance of varieties of appearance, therefore there must be another principle besides the matter, to order the motion of it so as may make these varieties to appear'.[3] Significantly, both instance the phenomenon of gravitation, and Bentley refers to his indebtedness to Newton's work, just as earlier More makes the same assumption that science assists theology, when he refers to Boyle's *New Experiments Physico-Mechanical touching the Air'*.[4]

More then leaves the larger canvas of nature to consider its details, and he remarks that beauty, symmetry and proportion, as for example in flowers and trees, are 'the proper object of the understanding and reason, for these things be not taken notice of by the beasts', and the absence of 'any ineptitude in anything . . . is a sign that the fluidness of the matter is guided by the overpowering counsel of an Eternal Mind'.[5] He considers how animals are adapted to their circumstances,[6] emphasising their usefulness and their beauty, and it is of interest that while More gives credence to the old idea of spontaneous generation 'out of such kind of matter as will never fail', as of eels from mud,[7] or 'by putrefaction',[8] as in the case of frogs and mice and certain birds, Bentley is at pains to refute this in detail in the light of its denial by scientists in his own day. Having surveyed the plants and their uses,[9] More turns to the human frame, of which 'the contrivance of the whole and every particular is so evident an argument of exquisite skill in the Maker',[10] and he illustrates an argument from design from the various parts of the body. Bentley, in the third, fourth and fifth of his lectures, follows the same plan, and draws the same conclusions. He is, of course, indebted, as he acknowledges, to Newton,

1. *Ib.* Bk. I, Chap. XI, 7, 13.
2. *Ib.* Bk. II, Chap. I, 1.
3. *Ib.* Bk. II, Chap. I, 2.
4. *Ib.* Chap. II, 7.
5. *Ib.* Chap. V. 6.
6. *Ib.* Chap. VIII.
7. *Ib.* Chap. IX, 6.
8. *Ib.* 7 and Bk. III, Chap. XV, 8.
9. *Ib.* Chap. V, VI, VII.
10. *Ib.* Chap. XII, I.

while More shows traces of a more transitional period of thought, but their method is the same. While it is probable that this is the model for Bentley's treatment, what is more significant is that a theological method, to which he was considered as having given its first full expression at the end of the century, is found to have been fully stated and active almost forty years earlier. In view of this, it seems difficult to overstress the connection of the Cambridge Platonists with the new philosophy, or to rate too highly their rôle in the development of theological method. Perhaps their apartness is more evident now than it was to their contemporaries, since the influence of university teachers is diffused rather than concentrated, and is necessarily hidden in part from later times by its very nature, except when some link can be established.

It would not be easy to say with exactness, although it seems likely in the circumstances, whether More's book was one of those that started people thinking along those lines, or whether its reappearance as part of his collected works in 1679 served to give fresh impetus to a way of thinking that must by then have been gaining ground. It certainly was the starting-point of John Ray's *The Wisdom of God, manifested in the Works of Creation* which was published in 1691 and which Derham took as the basis of his Boyle Lectures in 1711. In any event, it seems probable that it contributed to Bentley's ideas in the first series of Boyle Lectures which appeared in the year after Ray's book. More's significance is to be gauged by the fact that he had accurately assessed the situation and the method of approaching it shortly after the beginning of the second half of the century.

As they endeavoured to understand and explain the natural world, the Cambridge Platonists, influenced by their philosophical background, came to describe it in terms which showed that they saw it as plastic rather than mechanical. This brought them into disagreement with the position of Descartes, since they saw nature not as divided into compartments, each separately analysable, but as 'an abundance of varieties of appearances', in More's phrase, governed by an internal vital principle, plastic nature. This was 'a substance incorporeal, but without sense and animadversion, pervading the whole matter of the universe, and exercising a plastical power therein according to the sundry predispositions and occasions in the parts it works upon, raising such phenomena in the world, by directing the parts of the matter and their motion, as cannot be resolved into mere mechanical powers'.[1] In the general preface, he describes it again as 'a substance incorporeal that does interesse itself in the bringing about some more general phenomena in the world', referring to 'all the plastic services it does both in plants and animals'. It is an imperceptive, imprisoned reason, implanted in matter: 'This therefore being a mute copy of the eternal Word . . . is in every part naturally appointed to do all the best services that matter is capable of, according to such or such modifications, and according to that platform of which it is the transcript . . . This spirit need not be perceptive itself, it being the naural transcript of that which is knowing or perceptive, and is the lowest substantial activity from the all-wise God, containing in it certain general modes and laws of nature for the good of the universe. But the eye of particular providence is not therein. Else why does a tile fall upon the head of him that passes by in the streets, go he either to play or sermon? And how come those bungles in monstrous productions, or those inept and self-thwarting attempts of this spirit in certain experiments about the finding out a vacuum? . . . Wherefore neither omnipotency nor omnisciency acts in such cases, but this imperceptive spirit of nature'.[2]

Its place is secondary and its function is that of a medium or as More puts it elsewhere, that of a vicarious power acting upon 'this great automaton, the world'.[3]

The influence of Cudworth and More upon Ray is strong in this connection, although he owed to them and to Whichcote a general debt. C. E. Raven has shown how Ray echoes Whichcote in one of his phrases, and is it not also possible to see More's description of speculative enquiry as 'a Holy-day and Sabbath of rest to the soul'[4] reflected in Ray's picture of scientific studies as 'part of the business of a Sabbath-day?'[5] Confronted with the uneven and the incomplete, Ray, as a candid observer of the natural world, saw that these problems were by-passed or ignored by the accepted view of its origin, but that there was an explanation in the idea of a plastic nature which he had learned from Cudworth and More. This is seen in the book which has been

1. *Immortality*, Bk. II, Chap. XII.
2. *Ib.* pp. xv–xvi.
3. *Antidote*, Bk. II, Chap. II.
4. *Explanation*, Preface, p. v.
5. *The Wisdom of God, manifested in the Works of Creation* (4th ed.), p. 199.

described as his most popular and influential achievement, of which C. E. Raven writes that 'it was reissued many times during the next century; it formed the basis of Derham's Boyle Lectures in 1711–12; it supplied the background for the thought of Gilbert White and indeed for the naturalists of three generations; it was imitated, and extensively plagiarised, by Paley in his famous *Natural Theology*; and more than any other single book it initiated the true adventure of modern science, and is the ancestor of the *Origin of Species* or of *L'Évolution Créatrice*.[1]

This influential work had as its acknowledged starting-point More's *Antidote* and while Ray's attitude, because of the accumulation of fresh information and his own specialised studies, is more scientific, the form and major ideas of both books are the same. By reason of his training as a naturalist in observation and classification, Ray disregards entirely the third book of the *Antidote*, in which More deals with those psychic questions to which he was drawn by his own mystical and meditative temperament, but it is clear that More has again left an impress. This time he gave to the naturalists and scientists a theology of synthesis, in which philosophy and accurate observation have a part, while to the theologians he had suggested a method which made use of the new science. This was the deliberately chosen direction taken in the *Antidote*, and More's contribution is further emphasised, if in the case of Bentley, the surmise concerning the latter's indebtedness to it for the form and plan of his own lectures be accurate.

More's criticism and final abandonment of Descartes was inevitable as a result of his insistence on the unity of spirit and matter and on the necessity of taking full account of the life of the natural world. Descartes' position was that pure thought was essential to mental substance, and that extension is essential to corporeal substance. If this is granted, it follows that anything which does not possess the former attribute must be relegated to the sphere of matter. One of the immediate consequences of this view is that animals are mere automata. This was in opposition to the basic idea of the unity of life and experience as held by the Cambridge Platonists, and More rejected the idea of extension and the belief that animals are mere machines.[2]

More's books are in fact a coherent attempt to show the unity

1. C. E. Raven, *John Ray*, p. 452.
2. *Immortality*, Bk. II, Chap. V, 10.

of life as it exists at different levels. In the *Antidote*, which he calls 'a careful draft of natural theology or metaphysics',[1] he draws his arguments from natural phenomena and the use of reason, and his theme is that men's faculties convince them that the visible world is not explicable in terms of matter only. More and Wilkins may indeed be regarded as the originators of the natural theology which was a feature of Latitudinarian writings. Wilkins's approach was more simplified but his method was the same as More's and it had its effect on the work of Stillingfleet and Tillotson.

In the *Immortality*, More develops other aspects of this. 'Whatever things are in themselves', he writes, 'they are nothing to us, but so far forth as they become known to our faculties or cognitive powers',[2] and similarly, 'Whatsoever is unknown to us, or is known but as merely possible, is not to move us or determine us any way, or make us undetermined; but we are to rest in the present light and plain determination of our own faculties'.[3] He adds that 'all our faculties have not a right of suffrage for determining of truth, but only common notions, external sense, and evident and undeniable deductions of reason',[4] and what is 'not consonant to all or some of these, is mere fancy'.[5] The essence or substance of a thing, however, cannot be apprehended by the faculties, so that it follows that 'if the naked substance of a thing be so utterly unconceivable, there can be nothing deprehended there to be a connexion betwixt it and its first properties. Such is actual divisibility and impenetrability in matter . . . These are immediate properties of matter',[6] and being immediate, they are indemonstrable. The immediate properties of an immaterial substance are then penetrability and indivisibility.[7] More maintains that such a notion is just as intelligible as that of a material substance,[8] and that such immaterial substances are seminal forms, animals, and human and angelic spirits. He defines the first of these as 'the first degree of particular life in the world', and as 'a created spirit organising duly prepared matter into life and vegetation proper to this or the other kind of plant'.[9] Animals have the further 'intrinsecal power' of sensation, and men have this and reason as well.[10]

1. *Ib.* Dedicatory letter.
2. Bk. I, Chap. II, 2.
3. *Ib.* 3.
4. *Ib.* 4.
5. *Ib.* 5.
6. *Ib.* 10.
7. *Ib.* II.
8. *Ib.* Chap. III, I.
9. *Ib.* Chap. VIII, 4.
10. *Ib.* 5.

The phenomenon of motion argues the existence of immaterial substances, for 'if matter be utterly devoid of motion in itself, it is plain it has its motion from some other substance'.[1] The order of the universe is an additional argument, for 'suppose matter could move itself, would mere matter, with self-motion, amount to that admirable and wise contrivance of things which we see in the world'.[2] Having demonstrated that there is no contradiction in the notion of spirit, but that 'there are incorporeal substances really existent in the world', he attempts to show, drawing support from considerations of personality and physiology, that 'there is such an immaterial substance in man'.[3] He examines Hobbes's view that 'all our actions are necessitated', and endeavours to consider the problem 'that has exercised the wits of all ages',[4] the reconciling of free-will with decrees and foreknowledge, in so far as it is concerned with his general purpose. While liberty of will exists, it is frequently circumscribed, in that many people's reactions in given circumstances are predictable.[5] Freedom of action 'is properly there, where we find ourselves near to an aequiponderancy',[6] and the influences in either direction may be such that, in fact, there is no 'liberty of going indifferently either way'.[7] His conclusion is: 'That this knowledge is most perfect and exquisite, accurately representing the natures, powers and properties of the thing it does foreknow. Whence it must follow, that if there be any creature free and undeterminate, and that in such circumstances and at such a time he may either act thus or not act thus, this perfect knowledge must discern from all eternity, that the said creature in such circumstances may either act thus, or so, or not. And further to declare the perfection of this fore-knowledge and omniscience of God; as His omnipotence ought to extend so far, as to be able to do whatsoever implies no contradiction to be done; so his praescience and omniscience ought to extend so far, as to know precisely and fully whatever implies no contradiction to be known. To conclude therefore briefly; free or contingent effects do either imply a contradiction to be foreknown, or they do not imply it. If they imply a contradiction to be foreknown, they are no object of the omniscience of God; and therefore there can be no pretence

1. *Ib.* Chap. XI, 3.
2. *Ib.* Chap. XII, 1.
3. *Ib.* Bk. II, Chap. I, 1.
4. *Ib.* Chap. III, 15
5. *Ib.* Bk. II, Chap. III, 16.
6. *Ib.* 17.
7. *Ib.* 18.

that his foreknowledge does determinate them, nor can they be argued to be determined thereby. If they imply no contradiction to be foreknown, that is to acknowledge that Divine praescience and they may very well consist together. And so either way, notwithstanding the Divine omniscience, the actions of men may be free.

The sum therefore of all this, that men's actions are sometimes free and sometimes not free; but in that they are at any time free, is a demonstration that there is a faculty in us that is incompetible to mere matter.'[1]

In the preface to the *Explanation*, More describes the subject-matter of his various books, and shows how the theme of the present work fits into the general design. The attempt to group the work as a whole is unusual in a writer of the period, and is dictated by the conviction of the underlying unity of things, and by the necessity of showing experience to have meaning. Unusual also are the auto-biographical references to incidents such as the illness which impelled him to write first the *Immortality* and then the *Explanation*, and to the details of his own inner development and experiences. In fact, the stress on experience is as striking as the emphasis on reason, and it conveys an impression of completeness and reality such as emerges only when a balance is kept. More's interest in the mystical aspect of things is balanced by the certainty that 'the light within must be reason', and also by the fact that it begins with an apprehension of nature, with 'the contemplation of this outward world, whose several powers and properties touching variously upon my tender senses, made me such enravishing music, and snatched away my soul into so great admiration, love, and desire of a nearer acquaintance with that Principle from which all these things did flow'.[2]

This mysticism through nature, as opposed to nature-mysticism, is to be found also in the poetry of Thomas Traherne, between whom and More there are parallels of temperament and outlook. Traherne shows the same wonder and delight in the visible world that is to be seen in More's poems. As with More, there is no diffused pantheism but rather apprehension of reality through nature and understanding of the Creator through the creation. His editor describes him as being 'penetrated with a sense of the glory of the universe, and of the infinite greatness of its

1. *Immortality*, Bk. II, Chap. III, 20, 21.   2. *Ib*. Preface, 2.

Creator'.[1] Traherne writes: 'In the meantime I was sometimes, though seldom, visited and inspired with new and more vigorous desires after that Bliss which nature whispered and suggested to me',[2] revealing the same outlook and approach as does More in the passage already quoted. They share the same vitality, the same looking for simplicity and the same idea of the unity of things. It is not surprising to find that the book which most influenced Traherne 'was that ancient mystical and philosophical work which is attributed to Hermes Trismegistus',[3] which More also had read.

There is a further parallel in that, for More, the possibility of quietism, of withdrawal, is excluded by the centrality in his thought of what he calls the divine life, and by the conviction that no state of feeling is significant unless it bears on this. Inward and outward are related through charity, faithfulness, obedience, 'abundance of kindness', justice, 'mutual forbearance'.[4] Traherne too is firmly based on practical theology, and in his *Christian Ethicks* which, as his editor pointed out, is full of 'the spirit of poetry',[5] he writes of such subjects as magnanimity, courage, love, knowledge, with shrewdness and understanding of men's situation. He expresses himself with a delicate and beautiful imagery which does not distract but illuminates the subject with insights of reality.

In this connection, the outstanding characteristic of More's writing must be judged to be balance, for he rightly discerns that such experience cannot be severed from the historical content of the New Testament which validates it: some 'have become . . . misbelievers of the whole history of Christ, and . . . look upon the mystery of Christianity as a thing wholly within us, and that has no other object than what is either acting or acted in ourselves'.[6] Equally mistaken is the concern with the objective and historical aspect which minimises 'all obligation to the divine life, that mystical Christ within us', and the clear testimony of reason and Scripture demonstrates not only the truth but the necessity of both.[7]

1. *The Poetical Works of Thomas Traherne*, ed. Gladys I. Wade; Introduction, B. Dobell, p. lxxxiii.
2. *Ib*. p. xxxiv.
3. *Ib*. p. lxxvi.
4. *Immortality*, Preface, 19.
5. *The Poetical Works of Thomas Traherne*, p. lxvi.
6. *Immortality*, Preface, p.9.
7. *Ib*.

Traherne, of whom it was said that he found in the Church his ideal Church,[1] was born about 1636 and went to Brasenose College, Oxford, where he graduated in 1656. He was rector of Credenhill in Hereford, his native county, for more than nine years when he became chaplain to the Lord Keeper of the Seals, Sir Orlando Bridgman, who died in 1674, a few months before Traherne.

The similarity of temperament and outlook in More and Traherne, the basic agreement in their approach, and their recourse, in one connection, to the same sources, is noteworthy not because of any apparent influence of the one on the other, for there is no indication of this. What is significant is that the atmosphere in which their thought expresses itself is totally different to that of the systematic theology of their time. They are contributing to the emergence of a theological method which seeks its terms of reference in a mystical experience mediated partially in and through the contemplation of nature but which they do not hesitate to validate by the historical element in religion, and in a moral and ascetic theology the primary concern of which is with the practicality of life. To these two terms of reference they added a third which included both, a concept of reason as the distinctive human quality, something more than ratiocination which involved almost the whole personality, and which reached out also to an awareness of the implications for theology of the new knowledge about the created world. Behind it all lay a conviction of the unity of truth and of the wholeness of experience.

Inevitably, in view of his general position, More found himself in disagreement with 'the opinions of solifidianism and eternal decrees', and he notes that they are not acceptable to all, 'and that for my own part I am one of that number'.[2] Some 'have made their own inventions and argumentative conclusions articles of faith',[3] and More considers that 'imputative righteousness . . . is nothing . . . but a mere phrase, if you prescind it from what is comprised in remission of sins'.[4] In his view, there is misunderstanding of various passages which might seem to imply that 'an empty belief' is sufficient.[5] If this interpretation is seen not to be consonant with reason and with the general sense of the New Testa-

1. *The Poetical Works of Thomas Traherne*, p. xxxix.
2. *Immortality*, Preface, 27.
3. *Ib.*
4. *Ib.* 28.
5. *Ib.* Bk. VIII, Chap. V, 3.

ment, it should be relinquished, and it is in this direction that an examination of 'the terms faith, righteousness, justification, imputation, and the like' points.[1] His conclusion is that the righteousness of faith is no figment, but obedience, the observance of man's two-fold duty.[2]

He regrets as arbitrary and unjust the condemnation of those who have never had the opportunity of hearing about Christianity,[3] and he condemns the point of view which treats all who do not subscribe to these opinions as 'poor moralists, mere natural men'.[4] Election and reprobation which exclude free-will, he characterises as 'the worst news and most mischievous that ever was communicated to the world', for it destroys the 'divine life' and 'slakes all endeavour'.[5] His own view is 'a middle way betwixt Calvinism and Arminianism', and is simply that the majority of men are probationers: 'I profess therefore, and do verily think, that there is such a thing as discriminative grace, as they call it, in the world, and that to such a difference for good, that some few of mankind by virtue thereof will be irresistibly saved, but that the rest of the world are probationers, that is, have free-will and are in a capacity of being saved, some greater, some less'.[6]

For More, the life of the created order is a unity within which there is a progressive gradation, beginning with that which men and animals have in common, 'which at large consists in the exercise of the sense', and the instincts directed towards the good of the individual and the conservation of the species.[7] The basic element in them is self-regard, 'a right and requisite property of life',[8] and from this stem the natural emotions and the satisfying of bodily requirements such as hunger.[9]

There is then what he calls a middle life, which is 'such as that with which it is conjoined'[10] and 'which if we might name by the general principle or common root thereof, we may call it reason'.[11] Its branches are many and include such things as 'the skill of natural philosophy, or arithmetic and geometry, the power of speech . . . a capacity of civil education',[12] and in these activities

1. *Ib.* 6.
2. *Ib.* Chap. VI, 4; Bk. VIII, Chap. XIV, 2.
3. *Ib.* Bk. X, Chap. I, 1.
4. *Ib.* Chap. IV, 4.
5. *Ib.* Bk. X, Chap. IV, 3.
6. *Ib.* Chap. V, 2.

7. *Ib.* Bk. II, Chap. IX, 1.
8. *Ib.* 2.
9. *Ib.* 3.
10. *Ib.* Bk. II, Chap. XI, 3.
11. *Ib.* 1.
12. *Ib.* 2.

the operations of reason are 'tinctured'[1] with the quality of the thing upon which it is engaged.

Just as the root of animal life is self-regard and of the middle life is reason, that of the 'divine life' is obediential faith,[2] the branches of which are 'charity, humility and purity',[3] and which include justice, temperance, fortitude and prudence.[4] For More, the fashioning of this life in man and the transforming of human capacities are central.[5] It is in the combination of practicality and inwardness that his depth is discernible, for in his writings there is nothing of superficial mysticism but an awareness based on experience, and a quality, fundamental, centred and fixed.

Because of the extent of his interests and influence, and the contribution which he made to the evolving of a new method, a contemporary such as Baxter regarded him as the most important of those whose views had been affected by the study of Plato and Descartes,[6] while a modern writer like Cassirer looks on More's slightly younger contemporary Cudworth as the real theoretical founder of the school.[7]

1. *Ib.* 4.
2. *Ib.* Chap. XII, I.
3. *Ib.* 2.
4. *Ib.* 9.
5. *Ib.* 4, 10.
6. *Autobiography of Richard Baxter*, ed. Lloyd Thomas (Everyman), p. 177.
7. Ernst Cassirer, *The Platonic Renaissance in England*, p. 42.

CHAPTER IV

THE CAMBRIDGE PLATONISTS (*continued*)

CUDWORTH, who was somewhat younger than More and Whichcote, was a graduate of Emmanuel College. He became Master of Clare Hall in 1645 and Regius Professor of Hebrew in the same year, and in 1654 he was appointed Master of Christ's College.

More's diverse works undoubtedly influenced the thought of his times in various ways, yet Cudworth's lengthy but incomplete book, *The True Intellectual System of the Universe*, by its very exhaustiveness and by its investigation of ancient sources has more of the nature of an attempt to establish a theoretical basis. Large as it is, it represents only part of the original plan, 'we being surprised in the length thereof', but as it stands, it is 'no piece, but a whole'.[1] It is digressive and tends to repetition and it is more specifically philosophical than are the writings of the other members of the group. There is the same attitude to reason and experience, the same appreciative awareness of the visible world, and the vitalism which rejects 'a kind of dead and wooden world, that hath nothing either vital or magical at all in it'.[2]

Like More, he had been brought up a Calvinist. He became a member of the Royal Society, and his interest in bringing together the new science and the older philosophical tradition is clear. He wrote that 'Galen professed he could never enough admire the artifice which was in the leg of a fly, and yet he would have admired the wisdom of nature more, had he been acquainted with the use of microscopes',[3] for he was in substantial agreement with the new philosophy, influencing Ray and probably Grew. Nevertheless, there are signs in his work of the transition from one period to another, from one way of thinking to another. His subject-matter, being an examination of ancient philosophy, tends to impart an anachronistic air to his writing which is altogether absent in the works of Smith or Whichcote. But this is to some degree inevitable since he is endeavouring to show that the philosophers of antiquity largely support his central and contemporary theme of the

1. *The True Intellectual System of the Universe* (1678), Preface.
2. *Ib*. Chap. III, xxxvii, 3.
3. *Ib*. Chap. III, xxxvii.

liberty of actions. The impression is further modified by the way in which he relates this to the work of Descartes. Nevertheless, although Raven holds him to be 'wholly free from More's belief in witchcraft and spiritualism',[1] Cudworth did in fact write of psychic phenomena, that 'though there be much of fabulosity in these relations, yet can it not reasonably be concluded, that there is nothing at all of truth in them'.[2]

In its present form, the book was finished in 1671, but it did not make its appearance until 1678. His other work, the *Treatise concerning Eternal and Immutable Morality*, of which the editor wrote that 'a book of sound sense and true learning is, at all times, in fashion',[3] was prepared in part for the press by Cudworth, but was published posthumously in 1731.

Cudworth attempts to establish freedom against the position of materialist philosophy by examining three statements which 'taken all together, make up the wholeness and entireness of that which is here called by us, the true intellectual system of the universe'. These three statements are 'that all things in the world do not float without a Head and Governor'; 'that this God being essentially good and just', just and unjust are immutably so in their own nature, and not so simply by arbitrary will, and that men are so constituted that they are masters of their own actions, and 'accountable to justice for them'.

His original intention had been 'a discourse concerning liberty and necessity, or to speak out more plainly, against the fatal necessity of all actions and events', but consideration showed that he had underestimated the extent of the survey required. There appeared to be three kinds of fatalism or, as we should say, determinism, namely, 'the Democritan fate', which makes material being to be the source of everything, and a theism which holds that things are not just and unjust in their own right, but are so 'by arbitrary will', and a theism which, while accepting the immutable nature of things, saw 'no liberty from necessity anywhere, and therefore no distributive or retributive justice in the world'. He therefore designed a book which would handle the matter in its entirety, but only the first part was written, which, however, he maintains is a unity in itself.

1. C. E. Raven, *Natural Religion and Christian Theology*, I, p. 112, n.3
2. *The True Intellectual System of the Universe*, Chap. IV, p. 700.
3. Preface.

Cudworth thinks in terms of 'the recovery of that nature and life of his which we have been alienated from',[1] and the preference of Cudworth and Smith for Origen amongst the patristic writers is significant in connection with this idea of a participation by which human nature is restored, for it is a preference shared by Colet and Erasmus. Compared with the Augustinianism re-emphasised in the Reformation period, it was an atmosphere obviously more congenial to those who looked back to Plato and who saw natural capacities in another light.[2] Cudworth, like Smith, considered that faith 'is not a mere believing of historical things, and upon inartificial arguments, or testimonies only; but a certain higher and diviner power in the soul', which is but another aspect of the view of human nature held by the Cambridge Platonists. This is further confirmed by his agreement that when to faith is added knowledge it is made 'more firm and steadfast'.[3]

The importance for theological method of his chief purpose of defending freedom against all forms of fatalism is that it faces the arguments both of the materialists and of the upholders of the doctrines of the decrees. Writing to Limborch in 1668, he had indicated that this view, being dependent on the idea of 'arbitrariousness', could not be maintained once it was recognised that good and bad were so by a changeless nature, and that as a result man had a real freedom. They are qualities that cannot be evacuated of meaning in themselves and made to depend on absolute will, so that 'we are so far forth principles or masters of our own actions as to be accountable to justice for them'.[4] There is little to choose between the Democritan fate or materialistic determinism, which reduces all to a basis of mechanism, and a theological fatalism, a 'divine fate immoral' as he calls it, that is to say, the determinism of predestination, for both endeavour to empty immutable qualities of value in themselves. Cassirer has noted the shift of emphasis away from Augustinianism towards the teaching of Aquinas that grace does not abolish natural powers but perfects them, and he writes: 'between the beginning and the end, there is now a middle ground within which natural powers are recognised as enjoying rights of their own and a relative independence'.[5] It is at this point that the underlying ideas of the Cambridge Platonists may be

1. Preface.
2. Cp. Cassirer, loc. cit. pp. 90–93, 105–6.
3. Preface.
4. Preface.
5. Cassirer, loc. cit. p. 90.

discerned, for they look back beyond the restoration of Augustinianism to the Renaissance and the revival of Platonism.

It has been pointed out by Louis Bouyer that two currents of
philosophy of opposite trends originated with the Renaissance.
On the one hand was the naturalism which issued in the encyclo-
paedist philosophy of the eighteenth century, and on the other hand
was the idealism which stemmed from the platonic academy of
Marsiglio Ficino. Of the latter he writes: 'It reached England first
with Grocyn and Linacre, and later inspired Pole, St. Thomas
More, the metaphysical poets of the seventeenth century, and the
Cambridge Platonists. Through Henry More's occultism it continued in the immaterialism of Berkeley . . . and Cartesianism derives from it'.[1] This is something peculiar to the Cambridge
Platonists, or rather which made its impact on theological method
in the seventeenth century through their contact with a source not
used by Hooker. They had undoubtedly been influenced by
Hooker, sharing with him and with Hales and Chillingworth, the
same ideas and a similar approach. But Hooker's rationalism was
something more clear-cut, deriving as it did from the system of the
Summa Theologica, a system less compact than that of Calvinism
and quite different in essence since it sought to achieve a synthesis of faith and reason, but nevertheless more sharply defined
in its terms than was the Cambridge Platonists' view of reason.
Hooker, moreover, was reacting from an ecclesiastical polity as
much as from the theology which accompanied it, while the Cambridge Platonists, like Hales, were in reaction from a system in
which everything was defined in relation to the idea, 'soli Deo
gloria'. It is here that the difference is to be seen, for it is at this
point that there appears what may be called, for want of a better
word, an element of humanism the effect of which on their outlook
was a pervasive one. In this particular connection, it may be seen
in that view of natural powers indicated by Cassirer, and which
Whichcote's editor regarded as the main scope of his endeavour
and a characteristic of the Anglican theological approach.[2]

Cudworth maintained that those who hold the necessity of all
human actions and events do so either because they regard necessity as 'inwardly essential to all agents' and contingent liberty to be
an impossibility, or else because, while granting the existence of

1. Louis Bouyer, *Erasmus and the*   2. Preface (1698 ed.).
   Humanist Experiment, pp. 26–7.

the latter, 'yet they conceive all things to be so determined by the will and decrees of this Deity, as that they are thereby made necessary to us'.[1] He describes the materialist position as founded on 'the atomical physiology' which 'supposes that body is nothing else but . . . extended bulk; and resolves therefore that nothing is to be attributed to it, but what is included in the nature and idea of it, viz. more or less magnitude with divisibility into parts, figure and position, together with motion or rest, but so as that no part of body can ever move itself; but is always moved by something else'. Nothing further was needed in this view to explain corporeal phenomena 'besides the results, or aggregates of those simple elements, and the disposition of the invisible parts of bodies in respect of figure, site and motion'.[2] Cudworth holds that while Democritus and Leucippus were the first to make this physiology into a philosophy by deriving all things from atoms, yet the atomists before them 'were asserters of a Deity and substance incorporeal'.[3]

Having endeavoured to show this, he goes on to maintain that by its very constitution this philosophy requires that its upholders should also admit of incorporeal substance since if, as they assert, body is 'included in the idea of a thing impenetrably extended, or can clearly be conceived to be a mode of it, as more or less magnitude with divisibility, figure, site, motion and rest, together with the results of their several combinations', then life and cogitation are excluded as qualities of body and must therefore be attributes of some other substance. The problem was whether the origin of motion was to be looked for in matter or in an incorporeal source: 'Since no body could ever move itself; it follows undeniably, that there must be something else in the world besides body, or else there could never have been any motion in it'.[4]

Cudworth maintains that according to this philosophy, physical phenomena cannot be explained 'by mechanism alone without fancy. Now fancy is no mode of body, and therefore must needs be a mode of some other kind of being in ourselves, that is cogitative and incorporeal'.[5] He adds further that, 'sense itself is not a mere corporeal passion from bodies without, in that it supposeth that there is nothing really in bodies like to those phantastical

1. *True Intellectual System*, Chap. I (I).   4. *Ib*. Chap. I (XXXVIII).
2. *Ib*. Chap. I, (V).   5. *Ib*.
3. *Ib*. Chap. I, (XVII, XVIII).

ideas that we have of sensible things, as of hot and cold . . . and the like, which therefore must needs owe their being to some activity of the soul itself, and this is all one to make it incorporeal'.[1]

There is in his work a determination to assert the originality of mind, and the freedom of spirit from the fatalism of matter. Knowledge is active and creative: 'Lastly, from this philosophy, it is also manifest, that sense is not the criterion of truth concerning bodies themselves, it confidently pronouncing that those supposed qualities of bodies, represented such by sense, are merely phantastical things; from whence it plainly follows, that there is something in us superior to sense, which judges of it, detects its phantastry, and condemns its imposture and determines what really is and is not, in bodies without us, which must needs be a higher, self-active vigour of the mind, that will plainly speak it to be incorporeal'.[2] For the Cambridge Platonists it is then of the first importance that intellect should be seen to precede sense-perception and the knowledge of objects perceived by it, just as spiritual must be seen as preceding corporeal.[3] Cudworth writes that 'life and sense could never possibly spring out of dead and senseless matter . . . much less could understanding and reason in men ever have emerged out of stupid matter, devoid of all manner of life'. His criticism extends equally to the qualified view held by some in his own day who were by no means materialist in outlook, 'that sense may rise from a certain modification, mixture, or organisation, of dead and senseless matter; as also that understanding and reason may result from sense: the plain consequence of both which is, that senseless matter may prove the original of all things'.[4]

His pupil Smith deals with the same question, showing that motion cannot arise from matter, and that neither reason nor the power of sensation can be derived from it. He endeavours to demonstrate that human knowledge cannot have its origin in sense, and that there exists a faculty which controls sense and both collects and unites the perceptions of the several senses. 'But yet', he writes, 'if our senses were the only judges of things, this reflex knowledge whereby we know what it is to know, would be as impossible as Lucretius makes it for sense to have innate ideas of its

1. *Ib.*
2. *Ib.* Chap. I (XXXVIII).
3. Cp. Cassirer, loc. cit. pp. 137–8.

4. *True Intellectual System*, Chap. V, p. 728.

own, antecedent to those stamps which the radiations of external objects imprint upon it. For this knowledge must be antecedent to all that judgment which we pass upon any sensatum, seeing except we first know what it is to know, we could not judge or determine aright upon the approach of any of these idola to our senses'.[1]

Cudworth concludes his survey of the atomical physiology of the ancients by pointing out its advantages, which are, 'that it renders the corporeal world intelligible to us',[2] and, by defining the notion of the body, it makes it easier to demonstrate the nature of incorporeal substances.[3] He holds that the ancients would have rejected the idea that 'life and sense and reason and understanding were really nothing else but local motion and consequently that themselves were but machines and automata', and 'that animals also consisted of mere mechanism'.[4]

It is this line of thought stemming from neo-Platonist sources such as Plotinus that is the particular distinguishing mark of the Cambridge Platonists. It is the chief element in the philosophy which they offered as an alternative to empiricism and to materialism, and it helped to form the theology of enlightened or illuminated reason which they substituted for the theology of system which found its expression in the decrees.

Yet there is paradox here, for if this trend in their thinking meant that they were ahead of their time with regard to the relationship of faith and reason, it seemed to militate against their entering into a full understanding of that science in which they were individually interested, and to the progress of which they made a considerable if largely indirect contribution. Cassirer's view is that, by returning to a form of the philosophy of nature outmoded by mathematical physics, and by turning away from Descartes's philosophy of nature, they broke 'with the strongest and most fruitful scientific force of the seventeenth century, exact mathematics'.[5] He considers also that while they lacked both the method and the mathematics of science, they lacked also 'the plain concept of the scientific "fact" itself',[6] with the result that 'they were constantly gathering scientific knowledge, but they did not

1. John Smith, *Select Discourses*, IV, Chap. III, p. 72.
2. *True Intellectual System*, Chap. I (XXXIX).
3. *Ib.* XL.
4. *Ib.* XLI.
5. loc. cit. p. 133.
6. *Ib.* p. 130.

differentiate within it. They had no norm for the critical examination and evaluation of individual observations'.[1] Cassirer regards
the Cambridge Platonists as rational in their general outlook, but
mystical in their attitude to nature.[2]

There is certainly, as he suggests, an element of mysticism in
their approach to the visible creation, but it takes the more positive form of a wonder at its diversity and complexity, and this is
not exclusive of curiosity and observation. What differentiates
their attitude to nature from that of Descartes or Hobbes is the
conviction that, informing the physical universe is an underived
life, underived, that is to say, from any aggregation of physical
elements. Like Cudworth, More wrote of the 'vitality' which
moves the 'inert materiality of great and little worlds'.[3] It is found in
all the forms and at all the levels of natural being, so that the universe appears as a series of organisms rather than as a machine. It
was because the Cambridge Platonists saw nature in terms of a
philosophy of organism that they elaborated the idea of a plastic
nature which is to be found also in the works of Ray. It did not,
however, find much favour with Boyle who was reluctant to stress
'such indeterminate agents, as the soul of the world, the universal
spirit, the plastic power, and the like'. It was not so much that the
idea was unacceptable, as that it gave no information in respect of
the scientific fact: 'Though they may in certain cases tell us some
things, yet they tell us nothing that will satisfy the curiosity of an
inquisitive person, who seeks not so much to know, what is the
general agent, that produces a phenomenon, as, by what means,
and after what manner, the phenomenon is produced'.[4] Possibly
the idea of a plastic nature would be more congenial to a naturalist
whose work moved outward to the understanding of the general
setting by relating various particular instances of observation to
each other, than to a physicist whose work tended towards the
isolating of individual phenomena the better to understand their
immediate causes.

Cudworth's determination not to lose sight of teleology is
apparent in the preference expressed for Aristotle's philosophy of
nature instead of 'the Cartesian hypothesis itself, which yet plainly
supposeth incorporeal substance. For as much as this latter makes

1. *Ib.* p. 131.
2. *Ib.* p. 132.
3. *Philosophical Poems*, p. 108.

4. *The Excellency of Theology compared
   with Natural Philosophy* (1671),
   V, 16.

God to contribute nothing more to the fabric of the world, than the turning round of a vortex or whirlpool of matter; from the fortuitous motion of which, according to certain general laws of nature, must proceed all this frame of things that now is, the exact organisation, and successive generation of animals, without the guidance of any mind or wisdom. Whereas Aristotle's nature is no fortuitous principle, but such as doth nothing in vain, but all for ends, and in everything pursues the best; and therefore can be no other than a subordinate instrument of the divine wisdom, and the manuary opificer or executioner of it'.[1] While he holds that it is not possible to 'banish all final, that is all mental causality, from philosophy, or the consideration of nature',[2] he sees no opposition between mechanism and purpose, but 'that there is a mixture of life or plastic nature together with mechanism, which runs through the whole corporeal universe'.[3]

Whether the general line taken by the Cambridge Platonists affected the final value of their view of the natural world, or whether it simply affected for their own time their active participation in all aspects of the movement which was going on, the fact that they gave so much time and thought to the problems raised was of benefit to theological method. New facts and their implications were being faced, the idea of a line drawn between the mutually exclusive areas in which faith and reason could be active was no longer being accepted, the rarefied atmosphere of theological speculation was being exchanged for one in which reason could take account of experience, and if there were deficiencies, an attempt was being made to show that theology was relevant 'in an age so philosophical'. There were dangers, but they were the inevitable concomitant of new discoveries and new disciplines, and that the Cambridge Platonists were wise to concern themselves with the issues raised is shown by the turn of events during the following century when the gap which they had tried to bridge grew wider.

It must also be asked whether the view of nature which they held was more than merely a by-product of their Platonism, and was in fact something more coherent, if incomplete—'a philosophy of organism',[4] which is relevant at the present time.

When Cudworth wrote of the form and parts of every animal as

1. loc. cit. Chap. I (XLV).
2. Ib. Chap. V, p. 682.
3. Ib. Chap. III (XXVII), 3.
4. C. E. Raven, *Organic Design*, p. 8.

'being as it were a little world',[1] he was expressing a considered conviction about the nature of the created world which he shared with the other Cambridge Platonists, but which he formulated in more detail and passed on to Ray. Following Cudworth, Ray stresses the fact that all creatures are alive, with some degree of freedom, and are not automata or puppets, and he is more interested in the organic with its quality of response than in questions of structure. It is here that C. E. Raven, in a lecture, *Organic Design*, sees the point at which change came about in scientific opinion during the period between the publication of Ray's work in 1691 and Paley's *Natural Theology* in 1802. He maintains that many scientists are recognising purpose in evolution because they see that the complexity and sequence in natural processes makes 'the concept of randomness statistically absurd'.[2] This is emphasised by the consideration that 'simultaneous accomplishment of a number of separate developments involving the transformation of the whole organism at one and the same time still more definitely rules out the possibility of chance'.[3]

There have been many, he writes, who hold that the alleged contrast between teleology and mechanism was meaningless, since the structure and operation of every mechanism implies purpose, but who regarded the traditional analogy of the watchmaker and the watch as inadequate.[4] What concept of design can be substituted that does more justice to all the facts, such as irregularities and errors, which a mechanistic teleology seems to ignore by its assumption that the course of nature is a smooth-running and mechanically-regular sequence?[5]

Ray's studies in botany and zoology helped him to develop a general philosophy which was indebted to Cudworth's work, and Raven describes it as a view of the universe as a school, and of its history as an educational process, which is that of Origen and Clement of Alexandria. 'From this standpoint', he writes, 'Ray was able to criticise, and in many respects replace, the mechanistic doctrines of Descartes'[6] by a position in which stress was laid on plastic nature, and on a continuous process or operation within the universe. The complexity and imperfections of natural pro-

1. *True Intellectual System*, Chap. V,   4. *Ib.*
    p. 676.   5. *Ib.* p. 12.
2. *Organic Design*, p. 5.   6. *Ib.* p. 7.
3. *Ib.* p. 6.

cesses did not fit in with the traditional teleology, and acquaintance with the living organism in its natural environment did not support the mechanistic view, so that the situation could best be understood in terms of what Raven calls organic design. This lead, however, was not followed up, and the emphasis in biological studies shifted from interest in behaviour and in the living organism to concern with matters of structure, weight and measurement: 'collecting and nomenclature had taken the place of observation and research'.[1] The result was that when Paley came to write his book, he did so in terms more mechanistic and superficial than those of Ray. The chief concepts in science were mathematical and mechanistic, and Raven notes the disappearance of 'the curiosity . . . and wonder'[2] which are associated with Ray and Whichcote. In consequence, Paley relies on contemporary biologists who regard the organism from the point of view of its complex mechanism and its intricacy of function: 'He is seldom concerned with its habits or life-history or with the extent to which it displays freedom of choice or intelligent responses to its environment . . . the watchmaker and the watch are for him a sufficient parallel'.[3] For Cudworth and Ray this begged the whole question, because if it were a true analogy, the irregularities of natural processes 'were surely reflections either upon the power or upon the will of the divine artist and artificer. It was this element of imperfection with its consequences of struggle and effort, of victory or defeat, which led the two seventeenth-century thinkers to posit a "plastic nature", an imminent nisus or élan, which inspired and energized the creature in its attempt upon the adventure of life'.[4]

While the inability of the Cambridge Platonists to understand the scientific fact belonged to a mode of thinking which differed from their attitude of reason, they turned aside from the mechanistic explanation less because of this than because they desired to relate mechanism to purpose within a setting of life and freedom, so that Cudworth could describe his work as a discourse concerning liberty and necessity. Raven concludes that 'it must be admitted that neither Cudworth nor Ray reaches a fully satisfying exposition; so long as the belief in creation as an act or series of acts, rather than a continuous process still in the making, prevailed, the deeper significance and necessity of these seeming de-

1. *Ib.* p. 9.   3. *Ib.* p. 12.
2. *Ib.* p. 10.   4. *Ib.* p. 13.

fects could not be acknowledged. But, holding as they did an organic not a Cartesian doctrine, they held also a clue to the right appreciation of these elements in the design'.[1]

It is of considerable interest to compare the line of approach in de Chardin's *The Phenomenon of Man*, which has been characterised as a very remarkable work in which the author 'has effected a three-fold synthesis—of the material and physical world with the world of mind and spirit; of the past with the future; and of variety with unity, the many with the one'.[2] It is not simply that de Chardin, as scientist and theologian, is drawn by the nature of his studies to interests similar to those of the Cambridge Platonists, but there are between them some significant parallels, the existence of which is not affected by the great disparity in the state of scientific knowledge during their respective periods. Despite an immeasurably different scientific stand-point, the cumulative result of the work of the centuries between, their general purpose seems to have much in common, for like the earlier writers, de Chardin's work maintains the unity of thought and experience: 'He has both clarified and unified our vision of reality. In the light of that new comprehension, it is no longer possible to maintain that science and religion must operate in thought-tight compartments or concern separate sectors of life; they are both relevant to the whole of human existence'.[3]

One may note individual similarities, as when de Chardin emphasises 'seeing' as 'the whole of life . . . if not in end, at least in essence', and when he writes that 'this work may be summed up as an attempt to see and to show what happens to man, and what conclusions are forced upon us, when he is placed fairly and squarely within the framework of phenomenon and appearance'.[4] There is here a more than merely verbal resemblance to Whichcote's phrase, 'men are wanting to themselves if they do not see with their own eyes'. Moreover de Chardin thinks in the same terms as Smith when he describes being reflective as the evolutionary lot proper to man, and he uses the same expression, 'to know that he knows'.[5] For de Chardin, in order 'to give man his natural position in the world of experience, it is necessary and sufficient to consider the within as well as the without of things',[6] and he comments on

1. *Ib.*
2. English translation (1959), Introduction by Sir Julian Huxley, p. 11.
3. *Ib.* p. 26.
4. *Ib.* p. 31.
5. *Ib.* p. 165.
6. *Ib.* p. 164.

the fact that 'for the Cartesian only thought existed; so the animal, devoid of any within, was a mere automaton'.[1] There is agreement as to the primacy accorded to the psychic and to thought in the material of the universe, which de Chardin regards as one of the two basic assumptions which 'govern every development of the theme'.[2] The importance of personality in the scheme of things, and the emphasis on knowledge and love as the conditions through which the world's future possibilities may be realised, which in Huxley's view represent the distillation[3] of de Chardin's book, are equally to the fore in the Cambridge Platonists.

In addition, the picture of the evolving creation outlined by him presents certain features which in a general way resemble the organic outlook noted by Raven as characteristic of the Cambridge Platonists, for it is one of growth, movement, becoming, life and autonomous development.[4] Writing of what he calls the general movement of life as it becomes regular but before it reaches the sphere of the person, de Chardin endeavours to isolate certain aspects of it: 'groping profusion; constructive ingenuity; indifference towards whatever is not future and totality;—these are the three headings under which life rises up by virtue of its elementary mechanisms. There is also a fourth heading which embraces them all—that of global unity. These we have come across already —first in primordial matter, then on early earth, then in the genesis of the first cells. Here it appears in a still more emphatic way. Though the proliferations of living matter are vast and manifold, they never lose their solidarity. A continuous adjustment coadapts them from without. A profound equilibrium gives them balance within. Taken in its totality, the living substance spread over the earth—from the very first stages of its evolution—traces the lineaments of one single and gigantic organism'. The emergence of new organisms is by groping: 'try-out follows try-out, without being finally adopted. Then at last perfection comes within sight, and from that moment the rhythm of change slows down'.[5]

These are but features from a book of great originality and depth, but they indicate sufficiently its scope and direction, and suggest that the analogy in respect of certain facets of the thinking of the Cambridge Platonists is a thought-provoking one with regard to the

1. *Ib.* p. 166.
2. *Ib.* p. 30.
3. *Ib.* p. 28.
4. *Ib.* p. 115.
5. *Ib.* p. 116.

presuppositions of theological method in the future. It may even appear that despite the acknowledged inadequacy of their concept of the scientific fact noted by Cassirer, the general terms in which they formulated their ideas of nature may ultimately be as productive in other times as their view of reason was in their own. It certainly seems difficult to avoid the conclusion that, in an age increasingly absorbed in the results of scientific discovery, a fresh vindication of natural theology must rank among the priorities. To one who has not the necessary scientific training to understand much of de Chardin's work it comes as a confirmation of something felt rather than worked out in detail, that C. E. Raven in his *Teilhard de Chardin, Scientist and Seer* (1962), published after these lectures were delivered, places de Chardin in the succession of the Cambridge Platonists.

The philosophy of nature and the general theological position of the Cambridge Platonists are not separate, but have a common link in reason, for to Cudworth, the plastic nature is 'reason immersed and plunged into matter'. This reason is not original but 'ectypal': 'it is a living stamp or signature of the Divine wisdom, which though it act exactly according to its archetype, yet it doth not at all comprehend nor understand the reason of what itself doth'.[1] It is something used, 'a manuary opificer',[2] and it cannot 'act electively or with discretion'.[3] The materialist position was that everything, including mind and understanding, are 'sprung up from senseless nature and chance, or from the unguided and undirected motion of matter'.[4] Just because he was writing about the different forms of fatalism, Cudworth was as concerned to show that things were not materially determined as he was to show that they did not happen by chance. The idea of a plastic nature seemed to allow for the elements both of purpose and autonomy, for unless there be such a thing, acting 'for the sake of something, and in order to ends, regularly, artificially and methodically', then either of two conclusions only can be drawn. Either everything happens by chance, or else, every phenomenon is the result of a specific intervention. Inanimate things are not governable 'by the mere force of a verbal law or outward command',[5] and therefore there must be some other agent which acts immediately to produce any effect.

1. *True Intellectual System*, Chap. III (XXXVII, II).
2. *Ib.*
3. *Ib.* 12.
4. *Ib.* Chap. II (XXII).
5. *Ib.* Chap. III (XXXVII), 2.

Not to accept a plastic nature, but to hold a direct divine agency in all things makes belief in the latter to be entertained with greater difficulty, and it would mean that all things are done 'either forcibly and violently, or else artificially only, and none of them by any inward principle of their own'. The idea of a plastic nature also explains 'those errors and bungles which are committed, when the matter is inept and contumacious'.[1] He describes it as 'art itself, acting immediately on the matter, as an inward principle'.[2] His characteristic vitalism appears in a definition of nature as art 'incorporated and embodied in matter, which doth not act upon it from without mechanically, but from within vitally and magically'.[3] Just as de Chardin, from the scientific stand-point, but using the same terms, insists as against the Cartesian explanation on the recognition of the within and the without as the key to understanding the natural order, so also Cudworth reacts against Descartes, emphasising life as the central factor. It is the basis of his criticism that 'they make a kind of dead and wooden world, as it were a carved statue, that hath nothing either vital or magical at all in it. Whereas to those who are considerative, it will plainly appear, that there is a mixture of life or plastic nature together with mechanism, which runs through the whole corporeal universe'.[4] Plastic nature is not regarded as something almost personalised, but is looked on as life expressing itself in a rich variety of forms and with some element of autonomy. Its instrumental and subsidiary character is apparent in the way it acts not by knowledge 'but fatally, magically and sympathetically'.[5] The recurring words 'vital' and 'magical' go together and refer not to magic in the accepted sense but to the spontaneity and vitality in the world, qualities which Cudworth regarded as ultimately underived from matter. The words seem to carry an undertone of the feeling of wonder which was transmitted to Ray.

In view of the purpose of his book which is to provide an answer to all forms of fatalism, Cudworth's use of the word 'fatal' to describe the action of plastic nature requires explanation. In this context, he employs it to indicate the unconscious conforming to patterns in the natural process. He instances bees, spiders and birds, whose instincts 'are nothing but a kind of fate upon them',[6] and he refers to plastic nature as 'the true and proper fate of mat-

1. *Ib.* 4.   3. *Ib.* 9.   5. *Ib.* 18.
2. *Ib.* 8.   4. *Ib.* 3.   6. *Ib.* 14.

ter'.[1] The impression that this resembles Hooker's idea of law as an implanted directive by means of which all things aspire to their own perfection, is confirmed by Cudworth's assertion that 'fate, and the laws or commands of the Deity, concerning the mundane economy (they being really the same thing),' cannot be understood as promulgations ('verbal things') nor as 'mere will', but 'as an energetical and effectual principle constituted by the Deity, for the bringing of things decreed to pass'.[2] In fact, the same view of nature as 'an instrument' and of natural agents keeping 'the law of their kind unwittingly' is found in Hooker's work.[3] He too agrees 'that each thing both in small and in great fulfilleth the task which destiny hath set down'; and concerning the manner of executing and fulfilling the same, 'what they do they know not, yet it is in show and appearance as though they did know what they do; and the truth is they do not discern the things which they look on'.[4] But as to defects and imperfections in nature, Hooker can only see in these a kind of penalty imposed because of human sin on the creatures made for mans' use.[5]

The rational life in man is for Cudworth a far higher degree in the scale of life than the plastic life of nature, but 'though the plastic life of nature be the lowest of all lives, nevertheless since it is a life, it must needs be incorporeal; all life being such'.[6] The inference then is that since body is 'nothing but mere outside . . . together with passive capability',[7] the life, the within, which moves and completes it, is not derived from matter. In itself the plastic life of nature is 'but the mere umbrage of intellectuality, a faint and shadowy imitation of mind and understanding . . . so that if there had been no perfect mind or intellect in the world, there could no more have been any plastic nature in it'.[8] It is but as the shadow is to the body or the echo to the voice.

It was inevitable, once they understood what it implied, that More and Cudworth should find themselves in disagreement with the system of Descartes, not 'as to the mechanic part of it',[9] as Cudworth took care to note, but chiefly in respect of the way in which it regarded non-reflective life as simply mechanism.

The importance of the position reached by the Cambridge

1. *Ib.* 18.
2. *Ib.*
3. *Ecclesiastical Polity*, I, III, 2, 4.
4. *Ib.* 4.
5. *Ib.* 3.
6. *True Intellectual System*, Chap. III (XXXVII, 19).
7. *Ib.* 20.
8. *Ib.* 26.
9. *Ib.* Chap. III (XXXVIII).

Platonists is not inconsiderable, for it meant that theology was no longer occupied for the most part with questions that were largely theoretical, but was ready to look at the created order as a whole, and to interpret experience in such a way that it could be seen to be meaningful. They linked theology not only with philosophy but also with the practical side of things, and performed for it a double service by ensuring that it was neither isolated from contemporary thinking nor from experience. The 'free, uncaptivated, universality of mind'[1] to which Cudworth refers, and to which they attached such importance, was more than the natural reaction from a system, it was the opposite of the kind of thinking which could only find its expression in a system.

The writer of the preface to Cudworth's second book suggests that it may be regarded as a partial sequel to the unfinished project begun in his first work.[2] The subject of the latter was the materialist idea of fate, and the second book is concerned with what Cudworth called theological fatalism, the idea that good and evil, just and unjust, are not so immutably in themselves, but are 'the arbitrary productions of will'.[3] The preface also makes it clear that the book would have been particularly useful if instead of being published posthumously, it had appeared when it was completed, at the time when Hobbes was putting forward his views on the contract between individuals as the basis of the state, a contract which was freely made, but once entered upon, became permanently binding so that the state is the source of authority and law. For the Cambridge Platonists, the basis of society was not pacts and covenants, as Cudworth pointed out,[4] but the underlying, immutable realities of natural law which precede all positive law and contract. He propounds an idealist philosophy instead of the naturalism of Hobbes, and so brings it into contact with another far-reaching development of the thought of his times, the investigation of the nature and basis of society. The attempt to understand this is parallel to, and involved with, their concern to understand physical being. That they saw the necessity of examining the implications of these questions for theology is the measure of their importance. To compare the subject-matter of their works with that of many of their contemporaries is to see that the

1. *Ib*. Chap. V, p. 670.
2. Preface to *A Treatise concerning Eternal and Immutable Mortality* (1731).
3. *Ib*.
4. *Ib*. Bk. I, Chap. I, p. 6.

Cambridge Platonists were beginning to move in a different atmosphere. There is a greater awareness of the gradual appearance of a profound change of attitude, and they seem to have perceived, however dimly, that the subjects now beginning to be examined in their own day would somehow create this new attitude in the future. They were convinced that a true view of life was one into which philosphical and scientific discoveries could be integrated, and they were convinced of the necessity of providing it. So by means of their theological method in which there was a synthesis of faith and reason, they were enabled to relate to this purpose such questions as the relation of life to matter, the unity of life and spirit, and the nature of thought and perception, in order to provide a unified conception of reality.

In not granting that things are just or unjust 'only by law and not by nature', that they are 'positive, arbitrary and factitious only',[1] Cudworth is in opposition to that preoccupation with power which was a feature of the thought of the period.[2] It is not possible, he writes, for a thing to be made anything simply by mere will, without a being or nature, for a thing is immutably determined by its own nature. The Divine will and power have unlimited command over all things to bring them into existence, but once they are created, 'they are what they are, this or that, absolutely or relatively, not by will or arbitrary command, but by the necessity of their own nature'. There is no such thing as a kind of arbitrary essence which may be made into anything at pleasure.[3]

He maintains that the distinction between things that are commanded because they are good and just, and things that are good and just because they are commanded, requires this qualification, that the obligation to do things that are positively commanded arises not from the will of the person who commands, but from the intellectual nature of the person commanded. The real difference is that some things are good and just in themselves, so that the intellectual nature has an inherent and permanent obligation to them. Other things the intellectual nature only obliges to by accident, when things in themselves indifferent come for some reason under an absolute heading, 'acquiring a new relation to the intellectual nature'.[4] This has direct bearing on the questions raised by Hobbes in connection with the basis of the state and society.

1. *Ib.* pp. 2, 3.   3. *Ib.* Chap. II, 2.
2. *Ib.* p. 10.   4. *Ib.* 4.

In this book, Cudworth emphasises again that sense by itself is not an adequate criterion 'of what does really and absolutely exist without us, but that there is a higher and superior intellectual faculty in us that judges of our senses, which discovers what is fallacious and fantastical in them, and pronounces what absolutely is and is not'.[1] Knowledge is free and creative, not passive reception, 'an inward and active energy of the mind itself, and the displaying of its own innate vigour from within, whereby it doth conquer, master and command its objects'.[2] The intellect contemplates the objects of the created world, and deduces something not in the objects themselves, namely, that the arrangements of the whole is evidence of purpose and wisdom. He likens the universe to an orchestra playing, pointing out that the harmony of all the parts implies a composer of 'the plot of the whole mundane music', a different idea to that of the watchmaker in Paley's book.[3] Cudworth pursues this thought of the universe with all its 'proportions . . . and correspondences of things to one another', as being something 'musically and harmonically composed', an idea similarly expressed by More, and he stresses the fact that it can only be appreciated by mind, which will be 'transported' by it and will find itself in tune with 'nature's intellectual music and harmony'.[4] 'The book of nature, the whole visible and material universe', writes Cudworth, using a term to which he and More gave currency, 'is legible only to an intellectual eye'.[5] His conclusion is that 'everything is necessarily and immutably to science and knowledge what it is, whether absolutely or relatively', since the intelligible natures of things are neither alterable by will nor changeable by opinon.[6]

When Whichcote was at work in Emmanuel College, Cambridge, Nathanael Culverwel, another of the Cambridge Platonists, was an undergraduate at the College. It is not certain that he was a pupil of Whichcote, as Smith was, but the reflection of Whichcote's ideas, to say nothing of his phrases, is everywhere in the works of both.

Little is known of Culverwel, save that he came from Northamptonshire, and entered Emmanuel College in 1633, became a Fellow, and died in 1650 or 1651.

1. *Ib*. Bk. II, Chap. VI, 3.
2. *Ib*. Bk. IV, Chap. I, 1.
3. *Ib*. 13.

4. *Ib*. 15.
5. *Ib*. 16.
6. *Ib*. Bk. IV, Chap. VI, 3.

His book, *An Elegant and learned Discourse of the Light of Nature*, appeared after his death in 1652, being prepared for publication by William Dillingham to whom his papers had been given. Ironically, in view of Tuckney's exchange of letters with Whichcote, it was dedicated to him as Master of Emmanuel and to the Fellows. The preface to the reader records that the material had been written six years previously, with the double purpose of vindicating the use of reason and of providing an answer to Socinus by giving to reason and faith a proper relationship. In this respect, the editor asks that the book be judged as a whole, when it will be seen that a due balance is kept. The preface, and a preface by Culverwel's brother, betray a good deal of sensitiveness on this point, as if the matter were a subject for criticism and debate. Dillingham notes that the book was the beginning of a projected undertaking which Culverwel's death prevented from being completed.[1] Smith was more fortunate in that he was able to achieve a fuller investigation of the different elements in religion, but he had in addition a psychological insight which was ahead of his time, and which Culverwel did not share. Because he was able to go further in the subject, Smith effected a better balance in his work by emphasising the unity of truth and goodness, which 'live in one another' and should 'never be disunited'. For him, it is all-important that knowledge should issue in life and practice, and this cannot happen if 'it is but a thin, airy knowledge that is got by mere speculation'.[2] Culverwel had in mind work along similar lines, as the *Discourse* is but an introduction which was never followed up, but despite a tendency to rhetorical writing at the beginning of the book, it has about it that clear and imaginative quality with a hint of modernity, which in varying degrees is encountered in all the Cambridge Platonists.

Culverwel sets out to show that the separation alleged between faith and reason cannot exist since 'they both spring from the same fountain of light'.[3] He has nothing in common with the attitude which treats reason as something complete and sufficient in itself, but he points out that because Socinus and his followers made extravagant claims for reason, this is no grounds for men to go to the opposite extreme and reject it. To do so would be to be 'banished from their own essences'.[4] Reason is something derived

1. *Ib*. Preface.   3. *Discourse*, Chap. I, p. 2.
2. *Select Discourses*, p. 4.   4. *Ib*.

and it is the means by which natural law is apprehended, and nothing revealed is contrary to it.[1] The first requirement is to define nature, and it is not easy to find a comprehensive definition.[2] Aristotle was influential in forming later ideas on the subject, but Culverwel considers that he only represents nature veiled,[3] and that by most writers the word is 'restrained to corporeal beings'.[4] Plato went further by describing nature as the channel of being which flowed from the divine fountain.[5] Culverwel enquires why body should be the only subject of natural philosophy, and why the term nature should exclude spirit.[6] He likens the world to an organ, tuned, 'yet not so as that it could play upon itself . . . and thus nature is that regular line, which the wisdom of God himself has drawn in being'.[7] For him, nature includes spirit as well as physical phenomena, as it does in the writings of Cudworth and More. In order to explain the law of nature, he outlines first the nature of law in general, and there is a resemblance to the way in which the subject is treated in the *Ecclesiastical Polity*. Only a rational creature, he writes, following Aquinas, is 'capable of a law',[8] and 'the law of nature is nothing but . . . the copying out of the eternal law, and the imprinting of it upon the breast of a rational being'.[9] It is 'that law which is intrinsecal and essential to a rational creature',[10] for there are stamped upon human nature 'some first and alphabetical notions; by putting together of which it can spell out the law of nature'.[11] Reason resembles 'an intellectual eye', exactly proportioned to the light of natural law, but it is still only the means by which law is apprehended. It does not publish the law, and is only its printer.[12] Culverwel refers also to the consent of nations in that, without pre-arrangement, they tacitly and spontaneously agree in the observance of natural laws.[13]

He then turns to the nature of reason, making clear that it is derived, since 'none can think that light is primitively and originally in the candle'.[14] Taken by itself, it is a diminutive light, so that 'you may see Socrates in the twilight',[15] but it is 'a certain

1. *Ib*. p. 9.
2. *Ib*. Chap. III, p. 14.
3. *Ib*. p. 15.
4. *Ib*. p. 16.
5. *Ib*. p. 18.
6. *Ib*. p. 15.
7. *Ib*. p. 18.
8. *Ib*. Chap. VI, p. 21.
9. *Ib*. Chap. V, p. 29.
10. *Ib*. Chap. VI, p. 34.
11. *Ib*. Chap. VII, p. 55.
12. *Ib*. Chap. IX, p. 69.
13. *Ib*. Chap. X, p. 77.
14. *Ib*. Chap. XI, p. 87.
15. *Ib*. Chap. XII, p. 128.

light'.[1] He regards the understanding and the will as being so closely linked as to 'make up one simple and entire print and signature of reason',[2] and he writes 'the will doth but echo to the understanding'.[3]

As to the place of antiquity and tradition, Culverwel thinks that there is 'more security in resting upon genuine reason', because, with the exception of the Scriptures in which certainty depends on content rather than on universal tradition, any 'historical conveyance' is open to uncertainty. Antiquity commands respect, but if it 'shall stand in competition' with reason, then the choice will fall on 'reason, a daughter of eternity, before antiquity which is the offspring of time',[4] 'the position of Hales, Falkland and Chillingworth. That Culverwel felt the pressure of contemporary Augustinianism is clear from the preface, and also from the fact that he is at pains to point out that his treatment of the subject of nature and grace will contain 'nothing but what an Augustin, or a Bradwardin, . . . would willingly set their seals unto'.[5] Despite this carefulness, he shares completely the view of the other Cambridge Platonists that reason and faith, far from being prejudicial to each other, are complementary and necessary to each other. 'Grace doth not come to pluck up nature as a weed, to root out the essences of men',[6] and whatever is revealed 'must needs be true; and this common principle is the bottom and foundation of all faith to build upon'.[7] He is at one also with them in their attitude to the philosophers, commenting after the manner of Whichcote, that the work of Plato and others was more effective than that of 'some that would fain be called Christians'.[8]

Inevitably, by reason of the circumstances, Culverwel's work is not of the same importance as are the writings of the better-known Cambridge Platonists. He was less fortunate than Smith, who although he too died at an early age only a year after Culverwel's death, was not incapacitated by illness as was the latter during the last few years of his life. In any event, it would hardly be claimed that he was of equal calibre with Smith who was in many ways the most original and attractive of them all, with a maturity out of all proportion to his age. Nevertheless, his work has clarity

1. *Ib*. Chap. XIV.
2. *Ib*. Chap. XI, p. 87.
3. *Ib*. Chap. XV, p. 155.
4. *Ib*. Chap. XV, pp. 160–1.
5. *Ib*. Chap. III, p. 14.
6. *Ib*. Chap. XVI, p. 168.
7. *Ib*. p. 170.
8. *Ib*. Chap. XVIII, p. 201.

and individuality, and although it is closer than the others to Hooker in his writing on law, it identifies itself completely with the general position of the Cambridge Platonists in respect of theological method. The suggestion, not infrequently made, that the work of the Cambridge Platonists is academic begins to recede into the background according as it is realised to what an extent they entered into the thinking of their times, and in some respects outdistanced it.

They followed on from Hooker's basic affirmation that the source of authority was law and that law was apprehended by reason. Hooker's liberal method confronted the Scriptural authoritarianism of his day, and, in effect, established the position that authority, if it were to command allegiance, must be able to stand the test of free and rational discernment. It is part of the abiding quality of *The Ecclesiastical Polity* that it recognises that reason and the appeal to Scripture and respect for the councils, traditions and practice of the early centuries, all taken in conjunction with the fact of the Church, cannot be isolated from each other. Taken together they fertilise and check one another, producing a balanced unity.

The advance of the Cambridge Platonists on this position was in respect of the richness of content which the word reason came to hold for them, and in the way in which they related it to the totality of experience. Their understanding of personality was something fresh and helped to impart a new dimension of depth to theological method. Their insistence on the freedom of reason, and of its essential congruity with faith stood over against the theology in which they had been reared. In their day, the necessary emphasis in the latter on the transcendent had slipped over into a too heavy emphasis on sovereignty as expressed in terms of the decrees. This seemed to the Cambridge Platonists to be contrary to freedom and reason. Like Andrewes and Hales, they wished to distinguish between what they regarded as speculative and what was plainly fundamental.

They moved with the thought of the times in their endeavour to keep the lines of communication open between theology and the new science, and although they were handicapped by an inadequate appreciation of the scientific fact, the broad lines of their philosophy of organism had certain superiorities over the mechanistic view.

Their opposition to materialism, and to the idea of a divided reality, was both valuable and timely. Nor did they allow theology to become out of touch with the questions which were now beginning to be raised concerning the nature of society.

Their constant recurring to the idea of life, to the unity of goodness and truth, to the practical obedience of life and simplicity, in the inwardness of Smith's writings, the mysticism of More, and the astringent quality of Whichcote's work, gave a feeling of reality to their writings.

Their attitude to the natural world, while fresh and enquiring, was not deficient in that sense of wonder which Raven felt to be missing at a later date. One of their loveliest characteristics which they helped to transmit to men like Ray and Boyle, was that they were entranced by the invisible reality enmeshed in the visible system of things. They are of those who, like Thomas Traherne, saw the world as 'the beautiful frontispiece of eternity' and valued it as 'a grand jewel of delight'.

Both theology and the new philosophy were influenced by their attitude to nature which was as religious as it was enquiring, and was at once a medium and an anchor of their highest aspirations.

It is hardly possible to understand the Latitudinarians and the scientists apart from them, and from their work something distinctive and permanent passed into theological method.

The connections between them and such men as Barrow, Ray, Rust and others are to be seen in John Worthington's letters to Hartlib, which reflect through the tastes and interests of the two correspondents, the advances being made in scholarship, theological studies, scientific matters, botany and many other matters. There is nothing of modern specialisation in this correspondence, for Worthington and Hartlib are interested in everything, and seem to have time for it.

The letters are a contemporary commentary illustrative of the change in theological method and emphasis, and are more eloquent by their silence concerning the once-burning questions than any dissertation on the subject. They were written in 1660-1, and Worthington, to whom we owe the edition of Smith's *Discourses*, is at one with the Cambridge Platonists in his general outlook. He also collected and edited the work of their forerunner Mede. A Cambridge Fellow himself, his 'publicness of spirit' and his desire to be 'useful to the world' are commented on by Tillotson, who observed how 'inquisitive' he was after the work of scholars so that it could be published and made available.[1] The letters contain many instances of his personal acquaintance with More, Whichcote, Cudworth and others, and of his interest in their work. They reveal also that he was in frequent touch with Ray, and there are other indications of his own interest in natural history and science. He tells Hartlib that Bochart's book is to be printed in England, and recommends to him a book by J. Childrey on *Natural Rarities of England, Scotland and Wales*.[2] He asks 'what doth the society at Gresham College?', and he observes that Dr Cowley's book of proposals for the founding of a philosophical college is dedicated to them.[3] In reply to a query from Hartlib, he had not heard of any 'new discourses of Mr Boyle's' but enquiry has since revealed that 'they are much desired, and enquired for, at Cambridge'.[4] Worthington writes from Ditton, and notes that he stirs 'but seldom to Cambridge',[5] but he contrives to keep up with developments. The extent of his information and the variety of his interests are remarkable, and they reflect clearly the method and the changed pre-occupations of theology at the time of the Restoration. That this had come about in such a comparatively short space of time was due as much to the influence of the Cambridge Platonists as it was to the normal processes of reaction and to the contemporary movements in science and in thought generally.

Worthington sends his correspondent a list of some of Spenser's poems, of which he prefers the *Faery Queen*,[6] and he comments on a work of Petraeus on Ruth and a homily of Chrysostom in Ethiopic,[7] and a new edition of Eusebius.[8] Glanvill's book on *The Vanity of Dogmatizing* has appeared, and his comment that the author was 'a great valuer of Descartes and Dr More'[9] is of interest because of the way in which the two names are linked, and because it indicates the direction in which writers like Glanvill were moving. A friend of Hartlib's is in search of a manuscript of Josephus, and Worthington remarks on Ussher's discovery of an 'old Latin Ignatius in manuscript' at Cambridge, by means of

1. Preface to *Miscellanies*, by John Worthington (1704).
2. *Ib*. I.
3. *Ib*. XI.
4. *Ib*. VIII.
5. *Ib*.
6. *Ib*. III.
7. *Ib*. II.
8. *Ib*. XV.
9. *Ib*. VII.

which 'he found out the false additionals of some Greek passages in his epistles',[1] and later he reports the existence of a manuscript of Josephus at Cambridge.[2] Hartlib having sent him the forms of service used by the Bohemian Unitas Fratrum, he finds them more agreeable to the Prayer Book services 'than the bare and thin forms'[3] in use in most reformed Churches of the Continent, and he enquires what steps are being taken 'to keep up the succession'[4] amongst them. Worthington would have seen the restoration of the episcopate at home at this time by the consecration of five bishops in October 1660, seven in December, and four in the following month when twelve bishops were also consecrated together in Ireland. Hyde, who had belonged to Falkland's liberal group, had become anxious about the succession during the years immediately preceding the Restoration, and the story of his efforts to have consecrations performed during the Commonwealth is told by R. S. Bosher.[5] In view of his background, the anxiety he shows and the importance he attaches to the matter in some of his letters, is of particular interest in showing how vital the question of the succession was for Anglicans of all types. Hyde wrote that there were many at home and abroad who knew the names and ages of the surviving bishops, and who 'value themselves very much upon computing in how few years the Church of England must expire.'[6]

Not many matters appear to escape Worthington: he has heard that Mr Pocock at Oxford is at work on the geography and history of Arabia:[7] he makes enquiries about Armenian and Lithuanian translations of the Bible, the latter being at the press in London.[8] He has read Dr Basire's book, and wishes that the author, whose travels and whose contacts with the Patriarchs of Constantinople, Antioch and Jerusalem, and with the Armenians, were so considerable, might be encouraged to 'give an account of the state of Christendom' and to 'publish his travels'.[9]

He is deeply interested in proverbs, as was Ray, who published a collection of them, and he sends a collection of fifty Turkish proverbs to Hartlib.[10] He wonders what has become of a large

1. *Ib.* V.
2. *Ib.* IX.
3. *Ib.* I.
4. *Ib.* VI.
5. *The Making of the Restoration Settlement*, R. S. Bosher, pp. 90–100.
6. *Ib.* p. 97.
7. *Miscellanies*, VII.
8. *Ib.* VIII.
9. *Ib.* IX.
10. *Ib.* XIII.

collection made by a Mr Alexander. If the author of it has grown weary of the project, why should all his labour be lost, and would it not be advisable for him to hand over his work to someone who could finish it? 'It is no trivial or inconsiderable thing, but of very much use, if done with care and judgment'.[1] Worthington draws his correspondent's attention to Howel's dictionary of four languages, which has 'an appendix of proverbs, especially of the old sayings of the Welsh'.[2] There are naturally personal touches in the letters, private messages, exchange of news concerning the health of the two correspondents, matters of topical moment, such as a storm, worse than any since that of 1636,[3] or the necessity of 'candour, charity and moderation' in those 'that are appointed to review the liturgy',[4] a reference to the Savoy conference.

But the chief interest of the letters for the present subject is, of course, the way in which Worthington's account reveals the contacts between the Cambridge Platonists and men like Dillingham, Culverwel's editor, Patrick (later to become one of the better-known Latitudinarians), Barrow, Taylor, Rust, Ray and Willughby. By showing them in actual contact, and their work as touching at different points, the letters form a striking postscript to the influence of the Cambridge Platonists on the outstanding writers among the scientists and Latitudinarians. They demonstrate by their content and tenour the changes which were coming about in theological method, underlining the part played in this by the Cambridge Platonists.

Worthington was in frequent touch with More, commenting in his first letter on one of his books, and in his second recounting a meeting with him. He tells Hartlib that More's books are best at a second reading, and adds 'it were to be wished indeed, that it were done into Latin for the information (amongst others) of those to whom Calvin's *Institutes* and some pieces of Luther are oracular'.[5] Hartlib then writes to More, who tells Worthington, and the latter in his next letter passes on the information that More is being asked to combine a number of his books, including the poems, in a single volume. One of his books was never presented to the King, which some of his friends think should be done, but Worthington does not see 'the author solicitous about it, as having

1. *Ib.*   3. *Ib.* XXIV.   5. *Ib.* II.
2. *Ib.*   4. *Ib.* I.

no design of ambition or advantage to himself',[1] a trait he shared with Smith, Whichcote and Cudworth.

The following letter informs Hartlib that More is in London on College business, and will probably visit him. Worthington has heard that the Queen of Bohemia has arrived, and he wonders if her daughter the princess Elizabeth is with her: 'If she be, I believe Dr More would rejoice at that good news: he having a great esteem for her from the high testimony of Descartes and others concerning her'.[2]

A later letter mentions More in connection with Barrow; 'Dr More is lately returned. I hope to have some discourse with him today, as also with Mr Barrow, who preached a sermon at the Commencement, which was practical, and much commended. He is Greek Professor, as I have perhaps heretofore told you'.[3] Barrow was a close friend of Ray and Wilkins which further emphasises the connection. Barrow's chief characteristic was practicality, and it is interesting that this was commented on by his contemporaries.

Further information is given, but it is to be regarded as private for the time being, concerning More's revision of his philosophical treatises which are being published together and with some fresh material on Descartes as well as the letters to him.[4]

Towards the end of the correspondence, Worthington is anxious that More's letters to Hartlib, some of which have apparently been lost, should be sent to him, and he notes that, despite delays, More's book is almost ready.[5]

The allusions to Whichcote are more personal, partly because of their relationship and because he had an illness during some of the time covered by the exchange of letters, and partly by reason of the fact that he did not publish anything during his lifetime. Worthington writes: ' I received a letter from Dr Whichcote, who is sorry that he cannot move abroad in your behalf, by reason of his illness. He has been under the hands of physicians and chirurgeons'.[6] The reference seems to be to the possibility of Hartlib obtaining a post in England.

Whichcote is next mentioned in conjunction with Patrick: 'I was glad of the last clause in your letter about Mr Patrick. Dr

1. *Ib.* VII.
2. *Ib.* VIII.
3. *Ib.* XII.
4. *Ib.* XIV.
5. *Ib.* XIX, XXIII.
6. *Ib.* III.

Whichcote writes he found him most ready upon intimation given. I formerly wrote to you about those useful books published by him'.[1] Worthington evidently had a high opinion of Patrick, for in a later letter he writes: 'I am glad that you have an interest in the acquaintance of Mr Patrick, whom I mentioned to you. You told me you would write to him for the favour of his books; which I suppose you have received, and found to be worthy of perusal'.[2]

Whichcote's name occurs on five other occasions in connection with visits he makes to London and Cambridge, and in three of them there are references to his health. In one of these passages, he and Barrow are both mentioned: 'Dr Whichcote goes this week to London. He hath had a quartan-ague, and is not likely to be free from it till the spring. He hath taken an house upon Bednall-Green... Mr Barrow hath begun this term his Greek lectures . . . I wish he would publish his great and long travels (as you wish Mr Ray would his shorter ones)'.[3] Barrow had signed the Engagement to be loyal to the Commonwealth in 1649, but immediately after had removed his name, and henceforth made no effort to conceal his political sympathies. In 1655 the College granted him permission to travel with an allowance for three years, and he went as far as Constantinople, writing from time to time to give an account of his journeys.

In the next letter, Worthington has heard from Whichcote that the 'ague . . . continues to afflict him sorely',[4] and in the second last letter, he writes that 'Dr Whichcote made a step down into this country (his presence being necessary) and he returns by coach this week. His ague seems to have shaken him much'.[5]

Cudworth's name occurs only once in the correspondence, when in reply to a query from Hartlib about a book, Worthington writes: 'I never saw that tract of Leo Modena's of the temple, in French, but in Dr Cudworth's study, and he told me it was Dr Wall's'.[6] There is a solitary reference to Dillingham,[7] and the news of Rust's appointment is given: 'Mr Rust . . . is going over in to Ireland, to be Dean of Down, being invited thither by Dr Taylor the bishop; and Mr. Marsh (sometime my pupil, and Fellow of Caius College) is there already, and made Dean of Armagh. They are both excellent persons, and preferred to these places by

1. *Ib.* XI.   4. *Ib.* XIX.   7. *Ib.* XVI.
2. *Ib.* XVIII.   5. *Ib.* XXIII.
3. *Ib.* XVIII.   6. *Ib.* XV.

the care of the above mentioned bishop'.[1] A further note records that 'Mr Rust is lately gone out of London for Ireland. He goes in the ship with the Lord Conway. By the news-book I perceive Dr John Finch (the Lady Conway's brother) is knighted by the king. He was Dr More's pupil, and one of excellent improvements when at Christ's College, and he hath gained much reputation abroad. He is furnished with all things convenient for the making experiments in the way of physic by the Duke of Florence'.[2] Taylor had a long and close connection with Lord Conway, whom More knew well, and Taylor and More had been friends for many years, while Rust was not only More's friend but a former pupil. There can be little doubt of the influence of More, and of the Cambridge Platonists generally, on Taylor who for all that he actively sympathised with the Laudian position, had studied Plato and Descartes and had much of the Latitudinarian in him. His earlier friendship with Chillingworth is significant in this respect. In any event, there were at this stage none of the clearly-marked lines of distinction between groups which became evident later. At this period of theological development the claims of reason and tradition were still the complementary parts of a single outlook, before the swing of events separated them and made of the sundered elements the basis of two conflicting points of view, not again to be reunited until the development of biblical criticism, the rise of idealist philosophy, and a renewed emphasis on the Church, coming together towards the close of the nineteenth century, forced a reappraisal.

'It is from Worthington', writes Raven, 'that we get our only description of Ray in his Cambridge days',[3] and the picture drawn in the letters is certainly an attractive one. Worthington sends to Hartlib a letter from Ray, with a copy of one of his books in which Hartlib is mentioned: 'He told me that he had thoughts heretofore to have sent you his book; and nothing hindered but modesty, he being a stranger to you. He is a person of great worth; and yet humble, and far from conceitedness and self-admiring. He is a conscientious Christian; and that's much said in a little'.[4] The book was the important *Cambridge Catalogue*, of which Raven gives it as his opinion that 'no book has so evidently initiated a new era in British botany'.[5] An account of the book follows in the

1. *Ib*. VI.
2. *Ib*. XI.
3. C. E. Raven, *John Ray*, p. 37.
4. *Miscellany*, X.
5. *John Ray*, p. 81.

letter, and the extract merits quotation because of Worthington's
own interest in the subject, which illustrates the development of
the trend largely initiated by More by which the full significance
of natural knowledge for theological method is appreciated. He
writes 'The expressing of the many little appurtenances to plants
required one (i.e. an author) of a great perfection in the Latin
style; and you will find the whole properly expressed. I believe he
hath made good preparations for such a work; but he is not hasty
to publish it, as he was not to publish this *Phytologia Canta-
brigiensis*; he would spend more time about considering it. I wish
other writers would express the like care, exactness and caution
about their books.'

This is not only a record of Ray's technique, but it shows how
Worthington discerned both the beginnings and the importance
of a new discipline of exact observation. He adds: 'In short, I
think there are not many that have attained to so great a knowledge in this part of natural philosophy; which he is still adding to.
He hath a little garden by his chamber, which is as full of choice
things as it can hold'.[1] There is more in the letters about this little
garden, in itself a symbol of the new method of patient observation
and deduction, when Worthington discusses Ray's projected
northern journey: 'I hope Mr Ray will meet with some new discoveries in his travels, which may help towards the further fur-
nishing of his garden; which though it be but a little spot of ground
belonging to his chamber in the College, yet hath at least seven
hundred plants in it'.[2]

Another reference[3] to the journey links Ray and Willughby
who travelled with him, worked with him, and assisted him not
least by his generosity. A man of means, talent and originality,
Willughby was representative of many men of his class and time
who turned with relief from the unending logomachy of theological
systems to the new science and study of nature as to a refreshment
and a restating of the meaning of experience.

Worthington gives various details of Ray's journey, and notes:
'They were in the Bass Island, and both saw and fed on the Soland
geese; but they found all was not true which is usually reported
of them'.[4] Doubtless this refers to the current belief, accepted in this

1. *Ib*. X.   3. *Ib*. XIV.
2. *Ib*. XII.   4. *Ib*. XVII.

instance and others by More, that these birds, as well as frogs and mice, were spontaneously generated 'by putrefaction'.[1]

With theology standing on the threshold of modernity, and looking into a changing world, or rather a world being revealed in a richness of design hitherto unimagined, it can be seen that the Cambridge Platonists did much to lay the foundation of a method which would be in a position to appraise the true and ultimate significance for theology of new knowledge and the new ways of obtaining it. In all this it is easy to overlook their essential orthodoxy, and the fact that they made no concessions to the spirit of the age in respect of credal declarations, but rather regarded themselves as reinterpreting these in the light of the new situation in order to avoid the difficulties for belief which would inevitably arise if these questions were not faced.

Hooker combined his interpretation of authority in terms of law and reason with Scripture, tradition and the Church, and mention has been made of the parallel between this and the position of Gore and his fellow-contributors in 1889. The parallel can be continued, and in some respects becomes more marked, between the Cambridge Platonists and the *Lux Mundi* writers, both in method and in the similar situations in which they worked. What emerges from the comparison is the element of permanent value in the method of the earlier writers, for the later situation reveals a revival and a restatement of the points they emphasised. This is brought out by comparing the way in which the seventeenth century related theology to new movements of thought with an analysis in two recent books of the work of Gore and his associates in relation to developments at the end of the nineteenth century.[2]

In pointing out that Gore's indebtedness to nineteenth-century thought was most noticeable in his understanding of the nature of reason, James Carpenter writes: 'He found scholastic reason untenable, and he also rebelled against the arid rationalism of the eighteenth century. Reason for the eighteenth century meant largely the common human understanding; it failed to appreciate a wide range of man's powers of spiritual perception that had been emphasised by the Cambridge Platonists and that was to be

1. Henry More, *Antidote*, Chap. XVI, pp. 136, 187.
2. *Gore, a Study in Liberal Catholicism*, by James Carpenter, and *From Gore to Temple*, by Arthur Michael Ramsey.

stressed again by the characteristic thought of the nineteenth century'.[1]

Gore insisted that faith and reason were in close relationship, a subject that was treated in detail by R. C. Moberly and J. R. Illingworth, and he was firmly rational in his approach to questions, referring to himself as 'a free-thinker' in this respect.[2]

The *Lux Mundi* writers desired to face the spirit of scientific enquiry and current evolutionary theories, and the views of personality beginning to appear, and Gore regarded scientific disclosures as, in a sense, something revealed. 'Closely allied with this' writes Carpenter, 'is his dictum "truth is one", and because this is so, "there can be no conflict between matters of faith and the conclusions of knowledge".'[3] There is a similarity of outlook here with the Cambridge Platonists, and Gore's preference for Butler in this connection points in the same direction, for as Raven has indicated, it was Butler who 'expounded the implications of Ray's work'.[4]

A further parallel between the two groups exists with regard to the extensive use made of a philosophy reconciling spirit and matter, and emphasising personality. The *Lux Mundi* group, as Scott Holland observed, owed much to the influence of T. H. Green whose philosophical idealism released the period from agnostic mechanism.[5] 'In the face of the mechanistic interpretation of the world urged upon man's acceptance by some of the leading secular thinkers of the time, idealism, with its concept of personality as an intelligent, purposeful centre of consciousness emerging from matter yet not attributable to matter, offered at the very least the possibility of an effective apologetic, and an apologetic that might reconcile faith and a philosophical viewpoint that seemed destined to capture a large area of the field of vision in contemporary thought'.[6] This has only to be compared with More's or Cudworth's outline of the position in their time to see that the analogy between the two groups does not stop short at method but extends also to the situation in which they worked. There was in each case an alliance with philosophy against a materialist viewpoint, an alliance in which the same points are made use of, just as scientific discoveries are utilised. Carpenter notes that by the

1. *Gore*, by James Carpenter, p. 68.
2. *Ib.*
3. *Ib.* p. 61.
4. *John Ray*, p. 477.
5. James Carpenter, loc. it., p. 28.
6. *Ib.* p. 148.

1870s evolution had become the category of the age, and that Gore
had played a large part in taking account of this.[1] In both periods
there was resistance to similar categories of ideas, and the pressure
of traditional views was strong. The Archbishop of Canterbury
sees the authors of *Lux Mundi* as men of synthesis, combining
Tractarian churchmanship and the critical spirit, 'the use of contemporary philosophy and a faith drawn from the Bible and the
Fathers', and he comments both on their otherworldliness and the
fact that their influence was more than academic and extended to
the general life of the Church.[2]

Their resemblance to the earlier group is noteworthy, and P. E.
More's comment, made twenty-five years ago, may be recalled,
that the real thread of continuity runs from the seventeenth century to *Lux Mundi* and not to the Tractarians.[3] One has only to
contrast the rigidity and the refusal to consider certain possibilities
which marked the outstanding and admirable leaders of the first
and second generations of Tractarianism, with the candour and
depth of the Cambridge Platonists and the later essayists, to see
the justice of this. For both groups shared an outlook, and to some
extent limitations, but they were determined to face the issues
raised by contemporary knowledge, being equally convinced that
what was needed was not concession in regard to fundamentals,
but restatement, and refusal to add to them. This synthesis was
primarily effected for Gore through the medium of his concept of
authority which was framed in terms of reason: 'Throughout his
development of his theory of authority, the real thread of continuity is confidence in reason'.[4] Gore himself wrote that Anglicanism
does not acquiesce in the severance of reason and authority, and
he gave a firm adherence to the three-fold combination of Scripture, tradition and reason.[5]

He considered it the advantage and attraction of Anglicanism
to have retained hold on the 'ancient structure of the Church',
while at the same time welcoming 'the new learning, the new
appeal to Scripture, the freedom of historical criticism and the duty
of private judgment'.[6] He set great store by the appeal to Scripture, stressing the value of antiquity, and he gave it as his opinion

1. *Ib.* p. 27.
2. *From Gore to Temple*, p. 11.
3. *Anglicanism*, ed. P. E. More and
   F. L. Cross, p. xxxiii.
4. Carpenter, loc. cit., pp. 136–7.
5. *Ib.* p. 31.
6. *Ib.* p. 57.

that 'it is this appeal ... which qualifies the Catholicism of the Church of England as scriptural or liberal',[1] for it prevents any misuse of authority and checks the tendency to accumulate formularies. It may also be noted that Gore's strong sense of the historical pointed in the same direction.

It is worth noting too that Gore's phrase 'liberal Catholicism'[2] drew its essential meaning from these pervading ideas of scripturalness, historicity and rationality, so that when using it he was in fact describing 'the historic position of Anglicanism' and 'he did not have theological liberalism in mind at all'.[3] In fact, the word liberality with its absence of particular associations, describes more faithfully that which was common to the Cambridge Platonists and the *Lux Mundi* essayists, and which was not found to any extent in the situations in which they commenced their work. A. R. Vidler uses the word to distinguish between nineteenth-century Liberalism and a quality which is not a set of philosophical assumptions, the opposite not of conservatism but of intransigence, a quality with which he associates flexibility and vitality. In his view, certain periods of history are more favourable to its appearance than others, and while he recognises its limitations, he maintains that it has a lasting value.[4]

The Archbishop of Canterbury indicates how Gore's temperament set a limit to the liberality of which he had been a pioneer,[5] but basically it remains an element re-affirmed in his work and in that of his fellow-essayists as it was affirmed by the Cambridge Platonists in a similar situation. The latter referred to it as 'universality' of mind, but they meant the same thing.

1. *Ib.*
2. *Ib.* p. 56.
3. *Ib.* p. 61.

4. A. R. Vidler, *Essays in Liberality*, pp. 21–28.
5. A. M. Ramsey, *From Gore to Temple*, p. 14.

CHAPTER V

THE LATITUDINARIANS

THE rise of the new philosophy, as contemporaries termed the new movement in the study of science and nature, was important for theological method in two ways. In the first place, it meant the beginning of the end for Aristotelianism which, in one form or another and in varying degrees, had dominated thought and which, despite the contribution it had made, was now becoming petrified. Its grip on University teaching had been firm and lasting. In the second place, the new philosophy, with what G. R. Cragg calls 'its patient waiting upon fact and its repudiation of all presuppositions',[1] had helped to create an intellectual atmosphere in which a theological method which took no account of the unfolding universe and the implications of new discoveries was deemed irrelevant. The fact that the scientists and naturalists were all Churchmen, and that many of them were clergy, is sufficient comment on contemporary awareness of this.

C. E. Raven writes: 'a brilliant generation nourished upon exaltations and agonies turned away from the squabbles of the sectaries and the intrigues of the politicians to the systematic exploration of the new world which telescope and microscope were revealing. It is in the work of John Ray, Francis Willughby, Nehemiah Grew, of Richard Tower, John Mayow and Thomas Sydenham; of Robert Hook, Edward Lhuyd and John Woodward; of Isaac Newton, John Flamstead and Edmund Halley, that the symbolic and epoch-making struggle of the Stuart period has its brilliant outcome'.[2]

This outlines the position, and indicates the direction in which things were moving, so that the two reasons already referred to with regard to the importance of the new philosophy for theological method might be described as positive and negative aspects of the fact that the post-Restoration period was a significant time of creative change and revision.

Confronted by a steadily augmented range of observable data concerning the physical universe, it was necessary not only to

1. *From Puritanism to the Age of Reason*, p. 99.
2. *Science, Religion and the Future*, p. 27.

consider the implications for traditionally accepted ideas, but to assimilate the fact that what Hales had called 'the truth of things' was in fact very different from what had been accepted hitherto. The new philosophy began to take effect not alone on the presuppositions but on the way in which theological questions were considered. Turning aside from empiricism, the Cambridge Platonists had endeavoured to provide a method which would take account of reason, faith and experience within the framework of a unified concept of reality. As the method appeared, Hooker came into his own as did the constructive aspect of the work of Chillingworth, Hales and Falkland, but something else had been acquired which was of considerable assistance in a time of transition.

The position after the Restoration was that Calvinism and the Independent influence no longer made the same impact on the situation, and the value of Hooker's legacy, exaggerated by some and underestimated by others during the intervening years, became apparent. For there was in existence a tradition which, adhering firmly to antiquity and the ancient structure of the Church, gave a high place to reason and fostered a liberal method while standing firm on essentials. Largely in consequence of this the Church of England was able to hold the enthusiastic support of men like the imaginative Sir Thomas Browne in whose attractive pages may be discerned that curiosity and growing tolerance of spirit which mark his younger contemporaries Wilkins, Francis Bacon and Ray, whose *Methodus Plantarum* was published in the year that Sir Thomas died.

Events had prepared for the work of the Latitudinarians and the new philosophers who were indebted to the Cambridge Platonists, so that the stage was set for the further development of theological method. It was indeed fortunate that, as society turned the first corners on the way to modernity, theological method was at once sufficiently flexible and sure of its presuppositions to accept new findings, and sufficiently sure of itself to be able to think in terms of assimilation.

Subsequent generations have tended to depreciate the Latitudinarian movement, and it would be idle to deny that a certain measure of criticism was justified. Just as the spirit of the movement seemed unable to capture and to pass on that which was finest in the Cambridge Platonists, so, as it developed, it seemed

in its later stages to quench the fire and to set a premium on dullness. The Latitudinarian movement is Cambridge Platonism minus
the sense of wonder and the genius. It ought to be borne in mind,
however, in this connection that the movement was partly the child
of a historical process of reaction. After the excessiveness of individuals such as Nayler,[1] a victim of messianic delusions, and of
various groups during the Commonwealth period, a sober spirit and
a reasonable theology were not only much to be desired, but were
a much-needed means of rehabilitating religion. Furthermore,
when it is held against the Latitudinarians that they turned the
Cambridge Platonists' idea of reason as something involving the
harmonious action of the personality into the idea of what is
reasonable, it must be remembered that they considered themselves as commending religion to the intelligent man in contemporary terms which he could respect. They wished to reinforce a
reasonable faith by means of the new intellectual medium now
provided, and they missed the point, which the Cambridge men
had not failed to appreciate, that truth is not necessarily synonymous with a specious plainness. Frequently one has the impression,
inaccurate in fact, that for them the word reasonableness means a
cautious self-interest, and this to the extent that they seem at times
to be caricaturing their own views, but this raises a question of the
use of terms which must be considered presently. This is not to
imply that the Latitudinarians were not competent, sincere and
vigorous. Their theology was orthodox and their method liberal,
and inevitably in such a period they had to be content with a certain amount of misunderstanding. But they exercised considerable
influence, particularly in London before 1688, after which,
through the happy coincidence of their views with those of
William of Orange, their position grew in strength. Distinguished
names are to be found in their ranks—Stillingfleet, Tillotson,
Sprat, Tenison, Patrick, Glanvill, Lloyd and Burnet. In the things
which they opposed they were progressives. In some of the things
which they supported they were mistaken. In the overempha-
sising of natural religion they unconsciously formed a stepping-
stone to the deism of certain circles in the eighteenth century. But it
is unfair to regard them as directly responsible for this since in
actual fact they maintained that natural religion could only find

1. For an account of Nayler, see *James Nayler, The Rebel Saint, 1618–1660*
(1931), by Emilia Fogelklou.

its completeness in revealed religion, and that reason must be supplemented by faith and that its exercise confirmed revealed truth.

Many of their contemporaries considered that the Latitudinarians failed to produce anything positive, and that their work was conducive to uncertainty. While the charge of vagueness is not without some foundation, it is also true that they were men who tried to speak to their contemporaries in terms which showed an awareness of the things that their contemporaries were thinking and hearing.

As has been indicated, the Latitudinarians had close connections with the Cambridge Platonists from whom they derived directly their views on tolerance and reason. The inspired quality, the depth and the power of attraction and the capacity for mysticism which pervade the writings of the earlier group are doubtless incommunicable in the last resort. The Latitudinarians inherited also the imaginative moralism of the Cambridge Platonists, but because of the combination of a certain type of practicality and restraint in their outlook it almost becomes moralising, for some things cannot be passed on.

Nevertheless in that which they assimilated the new school endeavoured to match the contemporary situation, when, as it is well to recall, the Age of Reason was only just around the corner. In one sense, their teaching and preaching were responsible for that Mr Holton, who as the Woodforde Diary records,[1] preached in Cary Church in 1762 'concerning private interest giving way to public good in regard to our having a water engine to prevent fire spreading', or for the late eighteenth-century bishop who relates with satisfaction how he planted larches and also planted in the hearts of his children 'principles of piety, benevolence and self-government'.[2] In another sense, they were simply involved in the larger movement of Western European thought, and they made a contribution as candid as it was practical which was both needed by the times and was conveyed in terms that were intelligible to them.

On the credit side must be placed their undeviating reasonableness, which, coming after a period when exaggeration and enthusiasm had succeeded in upsetting the balance of faith and reason and of the relation of the individual to the corporate, did not fail in its effect. Also their practicality in advancing beneficial

1. Entry for August 1st, 1762.
2. *A Short History of the Oxford Movement*, S. L. Ollard, p. 19.

projects had a realistic quality. They had a simple and uncomplicated approach and a directness of appeal. They were, as their
writings show, very much aware of contemporary advances in
knowledge and with the consequent problems of relevance and
communication. With Tillotson, they considered 'the Church of
England to be the best constituted Church this day in the world',[1]
and if the ground of their admiration was the contrast occasioned
by its 'sober' quality as contrasted with the vagaries of enthusiasm, they were clear that this arose from the consonance of its
tenets with Scripture and reason.

On the debit side, they too often allowed their plainness to become
pedestrian, and their desire for simplicity and clarity led them into
shallowness at times. There is in their writings a certain vagueness
and dispassionateness, due to an honest endeavour to be impartial
and to achieve contact with the mind of the times, but frequently
their very magnanimity seems to topple over into coldness and
indifference. Yet it is no small tribute to the Latitudinarians that
at the bottom of the criticisms levelled at them lies a disappointment that most of their best qualities suffer this declension and
modification. This may be due in part to the absence of that species
of sustaining inwardness so noticeable in the Cambridge Platonists,
and possibly also to the fact that the Latitudinarians were not so
much thinkers as preachers, so that they were constantly in danger
of indulging in over-simplification with its inevitable loss of
depth.

Yet when the balance is struck, there can be seen to have been
absorbed into Anglican theological method a practicality which
expresses itself in a concern with charitable objects. It joined itself
to the practicality of the Cambridge writers, which was an inward
simplicity and devotion expressing itself in obedience, and for the
Latitudinarians as well as for their predecessors there was the
sense of the responsibility for being meaningful, and for establishing contact with those movements which were beginning to make the
world look so different to the thinking man.

In 1670 there appeared a book by E. Fowler, *The Principles and
Practices of certain Moderate Divines of the Church of England,
abusively called Latitudinarians*. It is cast in the form of a dialogue
between Philalethes, a friendly enquirer, and Theophilus who

1. *Sermons* (7th ed. 1688), Vol. II, S. III, p. 86.

undertakes to explain the position of the Latitudinarians, and it pinpoints certain aspects of the current reaction to their views. Philalethes has heard so much about them, including the definition of a Latitudinarian—"'tis this short one, he is a gentleman of a wide swallow'[1]—that he is anxious to find out what they really hold. Theophilus at once gets down to the fundamental antithesis between adherence to a formulated system and the freedom of reason. The concern of religion is with the realities of men's existence, 'not to intoxicate their brains with notions, or furnish their heads with a system of opinions'.[2] The Latitudinarians are therefore concerned to demonstrate that religion is able to commend itself to men's free acceptance by its reasonableness, although Theophilus is well aware that there are many who will give one little thanks 'for insisting on that topic', arguing as they do that such acceptance is by means of faith only without the use of reason.[3]

Philalethes then puts the question, 'doth not what hath been said tend to disparage the Gospel, and make it the very same, excepting two or three precepts with a mere natural religion?'[4] This was of course the fundamental difficulty then and since for many with regard to the views of the Latitudinarians, for by their emphasis on reasonableness they contrived to convey the impression that religion was chiefly a matter of acquiring and practising justice, honesty, sincerity and charitableness. These things were recognisably reasonable and it was to man's immediate and ultimate interest to acquire them, and it was the fruit of common experience that this was for man's happiness as well as his interest. This impression was in fact only partly true, for the Latitudinarians said a great deal more than this. It is easy to see however why this aspect of their approach made the impression that it did. In the first place, it was diametrically opposed to the trend of that theology which had been dominant for a considerable part of the seventeenth century in England, the basic presuppositions and method of which had been questioned by Hooker, Hales, Hammond and the Cambridge Platonists. Although the days of that system were now numbered, its effect on popular thought was still to be reckoned with, and the effect of current fiduciary ideas in various

1. (2nd ed. 1671), Pt. I, p. 10.   3. *Ib.* Pt. I, XIV, p. 42.
2. *Ib.* Pt. I, VII, p. 18.   4. *Ib.* Pt. I, XXXII, p. 86.

forms supplemented it so that the reaction to such preaching in the circumstances of the time would naturally be to query whether the Latitudinarians attributed anything to the work of faith or allowed for any intrusion of grace on the orderly process of assimilating religion by reason.

In the second place, fairness to the Latitudinarian viewpoint must always recognise that it is born not only of reaction to the conditions which preceded it, but also of sympathy with the new philosophy which began to make its influence felt at the same time, and with which its agreements were far from superficial. Latitudinarianism performed a necessary function for theological method by stressing the place of order and reasonableness and practicality in contrast to the disorder, enthusiasm and individualism of the period now drawing to a close, and if some inner vigour was lost in the process, or temporarily mislaid, this was only to be expected. The new philosophy was moving in exactly the same direction, that of order and reason and deduction, and the strength and importance of the Latitudinarians lies in their prophetic perception that soon ordinary people would be accepting without question the scientists' view of reality. They considered that it was essential therefore that religion should be able to commend itself on the same ground of reasonableness, or else become excluded from what reality would mean for ordinary people.

There can be little doubt that they succeeded in their immediate object, even if ultimately they partially failed, and it may be the destiny of the Latitudinarians to act as a reminder of the need for balance between faith and reason in theological method.

The sad part is, from their point of view, that fundamentally they accepted this balance, but failed to convince others that this was the case. Replying to the criticism that they almost identified natural and revealed religion, Theophilus says that to commend something as reasonable is a high commendation, and that, in any case, religion 'is not made up altogether of agenda', but there are 'relations of matters of fact', and many things to be known, and while it contains all that is to be found out by reason, it gives 'far greater helps', and because of the events which the New Testament records, much stronger reasons.[1]

Philalethes then wishes to know whether, in addition to showing

1. *Ib.* Pt. I, XXXII, p. 86.

that the agenda are reasonable, the Latitudinarians endeavour to apply the same test to the credenda. The reply made to this is a fair statement of the Latitudinarian position. They attempt, says Theophilus, to show that they are 'consistent with reason', and that 'they are suitable to the reason of men's minds, being revealed'.[1] This certainly preserves the essential balance, and is but another way of putting Whichcote's aphorism, 'that is not revealed which is not made intelligible'.

Their method, says Theophilus, is plain and they react against 'turning everything almost into allegories'.[2] Philalethes has heard the words rational and moral used as a sort of accusation against the Latitudinarians, and has heard them referred to as mere moral preachers, and he and Theophilus consider it strange that such words should be capable of being reckoned as opprobrious.[3] What then, asks Philalethes, of imputed righteousness? Theophilus replies, 'they do not use the phrase, at least not often . . . but they believe the thing, and preach it too, in that sense, that I dare say you do'.[4] It is clear from what follows that the Latitudinarians do not accept the idea of a righteousness transferred and 'completely made theirs' on condition only of believing, which according to Theophilus means in this case 'strongly fancying'.[5]

As to authority, he writes, 'nor will an ipse dixit be admitted by them as a sufficient argument to prove any doctrine by', and he says that the Latitudinarians regard it as unreasonable to make human authorities a standard, or 'to deprive each other of their liberty to judge for themselves'.[6] The practice of referring to the ancient fathers is not of much assistance, 'they differing so much among themselves, as it is well known they do'.[7] They do not value general councils less than does Article XXI, and they maintain that submission to the Articles themselves is enjoined 'as to an instrument of peace'.[8] The sentence 'let us not magisterially impose one upon another' echoes Whichcote, 'let us lay aside imposing one upon another'.[9]

While there can be little doubt that the most influential of the Latitudinarians was Tillotson, the work of his younger contem-

---

1. *Ib*. Pt. I, XXXV, pp. 93, 102.
2. *Ib*. Pt. I, XLIV, p. 105.
3. *Ib*. Pt. I, XLIX.
4. *Ib*. Pt. I, LV.
5. *Ib*. Pt. I, LVII.
6. *Ib*. Pt. II, XXXVIII.
7. *Ib*. Pt. II, XL.
8. *Ib*. Pt. II, XLIII, XLIV.
9. *Ib*. Pt. II, XLIX.

porary Joseph Glanvill, whose book and whose admiration for Descartes and More are mentioned by Worthington, is significant for the development of theological method. This is so because Glanvill was a Latitudinarian who rejected the idea of a theological system, and he was also an ardent supporter of the new philosophy, seeing in its discipline of exact observation a new approach to the understanding of reality. He was therefore in opposition not only to the authority of a system, the conclusions of which were treated as if they were almost definitive, but to the authority of Aristotelian philosophy in those realms where for so long its sway had been unquestioned. In fact, his first book, published in 1661 and referred to by Worthington, and reappearing in somewhat altered form in 1665,[1] is a plea for the new philosophy, and he writes that 'the Aristotelian philosophy is inept for new discoveries; and therefore of no accommodation to the use of life'.[2]

Born in 1636, Glanvill was one of those who grew up under the Commonwealth, and his reaction in the direction of Latitudinarianism and the new philosophy from all that the Commonwealth period connoted was complete. It is significant that he records that 'in my first education I was continually instructed into a religious and fast adherence to everything I was taught, and a dread of disputing in the least article'.[3] He was made a Fellow of the Royal Society, and he died in 1680 and was buried in the Abbey Church in Bath, where he had been appointed in 1666.

For Glanvill the foundation of the new philosophy is 'modest, impartial enquiry' which leads not to scepticism, but to 'so much caution in our disquisitions, that we do not suddenly give firm assents to things not well understood, or examined'.[4] Such a method cannot but be of service, since so many facts are misunderstood or imperfectly understood that understanding depends on 'suspending our assent from all, till the deserts of each, discovered by a strict enquiry, claim it'.[5] This is not scepticism but the way of enquiry, and it is ultimately the answer to materialism. Benjamin Jowett once said that 'the search for truth is one thing: fluttering after it is another', and Glanvill's work did not belong to the latter class, for his outlook was steadily consistent and he was convinced

1. *The Vanity of Dogmatising or Confidence in Opinions* (1661); *Scepsis Scientifica* (1665).
2. *Scepsis Scientifica*, Chap. XXI.   4. *Philosophia Pia* (1771), Chap. V, III.
3. *Plus Ultra*, p. 142.   5. *Scepsis Scientifica*, Chap. X.

that the new philosophy was advantageous to religion by reason
of the fresh evidences of purpose and design which it discovered
in the created world. Indeed it is apparent from his whole handling
of the subject that Glanvill sees this enquiry not only as the necessary approach to experimental philosophy, but as a contribution to
theological method. There is an indication of this in the sub-title,
to *Philosophia Pia, a discourse of the religious temper and tendencies
of the experimental philosophy, which is professed by the Royal Society
to which is annexed, a recommendation and defence of the reason in
the affairs of religion.*

*Scepsis Scientifica, or confessed ignorance the way to science; in an
essay of the vanity of dogmatising and confident opinion* is a rare
book, owing to the greater part of the impression having been
destroyed in the great fire of 1666. It is of interest that the address
to the Royal Society with which it begins claims that their work
helps to refute the mechanistic view. Their aim, says Glanvill, is
'the improving the minds of men in solid and useful notices of
things, helping them to such theories as may be serviceable to
common life, and the searching out the true laws of matter and
motion, in order to the securing of the foundations of religion
against all attempts to mechanical atheism'. Denying 'that the
knowledge of nature tends to irreligion', he enquires what will be
the result if 'the whole fabric of religion is built upon ignorance of
things'. An attitude of enquiry, with suspended judgment until the
facts are proved, is the only reasonable approach to things.[1]

Too much regard for antiquity has been a hindrance, and it has
been to the advantage of mathematics and mechanical studies
generally that no tradition exists in them. Opinions are not an
entail, and ''tis no discredit to the telescope that antiquity ne're
saw in it'. The practice of constantly quoting authors only brings in
'authority in things neither requiring, nor deserving it'.[2]

He considers that the new philosophy will lead to fresh discoveries, and looking forward he foresees in general and prophetic
terms some of the characteristics of the future: 'And I doubt not
but posterity will find many things, that are now but rumours,
verified into practical realities. It may be some ages hence, a
voyage to the southern unknown tracts, yea possibly the moon,
will not be more strange than one to America. To them that come

1. *Ib.* Chap. X.   2. *Ib.* Chap. XVII.

after us, it may be as ordinary to buy a pair of wings to fly into remotest regions; as now a pair of boots to ride a journey. And to confer at the distance of the Indies by sympathetic conveyances may be as usual to future times, as to us in a literary correspondence'.[1]

Glanvill regards the idea that philosophy leads to unbelief as due to a misunderstanding of nature and of second causes: 'the students of nature, conscious of her more cryptic ways of working, resolve many strange effects into the nearer efficiency of second causes; which common ignorance and superstition attribute to the immediate causality of the first: thinking it to derogate from the Divine power, that any thing which is above their apprehensions should not be reckoned above nature's activity; though it be but his instrument, and works nothing but as empowered from him'.[2]

With the advent of Latitudinarianism and the new philosophy, the preoccupation of seventeenth-century theology with power disappears, and for it is substituted a preoccupation with wisdom. The consequent loss of the concept of arbitrariness was gain, but it was not all gain, for the sense of the imperative and of the transcendent tended to become weakened. The emphasis on knowledge is characteristic of the period, and is indicative of the impact of science on theological method. Thus the subject-matter of the *Philosophia Pia* is that man is to praise God for His works, and in order to do this he must study them. The study of nature is therefore serviceable to this purpose, and far from discouraging it men ought to promote it in every way.[3] The naturalist who 'discovers of the accurateness, and art that is in the contexture of things' will see in it the evidence of wisdom and design: 'for if we look upon any of the works of nature through a magnifying glass that makes deep discoveries, we find still more beauty, and more uniformity of contrivance'. By contrast, if the same thing is done with 'the most curious piece of human ingenuity' it will reveal the flaws and imperfections 'in our most elegant mechanics'.[4] The spirit of investigation and of wonder passed on from the Cambridge Platonists to the new philosophers, and if the second element is less noticeable in the Latitudinarians, it is still there to some degree.

The emphasis on wisdom, design and the usefulness of the new

1. *Ib*. Chap. XXI.
2. *An Apology for Philosophy*.
3. Chap. I.
4. *Ib*. Chap. II, I.

philosophy's method in theological matters, is apparent when Glanvill writes: 'if we know no further than occult qualities, elements, heavenly influences and forms, we shall never be able to disprove a mechanic atheist, but the more we understand the laws of matter and motion, the more shall we discern the necessity of a wise mind to order the blind and insensible matter'.[1] Worthington's comment on Glanvill's admiration for More is underlined here for he is indebted to him for the outlines of his thinking, as were others, such as Ray and his fellow-workers.

For Glanvill, the basis of the supposed antithesis of reason and religion is 'by an implicit assent to the systems, and dictates of those who first instructed them'.[2] The fact that he draws attention to Jeremy Taylor's defence of reason would seem to indicate that he wishes to show that this is a characteristic of Anglican writing generally and not just a fad peculiar to the supporters of the scientific movement.[3]

He holds that there is no truth in the suggestion that the study of philosophy results in neglect of Scripture, and offers as proof the works on this subject by two well-known philosophers, Boyle and Ward.[4] It is not the purpose of Scripture to instruct in 'the affairs of nature' so that various expressions about nature will be found to be accommodated not to exact terminology but to ordinary speech and meaning.[5]

Glanvill's *Essays* which appeared in 1676 deal with different aspects of the relationship between the new philosophy and theology, such as 'modern improvements of knowledge' and 'the usefulness of philosophy to theology'. In the introduction to Rust's *Discourse* he comments on the mistaken method of excluding from the discussion of theological questions 'arguments taken from natural notions'. The names of Glanvill and Rust are connected in an incidental way by the fact that they are both mentioned in Worthington's letters to Hartlib, but the introduction is a more substantial link, and the assertion that there are 'immutable respects in things' shows the basis upon which they were agreed.

In one of the essays, Glanvill describes 'the proper notion of reason', distinguishing between 'reason in the faculty, which is the understanding', and 'reason in the object, which consists in

1. *Ib*. Chap. II, II.
2. *Ib*. Chap. V, III.
3. *Ib*.
4. *Ib*. Chap. VI, III.
5. *Ib*. Chap. VII, IV.

those principles and conclusions by which the understanding is informed'.[1] It is the latter sense of the word which is implied in discussions about reason and religion, and he points out that 'reason in this sense, is the same with natural truth, which . . . is made up of principles and conclusions'.[2] It is this identification which lies behind the continued emphasis by the Latitudinarians on natural religion, and on the new philosphy which, in their view, helped to clarify this 'natural truth'. By principles, Glanvill meant very much the same as what earlier writers implied by the fundamental and universally accepted provisions of natural law such as command 'a sudden assent', and are 'immediately lodged' in the mind, and are 'inbred' and 'implanted'. The conclusions are whatever can be 'inferred rightly from these', or which can be deduced from observation by means of them.[3]

Glanvill's enquiring mind is his own, but the movement originated by those he admired, and in which he took part, was gathering momentum, so that during the last two decades of the century, as Sprat recorded, the spirit of enquiry and the new philosophy spread: 'this searching spirit, and this affection to sensible knowledge, does prevail in most countries round about us'.[4]

Few periods present a more fascinating picture than that of the post-Restoration period confronting the gradual opening of what had hitherto been a closed world. In the words of Roger of Salerno in one of Kipling's stories as he first saw a drop of water through a microscopic glass, 'it is a new world'.[5]

The invention of the microscope and the telescope were of course instrumental, but in themselves such inventions were only a result of the new method of enquiry and observation. In all spheres the forward movement is discernible. The Copernican astronomy was arriving in England, though reaction against it continued until late in the century. Mathematics and physics which had disappeared in the universities began to come back in company with the new philosophy. Medicine began to move with more certainty as a result of discoveries such as that of the circulation of the blood. Chemistry and engineering came to the fore. All this curiosity and investigation were seen within the wider context of reason as the

1. *Essays on several important subjects in philosophy and religion*, V.
2. *Ib.*
3. *Ib.*
4. *History of the Royal Society*, T. Sprat (2nd ed. 1702), Pt. II, XXIII.
5. *Debits and Credits.*

human characteristic by means of which the unity of experience and the meaning of reality could be apprehended. The spirit of enquiry ran counter to the old method of authoritative deduction, and it was impossible but that theological method should be affected by it. In all the circumstances, it is to the credit of the Latitudinarians and philosophers that they allowed no suggestion of arrogance to creep into their view of reason, and that this is due in large part to the balance, uneven though it was, which the period preserved between revealed theology and reason, there can be little doubt.

It would obviously not be in accord with the facts to imagine that the clear and sterile light of a developing science began to play impartially on the whole Restoration period. Many were quite unaffected in their outlook by the new philosophy, and many were strongly opposed to it. Moreover, the views of the thinkers of the period revealed the fact that it was a time of transition. There is a credulity in the works of Wilkins and Burnet, side by side with evidence of their active interest in science and of their acceptance of the new way of looking at things.

The Royal Society owed its origin to the small group which in Commonwealth times met first in London and later in the house of Wilkins when he was Warden of Wadham. When he came to Cambridge, Boyle's house was for a time the centre for the meetings of the society which was incorporated as the Royal Society at the Restoration.

Sprat, subsequently Bishop of Rochester, records such names as Seth Ward, Robert Boyle, Wilkins, Sir William Petty, Matthew Wren, Wallis, Goddard, Bathurst, Willis, Rook, Christopher Wren: 'their first purpose was no more, than only the satisfaction of breathing a freer air, and of conversing in quiet one with another, without being engaged in the passions and madness of that dismal age. And from the institution of that assembly, it had been enough, if no other advantage had come, but this: that by this means there was a race of young men provided, against the next age, whose minds received from them, their first impressions of sober and generous knowledge'.[1]

Their intention, writes Sprat, is to deal with natural phenomena on the evidence, excluding a priori arguments, and this evidence

1. *History of the Royal Society*, Pt. II, II.

will help towards understanding the Divine nature. 'They have begun to establish these reformations in philosophy . . . by the . . . unanswerable arguments of real productions',[1] and if they have diminished the prodigies, 'they add to the ordinary works of the same Author. And those ordinary works themselves, they do almost raise to the height of wonders, by the exact discovery which they make of their excellencies'.[2] The importance of this changing outlook for theological method is considerable: 'the disciplines of natural science have become in effect an alternative approach to the ultimate questions of theology'.[3]

Although there were many who would not accept or did not sympathise with the new philosophy, like Robert South or Swift, many of the first members of the Royal Society were clergymen who by their interest 'have taken off the unjust scandal from natural knowledge, that it is an enemy to divinity'.[4]

Sprat held that respect for antiquity combined with 'trying all things' was as natural a way of procedure to the Church of England as it was to the Royal Society, and that, in consequence, the former 'can never be prejudiced by the light of reason, nor by the improvements of knowledge'.[5]

It may be considered that the contemporary evalution was over-optimistic, but from the point which they had reached it can hardly have seemed so, and the whole trend of thought as the period progressed showed less appreciation of the characteristic insights of the Cambridge Platonists, and a growing confidence in the accumulation of new knowledge. Sprat wrote that 'the Church of England will not only be safe amidst the consequences of a rational age, but amidst all the improvements of knowledge, and the subversion of old opinions about nature, and introduction of new ways of reasoning thereon.'[6]

Glanvill, as Worthington wrote to Hartlib, was an admirer of More, but he learned from him an attitude rather than a philosophy. He was also an admirer of Descartes, and he wrote 'I think the method of the most excellent Descartes not unworthy of its author',[7] for he was nearer to modernity, for better and for worse,

1. *Ib.* Pt. II, V.
2. *Ib.* Pt. III, XX.
3. G. R. Cragg, *From Puritanism to the Age of Reason*, p. 97.
4. Sprat, *History of the Royal Society.*
5. *Ib.* Pt. III, XXIII.
6. *Ib.*
7. *Scepsis Scientifica*, Chap. X.

than were those with whom his opinions originated. There is in fact a distinct shift of emphasis in Glanvill's work as compared with the view-point of the Cambridge Platonists. Glanvill has caught something of the new philosophy's spirit of enquiry, as distinct from the enquiring spirit of the older writers, and he has transferred it to theology. He is more concerned with finding out than with the sense of the mysterious in life or with the wholeness of experience. There is a suggestion of a pragmatic approach rather than of an alliance with idealist philosophy.

Glanvill's importance is not so much that he reflects a trend, as that he understood it. Sprat also understood it, and his History of the Royal Society was at once the apologia for and the exposition of the new method. In both of them, it is possible to catch a glimpse of the process by which theological method was influenced by the method of the new philosophy.

With the exceptions of Stillingfleet and Burnet the Latitudinarians did not produce books which were significant for or which outlasted their own generation. Yet, despite the relative unimportance of what they wrote, their influence was wide and pervasive and it cannot be ascribed solely to the fact that their sermons and addresses drew large crowds, for the latter came because the Latitudinarians had something to say. The extent of their influence was due primarily to the way in which they diagnosed the needs of the contemporary situation and attempted to meet them. In reaction from the past, and particularly from the more recent past, the popular desire was for simplicity, order and intelligibility. The Latitudinarians themselves shared in this wish, and were therefore favourably placed to speak to their contemporaries in a way that commended itself to them.

The most influential was Tillotson, of whom Burnet said that 'the nation proposed him as a pattern',[1] for both his style and his method were everywhere imitated, and in his sermons the Latitudinarian movement can be seen at its most characteristic. Tillotson is primarily a preacher, and the centre of interest for him has shifted to theological exposition and to the practical aspects of religion. Both his sympathy with the new philosophy and his indebtedness to the Cambridge Platonists show more in what he assumes than in any specific references, for natural theology and

1. Quoted in an article by Dr N. Sykes on *The Sermons of Archbishop Tillotson* in *Theology* (Vol. LVIII. No. 422, p. 297).

reason together with the Bible and its exposition constitute the chief elements in his sermons. For his contemporaries they represented a new kind of preaching, as Charles Smyth had indicated, which 'meant the emancipation of the Anglican pulpit not only from the metaphysical but also from the Puritan tradition. It involved a breach, not only with the homiletic conventions of the middle ages, but also with the homiletic conventions of the immediate past. On the one hand, Tillotson abandoned the use of exempla; on the other, he rejected the almost mechanical iteration of cant terms and phrases; for both alike he substituted the appeal to reason and to common sense, the careful, comprehensive argument, solid, unhurried, unadorned'.[1]

The elusive reason of the Cambridge Platonists tended to become a process of guaranteeing revelation by showing its consistency with rationality, a constant effort to show that religion before all else was reasonable. But in all fairness the question should be asked, what would have happened if men of the calibre of Tillotson, Tenison, Lloyd and Stillingfleet, had not done their work at this particular time, using this particular idiom and method.

Tillotson constantly stresses application, practicality, diligence, industry and charitableness. Controversial points are not infrequent; topical references occur, as to the plague and the fire of London; illustrations are often homely and effective; the approach is by way of reason and exposition, and most of the sermons conform to a simple plan.

A large sum of money was paid for the manuscripts of his sermons after his death, but they were equally sought after during his lifetime, one volume passing through seven editions by 1688. The general outline is to show the unreasonableness of materialism and the advantages of religion, and to persuade men to its practice both from its obligation and from the future rewards it brought with it.[2] The period did not betray any sensitivity on the subject of reward, or of what was termed 'interest'.

For Tillotson, the 'whole duty of man', a favourite subject with the Latitudinarians, is to be expressed in knowledge, faith, remembrance, love and fear.[3] Religion is made up of knowledge of

1. *Ib.*
2. *Sermons*, Vol. I (1688), preface.
3. *Sermons* (7th ed. 1688), Vol. I, I, p. 3.

principles, and practice, 'the first of which being speculative, may more properly be called knowledge; and the latter, because 'tis practical, may be called wisdom or prudence.'[1] In view of the suggestion not infrequently and not altogether inaccurately made, that the prudential plays too large a part in Latitudinarian thinking, contributing to indecisiveness, it is worth looking at this definition.

It seems clear, although this does not appear to have been recognised hitherto, that Tillotson's description of prudence as practical reason which is to be distinguished from speculative reason, is the traditional view as seen for example in the *Summa Theologica*, where both terms are used and prudence is defined as wisdom about practice.[2] Aquinas writes that it is the function of prudence to decide by what manner the mean of reason can be achieved in actions,[3] and it is in this sense that Tillotson uses the word in his definition. Such a description of prudence as practical reason fits in with the general Latitudinarian approach in terms of reason. When it is remembered that the description comes from the Latitudinarians themselves, it should help in preventing the too facile equation of what they meant by prudence with the modern use of the word prudential. It is not without relevance that in the *Summa* caution is only one of the eight parts of prudence, and memory, to which Tillotson refers in this connection, is another.[4] A third part is understanding, for says Aquinas, 'prudence is right reason applied to action',[5] or as the Latitudinarians thought, 'it is to be wise as to our main interest. Our chief end and highest interest is happiness'.[6] It is in this sense that Tillotson describes materialism as 'a most imprudent ... opinion', being against reason and happiness,[7] for the chief human need is for happiness.[8]

This is a recurring idea with the Latitudinarians, and it has been criticised as illustrating the comfortable categories of their thinking. It may well be that this sort of criticism has been somewhat overdone. It is inevitable that the extolling of reason should sound complacent in certain circumstances, and it can hardly be denied that there is something of this in the Latitudinarians as well as a tendency to a facile optimism, which may not have appeared so

1. *Ib.* I, p. 9.
2. Pt. II (Second Part), Q. 47, Art. 2.
3. *Ib.* Q. 47, Art. 7.
4. *Ib.* Q. 49.
5. Q. 49, Art. 2.
6. Tillotson, Vol. I, I, p. 16.
7. *Ib.* II, p. 68.
8. *Ib.* III. p. 141.

irritating at that stage of history as it does in the darker days of modern scientific enlightenment.

But the record of the good works of the Latitudinarians and of their sustained interest in different projects is more impressive than that of any others during the period, and hardly gives colour to the much-canvassed notion of their complacency. If they considered happiness to be man's chief end, they made every effort to contribute to the happiness of others.

Here again, questions of language are involved, for the suggestion often made then and since, that this continued reference to happiness as the chief end of man simply demonstrates the low temperature and inadequate goal of Latitudinarian thinking, shows a lack of theological perspective.

With regard to language, there is no ground for supposing that, by happiness, the Latitudinarians meant solely contentment or well-being though that notion would naturally be included in the word. With regard to theological perspective, the importance attached to happiness was not an invention of the Latitudinarians, for Aquinas had said exactly the same thing, that 'the last end of human life is happiness', and had devoted considerable space to the examination of the subject.[1] This fact, of course, adds nothing in itself to the truth or value of the idea, but it helps to fill in the perspective for a more accurate assessment of the Latitudinarian outlook. Religion, says Tillotson is then to man's 'plain and true interest',[2] and without it there would be more disorder in society than if human laws were the only restraint.[3] It makes for peace and tranquillity, health and industry, and enlarges the mind and the understanding:[4] 'all the precepts of it are reasonable and wise, requiring such duties of us as are suitable to the light of nature and do approve themselves to the best reason of mankind, such as have their foundation in the nature of God'.[5] In the situation which followed after the civil war, what was required was an outlook 'solid and substantial . . . plain and unaffected', and not 'the extremes of superstition and enthusiasm'.[6] The Christian religion is 'the best and most reasonable in the world'.[7] In Tillotson's view, 'speculative atheism is unreasonable . . . because it gives no

1. *Summa Theologica*, Pt. II (First Part), QQ I–IV.
2. *Ib.* Vol. VII, V, p. 130.
3. *Ib.* Vol. I, III, p. 142.
4. *Ib.* Vol. I, IV, pp. 152–63.
5. *Ib.* Vol. I, V, p. 186.
6. *Ib.* Vol. I, III, p. 149.
7. *Ib.* Vol. II (1696), p. 150.

tolerable account of the existence of the world. Nor does it give any reasonable account of the universal consent of mankind in this apprehension, that there is a God'.[1] Dealing with the concept of randomness, he asks for how long might twenty thousand blind men wander up and down England before they all met on Salisbury plain and fell into rank and file like an army: 'and yet this is much more easy to be imagined, than how innumerable blind parts of matter should rendezvous themselves into a world'.[2]

The real weakness lay in the way in which the Latitudinarians tended to whittle down the distinction between natural religion and Christianity. 'Excepting a very few particulars, they (natural law and Christianity) enjoin the very same things',[3] wrote Tillotson. It is hardly surprising that Swift considered Tillotson to have reduced the difference to the two sacraments, and to be the patron of the free-thinkers.

In an address on the new commandment, he adds 'not that it is absolutely and altogether new . . . for it is a branch of the ancient and primitive law of nature'. Besides its authority, 'we have a precedent obligation to it from our own nature, and from the reasonableness and exellency of the thing itself. The frame of our nature disposeth us to it, and our inclination to society . . . and equity also calls for it'.[4] All this is hardly to be disputed, yet it somehow contrives to appear irrelevant, and there cannot be much doubt that, whatever intellectual help may have been afforded by it to contemporaries, the near-equation of natural with revealed religion was one of the minimising tendencies and ephemeral aspects of Latitudinarian theology.

'Reason' wrote Tillotson, 'is the faculty whereby revelation is to be discerned',[5] and it was the purpose of revealed religion not to undermine natural religion, but to complete it.[6]

The Latitudinarians were rightly anxious to show that nothing that science had discovered affected the validity of traditional beliefs. In order to do this, they first demonstrated how the basic truths of natural religion were, if anything, strengthened by new knowledge, and were ascertainable by and in tune with reason, and they then proceeded to show how closely natural religion

1. *Ib*. Vol. I, I, pp. 18–19. 2. *Ib*. Vol. I, I, p. 42. 3. *Ib*. Vol. I, VI, p. 217.
4. *Ib*. Vol. III (3rd ed. 1691), II.
5. *Ib. Sermons at St Lawrence Jewry* (1693), II, p. 63.
6. *Ib*. Vol. IV (2nd ed. 1700), II, III, IV.

resembled revealed religion. Although this may have been, temporarily, a relief and a genuine help to many, it was soon evident that the Latitudinarians had overplayed their hand, and it became difficult to rebut the charge that the line they had taken made the way easier for their opponents. It was not that they were unorthodox, or that they said what was untrue. It was simply that, in this question, they had got the order of things inverted and the balance upset. Also they were operating with an idea of reason that was too shallow, but on the credit side, their partial failure was due in the first place to the fact that, unlike their critics, they had seen the need and tried to supply it.

There is nothing indecisive in the Latitudinarian attitude to the related matters of the decrees and justification by faith alone. Tillotson wrote that an obedient man had not 'the least ground to suspect any latent or secret decree of God against him to work his ruin'.[1] It is significant that the 'fides caritate formata' emphasised by the Cambridge Platonists is to the fore in Tillotson, whose view is that the faith which is the condition of justification is 'faith perfected by charity'.[2] He considers that 'though we be justified at first by faith without works preceding, yet faith without good works following it will not finally justify', and he quotes 'we may not think that we are justified by faith as it is separate from hope and charity' as the opinion of the English reformers.[3] He points out that, as used in the New Testament, the word faith includes both obedience and assent. Tillotson holds that 'justification in Scripture signifies no more than pardon and remission of sins', and that the use of metaphors in this connection should be avoided as confusing.[4] He denies that the Church of England gives any support to the idea that a man is justified by a bare faith, by believing himself to be justified.[5] Disagreement with this was not peculiar to the Cambridge Platonists and to the Latitudinarians, but goes back to the Articles.

As to the decrees, Tillotson cannot see how human concurrence impugns divine sovereignty, for there is no evidence that the latter consists in 'any inevitable decree to necessitate them to sin', or that there has been 'from all eternity . . . a secret design to circumvent the greatest part of men into destruction'.[6] He writes

1. *Ib*. Vol. II, VII, p. 201.   4. *Ib*. Vol. XII, VIII.
2. *Ib*. Vol. IV, V.   5. *Ib*. Vol. XII, X.
3. *Ib*. Vol. XI, VI.   6. *Ib*. Vol. VI, VII.

equally plainly of the idea of reprobation: 'if by reprobation be meant, either that God hath decreed, without respect to the sins of men, their absolute ruin and misery; or that he hath decreed that they shall inevitably sin and perish; it cannot be denied, but that such reprobation as this doth clearly overthrow all possible notions of goodness . . . But it is said, reprobation is an act of sovereignty in God, and therefore not to be measured by the common rule of goodness . . . we must not attribute such a sovereignty to God, as contradicts his goodness'.[1]

The chief characteristic of Latitudinarianism appears when he states: 'I know not how it comes to pass, but so it is, that every-one that offers to give a reasonable account of his faith, and to establish religion upon rational principles, is presently branded for a Socinian; of which we have a sad instance in that incomparable person Mr. Chillingworth . . . who for no other cause that I know of, but his worthy and successful attempts to make Christian religion reasonable . . . hath been requited with this black and odious character . . . I cannot imagine how men can do a greater disservice to religion, then by taking it off from the rational and solid basis upon which it stands, and bearing the world in hand, that men ought to believe without reason; for this is to turn faith into credulity'.[2]

There is something worth listening to here for the development of theological method. It is the call to be meaningful, and not to substitute terminology for thought. Such words as sovereignty and justification require to be looked at in context, and not regarded as talismans. The words reason and nature might at first sight be said to occupy a similar postion in the Latitudinarian outlook, but they did know what they meant by them, and what they meant implied no reversal of ordinary meanings or of accepted notions. Elsewhere, Tillotson quotes with approval the words 'whatever things are necessary are plain',[3] and notes that it is no new idea. Throughout he emphasises that the approach of the Church of England is that of Scripture and reason. His sermons, with their clear phrasing and everyday illustrations, sometimes doctrinal and sometimes on a topical theme, were practical and direct, but although he was practical, and admired practical people like Gouge, it was of Whichcote that he wrote, he 'was so wise, as to be

1. *Ib.* Vol. VII, III.   2. *Ib.* Vol. XII, VI.
3. *Ib.* Vol. III, III, and cp. the members of the Tew circle.

willing to learn to the last'.[1] Tillotson seems to echo Whichcote
when he says, 'men should never be earnest for, or against anything, but upon clear and certain grounds'.[2] When Turrettini,
a leading figure in Switzerland who corresponded with Wake,
came to England he met Tillotson and Burnet. The meeting
derived significance from the fact that a situation existed on the
Continent in which the questions which occupied the English
Latitudinarians were an important issue. Turrettini, with Werenfels
and Ostervald, formed a triumvirate of liberal thinkers in
Switzerland at the close of the seventeenth century and during the
first couple of decades of the eighteenth century. They did not
accept the strongly Calvinist *Formula Consensus* of 1675 which was
added to the *Confessio Helvetica*, and while it received general
assent in German Switzerland there was opposition to it in
Romance Switzerland. Norman Sykes, giving an account of the
way in which 'Basle in 1686 silently ceased to require subscription
to the Formula; whilst Zurich and Berne held stoutly to their
practice of compelling signature'; draws attention to the appearance
of what he regards as Swiss Latitudinarianism: 'during the interval
since the framing of the *Formula* moreover the Swiss Reformed
churches had experienced the rise of a movement, called by the
historian of the pays de Vaud 'l'orthodoxie liberale', which was
closely akin in fundamental principles to the Latitudinarianism
of the contemporary Church of England'.

Turrettini laid emphasis on the distinction between 'fundamental and non-essential doctrines in theology'. The correspondence with Wake reveals the tension between a liberal orthodoxy
and a systematic theology which imposed non-fundamental conclusions, and Wake's assessment, set out in a statement sent to
Turrettini, is fully dealt with by Sykes. It is an important expression of the Anglican attitude in which is stressed the prudence and
moderation of the sixteenth-century reformers in that 'they did
not think that anything should be conceded to any one's curiosity;
nor did they think it right to bind the faith of any one to the pious
though uncertain hypotheses of men concerning the divine
decrees', and they were not 'officious in the definition of non-
essentials'.[3] Wake's lengthy letter written in 1718 is an expression

1. *Ib.* Vol. III, VI.   2. *Ib.* Vol. II, XIII.
3. See Norman Sykes, *William Wake, Archbishop of Canterbury, 1657-1737*,
   Vol. II, pp. 24-58.

of an undeviating Anglican standpoint reiterated in a reply to another correspondent who had asked him to recommend a system of divinity suitable for students: 'as to your question about a system of divinity suitable to pupils, I know of none that I could recommend. Our Church stands upon a different bottom from most of those in which the system-writers have been bred'.[1] Properly speaking, this is not Latitudinarianism, as Sykes implied, but an essential element of Anglicanism to be found as much in Hooker and Andrewes, Sanderson and Hammond, as in the Cambridge Platonists and the Latitudinarians. It was the function of Tillotson and his age to give it fresh expression in a new context, but it was there before them.

It is Stillingfleet who can claim to be the chief writer among the Latitudinarians, for although Glanvill's work is important as a point at which the new philosophy and Latitudinarianism met, and Sprat and Burnet made their contributions, it is the *Origines Sacrae* which is the major, perhaps the only, book of size and importance produced by the Latitudinarians. His *Irenicum*, Stillingfleet's first book, and his *Unreasonableness of Separation* were also well known, the method of the former being of particular interest.

Like Tillotson who, according to Birch, regarded the new philosophy and its study as 'the most solid support of religion',[2] Stillingfleet made use of new knowledge to support Scriptural authority in *Origines Sacrae*. In one passage he links the names of Ray and Boyle with those of contemporary workers as he deals with a constantly recurring idea of the period, that of spontaneous generation. Stillingfleet writes, 'some of our most diligent enquirers, after all their searches, declare that they can find no such thing as a spontaneous generation of animals; and I remember I have formerly read a discourse in manuscript of Mr. Boyle's to that purpose. Our ingenious and learned Mr. Ray postively affirms, that there is no such thing in nature, as equivocal or spontaneous generation, but that all animals as well small as great, are generated by animal parents of the same species with themselves. And because some were offended at it, he goes about to justify his assertion, not only from reason, but from the authority of Malpighius as well as Redi, Swammerdam, and Lewenhoek, and many others, who have examined this matter carefully and circumspectly; and

1. *Ib.* Vol. I, p. 163.
2. *Life of Tillotson*, T. Birch, p. cxxvii.

therefore their authority sways more with him, than the concurrent suffrages of a thousand others; as he saith'.[1]

The point at issue here is that Stillingfleet has employed the new philosophy in this particular instance to support the contention that neither animals nor men appeared first by accident or by spontaneous generation. Even the structure of the lowest forms of life and their adaptation to their environment show purpose, a work of design, and the same is shown by the complex nature of the human frame.

Origines Sacrae is designed to be a 'rational account of the grounds of natural and revealed religion' which has as its purpose the establishing of the basic truths of religion and 'the authority of the Scriptures', and is a lengthy treatment of the subject. It is clear from Stillingfleet's preface that circumstances are presenting the old question of authority in a new form. Hooker had to show at the beginning of the century that the source of authority was not simply the Bible, as the Puritans held, but law in all its forms. Stillingfleet has to show at the end of the century that the Bible itself is a valid source of authority, and he sets himself in *Origines Sacrae* to reply to three contemporary arguments: 'the irreconcilableness of the account of times in Scripture, with that of the learned and ancient heathen nations; the inconsistency of the belief of the Scriptures with the principles of reason; and the account which may be given of the origin of things from principles of philosophy without the Scriptures'.[2]

Accordingly, the work is divided into three books, the first of which is concerned with the uncertainty and defects of history and chronology among different nations. The second book attempts to show 'the certainty of the writings of Moses', and 'the fidelity of the prophets succeeding Moses',[3] and the third contains an examination of certain basic ideas and of the origin of the universe.

Stillingfleet's view of man as first created is surprisingly not modern at all, but is practically identical with the traditional view as expressed, for instance, by Aquinas. No clearer indication could be given of the transitional nature of thinking generally at this time. Stillingfleet, like the other Latitudinarians, was interested in the new philosophy, and discerned something of its implications

1. *Origines Sacrae*, Bk. I, Chap. I.
2. *Origines Sacrae* (1701 ed.), Preface.
3. *Ib.* Bk. II, Chap. I, Chap. IV.

for the subject but the time seemed largely unaware of the degree of its own involvement with the past. When this is lost sight of, the result is a defective estimate of the Latitudinarians. Because they were in step with some contemporary developments, too much was expected of them, and their tacit acceptance of older ideas was not generally recognised.

Stillingfleet regarded man as having been created at first in a condition of perfection, in the image of God, as the book of Genesis puts it, so that he was, as it were, the reflection of the Divine 'on a dark cloud'. Nor was there then a great difference 'between the angelical and human life', for the one occupied 'the upper room in heaven' and the other 'the summer parlour in paradise'. He was created with a clear and distinct knowledge of his Creator, which was necessary, writes Stillingfleet, seeing that the end and purpose of the creature was 'to enjoy converse' with his Creator. This knowledge was 'more intellectual than discursive',[1] something intuitive and proper to his condition. He had also, by virtue of his superior postion 'a particular knowledge of the nature, being and properties of those things which he was to make use of, without which he could not have improved them for their peculiar ends. And from this knowledge did proceed the giving the creatures those proper and peculiar names which were expressive of their several natures'.[2] Because man was to be 'the standard and measure of all that followed, and therefore could not want anything of the due perfections of human nature', it followed that his knowledge should be of this kind.

Aquinas, describing man as created in the Divine image, also uses the word 'reflection': 'Where there is an image there is not necessarily equality, as we see in a person's image reflected in a glass'.[3] Stillingfleet adds, 'the similitude was the same, but the substance different'.[4] It was Aquinas's view that man at the first 'had a more excellent mode of knowledge regarding the angels than we possess, because his knowledge of intelligible things within him was more certain and fixed than our knowledge'.[5] Similarly, 'there was no need for the first man to attain to the knowledge of God by demonstration drawn from an effect, such as we need; since he

1. *Ib.* Bk. I, Chap. I, II.
2. *Ib.* Bk. I, Chap. I, III.
3. *Summa Theologica*, Pt. I, Q. XCIII, Art. I.
4. *Origines Sacrae*, Bk. I, Chap. I, II.
5. *Summa Theologica*, Pt. I, Q. XCIV, Art. 2.

knew God simultaneously in His effects'.[1] As to particular knowledge, Aquinas writes that 'the first man was . . . established in a
perfect state to instruct and govern others. Now no one can
instruct others unless he has knowledge, and so the first man was
established by God in such a manner as to have knowledge of all
those things for which man has a natural aptitude'.[2] In support
of this, he points out, as did Stillingfleet who quotes Plato to that
effect, that man named the animals and therefore knew their
natures, since 'names should be adapted to the nature of things'.[3]

The closeness of the parallel needs no emphasising, but when it
is seen that Stillingfleet, who was a member of the Royal Society
and who wrote on Descartes, regarded some matters in exactly
the same way as did Aquinas, a clearer estimate of Latitudinarianism is possible. It also extends in an unexpected direction
the area of information concerning the use made of the *Summa
Theologica* by seventeenth-century Anglicanism. Hardly enough
attention has been paid to the effect of this on theological method
during the period, and yet it is clear that many writers were well
acquainted with it. Sanderson made use of it, and Hooker's
Ecclesiastical Polity ensured that the characteristic aspects of its
thinking, mediated through a book the influence of which grew
with the passage of time, became widely current. It predisposed
Anglican writers to think in terms of reason and law, and may
therefore be accounted a determining factor in the resistance to
the system of Calvinism which discounted these elements. Just as
the *Summa Theologica* provided the basis for Hooker's writing on
law, so it gave Sanderson the framework for his views on human
acts and even furnished some illustrations, and at the end of the
century certain elements in it are met with in the books of
Stillingfleet and Tillotson. Even the contact with the Latitudinarians
is not so surprising seeing that Aquinas looked for a synthesis of
faith and reason.

While accepting the traditional view, which, he holds, explains
mankind's present condition.[4] Stillingfleet regards it as probable
that the flood was 'only over those parts where mankind inhabited'.[5]
This would account for the fact that there are animals in other
lands such as America, 'which have left no remainders of themselves in these parts of the world', and which in any event 'cannot

1. *Ib.* Art. I.   2. *Ib.* Q. XCIV, Art. 3.   3. *Ib.*
4. loc. cit. Bk. III, Chap. IV, I.   5. *Ib.* Bk. III, Chap. IV, IV.

live out of that particular clime wherein they are'.[1] Shrewd as this conjecture may be, his general attitude is that of attempting to justify as reasonable the details of the traditional account, as when he takes the supposition of 'the flood to have been over the whole globe of the earth',[2] and endeavours to show its possibility by calculations.

There is a passage in More's *Apology*, published in 1664, which bears on the same question, and the comparison is interesting. More agrees that the account of the creation is to be accepted, but suggests that in some respects it is adapted to the capacity of the hearer, and he questions the advisability of pressing 'the certainty thereof in every passage to men of more philosophical genius', even when a man is personally convinced of 'the historical truth of the symbols'. As to the details, some 'very sober and well-approved writers have affirmed some of them parabolical', and he instances the treatment of the serpent, the creation of Eve and the naming of the animals by some of the fathers such as Tertullian and by some later writers like Cajetan. In addition, 'Philo and other Jews, make several passages of these chapters parabolical', and it would be 'indiscreet . . . to avow to a philosopher that they are all of them really historical'[3] whatever a man may think of the matter himself.

It may be largely a difference of emphasis, for the attitude of the period was at all levels more or less literalist, but the fact in the foreground is that Stillingfleet's concern with historicity is but another aspect of the Latitudinarian concern with establishing the authority of Scripture. They wished to show that while what was revealed did not depend on reason, it was supported by it. Accordingly, Stillingfleet, having shown the defects of ancient history, turns to the 'credibility and certainty of that account which is given in Scripture'.[4]

In the first place, 'it stands to the greatest reason' that an account of things of such importance should not be left to the uncertainties of oral tradition, but should be preserved for posterity.[5] In the second place, there are as good guarantees 'that Moses was the author of the records going under his name' as there are of any facts of similar antiquity.[6] In support of this are the universal consent of those best qualified to know and 'the settling of a

---

1. *Ib.*
2. *Ib.* Bk. III, Chap. IV, V.
3. *Apology*, Chap. I, 9.
4. *Ib.* Bk. II, Chap. I, I.
5. *Ib.*
6. *Ib.* Bk. II, Chap. I, II.

commonwealth' upon his laws.[1] But the decisive proof for Stillingfleet is in miracles which he regards as the chief evidence confirming
what is revealed.[2] His argument is that only the 'power which
produced them' can 'alter the series of things', and whenever such
a power appears it authenticates 'the person who enjoys it. And
this is that which is most evident in the actions of Moses'.[3] In the
same way, miracles were 'necessary for confirming the truth of the
Gospel ... because the Gospel was to be propagated over the
world without any other rational evidence than was contained in
the miracles wrought for the confirmation of it'.[4]

Although the Latitudinarians saw it as part of their work to
maintain what they had learned, that 'that is not revealed which is
not made intelligible', they held that 'the immediate dictates of
natural light are no sufficient standard to judge of Divine revelation
by'.[5] That this is no merely formal concession to contemporary
orthodoxy is clear from Stillingfleet's argument, and from the fact
that he sees no 'contrariety between the foundation of faith and
knowledge'. He holds that 'both of them proceed on the same
foundation of certainty; all the difference is, faith fixeth on the
veracity of God immediately in reference to a Divine testimony;
knowledge proceeds upon it, supposing no Divine revelation as to
the things it doth discover'.[6]

References occur to the work of More, Boyle, Hobbes and
Descartes, and Stillingfleet outlines his position with regard to the
new philosophy. He writes that 'it cannot be denied by any
ingenuous man, that in our age a great improvement hath been
made in natural and experimental philosophy. But there is a great
difference to be made between those who have proceeded in the
way of experiments, which do great service as they go, and such as
have formed mechanical theories of the system of the universe'.[7]
It is evident that a better knowledge of nature has been the result,
and if certain qualities of bodies can be explained mechanically,
he can see no objection to this and agrees with Boyle's statement
of the case, which he sets out.[8] What he does not accept is the
independence of matter, the forming of phenomena by mechanical

1. *Ib.* Chap. I, IV.
2. *Ib.* Bk. II, Chap. III, III.
3. *Ib.* Bk. II, Chap. III, II.
4. *Ib.* Bk. II, Chap. IX, IX.
5. *Ib.* Bk. II, Chap. V, V.
6. *Ib.* Bk. II, Chap. VIII, IV.
7. *Origines Sacrae*, described as *Part of another book upon the same subject, written A.D. 1697. Published from the author's own manuscript*, and included in the 1702 ed. Bk. I, Chap. II, II.
8. *Ib.*

laws of motion, and like More and Cudworth he holds that
Descartes' explanation leads to materialism.[1] Nevertheless,
though he is critical of some aspects of Descartes' ideas, Stillingfleet points out that 'this great improver and discoverer of the
mechanical power of matter' supports More's view that matter is
not a self-moving principle.[2] He examines Descartes' work very
closely, and suggests that the identification of matter and extension
was the fundamental mistake of Descartes. He agrees with Du
Hamel that Descartes 'being a great mathematician, endeavoured
to reduce nature to geometry, and so considered nothing in body
but extension'. He notes that 'his mathematical notions ran so much
in his mind, that his endeavour to accommodate them to the nature
of things, was that which led him into such inextricable difficulties'.[3] Stillingfleet, among the Latitudinarians, shows most
clearly the influence of More by his interest in this aspect of contemporary thinking.

The fundamental awkwardness of the situation for Latitudinarianism appears where its greatest effort at reconciliation is made.
Confronted with the new movement in science and philosophy
with which they were in sympathy, they attempted not only to
assimilate fresh ideas, which was courageous and sensible, but
they attempted to reconcile them to a literalism on which they
mistakenly thought the authority of the Bible to depend. Thus,
side by side with philosophical analysis is found the statement that
mankind is derived from Adam, and that to suppose the contrary
is 'an introduction to atheism',[4] so that it is as a holding operation
that their attempt was of service in a time of considerable change.
Stillingfleet concludes by stating that, having examined 'all those
passages . . . which concern the history of the first ages of the
world',[5] it remains to consider the main purpose, 'the gradual
revelation of Himself to His people'.[6] Stillingfleet describes this as
a record of 'memorable transactions',[7] an account of the new covenant of grace made with man. Like Tillotson, he stresses practice
and 'the whole duty of man',[8] and as does Hales, he lays emphasis on
Scripture as revealing man to himself.[9] It is clear and authoritative,

---

1. *Ib.*
2. loc. cit. Bk. III, Chap. II, XVIII
3. *Ib. Origines Sacrae* (the second book),
   Bk. I, Chap. II, II.
4. loc. cit. Bk. III, Chap. IV, I, II.
5. *Ib.* Bk. III, Chap. VI, I.
6. *Ib.* Bk. III, Chap. VI, IV.
7. *Ib.* BK. III, Chap. VI, X.
8. *Ib.*
9. *Ib.* Bk. III, Chap. VI, VI.

and it resembles a telescope in that it discovers things 'of highest concernment' to men, and, like a microscope, it reveals to them 'the smallest atom' of their thoughts.[1]

Burnet says that Tillotson, Stillingfleet and Patrick 'read Episcopius much',[2] and it is possible to see traces of this influence in Stillingfleet's assertion that the Incarnation is the 'greatest expression of love' and is 'above all other discoveries of God's goodness'.[3] It was Episcopius's emphasis on this which Hales recorded as having a decisive effect in changing his own ideas. Momentarily, there breaks surface in the writing of Stillingfleet a suggestion of More or Smith.

Stillingfleet's method resolves itself into a kind of liberal conservatism, by means of which he makes a sustained effort to achieve a synthesis, and allowing for the stage of development in science and criticism, it conveyed the impression that new movements of thought were not detrimental to religion when the due claims of reason were met, and that authority was not impaired by allowing a proper freedom of manoeuvre to reason.

The presentation of his material, being naturally controlled by the design of a book intended to deal with the contemporary problems referred to in the preface, tends in consequence to be concerned largely with matters of reason and nature. Yet Stillingfleet gives expression to the sense of the uniqueness of Scripture, to its 'peculiar excellency'[4] as compared with other sources, to its 'depth and mysteriousness',[5] to its superiority to the works of philosophy which are 'jejune and unsatisfactory'[6] by comparison.

Compelled by contemporary requirements to concentrate on certain things, and convinced themselves of the necessity for stating the position in certain terms, the Latitudinarians were placed at a disadvantage by these conditions which tended to confine their work to a limited area. Within that area, the Latitudinarians made a real contribution to stability at a time when the fluidity of the situation and the existence of conflicting elements was becoming disquietingly apparent. The fact that, in *Irenicum* published in 1662, Stillingfleet treated of 'the particular forms of

1. *Ib*. Bk. III, Chap. VI, VIII.
2. G. Burnet, *History of His Own Time*, Vol. I, p. 324.
3. *Origines Sacrae*, Bk. III, Chap. VI, IV.
4. *Ib*. Bk. III, Chap. IV, X.
5. *Ib*. Bk. III, Chap. IV, VII.
6. *Ib*. Bk. III, Chap. IV, IV.

church-government' partly from the point of view of the law of nature is indicative of how far this kind of approach had taken hold.

Stillingfleet died in the last year of the century, having been made a bishop of Worcester ten years previously, and Tillotson predeceased him by five years as Archbishop of Canterbury. Burnet records Tillotson's great uneasiness and reluctance to accept, and comments that, at the time, instead of seeking preferment, 'men were sought after'.[1] He regarded Tillotson as 'the best preacher of the age', and notes that his generosity was such that he died poor.[2] Many would have wished Stillingfleet to succeed him, but because of his indifferent health, Tenison, with 'a more active temper', was chosen instead. [3]

Referring to the connection between the Latitudinarians and the Cambridge Platonists, Burnet writes, 'the most eminent of those who were formed under those great men were Tillotson, Stillingfleet and Patrick'. They were moderate men who 'continued to keep a good correspondence with those who had differed from them in opinion, and allowed a great freedom both in philosophy and divinity; from whence they were called men of latitude'. He adds that 'the making out the reasons of things being a main part of their studies, their enemies called them Socinians'. Tillotson had given the same reason for this being said of Chillingworth, and, doubtless the friendship of Tillotson and others with such as Thomas Firmin was a contributory factor, and another could be found in their views on toleration. In fact, there were no grounds for the suggestion as their writings show, and both Tillotson and Tenison made this clear. Burnet goes on to emphasise their loyalty to the constitution and liturgy of the Church, 'but they did not think it unlawful to live under another form'.[4]

The chief influence on the Latitudinarians, according to Burnet, was from Whichcote, Cudworth, Wilkins, More and Worthington. It is curious that he does not mention Smith who influenced himself, and it is of special interest that he includes Wilkins, whom he describes as 'a great observer and a promoter of experimental philosophy'. He notes the reaction of the Cambridge Platonists

1. G. Burnet, *History of His Own Time* (1734 ed. T. Burnet), Vol. II, p. 44.

2. *Ib.* p. 79.
3. *Ib.* p. 80.
4. *Ib.*

from 'the dry systematical way', and the way in which they introduced students to Plato, Tully and Plotinus.[1]

Burnet's reference to Episcopius points to another source, and
the correspondence between Limborch and More and Cudworth,
and later, with Tillotson, Stillingfleet, and Lloyd, also reveals
contact with the Arminians. Burnet himself visited Holland, and
writes of the reasonable and moderate views of the Remonstrants.[2]

His own Latitudinarianism came from the same influences, but
at second hand from an unexpected quarter through 'Mr. Nairn,
minister of the Abbey Church at Edinburgh', who 'led him . . .
into a new course of reading, by recommending to his perusal
Smith's Select Discourses, Dr. More's works, and the writings
of Plato and his followers: but no book pleased him more than
Hooker's *Ecclesiastical Polity*, from the principles of which he
never departed'.[3]

There is a distinct continuity increasingly confirmed, and the
various interconnections of Cambridge Platonists, Latitudinarians,
Arminians and the new philosophy, show clearly the evolving
pattern of a liberal method in theology, and the recurring influence
of Hooker is significant.

1. *Ib.*
2. *Ib.*

3. Life of the Author, by the Editor,
   Thomas Burnet (*History of His
   Own Time*, 1734), p. 4.

CHAPTER VI

THE LATITUDINARIANS (*continued*)

IT IS noticeable that the connections between the various writers at this time were not simply by way of the influence of their writings upon one another, but also through personal contact, as the references in the letters of Worthington show. It accounts for a type of inner similarity which is more than verbal, and amounts to the transmission and sharing of an outlook.

Burnet came to Cambridge a couple of years after the Restoration, when the political situation was beginning to be stabilised, and he met More, Cudworth, Whichcote and Wilkins. Smith, whose works had played a part in forming Burnet's ideas, was no longer alive, but Burnet made the acquaintance of Tillotson, Stillingfleet, Patrick, and Lloyd. His association with Tillotson began at this time, and he further emphasises the extent of this type of personal contact by noting the influence of Wilkins on Tillotson, who wrote an introduction to a posthumous collection of Wilkins's sermons.

Burnet regarded Simon Patrick as sharing with Tillotson and Stillingfleet the position of being the foremost among those who were influenced by the Cambridge Platonists, and certainly Patrick's work has significance in itself.

He did not share Tillotson's acknowledged place, nor did he come to be regarded, like Stillingfleet, as a thinker, but his numerous works represent the appearance of an undifferentiated Anglicanism, a central position in which the characteristic aspects of the Latitudinarian movement are integrated into Churchmanship. His literary output included not only more specifically theological work, but also devotional writings and a number of commentaries on books of the Old Testament. Up to the middle of the nineteenth century there appears to have been a demand for the latter, for Taylor notes that some of them are 'accessible to the public in a popular and serviceable form'.[1] It is clear from the titles of such works as the *Treatise on the Necessity and Frequency of Receiving the Holy Communion*, or the *Discourse concerning Prayer: Especially of frequenting the daily Public Prayers*, not to mention

1. *Works of S. Patrick* (ed. A. Taylor, 1858), Vol. I, Preface, p. lii.

others, that Patrick's thought moves naturally within the setting of the liturgy of the Church. It is not that Tillotson and Stillingfleet neglected to deal with such matters, but that Patrick seems more involved in the day-to-day actuality of its realised corporateness. His liberality lays equal stress on reason, but his work shows a heightened awareness of the implications of the living quality of membership. In his works there clearly emerges the traditional Anglicanism, conscious of the corporate aspect, historically-minded, conservative as to formularies, liberal in its attitude to contemporary advances, confident of its doctrinal presuppositions, but with a certain insularity which became a general outlook, having selectively absorbed the chief characteristics of the Cambridge Platonists and of those who followed them.

Patrick was rector of St. Paul's, Covent Garden, and later became Dean of Peterborough, being subsequently appointed Bishop of Chichester and then of Ely. During his long life-time his literary industry was very considerable, and with Tenison, he took an active part in founding charity schools. At the time of the plague he remained in his parish, and he records the kindness shown to him by the people because of his action in staying with them.[1] His story is told in an easy and pleasing style, with a good deal of biographical detail, which reveals the influences that formed his ideas.

His grandfather had been in easy circumstances, and had a taste for learning,[2] which his father also had.[3] His father's favourite reading was Sanderson,[4] and that of his mother was Lewis Bayly's *Practice of Piety*,[5] a book which had circulated very widely in the seventeenth century, and had been translated into several languages. Its approach was practical and detailed, and its simplicity and emphasis on the observances of the Prayer Book system had an effect on Patrick's writings. His unfavourable reaction as a boy to a sermon on reprobation indicated his future outlook which appears to have owed much to Smith who had transferred to Queen's College, Cambridge, in 1644, the year when Patrick entered the same College.[6] For him Patrick had 'a profound reverence',[7] and he was later to preach at Smith's funeral.

1. *A Brief Account of my Life, Works*, Vol. IX, p. 446.
2. *Ib*. p. 407.
3. *Ib*. p. 409.
4. *Ib*. p. 410.
5. *Ib*. p. 409.
6. *Ib*. p. 410.
7. *Ib*. p. 423.

He had applied to Whichcote and Cudworth to be taken as a sizar, having been recommended to them as his father was too poor to maintain him at the University. They received him with kindness, but being unable to take him themselves, arranged for him to go to Queen's College.[1] He received Presbyterian ordination, but on reading Hammond's work on Ignatius's epistles and Thorndike's *Primitive Government of the Church*, he decided to seek episcopal ordination from Bishop Hall, who ordained him 'in his own parlour at Higham about a mile from Norwich, April 5th 1654'.[2] Enquiry has shown that many others were similarly influenced.[3]

From the outset it is evident that two types of influence, that of the Cambridge Platonists and that of the Laudians, produced in Patrick an outlook in which freedom of reason and a consciousness of the Church were combined. This fusion appears, without any sense of strain and, as it were, incidentally, in the *Friendly Debate* and in the *Brief Account*,[4] for there seems to be no reason to doubt that S.P. of Cambridge is Patrick. Since it was Bishop Hall who ordained him, there may well be confirmatory evidence of authorship in a reference[5] contained in the *Brief Account* to an action by the authorities then in power in the University. They were reputed to have obtained a list of all who had been ordained secretly by the Bishop of Norwich with a view to stemming the rise of Arminianism. The reference in a booklet designed for wide circulation is sufficiently local to point in this direction when all the circumstances are taken into account.

These influences in maturity were joined with the influence of a home in which Sanderson, a moderate associate of such as Hammond and Sheldon, both of whom combined Laudian views with strong advocacy of the claims of reason, was read and the solid Anglicanism of Bayly was taken for granted, and resulted in a strong central position for Patrick.

The *Brief Account* takes the form of a letter in reply to a friend who writes that everywhere he hears of 'a certain new sect of men called Latitude-men' but that he cannot ascertain 'the explicit meaning' of the term, and that he can find 'nothing distinct

1. *Ib.* p. 413.   2. *Ib.* p. 423.
3. R. S. Bosher, *The Making of the Restoration Settlement*, p. 38.
4. *A Friendly Debate betwixt Two Neighbours, The one a Conformist and the other a Non-Conformist* (1668). *A Brief Account of the New Sect of Latitude-men: Together with some Reflections upon the New Philosophy* (1662).
5. *Brief Account*, 3.

concerning them, but that they had their rise at Cambridge, and are followers for the most part of the new philosophy'.

Those here referred to, writes Patrick in reply, were at the University during the Commonwealth period, and were under the disapproval of the University authorities both because 'they were generally ordained by bishops', and because they were opposed to 'the hide-bound spirit . . . that did then prevail', and this was the origin of the term.[1]

The *Brief Account* begins by making it clear that, as far as the Latitudinarians are concerned, there is no question of deviation from accepted standards in liturgy, church government or formularies. 'Our Latitudinarians therefore are by all means for a liturgy, and do prefer that of our own Church before all others', and their appreciation of it is such 'that they would be loth to adventure the mending of it, for fear of marring it'. With regard to rites and ceremonies, they prefer 'virtuous mediocrity' to extremes, and they consider the government of the Church to be not only the best in itself but the same as was practised in apostolic times. Their adherence to the teaching of the Church includes not only acceptance of the Creeds and the Thirty-nine Articles but also approval of the Homilies, and this agreement is general. They do not however accept the idea of 'absolute reprobation . . . which they do not think themselves bound to believe'.[2] It is in no way strange that they should find themselves in full accord with the position of the Church, since the source of their views is the same —not the Schoolmen, or 'Dutch systematics', or the Council of Trent, or the Synod of Dort, but 'the writings of the apostles and evangelists, in interpreting whereof, they carefully attend to the sense of the ancient Church, by which they conceive the modern ought to be guided: and therefore they are very conversant in all the genuine monuments of the ancient fathers, those especially of the first and purest ages'.[3]

This is the position found elsewhere in Patrick's writings, a position which was established through the works of Hooker and Andrewes and the controversies of their times, and through subsequent developments, and it is not inapposite to note its statement by a Latitudinarian. It possesses all the features of what later came to be regarded as the classical expression of Anglicanism. While it did not allow sufficiently for the difficulties inherent in the

1. *Ib.* 3.   2. *Ib.* 4.   3. *Ib.* 5.

appeal to antiquity, it was based on the view that Scripture and the
first five centuries constituted a standard of reference, a view which
the work of Andrewes had done much to make normative for
Anglicanism. It regarded this as the basis in which reason had a
place: 'Let no man accuse them of hearkening too much to their
own reason, since their reason steers by so excellent a compass, the
ancient fathers and councils of the Church'.[1] Defining reason as the
faculty by which judgments are made concerning everything,
Patrick affirms that things cannot be believed unless there be a
reason, which may be 'a deduction from the light of nature, and
those principles which are the candle of the Lord', or revelation in
Scripture, or 'the general interpretation of genuine antiquity, or
the proposals of our own Church consentaneous thereto, or lastly
the result of some or all of these'. Right use of reason implies taking
'all that is reasonable into consideration', and similar conclusions
are found to result from these several principles, for 'there is an
eternal consanguinity between all verity: and nothing is true in
divinity, which is false in philosophy, or on the contrary'. There is
here a deliberate integrating of some characteristic aspects of
Cambridge Platonism with something wider, namely, the active
acceptance of the implications of the historicity of the Church for
theological method: 'nor is there any point in divinity, where that
which is most ancient doth not prove the most rational'.[2]

As to the views of the Latitudinarians concerning the new philosophy, 'it cannot be denied, that they have introduced a new
philosophy; Aristotle and the Schoolmen are out of request with
them'.[3] He adds that it is true 'that ipse dixit is an argument much
out of fashion', a phrase echoed by Fowler, who similarly lays
emphasis on their adherence to the accepted standard, although
he comments more acutely on the uncertainties involved in referring to ancient writers. Patrick considers that it is the task of philosophy to explain the workings of natural processes. These have
been studied in animal anatomy, and by Descartes in respect of
'that vast machine, the universe'.[4] He writes, 'this farther I shall
add, in the behalf of new and free philosophy, that the theatre of
nature is much enlarged since Aristotle's time', as, for example, by
the invention of the telescope, which has shown the existence of
stars previously unknown[5]. Further knowledge about natural

1. *Ib.* 5.   3. *Ib.* 6.
2. *Ib.* 5.   4. *Ib.* 11.   5. *Ib.* 12.

processes has come through such experiments as those of Boyle,[1] through the improvement of anatomy, and through discoveries such as that of Harvey concerning the circulation of the blood[2] Patrick is aware of the implications of this for theological method: 'But methinks I hear some men say, all innovations are dangerous; philosophy and divinity are so interwoven by the Schoolmen, that it cannot be safe to separate them; new philosophy will bring in new divinity, and freedom in the one will make men desire a liberty in the other'. This argument had carried weight with the University authorities in the Commonwealth period, and 'the new philosophy was interdicted in some Colleges on that account. But what was the event? It was so much the more eagerly studied and embraced'.[3]

So great is the desire for knowledge that he concludes that it would be as easy to stop the tide as to prevent the spread of free philosophy, and he expresses the conviction common to all who shared his views, that 'true philosophy can never hurt sound divinity'.[4] The *Friendly Debate* is a discussion in which a conformist and a non-conformist contrast Anglicanism, with its nexus of Scripture, reason and tradition, and contemporary non-conformity, which at its best was a religion of Scripture interpreting, and interpreted by experience. The *Friendly Debate*, however, reveals that to either side, as so frequently happens, it is not the whole picture of the other side which is always communicated. The result is that for the non-conformist, it is the rational and practical element in Anglicanism which predominates, while to the conformist it seems not so much to be Scripture and experience which are in question, as a particular interpretation of Scripture, and a view of experience which confines it to the feelings. The non-conformist observes 'ours move my affections very much, and yours stir them not at all'.[5] Patrick, as his works show, does not attempt to exclude the emotions from the picture, but with treating them as a criterion in religion he does not agree. He holds that it leads to a disregard for 'sober and plain doctrine' which plainly sets out the two duties, and to concern with mysteries, speculations, and preoccupation with phrases and ideas which do not 'meddle' with reality.[6] The working ideas of Anglicanism, as

1. *Ib.* 13.
2. *Ib.* 14.
3. *Ib.* 16.
4. *Ib.* 16.

5. *A Friendly Debate*, *Works*, Vol. V, p. 277.
6. *Ib.* pp. 293, 295, Part II, p. 559.

stressed by the Cambridge Platonists and the Latitudinarians, reason, practical obedience, and faith working through charity, are emphasised by Patrick.

The non-conformist refers to the conformist's clergyman as 'a man of reason', and observes that he expounds Scripture not in 'a spiritual way, but only rationally'.[1] His own clergyman's sermons are nothing but Scripture, 'whereas yours are but rational discourses',[2] with which he contrasts the 'experimental' method, or way of experience.[3] The conformist enquires whether spiritual and rational are opposites,[4] and he maintains that this way of thinking involves a dangerously inadequate evaluation of the practical side of things.[5] The reply to this is that 'insisting so much upon good works is legal',[6] and the same applies to the constant reference to obedience, a favourite term with the Cambridge Platonists and the Latitudinarians.[7] The conformist answers that the faith which justifies 'is not an idle ineffectual faith . . . but that which works by love'.[8]

Patrick instances the experience of Bradshaw when people would not be satisfied with his solution of their difficulties unless he gave them Scriptural authority, a position familiar to Hooker, whom he quotes to show the needless perplexities that arise 'if the light of reason be suppressed'.[9]

Patrick's *Discourse about Tradition* is a further illustration of his central postion. Tradition means 'the matter which is delivered . . . either by writing or by word of mouth', and in this sense, Scripture is tradition, but ordinary usage now implies by it what has anciently been delivered by word of mouth or by other writings not possessing the same authority.[10] There are four considerations in assessing the value of such traditions, where they come from, their content, their authority, and the means there are of ascertaining whether they are what they claim to be.[11] As to where they originate, there are only four allowable sources, 'either from Christ, or from the apostles, or from the Church (either in general, or in part), or from private doctors in the Church'.[12]

It is accepted that Scripture was 'once unwritten', and therefore

1. *Ib.* p. 271.
2. *Ib.* p. 272.
3. *Ib.* p. 299.
4. *Ib.* p. 272.
5. *Ib.* p. 294.
6. *Ib.* p. 276.
7. *Ib.* p. 296.
8. *Ib.* p. 277.
9. *Ib.* Part II, p. 567.
10. *Works*, Vol. VI, p. 474.
11. *Ib.* p. 424.
12. *Ib.* p. 425.

was once tradition in the current sense,[1] and also that the Church preserved and delivered the Scriptures.[2] It is also agreed that 'the sum and substance' of what they contain has from the earliest times been delivered in other ways, as in the creeds, and in the services of the Church.[3] These may be referred to as traditions, but they are simply abridgements of what was delivered, and they add nothing new. There is also the unanimous tradition of the Church in all ages determining the meaning and sense of Scripture, but this adds nothing new and is in the nature of an unfolding and an explanation,[4] and the same may be said of the decrees of the first four general councils.[5] In addition, tradition is of assistance in points not specifically contained in Scripture, but which may be deduced from it.[6] When it may be seen that there has always been universal consent to something that may be proved from Scripture, though it may not be expressly stated in it, this may be accepted as 'confirming tradition', instances of which are infant baptism and the assertion of the authority of bishops over presbyters by divine right, which are confirmed by the perpetual practice and tradition from the beginning.[7] Whatever is not derivable from these sources may not be regarded as part of what was delivered, but some things which have been universally believed, not being contrary to Scripture, although they are not contained in it or to be deduced from it, may be taken as allowable opinions on the grounds of probability and general acceptance.

Traditions about rites and ceremonies are likewise accepted, but are alterable by the authority which instituted them.[8] As to individuals and particular Churches, their authority is their own so that its acceptance is limited by preference and other conditions.[9]

The position then is that the Church does not refuse to accept something as not being delivered because it is unwritten, but rather that it questions the nature and extent of the authority which so delivers it.[10] This is the basis of the refusal to accept as tradition anything that adds to the necessary articles of faith originally delivered.[11] It is another aspect of the question of authority, consistently treated, and showing signs of that growing

1. *Ib.* p. 478.
2. *Ib.* p. 481.
3. *Ib.* p. 484.
4. *Ib.* p. 484.
5. *Ib.* p. 487.
6. *Ib.* p. 487.

7. *Ib.* p. 488.
8. *Ib.* p. 489.
9. *Ib.* p. 490.
10. *Ib.* p. 490.
11. *Ib.* p. 496.

awareness of need for a critical handling of evidence, as when Patrick comments on the way in which 'so great a man as Thomas Aquinas' was misled into using as confirmatory various passages in ancient writers which in fact were not part of the original.[1]

The more typical aspects of Latitudinarianism are also found in Patrick's writings, for he is in full agreement with the general outlook of Tillotson and Stillingfleet, but for him the centre of interest is not the same. He writes that faith is 'the highest improvement' of reason and elevates the understanding,[2] and that the light of nature as well as Scripture shows the existence of fundamental laws 'engraven upon the tables' of human nature.[3] There can be seen 'some faint imitation of reason and discourse' in animals, but no sign of any 'sense of religion', and he modifies the accepted definition and describes man as a 'rational, religious creature'.[4] In his works, as compared with those of Tillotson and Stillingfleet, the reasonableness of natural religion and its completion in what has been revealed tends more to be taken for granted. His acquaintance with Aquinas is not inconsiderable, as can be seen in his discussion of several doctrinal questions.[5]

Patrick enters the eighteenth century with a fuller statement of Anglicanism than was made by the more prominent Latitudinarians, in that the general position in regard to reason and the new philosophy is assumed as part of the basis of a Churchmanship in which this liberality of outlook is blended with an active awareness of the Church as the living embodiment of its own past. Antiquity is a standard of reference in the past, but it is also a continuing, formative element in the present.

The significance of Patrick's work for the development of theological method is that he combined the particular insights of the Latitudinarian movement with something of the earlier Laudians and of Taylor and Sanderson, and passed it on to become part of the later climate of opinion. The stolid outlook of the eighteenth century has been somewhat misrepresented, and the evidence goes to show that throughout the period an untroubled acceptance of the appeal to antiquity, of episcopacy and of the necessity of the approach to things through reason, was widespread. That this balance was preserved was due in no small

1. *Ib.* p. 429.
2. *Works*, Vol. II, p. 616.
3. *Ib.* Vol. V, p. 193.
4. *Ib.* Vol. IV, p. 706.
5. *Ib.* Vol. VII, pp. 103, 121.

measure to the work of the Latitudinarians, and to the fact that the outward expression of membership was through a liturgy, for the effect of the Prayer Book was not only to stabilise but to give depth and a sense of continuity as well as a quality of everyday vitality which a theological method cut off from such a living association inevitably loses.

Reflection suggests that the rapid and successful spread of Tractarian ideas in the 1830's could not have taken place in a vacuum. It would be of interest to endeavour to disentangle the contributions made by the Prayer Book and by a continuing theological method to this. The effect on theological ideas of a liturgy constantly used is very considerable, though for the large part un-noticed. Most of the ideas canvassed by the Tractarians were to be found in the Book of Common Prayer, or were implicit in it, and had therefore passed into the minds of many over the years, and were, so to speak, latent until the Tractarian movement called them into activity. But it is also the case that the emphasis on antiquity and on the continuity of episcopacy never disappeared, and to this writers like Patrick made their contribution.

The emphasis on liberality and on maintaining contact with the movement of knowledge in other spheres found no answering echo until the end of the nineteenth century. Various factors contributed to this, not all of them theological. By the close of the eighteenth century, toleration was more or less an accepted fact, and the fluid situation obtaining between conformists and non-conformists in the years following the Restoration had been replaced by a situation in which these divergences had firmly set in the mould of denominational differences. The possibilities of drawing together again which had to some extent existed a century before were no longer inherent in a situation which had solidified, so that the general context of theological method was one in which everything seemed to have become immobilised. The idea of reason no longer appeared to have that strange vitalising quality it had momentarily possessed during the earlier period. It was no longer a candle lighted in the midst of the unfolding and uncertain human situation, and was concerned less with illumination than with demonstration. The same static condition was reflected elsewhere, and C. E. Raven referring to scientific studies has contrasted 'the amazing achievements of the seventeenth century' with 'the dullness and disappointment of the eighteenth',[1] He points out that the end of an epoch came by the second decade of the eighteenth century, and there was no one of the same calibre to succeed Ray, Willughby, Grew, Halley and others in the different subjects in which they had worked: 'the universities produced no one of any merit at all in the sciences and hardly anyone to be remembered in any field of scholarship'.[2] It was a period of systematisation and classification, and the absence of movement was more or less reflected in theology. The result, as far as the Evangelical and Tractarian movements were concerned, was that the aspect of theological method which the Cambridge Platonists and the Latitudinarians had emphasised was discounted in favour of what in the circumstances appeared more important. It was the movement of scientific thought which acted as a stimulus for theological method towards the end of the nineteenth century so that once again the necessary balance between its constituent parts was asserted. This is apparent from the reference in the preface to *Lux Mundi* to the need for bringing the creed 'into its right relation to the modern growth of knowledge, scientific, historical, critical', for 'reconciliation' with this new knowledge, which was perplexing and needed to be assimilated.[3] In an age of transformation, it is interpretation of what has been received that is required, so that theology can relate this to the new social and intellectual movements of each age, and this is its real development. The preface foresees 'great changes in the outlying departments of theology, where it is linked on to other sciences'.[4] One of the essays points out that contemporary treatment of various aspects of teleology has strengthened the evidence for design, in that the world is no longer regarded 'as a machine, but as an organism, a system in which, while the parts contribute to the growth of the whole, the whole also reacts upon the development of the parts'. Science has given a real as opposed to a notional 'apprehension of the manifold adaptations of stucture to function' and so provided a teleology more adequate than the mechanical view, and it is maintained that this has suggested to theology the need for a fresh appraisal of immanence.[5] As with the Cambridge Platonists, a similar situation produced the same effects.

Basically the Evangelical and Tractarian movements had much in

---

1. C. E. Raven, *Natural Religion and Christian Theology*, I, p. 145.
2. *Ib*. p. 151.
3. *Lux Mundi*, Preface (5th ed.).
4. *Ib*. Preface.
5. *Ib*. V.

common, for in different ways the doctrine of the Spirit was fundamental to them both. For the one, the terms of its statement were
conceived as being essentially corporate, and for the other, the
terms were individual and personal, but the distinction was a rough
and ready one and there was a good deal of overlapping. It was not
until the end of the nineteenth century that reason in its creative
and critical aspects was again seen to belong to this category, and
that Evangelical and Tractarian thinking on the Church and the
individual were incomplete without it. The Latitudinarians had
seen what the later movements had failed to appreciate, that the
Church did not exist in a vacuum, but in a changing world with
which it had to make contact. Tillotson, Stillingfleet and others
had established a tradition of co-operation, and Patrick had made
his own contribution. Tenison too had written on Scripture, tradition and reason, as constituting theological method, and actually
uses the word in the title of a booklet *The Difference betwixt the
Protestant and Socinian Methods*.[1]

He affirms that 'a man of this Church' considers Scripture in a
different way from those who make reason 'the rule of that rule'.
'Nothing contrary to true reason can be contained in the Scriptures'
and therefore what may appear incomprehensible is not so much
irrational as rational though mysterious. Tradition 'in concurrence with Scripture',[2] and also the early writings and councils are
component elements in this method.[3]

Seth Ward, who was one of the first Fellows of the Royal
Society, was characteristically Latitudinarian in many of his ideas,
and he shared with Barrow and Wilkins an interest in mathematics.
When he went to Sidney College, Cambridge, he found that the
study of mathematics was more or less in abeyance, and he applied
himself to the subject without any assistance. Although he was
ejected from Cambridge because he would not comply with the
Covenant, he had acquired sufficient distinction in this line of
study to be appointed to the Savilian Professorship at Oxford in
1648 through the influence of Sir John Trevor, a supporter of the
Parliament.

At the Restoration he was made Dean of Exeter, and shortly
afterwards became Bishop of Exeter, where he found the Bishop's
residence in a dilapidated condition and being used for trading
purposes, a situation which was to be repeated on his arrival at

1. 1687 ed.   2. *Ib.* p. 26.   3. *Ib.* p. 30.

Salisbury where he was appointed Bishop five years later. In 1674 he supported proposals for accommodation between conformists and nonconformists made by Tillotson and Stillingfleet. These proposals were more widely acceptable than those which had been put forward a few years earlier by Wilkins and Hale, being approved by Morley who had not favoured the latter.[1] Morley, who after the Restoration was second in influence only to Sheldon, was one of the leading Laudians, and R. S. Bosher has pointed out that most of the episcopal vacancies in 1661–2 were filled by members of this group.[2] Seth Ward's late affiliation with them was consistent with his earlier refusal of the Covenant, just as his support of proposals for accommodation in a form acceptable to Laudians like Morley was consistent with his general position. It is an indication of the way in which ideas now differentiated as Latitudinarian and Laudian could merge at certain points during the period. Patrick was a Latitudinarian, but his views on the apostolic succession were similar to those of Hammond who, in turn, laid emphasis on the rational aspect of theological method. It has been pointed out that the same is true of Burnet who was closely identified with Latitudinarian ideas and who wrote a *Vindication of the Orders of the Church of England*.[3]

As one who took an active part in the work of the Royal Society, Ward could counsel those who regarded themselves as being in the vanguard of new ideas to undergo the discipline of learning about experiment and demonstration.[4] If they understood this, they 'would not call for experiment in a subject uncapable of it', and they would find that to look for evidence of an experimental nature to establish propositions other than 'universal propositions in materia necessaria, whose contrary positions imply a contradiction', is injudicious and 'contrary to the reason of mankind'. He maintains that such a method is quite irrelevant and therefore cannot lead to any conclusion.[5]

Like Stillingfleet, he sees the necessity of establishing the authority of 'the original books of the canon of the Old and New Testament' in a situation where some accept the latter but not the

1. George Every, *The High Church Party 1688–1718*, p. 10.
2. R. S. Bosher, *The Making of the Restoration Settlement*, p. 183.
3. George Every, *The High Church Party 1688–1718*, p. 16.
4. *Six Sermons* (1672), p. 123.
5. *Ib.* p. 124.

former, and others accept matters of fact related in the New
Testament but do not look on it as constituting authority, while
others do not accept the facts or the authority.[1] He considers that
there is a completeness as between the Old and the New Testaments, for the later writers see the events which they record in
terms of fulfilment.[2] In common with the general Latitudinarian
position he maintains that acceptance of this authority is 'most
agreeable to reason'.[3] It is 'the fatal paradox' that while man's
'being consists in rationality', he acts contrary to it.[4]

There are references to the situation at the time of the Restoration, and he describes it as a characteristic of the Church now
restored that it adheres to 'obedience without base restrictions and
limitations',[5] and this is for him an essential part of the Anglican
spirit. He writes of the work of Hobbes[6] and of the two great
catastrophes of the fire and the plague.

On the question of the authority of the Old and New Testaments, his approach is typical in that he considers that it is necessary 'to have recourse to the original reason of things, and the
common grounds whereupon mankind doth proceed in matters of
this nature'. Authority is authenticated by reason and not by
conciliar decrees or edicts of state, and like Stillingfleet he is of the
opinion that the historical relation of matters of fact in the Bible
has 'far greater advantages than any other history', among ancient
records.[7]

That they were able to combine this emphasis on reason with a
practical outlook and an uncomplicated method, and often with a
better understanding of the Church and of the meaning of membership than that with which they have been credited, was the significant aspect of the work of the Latitudinarians. For if the negative
side is seen in the unwelcome approval of their attitude to reason
shown by their opponents, the positive side is seen in the way
in which they maintained that there was an accord between religion
and the new philosophy. These qualities together with their
simplicity of approach in religious questions and the plainness of
their preaching made them to be a considerable force in their own
time. It is also true that without their contribution theological

1. *Ib.* p. 85.
2. *Ib.* p. 88.
3. *Ib.* p. 126.
4. *Ib.* p. 350.

5. *Ib.* p. 78.
6. *Ib.* p. 180.
7. *Ib.* pp. 164–6.

method would have been less stable and the Church would have been less sure of the grounds of its position in the eighteenth century.

When Ward went to Exeter he was succeeded at St. Lawrence Jewry by Wilkins, who with the Cambridge Platonists, as Burnet noted, had helped to shape the ideas of Tillotson, Stillingfleet, Patrick and others. The connections were close and Tillotson was his son-in-law, at whose London house Wilkins died in 1672, and the sermon at the funeral was preached by William Lloyd, then Dean of Bangor.

Wilkins tends to be remembered by later generations as Cromwell's brother-in-law and as a supporter of the new philosophy whose works such as *The Discovery of a New World*, in which are discussed the possibilities of the moon being habitable and of its being reached from the earth, caught the imagination of the times. This aspect of his work and the part which he took in public affairs has altogether overshadowed the fact that both in respect of his own writings and his effect on the Latitudinarians, he occupied a significant place in the development of theological method in the seventeenth century.

The son of Walter Wilkins 'citizen and goldsmith of Oxford', he was born at Fawlsby near Daventry at the house of his maternal grandfather John Dod, a learned man.[1] Lloyd, who notes that Dod leaned to dissenting opinions in some things, conjectures that he influenced Wilkins,[2] for after taking his degree 'upon the breaking out of the civil war, he joined with the parliament, and took the solemn league and covenant'.[3] He was appointed Warden of Wadham College in 1648 and some eight years later he married Robina French, widow of a former canon of Christ Church and sister of Cromwell. The year before the Restoration he was made head of Trinity College, Cambridge, but at the Restoration he was removed from this position, and was appointed to St. Lawrence Jewry. About this time he became a member of the Royal Society, and was later made Dean of Ripon and subsequently Bishop of Chester. At his consecration in 1668 in the chapel of Ely House, Holborn, the sermon was preached by Tillotson.

1. *The Mathematical and Philosophical Works of the Rt. Revd. John Wilkins*, (1802), Vol. I, p. iii.
2. Sermon by William Lloyd, added to *The Principles and Duties of Natural Religion* (1675), p. 46.
3. *Works*, Vol. I, p. iv.

The author of the biography prefixed to the edition of the mathematical and philosophical writings considers that Wilkins regarded moderation as of the first importance. Those who looked on this as 'unsteady principles' did so because they were strangers to moderation themselves, and therefore he was not fairly represented by men like Sheldon, Fell and Dolben.[1] Nor did they understand that he would be naturally well-disposed to those who had not conformed because of his upbringing by his grandfather, who although opposed to extremism, sympathised with nonconformist views.[2] Wilkins was a complex individual and can hardly be disposed of adequately in summary terms. While he certainly subscribed to the Covenant and the Engagement, and was removed from his position in Cambridge at the Restoration, he continued consistently to advocate comprehension and accommodation when he went to Chester as bishop. Lloyd wrote of him that he did not look for profit or advancement,[3] and that his support of the Church was such that he brought others to conform.[4] He concludes that 'he conformed himself to everything that was commanded. Beyond which, for any man to be vehement, in little and unnecessary things, whether for or against them, he could not but dislike; and as his free manner was, he hath oft been heard to call it fanaticalness. How this might be represented I know not, or how his design of comprehension might be understood'.[5]

The impression is less that of one who was pliant than of one who had a different set of priorities, and for whom polity and the differences of administration in public affairs were not of compelling importance. It is clear from Lloyd's noncommittal remark about Wilkins's design of comprehension, that he did not share these ideas, since he himself refers to 'the apostles . . . and to the bishops their successors'.[6] While he describes Wilkins's prudence as great, he describes him also as being extremely open and of a natural sincerity of manner,[7] a judgment confirmed by the policy followed by Wilkins. He was averse to 'the eager pursuit of small . . . designs' and his interests were not specialised.[8] It is a safe deduction that his preaching was the original for the Latitudinarians and Lloyd characterises it as 'solid . . . with as little show of art as was

1. *Ib.* p. viii.
2. *Ib.* p. viii.
3. Sermon added to *The Principles and Duties of Natural Religion*, p. 42.
4. *Ib.* p. 50.
5. *Ib.* p. 49.
6. *Ib.* p. 8.
7. *Ib.* p. 41.
8. *Ib.* p. 36.

possible', remarking on its plainness, on the natural way in which subjects were presented, and on the manner in which Wilkins addressed himself rather to the 'understanding than affections'.[1] The style of his writings was 'judicious and plain',[2] and there can be little doubt of his influence in this respect on the Latitudinarians, for his son-in-law Tillotson and others made this style their own just as they incorporated into their theological outlook the specific emphases which mark Wilkins's work.

Referring to his wide interest in a variety of subjects, Lloyd comments that if in these studies 'he went sometimes beside his profession, it was in following the design of it', for the aim of all knowledge is to be of benefit to men.[3] This was particularly the case in respect of his interest in the Royal Society, and Lloyd remarks that Wilkins's purpose was 'to promote modern knowledge' without in any way derogating from the work of great men in former times.[4] That this was his method is to be seen in his combination of a concern with the new philosophy with the use of older writers.

He was active and practical, of an enquiring mind, and greatly given to study,[5] and in many ways shared the views of the Cambridge Platonists. Yet there is a difference as well as a resemblance, for in his works Latitudinarianism as distinct from Cambridge Platonism begins to appear, and the influence of Aquinas, no trace of which can be detected in their writings, is a noticeable element. Wilkins is closer at some points to Hooker than to the Cambridge Platonists although the new philosophy has appeared in the intervening period. Again, he is closer in some ways to the Cambridge Platonists than to the Latitudinarianism of Patrick or Lloyd for whom the form of the Church and ministry is something quite different from that which is implicit in Wilkins's view of comprehension. The kinship on all sides is there, but just as certain aspects of Latitudinarianism cannot be explained apart from the influence of the Cambridge Platonists, so other features in it derive from the work of Wilkins.

As one who was a mathematician, a student of astronomy as well as of mechanics, Wilkins's interest in the new philosophy took various forms, and in addition to the *Discovery of the New World*,

1. *Ib.* p. 38.
2. *Ib.* p. 39.
3. *Ib.* p. 39.
4. *Ib.* p. 40.
5. *Works*, Vol. I, p. ix.

he wrote on the probability of the earth being one of the planets, on communicating thoughts at a distance, *Archimedes; or Mechanical Powers*, and *Daedalus; or Mechanical Motions*. The last two were printed together under the title *Mathematical Magic*.[1]

This aspect of Wilkin's work shows something of the effect of the new philosophy on theological method, and in certain ways illustrates the transitional nature of the period.

In *The Discovery of a New World*, Wilkins disposes at the outset of the old argument from inertia, that because an opinion is new it should be rejected, and he reminds traditionalists 'how did the incredulous world gaze at Columbus, when he promised to discover another part of the earth'.[2] Why then should this be improbable? He is conversant with contemporary works on astronomy but the chief interest for the present subject is in the way in which he turns at once to the theological implications: 'and because the suppositions implied in this opinion may seem to contradict the principles of reason or faith, it will be requisite that I first remove this scruple, showing the conformity of them to both these'.[3] It was the accepted opinion that there could not be a 'plurality of worlds',[4] and the argument advanced was that the Old and the New Testament refer only to one world, in the singular. Wilkins observes that this is the argument of Aquinas who thinks that it will be opposed only by those who hold that all things are brought about not by design but by chance. Aquinas also considers that the opinion involves a dilemma, since to assume that there is more than one world of the same kind argues improvidence, and if they are of different kinds, one of them could not be called the world or universe, since it did not contain universal perfection.[5] As to this, Wilkins regards the argument as not being effectual on either side, and he maintains that the 'negative authority of Scripture' does not apply to things that are not fundamental or essential,[6] and that the world means the universe.[7] To make the same body a world for habitation and a moon for others does not 'derogate from the divine wisdom (as Aquinas thinks) but rather advances it'.[8]

1. *Mathematical Magic: or the Wonders that may be performed by Mechanical Geometry* (1680). The book discusses mathematical and mechanical matters, and such possiblities as those of flying and submarine nagivation.
2. *Mathematical and Philosophical Works* (1802), Vol. I, p. 4.
3. *Ib.* Vol. I, p. 12.   6. *Ib.* p. 18.
4. *Ib.* p. 13.   7. *Ib.* p. 21.
5. *Ib.* p. 17.   8. *Ib.* p. 22.

In the discussion of the possibility of the earth being a planet, Wilkins contrasts the 'safest method' in theological matters, which is to look first to authority, with the procedure required in examining philosophical questions. In the latter case, it would be a reversal of the proper course to begin with the opinion of others and then to proceed to the 'reasons that may be drawn from the nature and essence of the things themselves'. In such matters, arguments that do not adduce factual evidence can serve only as confirmatory.[1]

He has to reckon with contemporary arguments advanced from Scripture against the conclusions of the new science, and he does so only to avoid reproaches and to prevent confusion arising from misunderstanding.[2] His general reply to this type of argument is that these expressions are accommodated to 'the usual opinion'[3] and are used 'in reference to the appearance of things'. They are not applied to 'things as they are in themselves, but as they appear unto us'.[4] It is not possible to establish a basis of science on forms of expression not designed for that purpose, and he instances mistakes in this connection in earlier writers such as Augustine and Aquinas as a result of adherence to 'the letter of the text'.[5] His conclusion is that 'it were happy for us, if we could exempt Scripture from philosophical controversies: if we could be content to let it be perfect for that end unto which it was intended'.[6] The last part of the sentence echoes Hooker.

There is a good deal of bearing on his relationship with the Latitudinarians in Wilkins's book *Of the Principles and Duties of Natural Religion*[7] which was published with a preface by Tillotson who acted as literary executor. It has much in common with the writings of the Cambridge Platonists but there is an admixture of an individual element which gives it a quality of its own and which foreshadows aspects of the work of Tillotson and Stillingfleet.

It had been Wilkins's intention to publish the book, and the first twelve chapters were complete, but the rest was in unfinished form at the time of his death. Tillotson describes its design as threefold, to establish fundamental principles 'by showing how

1. *Ib.* p. 135.
2. *Ib.* p. 149.
3. *Ib.* p. 150.
4. *Ib.* p. 158.
5. *Ib.* p. 177.
6. *Ib.* p. 149.
7. 1675 ed.

firm and solid a foundation they have in the nature and reason of mankind'; to show the indispensable obligation of the two duties which does not depend simply on what is known from Scripture, for man was always under a law; and to show the necessity for putting this into practice. Tillotson adds that nothing is more likely to carry weight with thoughtful people than to be convinced that 'religion and happiness, our duty and our interest, are really but one and the same thing considered under several notions'.[1] These are the familiar ideas of Latitudinarianism, and it is obvious from the preface and from the fact that Tillotson wrote it that these ideas were first stated by Wilkins and that their dissemination owed much to his work and personal influence.

The first book is designed to show the reasonableness of the principles of natural religion, and begins with an outline of the different kinds of evidence by which knowledge of things is established.[2] The assent which proceeds from the acceptance of such evidence is either of the nature of knowledge or certainty or of opinion or probability, depending on the evidence.[3] He then lays down two schemes of principles, and in doing so employs, as he points out, the mathematician's method of postulates, definitions and axioms.[4] This is interesting as one example of the effect of his studies in such subjects on his approach to theological questions, and in fact the influence of the new philosophy is felt throughout his work. His treatment of some matters is very close to that of More or of Cudworth, but combined with this is the effect of his acquaintance with the *Summa Theologica* which is often noticeable in the form and content of the book.

The first scheme is of natural principles, and its basis is that 'everything is endowed with such a natural principle, whereby it is necessarily inclined to promote its own perfection and well-being'.[5] As to the second scheme, the created world has an ascending order, inanimate and animate, vegetable and sensitive, animals and men: 'It is a greater pre-eminence to have life, than to be without it; to have life and sense, than to have life only; to have life, sense and reason, than to have only life and sense'.[6] That which constitutes and differentiates a thing is its form or essence, and the condition by which a thing achieves its perfection is 'the chief end

1. *Ib*. Preface.
2. Chap. I, p. 5.
3. *Ib*.
4. *Ib*. Chap. II.
5. *Ib*. Chap. II, p. 12.
6. *Ib*. Chap. II, p. 17.

or happiness of such a thing'.[1] The influence of the *Summa
Theologica* on Wilkins's book is of a diffused kind, showing itself
from time to time in the form taken by his ideas or in the presentation of his material, and occasionally in similarity of treatment.
It helps to explain the derivation of certain aspects of the work of
Tillotson, Stillingfleet and Patrick. Yet it is but one element in the
writings of Wilkins whose work in the final assessment is not
derivative but distinctive, containing most of what came to be
regarded as Latitudinarianism.

Having discussed the matter of evidence and the general composition of things, Wilkins turns to the fact that different kinds of
things, equally true in themselves, are not necessarily capable of
the same kind of demonstration. The propositions that there are
such places as America or China, or that we now see and are
awake, or that the three angles in a triangle are equal to two right
ones,[2] are accepted on the testimony of others, or through proof
offered by the senses, or because of mathematical demonstration,
respectively.[3] He concludes that 'nothing can be more irrational
than for a man to doubt of, or deny the truth of anything, because
it cannot be made out, by such kind of proofs of which the nature
of such a thing is not capable'.[4] He quotes 'the Philosopher', 'that
according to the divers natures of things, so must the evidences
for them be'.[5] The effect of this, as Ward also emphasised, is that
experimental proof is not to be required in matters of faith and
religion, but that the reason given for them should be such as can
freely command assent. This is not to suggest that such matters
are merely probable, but that their certainty is congruous with
their nature.[6] Having already shown that, given evidence of a certain kind, assent may be of the nature of opinion or probability, he
goes on to point out, as did Butler later, that in all the ordinary
affairs of life that which is most probable is the guide when undisputed certainty is not possible.[7] There is in the work of Wilkins
a strongly marked element of what the period called practical
divinity, as in this instance, where he seems to favour the tutiorist
solution 'if the probabilities can be supposed equal'.[8]

1. *Ib.*
2. *Ib.* Chap. III, p. 22.
3. *Ib.* Chap. III, p. 23.
4. *Ib.*
5. *Ib.* References to Aristotle in the *Summa Theologica* are always to 'the Philosopher'.
6. *Ib.* Chap. III, p. 31.
7. *Ib.* Chap. III, p. 34.
8. *Ib.* Chap. III, p. 37.

In the following section of the book is set out the main theme which is 'to prove the reasonableness and the credibility of the principles of natural religion'.[1] This he defines as that 'which men might know, and should be obliged unto, by the mere principles of reason, improved by consideration and experience, without the help of revelation'.[2] It includes three principal things which he lists as acknowledgment of the Divine existence, due apprehensions of the Divine perfections, and worship and obedience.[3]

Belief in the existence of God is confirmed by 'the universal consent of nations; the original of the world; that excellent contrivance which there is in all natural things; the works of Providence in the government of the world'.[4] In dealing with the first of these he quotes the Philosopher that 'what all men have generally consented to, hath for it the highest degree of evidence of this kind, that anything is capable of'.[5] He goes into the matter in detail, discussing natural evidence, and freely using writers such as Tully, Seneca and others, a tendency objected to by Tuckney in the writings of the Cambridge Platonists.

As to the second, either the world was eternal or it had a beginning, 'and if it had a beginning, this must be either from chance or from some wise Agent'.[6] Supposing that neither theory is impossible, there are only two proofs by which it can be decided, namely testimony and reason.[7] In his view, the testimony of different nations, the history of Moses, and later writers including Socrates, Plato, Tully and Seneca, give support to the belief that the world was created and had a beginning. It is difficult to explain how such an idea could arise so early and spread so widely if there were not 'a real ground for it'.[8]

The effect of contemporary limitations on the discussion of theological and scientific matters becomes apparent when he begins to examine the reason of things. Positions are taken which are mainly the result of the absence of any body of verified knowledge and information. For example, he argues that the world is unlikely to be older than 'the time assigned for it in the history of Moses', since no memorials of such times are extant or 'some real evidence that there had been such'.[9] Similarly, he takes Seneca's point that

1. *Ib*. Chap. IV, p. 39.
2. *Ib*.
3. *Ib*. Chap. IV, p. 40.
4. *Ib*. Chap. IV, p. 41.
5. *Ib*.
6. *Ib*. Chap. V, p. 62.
7. *Ib*. Chap. V, p. 63.
8. *Ib*. Chap. V, pp. 64–70.
9. *Ib*. Chap. V, p. 71.

the arts and sciences did not originate more than a thousand years before his time as proof that mankind had not 'lived for an infinity of ages', since successful attempts to produce such things would certainly have been made, and could hardly have vanished without leaving any indication. To the suggestion that this could be due to many general inundations 'by which former inventions might be lost and forgotten', necessitating fresh starts from 'a kind of simplicity', he replies that a mere possibility to the contrary does not affect the credibility of a thing.[1] He asks if the world had been eternal why is it not everywhere inhabited and cultivated, and how is it that much of it is probably still unknown?[2] His opinion is that, estimating its beginning by its present state of population and cultivation and allowing for natural devastations of various kinds, the time assigned to it in the history of Moses is more probable than the assumption that the world is eternal.[3] If the latter were the case, the world would be over-populated, and the reply to this, that there may have been several floods with only one family surviving, argues an Agent who can alter the course of nature.[4]

Wilkins emphasises that these arguments are not demonstrations, 'of which the nature of this thing is not capable', but that they are more probable than anything that can be put forward to the contrary.[5] Confined within the limits of inadequate and often incorrect information, his method is basically that of relating religion and the new philosophy to each other. As with the Cambridge Platonists there is the extensive background and the weighing of possibilities. There is the endeavour to bring together new ideas and a literalist way of thinking, as in Stillingfleet's treatment of similar subjects. There is the particular view of natural religion used by the Latitudinarians to make contact between theological method and the new philosophy, and as a basis to commend religion generally to a generation beginning to see the world and experience within a context of cause and effect, while at the same time querying the relevance of older ideas to the new situation.

In discussing the 'admirable contrivance of natural things', he points to their beauty, order and fitness for their purpose, as inferring them to be 'the productions of some wise Agent'. He quotes Tully that beauty and order are evidence of this, and he

1. *Ib.* Chap. V, p. 72. 4. *Ib.* Chap. V, p. 74.
2. *Ib.* 5. *Ib.* Chap. V, p. 76.
3. *Ib.* Chap. V, p. 73.

holds that 'this great volume of the world' has no error or 'imperfect essay'.[1] He instances as further evidence, day and night, the seasons, the growth of plants, the production of minerals and animals, and the law of natural instinct by which everything 'is inclined and enabled for its own preservation'.[2] Like Glanvill who had made the same comment,[3] he draws attention to the way in which the design of the smallest things in nature such as 'seeds and . . . minute creatures' surpasses anything produced by art, when seen with the microscope.[4] There is evidence of design particularly in the human body and, proportionately, in minerals and vegetables, and especially in insects, fishes, birds and animals, with their organs and faculties of sensation.[5] He treats the subject in the same way as More, but adds a further consideration from man's nature by which he is 'necessarily inclined to seek his own well-being and happiness',[6] and from the fact that 'nothing properly is his duty, but what is really his interest'.[7]

There is a specifically Latitudinarian quality in this, and Wilkins's work points to the *Summa Theologica* as the source of the Latitudinarian ideas of happiness as the human end, of reason and of prudence as practical reason. It is as if there were two strains mingling in his work, broadly coinciding as to purpose but not quite the same in respect of composition. He combines something of the Cambridge Platonists and of the new philosophy with the more sharply defined view of reason which brings him closer to the form of the *Ecclesiastical Polity*, since it stems from the effect on his thinking of the *Summa Theologica* and Aristotle, although he is not always in agreement with either. This fusion of ideas he passed on to Tillotson and Stillingfleet, and it may be that it is at this point of transmission that the mystical element in the Cambridge Platonists' view of reason disappeared for the Latitudinarians in favour of an adaptation of something which, if it had not the same depth of content, was more clearly drawn.

His appeal is to the 'considering man' as to whether all this can be 'reasonably ascribed' to chance or necessity or to a 'wise Agent'.[8] The shift of emphasis to reasonableness indicates the

1. *Ib*. Chap. VI, p. 78.
2. *Ib*. Chap. VI, p. 79.
3. J. Glanvill, *Philosophia Pia*, Chap. II, I.
4. Wilkins, loc. cit. Chap. VI, p. 80.
5. *Ib*. Chap. VI, pp. 81–2.
6. *Ib*. Chap. VI, p. 82.
7. *Ib*. Chap. VI, p. 83.
8. *Ib*.

subtle change as compared with the Cambridge Platonists, and it
marks the beginning of the distinctively Latitudinarian approach.
Turning to 'the works of Providence in the government of the
world',[1] Wilkins notes that it is neither necessary nor fitting that
temporal happiness and prosperity should inevitably follow good
actions by a 'physical or mathematical certainty'.[2] This would be
inconsistent with men's dependent condition, putting everything
within the reach of their own endeavours. It would also diminish
the liberty of actions and make them mechanical.[3] There have also
been various special dispensations, designed to particular purposes, of which the history of Israel is a case in point.[4] The existence of natural conscience and of natural law are further evidences,[5]
and he concludes that 'there may be an indubitable certainty,
where there is not an infallible certainty',[6] and even if the matter
could be reduced to equal probabilities on either side, which he
does not see possible, the 'rational and prudent man' should
choose what seems 'most safe and advantageous for his own
interest'.[7] It is not without significance in connection with this
kind of approach that he quite frequently quotes Francis Bacon,
whom he regards as 'a great Author',[8] and also that there are numerous references elsewhere in his work to Proverbs and Ecclesiastes.
The latter belong to what have been described as the documents of
Hebrew humanism, and the Essays, akin to the essays of
Montaigne, share the same outlook, and in this they coincide with
one aspect of Latitudinarianism.

Wilkins then considers the second part of natural religion as
defined, the ideas of God which are 'discoverable by the light of
nature',[8] and devotes the chapters which follow to what he describes as the incommunicable and communicable 'perfections of
the Divine nature'.[10] It is here that the extent and the limitation
of his use of the *Summa Theologica* are to be seen, for while the
list of attributes clearly derives from it, the method of treatment
is his own, despite occasional contacts with the *Summa Theologica*,
and conveys the impression of belonging to its own period. He
writes, 'I shall endeavour to explain and describe, what is meant by

1. *Ib*. Chap. VII, p. 85.
2. *Ib*. Chap. VII, p. 86.
3. *Ib*. Chap. VII, p. 87.
4. *Ib*. Chap. VII, p. 89.
5. *Ib*. Chap. VII, p. 90.
6. *Ib*. Chap. VII, p. 94.
7. *Ib*. Chap. VII, p. 96.
8. *Ib*. Chap. VIII, p. 100, Chap. VII,
   p. 91, Bk. II, Chap. I, p. 295.
9. *Ib*. Chap. VIII, p. 100.
10. *Ib*. Chap. VIII, p. 102.

each attribute; and then prove, that these attributes so explained, must belong to the natural notion of God. Which I shall make out, both by the consent of the wisest heathen, expressed by their declared opinions, . . . and from the nature of the things themselves; their congruity to the principles of reason'.[1] The method is that of Latitudinarianism, the use of the ancient philosophers being part of what derived from the Cambridge Platonists, to which Wilkins added something of that awareness of the *Summa Theologica* which is a recurring factor in so many writers of the period.

It is clear, says Wilkins, that 'the Divine nature is supposed to be the first and supreme good', and can only be thought of in terms of absolute perfection,[2] so that 'the most general notion that men have of God, is that He is the first cause, and a Being of all possible perfection'.[3] This in effect reproduces the *Summa Theologica*: 'Now God is the first principle, not material, but in the order of efficient cause, which must be most perfect',[4] and he enumerates as does the *Summa Theologica*, simplicity, unity, immutability, infiniteness, eternity, understanding, knowledge, providence, goodness, justice, love and power.[5]

If the form of this part of his book and the outline of his thought owe something to Aquinas, his method of treatment, as he has indicated, and the general contents are original and different. It is in the general concept of the work, and in some of the ideas by which he expresses it, that the resemblance is seen, but there are certain specific similarities which show that the contact is not a superficial one.

The necessity of the chief end of anything being such that will promote the perfection of the thing, that of rational beings consisting in 'a conformity unto the chief good' is expressed in the same terms as those used in the *Summa Theologica*.[6] There is a verbal similarity between Wilkins's sentence, 'the having of an end is . . . a natural principle, like that of the descent of heavy bodies; men must do so, nor can they do otherwise', and 'it comes to the same . . . than the appetites rest in good; thus it is owing to the same natural force that a weighty body is borne downwards and that it rests there'.[7]

1. *Ib.* Chap. VIII, p. 103.   4. Pt. I, Q. 4, A. I.
2. *Ib.* Chap. VIII, p. 101.   5. Wilkins, Chap. VIII, p. 102; *Summa Theologica*, Pt. I, QQ. I–XXVI.
3. *Ib.* Chap. VIII, p. 102.
6. Wilkins, Bk. II, Chap. I, p. 306.
7. *Ib.* Bk. II, Chap. I, p. 307; *Summa Theologica*, Pt. II, 1st Pt. Q. 2, A. 6.

Similarly, Wilkins writes of the meaning of omnipotence that 'some other things may imply contradiction, either directly, or by plain consequence. And of such matters it is not proper to say, that he cannot do them, as that they cannot be done', and that 'the object of power, must be that which is possible. And as it is no prejudice to the most perfect understanding, or sight, or hearing, that it doth not understand what is not intelligible, or see what is not visible, or hear what is not audible; so neither is it to the most perfect power, that it doth not do what is not possible. Every kind of faculty being necessarily determined to its own proper object'.[1] This may be compared with Aquinas: 'If, however, we consider the matter aright, since power is said in reference to possible things, this phrase, God can do all things, is rightly understood to mean that God can do all things that are possible'; and, 'it must, however, be remembered that since every agent produces an effect like itself, to each active power there corresponds a thing possible as its proper object according to the nature of that act on which its active power is founded'; and, 'therefore, everything that does not imply a contradiction in terms is numbered amongst those possible things, in respect of which God is called omnipotent; whereas whatever implies contradiction does not come within the scope of divine omnipotence, because it cannot have the aspect of possibility. Hence it is better to say that such things cannot be done, than that God cannot do them'.[2]

Defining simplicity as 'freedom from all kind of composition', Wilkins again uses the same term as the *Summa Theologica*, although his treatment of the subject differs from that of Aquinas,[3] and referring to unity both mention Pythagoras.[4] On this particular subject while there is little or no resemblance between Wilkins's arrangement and content and that of the *Summa Theologica*, he is in debt at one point to it for the form of his thought. Wilkins writes, 'to suppose two Gods, with several perfections, some belonging to one, and some to another, will plainly prove, that neither of them can be God, because neither of them have all possible perfections'.[5] This reproduces the passage from Aquinas; 'for it was shown above that God comprehends in Himself the

1. *Ib*. Chap. XI, p. 144.
2. *Summa Theologica*, Pt. I, Q. 25, A. 3.
3. Wilkins, *ib*. Chap. VIII, p. 104; *Summa Theologica*, Pt. I, Q. 3.
4. Wilkins, *ib*. Chap. VIII, p. 111; *Summa Theologica*, Pt. I, Q. 2, A. I.
5. Wilkins, *ib*. Chap. VIII, p. 114.

whole perfection of being. If then many gods existed, they would necessarily differ from each other. Something therefore would belong to one, which did not belong to another'.[1]

There are minor points such as Wilkins's use of the terms filial and servile fear,[2] and there is a connection between the following extracts. That from the *Summa Theologica* is as follows: 'One need not always be thinking of the last end, whenever one desires or does something: but the virtue of the first intention, which was in respect of the last end, remains in every desire directed to any object whatever, even though one's thoughts be not actually directed to the last end, Thus while walking along the road one needs not to be thinking of the end at every step'.[3] The second extract, from Wilkins's book resembles this: 'I do not say, that a man's thoughts are always to be taken up about the immediate acts of religion, any more than a traveller is always to have his mind actually fixed upon the thought of his journey's end . . . But yet, as he that is upon a journey, doth so order all his particular motions, as may be most conducible to his general end; so should men habitually, though they cannot actually, in every affair have respect to their chief end'.[4]

This selection of extracts, together with the fact that the shape of the first part of Wilkins's book owes something in its pattern to the *Summa Theologica*, is sufficient to show that its influence is a very distinct component of his thought. It suggests the explanation of and the understanding of certain concepts stressed by the Latitudinarians. But Wilkins, as has been previously indicated, is a complex writer, with more than a fair share of that 'universalised' spirit which drew him to other sources, such as the new philosophy in which he took an active and discerning interest, and the works of the philosophers and writers of earlier times with which he was clearly conversant. Influenced to some extent by all these, and doubtless by his contact with the Cambridge Platonists, he preserved his individuality, for his method of presenting the subject of natural religion, and his whole treatment of it, are original. He played a part in shaping Latitudinarianism, so that without being of the same calibre as More[5] or Cudworth, his

1. *Summa Theologica*, Pt. I, Q. XI, A. 3.
2. Wilkins, *ib.* Chap. XV, p. 217.
3. *Summa Theologica*, Pt. II, 1st Pt. Q. I, A. 6.
4. Wilkins, *ib.* Chap. I, Bk. II, p. 300.
5. With whose work he was acquainted, *Ib.* Bk. I, Chap. II, p. 12.

place in the development of theological method is far from being unimportant.

It is curious that while he gives the source of all quotations from such as Plutarch, Tully, Juvenal and others, and also from Aristotle, there is little or no acknowledgment of the use made of the *Summa Theologica*, save in the comments already referred to in *The Discovery of a New World*. In none of the parallels or similarities which have been noted in this chapter, does Wilkins make any reference either by way of comparison or as a source, to the *Summa Theologica*. This is the case also with those parts of Stillingfleet's work, where some parallels with the *Summa Theologica* have been noted. Similarly, there is no adequate indication in the *Ecclesiastical Polity* of the extent to which the book, in its earlier parts, was influenced by the thinking of Aquinas. A possible explanation may lie in the fact that in the seventeenth century material derived from the *Summa Theologica* was more widely used than has been thought, so that theologians of the period were so familiar with it that they tended to reproduce some of its ideas almost without comment, considering, perhaps, that what was plainly recognisable did not require indentification.

Having dealt with the first two elements in natural religion as he has described it, Wilkins examines the third, namely, the duties which are a natural consequence of the first two, since such consideration 'ought not to be terminated in mere speculation'. These duties he sees as naturally flowing from the consideration of the attributes he has discussed earlier,[1] and while they are not to be limited to the specific attributes with which he has linked them, there is a particular 'reference and correspondence' between certain 'affections and duties' and certain attributes.[2] The incommunicable attributes are associated with worship[3], and the 'communicable perfections belonging to the Divine understanding, will, faculties of acting', namely, wisdom, goodness and power, with faith, love, reverence and obedience.[4] Each of these forms the subject of a separate chapter, which makes the book much more of a compendium than its title implies. That Wilkins is conscious of a certain extension of his subject by the inclusion of these chapters is apparent, for while he notes his intention of adhering to the

1. *Ib.* Bk. I, Chap. XII, p. 176.   3. *Ib.* Bk. I, Chap. XII, p. 177.
2. *Ib.* Bk. I, Chap. XII, p. 178.   4. *Ib.* Bk. I, Chap. XIII, p. 189.

same method of basing his conclusions on natural reason,[1] he admits that the writings of antiquity cannot, in the nature of things, be expected to provide as much material on this point as they do on others. Referring to the subject-matter of these chapters, he maintains that although the obligation to them is 'deducible from the light of nature and the principles of reason, and consequently must be owned by the heathen philosophers; yet they do in their writings, speak but sparingly, concerning those kind of virtues which are of a more spiritual nature . . . and on the other side, the Scripture doth most of all insist upon the excellency and necessity of these kind of graces'. This explains why he has varied his method in this respect, in these chapters.[2] He concludes the first book by recommending 'a sober enquiry into the nature of things, a diligent perusal of this volume of the world',[3] as did Glanvill with whom he agrees as to the theological advantages of the new philosophy.

The second book has as its title 'the wisdom of practising the duties of natural religion', and his object is to show how this is men's 'chief happiness and interest'.[4] He begins with what was to become a central phrase with the Latitudinarians, 'Fear God, and keep his commandments: for this is the whole of man', and he describes Ecclesiastes as 'a book, the main argument whereof is to enquire, wherein the chief happiness of man doth consist'. He regards this as summarising the position, so he examines the various renderings of the words 'this is the whole of man', noting that the Septuagint and the Vulgate give it as 'this is all', or 'everyman', the word duty not being in the original or in other translations.[5] He employs his usual method of 'clear principles of reason, attested to by several of the wisest heathen writers', and he proceeds to show how religion is of the essence of human nature, of the composition of society, and of happiness and well-being.[6]

In connection with this Wilkins writes that 'in the actions of many brute creatures, there are discernible some footsteps, some imperfect strictures and degrees of ratiocination; such a natural sagacity as at least bears a near resemblance to reason. From whence it may follow, that it is not reason in the general, which is the form of human nature; but reason as it is determined to actions

1. *Ib*. Bk. I, Chap. XII, p. 177.   4. *Ib*. Bk. II, Chap. I, p. 285.
2. *Ib*. Bk. I, Chap. XIII, p. 199.   5. *Ib*. Bk. II, Chap. I, p. 286.
3. *Ib*. Bk. I, Chap. XVI, p. 238.   6. *Ib*. Bk. II, Chap. I, p. 287.

of religion, of which we do not find the least signs or degrees in brutes'.[1] There is a similar passage probably derived from Wilkins in Patrick's writings on the same subject, and Wilkins points out that it is not a new opinion but was held by various ancient writers of which he gives examples.[2]

All things tend towards the perfection proper to them: 'that is properly said to be the chief end or happiness of a thing, which doth raise its nature to the utmost perfection of which it is capable, according to its rank and kind . . . the chief good belonging to a vegetable or plant, is to grow up to a state of maturity, to continue to its natural period, and to propagate its kind, which is the utmost perfection that kind of being is capable of. And whereas sensitive creatures, besides those things which are common to them with plants, have likewise such faculties, whereby they are able to apprehend external objects . . . therefore the happiness proper to them, must consist in the perfection of these faculties'.[3] For rational beings, this must consist in 'conformity unto the chief good',[4] and it is religion that effects it, which is, as he has shown, the position of the writer of Ecclesiastes.

The whole of the second book is concerned with different aspects of happiness as the chief end, and in respect of the development of the idea and the importance attached to it, Wilkins is in accord with the *Summa Theologica*. But a new element is present also for Wilkins having described 'the proper happiness of man', adds that his nature being such that it partakes of other capacities, it 'may stand in need of several other things, to render his condition pleasant and comfortable in this world, as health, riches, reputation, safety'. He considers that it is the great advantage of religion that, as well as effecting the main purpose, it is also 'the most effectual means to promote our happiness in this world'.[5] The *Summa Theologica* maintains that happiness does not consist in such things as wealth, honour or power, and while Wilkins does not actually assert the contrary, he states that these particular things are the 'usual ingredients' of it, and that they complete it.[6] His account of what he terms the general nature of happiness agrees with that given in the *Summa Theologica*, but he puts more emphasis on the fact that, as he expresses it, religion 'conduces to

1. *Ib*. Bk. II, Chap. I, p. 289.
2. *Ib*. Bk. II, Chap. I, pp. 290–2.
3. *Ib*. Bk. II, Chap. I, p. 304.
4. *Ib*. Bk. II, Chap. I, p. 306.
5. *Ib*. Bk. II, Chap. I, p. 305–6.
6. *Ib*. Bk. II, Chap. I, p. 311.

present happiness' as well.[1] He does not state in so many words that happiness consists in any of these things, but he holds that 'the happiness of our condition, in all these respects, doth depend on religion'.[2] It is his view that there is a close association between religion and temporal happiness, but he adds a caution to the effect that 'the meaning is not, that it is so necessary and so infallible a cause, as can never fail of its effect'.[3] Accordingly the following chapters develop this connection with external well-fare, health, liberty, safety, quiet, honour, and possessions, and with internal well-fare, which consists in the harmony of the faculties. These aspects of what he calls temporal happiness are involved with things like content, moderation, charity, forbearance, and liberality. It is the property of religion, he writes, that 'it changes the natures of men',[4] that it is said to be 'a participation of the Divine nature'.[5]

Considering this part of the book, and the persistence of something very similar in the writings of the Latitudinarians, it is not difficult to see how this particular emphasis affected the general estimate of them. There is a pragmatic and matter-of-fact element here, a kind of combination of practical divinity with something of the humanism which lay behind the Cambridge Platonists' view of the human situation. The source common to them and to Wilkins would have been writers such as Tully and Seneca, but Wilkins's interest in Bacon may point in the same direction. The frequent use he makes of Ecclesiastes and Proverbs indicates another influence of the same kind. Both in the sermons and in his book he refers to 'the wise man', much as he does to 'the Philosopher', and it is obvious that there is something here which coincides with his own outlook. This preference is hardly surprising when the nature of these books is considered, for they are concerned with humanity and the individual in his relationships, with happiness and the chief good, with reputation and wealth, with ordinary life and its preoccupations, with wisdom as it is related to everyday experience. This fitted in with one side of Wilkins's thinking, for it is not only in keeping with the influence on his work of Aristotle and the *Summa Theologica*, and with his interest in the new philosophy, but is part of a general reaction

---

1. *Ib*. Bk. II, Chap. II, p. 314.
2. *Ib*. Bk. II, Chap. I, p. 313.
3. *Ib*. Bk. II, Chap. II, p. 315.

4. *Ib*. Bk. II, Chap. V, p. 350.
5. *Ib*. Bk. II, Chap. VII, p. 374, a favourite phrase with More.

in the direction of a theological method which sets a premium on reason and practicality. In his view, it was the only positive and constructive line to take because the prevalent indifference was in large part due to 'that heat and zeal of men in those various contrary opinions, which have of late abounded'.[1]

The final chapter contains in outline a good deal of what came to be the classical Latitudinarian position. Wilkins recalls his purpose of showing that religion is firmly based in the nature and reason of mankind, but without taking away from 'the necessity and usefulness' of revelation, and 'rather to prepare and make way for the entertainment of that doctrine which is so agreeable to the clearest dictates of natural light'.[2] This is the characteristic Latitudinarian expression of the relation of reason to revelation: reason is incomplete without revelation, and revelation is agreeable to reason. The design of the chapter is to show 'the advantages of the Christian religion . . . above the mere light of nature'[3] on the grounds of its superior authority, evidence of which is seen in the Old Testament, by reason of its being the most ancient record of the beginnings of things,[4] and in the New Testament, corresponding as it does to 'the chief things of the Old Testament', because of the 'good certainty' that there is of the truth of its contents which is confirmed by miracles.[5] This was also the position maintained by Stillingfleet with regard to the same subject.

That the work of Wilkins shows itself to be the beginnings of Latitudinarianism is apparent not only from his book, for the sermons also contain an even more marked expression of the method and approach which came to be associated with Tillotson, Stillingfleet and others. For although publication was posthumous in 1675 and 1682, his influence, as Burnet and Tillotson recorded, did not wait on the work of the printer. In some respects, the impact of Wilkins's ideas on the Latitudinarians is more measurable than that of the Cambridge Platonists, with the qualification that Wilkins had much in common with the latter. The Latitudinarians took from the Cambridge Platonists an outlook, but they shared with Wilkins something more identifiable. It is a factor needing to be taken into account in the attempt to understand the sense of a break in continuity between the later writers

1. *Ib*. Bk. II, Chap. IX, p. 407.
2. *Ib*. Bk. II, Chap. IX, p. 394.
3. *Ib*.
4. *Ib*. Bk. II, Chap. IX, p. 400.
5. *Ib*. Bk. II, Chap. IX, pp. 401-2.

and the Cambridge Platonists. It is here contended that this identifiable element is a compound of a selective use of parts of the *Summa
Theologica*, an interest in the Wisdom books and in practical
divinity, all of which have a rational and practical aspect in common. This was joined to an active approval of the aims and method
of the new philosophy. Taken together, these constituted the basis
of Latitudinarian method, which, while it was negatively the product of reaction, was positively an attempt to achieve relevance
and realism in terms of reasonableness and practicality. This latter
emphasis led the Latitudinarians generally and Wilkins in particular to a choice of subjects in which practical divinity, as it was
termed in the seventeenth century, played a large part. That
Wilkins had given attention to the subject is clear from his
obvious acquaintance with the relevant parts of the *Summa
Theologica*, and it is not therefore surprising to find him giving an
estimate of practical divinity which he seems to have taken from the
sermons of Sanderson who used the same source. Wilkins, having
discussed the subject of various studies, adds, 'but yet when all is
done, 'tis this practical divinity, that must bring us to heaven, that
must poise our judgments, and settle our consciences, and strengthen our comforts, and save our souls'.[1] Although unacknowledged by Wilkins this is almost word for word the same as a passage
from a sermon preached in 1620 by Sanderson, where he is
writing on the same subject, the relative value of different studies.[2]
Considering the place occupied by Sanderson's work in practical
divinity, it is natural that Wilkins should have felt drawn to one
whose sermons, like his own, constantly reverted to some aspect of
the subject, and which in consequence spoke plainly to the condition of the times.

A further indication of his interest in practical divinity is seen
in the fact that he refers to Perkins's *Cases of Conscience*,[3] but the
subjects of his sermons all point in the same direction, for none
of the surviving addresses deals with anything remote or theoretical, but with the impact of religion on the setting and circumstances

1. *Sermons* (1682), VI, p. 192.
2. *XXXV Sermons* (1681), III, p. 58: 'But when all is done, positive and practick
   divinity it is must bring us to heaven; that is it must poise our judgments,
   settle our consciences, direct our lives, mortify our corruptions, increase our
   graces, strengthen our comforts, save our souls.'
3. *Sermons*, XI, p. 377.

of life. It is this which led Wilkins to Ecclesiastes and Proverbs, for he sees Proverbs as 'a miscellany of sentences full of various and profound wisdom', and suitable for the guidance of practical affairs. 'They concern all kind of matters', not only customs, behaviour and temperament, but 'the duties and business of life'. The value lies in the way in which the essence of these matters, from the practical aspect, is 'set down in plain and pithy sentences: and though some of them may at first glance perhaps seem to be but obvious and flat, yet upon a nearer and more considerate view' they will be found 'to have a special authority . . . in the guidance of affairs'.[1] The interest in Ecclesiastes is that it contains 'the different thoughts and attempts of men according to their several principles and tempers in the pursuit after happiness'.[2]

It is not difficult to see how for Wilkins the *Summa Theologica's* definition of prudence as practical reason fitted in with the constant references in these books to wisdom: 'for the description of the nature of wisdom, this is by Aristotle said to be that intellectual virtue whereby we are directed in our manners and carriage, to make choice of the right means in the prosecution of our true end. Tully describes it to be ars vivendi: and to the same purpose Aquinas, recta ratio agibilium, the skill of demeaning a man's self aright in practical affairs. And Solomon to the same purpose: the wisdom of the prudent is to understand his way'.[3] It is not simply that Wilkins recognises that the ideas are the same, but that there is a temperamental affinity between his outlook and that of the writers of the Wisdom books. The emphasis which he found there on happiness, prudence and moderateness was not only close to those leading ideas of practical divinity which were met with in Aristotle, Seneca, Tully and the *Summa Theologica*, but Wilkins saw in it the counterpart of what he had learned from the new philosophy. Writing of moderation, he observes that it is a thing not only 'reasonable . . . in itself' but also because of 'the fallibility of human judgment and the mutability of human affairs' and because of 'the difficulty and obscurity of things'.[4]

This similarity of outlook and extensive use by Wilkins of

---

1. *Ib*. VIII, p. 235, XII, p. 359.
2. *Ib*. VI, p. 166. Although unaware of the existence of editing in Ecclesiastes he notes that it is not 'easy to find out the particular connection in many parts of it', *ib*. IX, p. 263.
3. *Ib*. VII, p. 199.   4. *Ib*. XIII, p. 407.

Proverbs and Ecclesiastes is in part the origin of the Latitudinarian stress on prudence, practicality, moderateness and happiness.
To the same source may be traceable the attempt to put into perspective such subjects as 'temporal reward'[1] and well-being. This
is an aspect of Latitudinarianism which, perhaps understandably,
jars on modern susceptibilities, but which becomes more com-
prehensible once it is seen that it does not originate in complacency
and acceptance, but in the effort to understand the meaning and
implications of certain basic terms. Wilkins refuses to ignore the
questions raised, and suggests that the solution lies in the relation
of what he calls 'subordinate' to 'ultimate' ends. It is from this
angle that he approaches the question of reward, showing himself
to be aware of the sensitivity in this matter of many who doubt
'concerning their own sincerity' if they discover that this is 'that
which has the chief influence upon them'.[2] The existence of this
motive and not 'filial affections' suggests to them that they are in
a 'state of unregeneracy', and, in consequence, 'they . . . need-
lessly disquiet themselves and discourage others'.[3]

As a starting point, Wilkins takes the passage describing Moses
as having 'respect unto the recompense of reward', which he skil-
fully notes as occurring in a chapter, the chief scope of which is a
discussion of faith.[4] His purpose is to show that it is not only 'permissively lawful' for ordinary people, but that it is 'likewise
necessary for the most eminent . . . to support themselves . . . by
a special and particular regard to the recompense of reward'.[5] The
inference 'may seem unto many a bold paradox and mistake', being
the opposite of what had been so commonly held. It is his view,
however, that 'a mistake in this may prove of very dangerous consequence' to anyone suffering from 'dejection of mind', making it
difficult for him to be assured 'concerning his own sincerity'.[6]
Wilkins's preference, which he plainly indicates, has an objecti-
vity which he felt was needed in the contemporary situation. It is
an 'uncomfortable error . . . that it is not enough to prove our
sincerity, that we are able to do good out of love to the reward'.[7]
To the extreme statement of the position, that the individual was
bound in theory to desire his own ultimate condemnation if it

1. *Ib.* I, p. 6.
2. *Ib.* I, p. 1.
3. *Ib.* I, p. 2.
4. *Ib.* I, p. 2. *Heb.* XI, 26.
5. *Ib.* I, p. 4.
6. *Ib.* I, p. 5.
7. *Ib.* I, p. 33.

'might conduce more to God's glory', he replies with the 'advice of the Wiseman, Be not righteous over much, neither make thyself over wise'. This is to 'invent such precepts as the Scripture doth not prescibe', and to make such rules as cannot be conformed to.[1] The moderateness and reasonableness which came to be associated with the Latitudinarians, and which at times took forms that laid them open to being regarded as negative and vague, is here seen in sharp contrast. For Wilkins, the immediate source of this contrasting outlook is, in part, the Wisdom books with their attitude of reasonable moderation, conveying the impression of placidly playing down over-statements, which are contrary to wisdom.

Wilkins holds that reward is of two kinds as it is concerned with temporal or future happiness, and that there are subordinate and ultimate ends.[2] This means that 'temporal rewards may be the subordinate end in our obedience', and that 'temporal reward may at first be the chief occasion of men's being converted and following Christ', examples of which are certain healing miracles in the New Testament.[3] 'We must not propose temporal rewards as our chief end', for 'God Himself (in the phrase of the Schools)' is man's objective happiness and his formal happiness the 'enjoyment of Him'.[4] To attempt to effect a separation is to deny what is fundamental, that the chief human end is happiness.[5] This is a further indication that Latitudinarian views on such subjects as reward and well-being are to be explained by reference to the fundamental ideas of happiness and wisdom which figure so prominently in the *Summa Theologica* and the Wisdom books. Wilkins points out that 'to aim chiefly at our well-being, is not only permissively lawful ... but it is likewise essentially necessary'[6] to man's nature, since 'every created thing is by its most powerful and immediate instincts carried out to its own conservation'.[7] Like Hooker, he regards the law of nature as an implanted directive, a combination of laws 'suited to those several natures' and 'implanted in them', and, of these, the most universal principle is that of self-preservation which in man takes the form of making 'a state of happiness ... the supreme and ultimate end'.[8] With the *Summa Theologica*

1. *Ib.* I, p. 34.
2. *Ib.* I, p. 5.
3. *Ib.* I, p. 6.
4. *Ib.* I, p. 7.

5. *Ib.* I, p. 8.
6. *Ib.* I, p. 12.
7. *Ib.* I, p. 11.
8. *Ib.* I, p. 13.

he agrees that the only difference is as to its nature.[1] To look then for a reward is consistent with the 'prime and fundamental law of nature'.[2]

A second reason is that the promises 'so frequent in Scripture . . . are intended for this very purpose'[3] of encouraging obedience, and a third is the definition of faith as 'the substance of things hoped for' which 'doth chiefly refer to the rewards hoped for and not seen'.[4]

On the subject of wisdom, Wilkins writes that 'because learning is of two kinds, either of business or things; therefore Solomon makes a distinct enquiry into each. The first he calls wisdom, the other knowledge'.[5] The latter 'doth concern the speculation of nature in reference to causes and effects, the differences and properties of things'. Wisdom is defined as 'the art of business, directing a man in the practical affairs of life to what is fit and convenient, according to the variety of circumstances. It consists in a solid judgment to discern the tempers and interests of men, the state of business, the probabilities of events and consequences, together with a presentness of mind to obviate sudden accidents'.[6] Once again it is clear how, for Wilkins, the *Summa Theologica's* view of prudence as practical wisdom merges with the ideas of the Wisdom books, and, in fact, he makes the identification in another context. Writing of prudence, justice, fortitude and temperance, he describes 'wisdom or prudence' as consisting in the ability to make a true estimate of things, persons and events, and also in presence of mind and in experience of the 'usual and probable consequences of things'.[7] In itself it is differentiated by the end proposed and by the means by which this is to be attained.[8]

The combination of the Philosopher with Ecclesiastes and Proverbs is then constantly to be noted in Wilkins's description of wisdom. Its chief office is to direct, and 'this it doth both as to the end and the means', in connection with which he quotes Ecclesiastes that 'wisdom is profitable to direct'.[9] It also 'directs to consult about the means: this the Philospher calls, euboulia, which consists in a judicious investigation about the several ways, and a

1. *Ib.* I, p. 11. *Summa Theologica*, Pt. II (First Pt.), Q.I, A.7.
2. *Ib.* I, p. 11.
3. *Ib.* I. p. 14.
4. *Ib.* I. p. 16.
5. *Ib.* VI, p. 170.
6. *Ib.* VI, p. 171.
7. *Ib.* VII, p. 201.
8. *Ib.* VII, p. 205.
9. *Ib.* VII, p. 211. Cp. *Summa Theologica*, Pt. II (Second Pt.), Q. 47, A. 8.

choice of such as are more proper to the end'.[1] Four things are
required, namely, 'forecast and providence against want, wariness
and caution against danger, order and union against opposition,
sedulity and diligence against difficulties', and these are suggested
in Proverbs 30.24, by the ants, the conies, the locusts and the
spiders.[2] The opposites of wisdom are craft and folly, the former
being of the nature of guile or fraud, and the latter 'the deficient
extreme of wisdom'.[3]

Wilkins considers that knowledge, whether it be of the arts or of
history or 'real knowledge', by which he means the knowledge
which is the subject of the new philosophy, is imperfect, and he
refers to Bacon in connection with the 'ambiguity' and the
'obliqueness' in things, so that 'even sense itself . . . is fain to
wander up and down in uncertainties'.[4] Wisdom itself is imperfect,[5]
and this natural wisdom and knowledge needs what he terms other
ingredients and graces, and he quotes 'add to your knowledge,
faith, virtue, temperance, patience, goodness, brotherly kindness,
charity'.[6] It is at this point that he states the importance of practical
divinity as compared with wisdom and knowledge, which, in his
view, need 'the mixture' of faith which is 'wisdom unto salvation'
and 'the fear of the Lord, that is wisdom'.[7] He concludes with the
sentence from Ecclesiastes, 'Fear God and keep his commandments; for this is the whole duty of man',[8] which was to be the
recurring maxim of the Latitudinarians, just as significantly the
phrase from the Proverbs came to be associated with the Cambridge Platonists.

Reference has already been made to the comments by Lloyd and
by the author of the biography prefixed to the mathematical works
on Wilkins's attitude to moderateness and comprehension, which
attribute the latter in part to his personal background and associations, and to his dislike of too much importance being attached to
unnecessary things. His moderateness of view-point is mainly
connected with the recognition of the fact that 'nothing is more

1. *Ib.* VII, p. 212, Cp. *Summa Theologica*, Pt. II (Second Pt.), Q. 51, A. 2.
2. *Ib.* VII, pp. 213–6. Cp. *Summa Theologica*, Pt. II (Second Pt.), Q. 49, Artt. 4,
   6, 7, 8, where the same things are mentioned among others, but in a different
   way.
3. *Ib.* VII, p. 217. Cp. *Summa Theologica*, Pt. II (Second Pt.), Q. 55, Artt. 3–5.
4. *Ib.* VI, pp. 184–6.　　　　　　　7. *Ib.* VI, pp. 194, 196.
5. *Ib.* VI, p. 171.　　　　　　　　8. *Ib.* VI, p. 196.
6. *Ib.* VI, p. 193.

incidental' to the nature of man than mistakes and misunderstanding, and with the distinction between 'things essential ... and accidental'.[1] In things which are not essential, there should be mutual forbearance,[2] and he does not hold that this implies being 'indifferent to everything, as if there could be no certainty'.[3] He sees it as a matter of proportion, of considering 'the evidence and importance of the things in question'.[4] With regard to evidence, scepticism or dogmatism are to be avoided, 'to look on everything as doubtful' or to 'receive a whole system ... by the bulk'.[5] As for the relative importance of things, 'prudence will be required to distinguish aright'[6] between fundamental and secondary things. This differentiating between what Wilkins calls necessary things and things 'of a lighter consequence and more remote from the foundation',[7] is so much a part of theological method in the seventeenth century that it is almost taken for granted.

For Andrewes, Hales, Chillingworth and others, it is the real moderateness, imposed as Wilkins pointed out, by the differences in 'the evidence and importance of the things in question' and 'the several degrees amongst them'.[8] It is met with in Smith and Whichcote, and it was apparent to Andrewes in the matter of the Lambeth Articles, and to Hales as he surveyed the state of the question as regards theological liberality or a system of theology in his correspondence. For all of them, this moderateness was esentially a reasonableness demanded by the facts, or as Wilkins put it, by 'those bounds which are fixed by the nature of things in respect of their evidence and importance'.[9] It is from this awareness of the need for distinguishing between essentials and nonessentials, that Wilkins's moderation is partly derived, although both his early association with Dod and his later training in the new philosophy contributed to it. But it went deeper still, not simply as a principle of differentiation in matters theological, but as an attitude of gentleness and forbearance in practical affairs, 'a real sense of humanity'.[10] Some have questioned, he says, whether this is a single quality at all, but whether as effects or components,

1. *Ib.* II, p. 66.
2. *Ib.* II, p. 57.
3. *Ib.* III, p. 85.
4. *Ib.* III, p. 86.
5. *Ib.* III, p. 88.
6. *Ib.* III, p. 89.
7. *Ib.*
8. *Ib.*
9. *Ib.* III, p. 91.
10. *Ib.* XIII, p. 401.

there are associated with it such things as forbearance, kindness, gentleness.[1] These are 'the grand criteria' in the New Testament, and it is things of this nature which are moderation.[2] Wilkins defines it as 'a virtue inclining . . . to . . . a benign and equitable temper',[3] but his interest in practical divinity leads him to describe another aspect of it, a 'forinsecal notion of the word as it refers to positive laws, and the dispensation of justice'.[4] This is equity, or epieikia, and he notes that the Philosopher treats of it as a branch of justice, for laws cannot be framed to cover all eventualities, so that situations can arise in which literal application of the law can defeat its intention. Equity is 'to deal according to the equitable sense of the law, and to allow for such particular circumstances as may make a real difference in several cases'. It is a moderate interpretation between 'on the one hand, insisting too much upon the letter . . . and remitting too much from the true sense of it, on the other hand'.[5]

Not only the form but the substance of Wilkins's writings show his concern with moral theology, for without exception, his sermons deal with practical things, liberality, charitableness, justice, kindness, obedience, with the outward effect of interior qualities. In fact, his practice of discussing not only faith, humility, wisdom, for example, but their opposites and the things associated with them, means that he contrives to cover a very wide range. His use of terms also underlines his interest in the subject, as when he writes of prodigality as 'the exceeding extreme' of liberality, and churlishness as its 'deficient extreme'.[6] In the same way, writing of revenge, he refers to it not only 'according to the most usual acception of the word',[7] but also to the fact that it is 'by several authors used in such various and equivocal senses; sometimes for a passion of the mind, so Plato defines it . . . sometimes for a virtue, amongst the catalogue of which Aristotle doth reckon it . . . and so likewise Aquinas'.[8]

This is more than an incidental aspect of Wilkins's thinking, being rather a determining element in its form, giving to it a practical quality, which, expressed with plainness and restraint, merges with his exposition of natural theology and with his interest

1. *Ib*. XIII, p. 417.
2. *Ib*. XIII, p. 421.
3. *Ib*. XIII, p. 394.
4. *Ib*.
5. *Ib*. XIII, p. 393.
6. *Ib*. X, p. 299, cp. *Ib*. XIII, p. 393.
7. *Ib*. XIV, p. 433.
8. *Ib*. XIV, p. 432.

in the new philosophy. Having something in common with Hooker and with Sanderson and with the Cambridge Platonists, sharing Glanvill's ideas and influencing Ray, his work seems to be one of the immediate sources of the characteristic aspects of Latitudinarianism.

Not only the ties of friendship, but interest in practical divinity, in mathematics and in the new philosophy, linked Wilkins with one whose work seemed in turn to form, as his biographer has observed, 'a connecting link between the old and the new philosophy'.[1] Isaac Barrow, distinguished by reason of having lectured Newton, is nevertheless in his own right significant for the seventeenth century. In his outlook can be discerned a blend of the new philosophy and the older unspecialised culture, and a mingling of traditional views on episcopacy and acquaintance with patristic writings with what might be broadly described as a Latitudinarian approach to theological questions, in which, however, the more caricaturable aspects are absent. Sharing Wilkins's interest in the new philosophy, Barrow made original contributions to mathematics where Wilkins's function was rather to help the new outlook to establish itself. Where Barrow was a creative worker in a specific field, Wilkins was the gifted amateur of insight and imagination who grasped the implications of the new philosophy for the future. Barrow has the same practicality fully developed and the same tendency to look to Proverbs and Ecclesiastes, and his subject-matter and its treatment support P. H. Osmond's view that 'his rôle as preacher was to be an expounder of moral theology'.[2] In his attitude to reason he is one with Wilkins and the Cambridge Platonists: 'the proper work of man, the grand drift of human life, is to follow reason'.[3] Whichcote had been appointed Provost of King's in 1644, at the time when Barrow went to the University, and the influence of the Cambridge Platonists on Barrow's outlook can be seen not only in his idea of reason as a 'spark kindled' in men,[4] but in his general approach to the question of the decrees and allied questions. His method of handling subjects is that of combining Scripture, antiquity and practical application within the framework of a reasoned discussion. He has the impartiality and restraint associated with Latitudinarianism, but there is depth

1. P. H. Osmond, *Isaac Barrow, His Life and Times*, p. 1.
2. *Ib.* p. 170.
3. Quoted, *ib.* p. 76.
4. *Ib.*

and feeling, an acuteness in analysis and a perceptiveness which convey a clear impression not only of being on the level of reality but of understanding it. His Latitudinarian associations were with Seth Ward and Thomas Firmin as well as with Wilkins, and particularly with Tillotson who published a collected edition of Barrow's works in 1683–9. The fact that he also edited Wilkins's writings indicates Tillotson's awareness of the relationship of Barrow and Wilkins to the general position of Latitudinarianism.

In spite of a restrained collectedness, there is always the likelihood in Barrow's work of a glimpse of warmth and devotion, all the more convincing because of an obvious natural reserve. Joined with a capacity for understanding human characteristics and for high-lighting it in a telling sentence, this imparts a distinctive flavour to Barrow's writings. If he does not conform in this regard to the conventional picture of Latitudinarianism, neither does he do so in respect of his political views, for he was a Royalist who twice placed his future in jeopardy because of his attitude. In 1651, he had the courage to voice his sympathy with the Royalist cause and with episcopacy when he was chosen to make a Latin oration at the University. It is perhaps not irrelevant in this connection that he had contacts with Hammond. He graduated at Trinity College, Cambridge, in 1649, becoming a Fellow shortly afterwards in a predominantly parliamentarian academic society in spite of his known political views. In the same year he signed the Engagement but almost immediately had his name removed.

Barrow's inclination to the new philosophy did not preclude him from recommending the scholastics for the same reason that Bramhall did, because they showed 'how to unknot difficulties'. Like Henry More, he admired Descartes but was critical of a hypothesis of nature which excluded the spiritual and the immaterial. He held as did Cudworth that there was 'a vital spirit . . . diffused throughout the universe to preserve and sustain all things',[1] and there is a strong suggestion of something like the concept of plastic nature in the same passage. Barrow's versatility is reflected in the fact that he did pioneer work in geometry and mathematics and was Regius Professor of Greek as well as Professor of Mathematics. Newton attended his lectures in 1661, and P. H. Osmond notes that a study of his published lectures shows Barrow's influence on Newton in respect of the ideas of absolute

1. *Ib.* p. 30.

space and absolute time and suggests that these lectures had a place in Newton's invention of the differential calculus, on his theory of light and colour, and on the question of time: 'no one can read that discussion of time without noticing how profoundly it influenced the famous scholium of Newton'.[1]

In 1655, a Government Commission having been appointed to investigate University affairs, it was thought best that Barrow should be absent from the University for a time because of his political views, so he was given leave to travel and on arriving in France, 'among the ruined Royalist exiles at Paris, Barrow found his father'.[2] During the next four years his journeyings took him as far as Constantinople, and on his return the year before the Restoration he found that Wilkins had been appointed Master of Trinity College. This welcome association did not last, however, as Henry Ferne's prior claim nullified Wilkins's appointment apart altogether from the question of the appointing authority for Wilkins might have continued to hold the position after the Restoration 'had not a prior claim existed'.[3] Events also interrupted his friendship with John Ray who felt compelled to relinquish his Fellowship because of the Act of Uniformity. Barrow's close relationship with Wilkins continued nevertheless and when he applied for the professorship of geometry at Gresham College, Wilkins supported him.

Barrow was appointed Master of Trinity in 1672 and for the next five years until his death he was occupied with the work of administration and its details.

It is informative in respect of theological method to mark the parallel in more than one instance between Barrow and Wilkins. Both were concerned with the new philosophy, Barrow being a distinguished mathematician and Wilkins having had much to do with the beginning of the Royal Society. Yet little of this appears in the theological work of either except in their general attitude. Rather is the effect of their sympathy with the new philosophy apparent in the emphasis on reason and practicality, in the reaction from the speculative to the practical, and in a sense of the need for relevance and realism expressed in an active concern with rationality, experience and application. It is no more than a statement of fact to say that the most frequently recurring concept in Barrow's sermons is that of practice. It is the central idea upon which

1. *Ib.* p. 138.   2. *Ib.* p. 49.   3. *Ib.* p. 84.

depends his whole assessment of what constitutes the reality of the human situation. Yet it would be a mistake to imagine that a dry exposition of the duties was the sum total of Barrow's contribution to the needs of the times. He saw that for the post-Restoration period the urgent requirement was not preoccupation with the subtleties of speculation but with practice and 'obedience', two of his favourite terms. This is the solid basis of what he has to say, but his writing on prayer and thanksgiving shows his awareness that practice could not be separated from its source or sustained apart from that which invigorates it. In a sermon showing the nature of this relationship he writes that 'to maintain in us a constant and steady disposition to obedience . . . we do need continual supplies of grace from God'.[1] 'The life of practice',[2] he continues, consists in this, and he adds that 'devotion is that holy and heavenly fire which darteth into our minds the light of spiritual knowledge, which kindleth in our hearts the warmth of holy desires: if therefore we do continue long absent from it, a night of darkness will overspread our minds, a deadening coldness will seize upon our affections'.[3] Barrow's Latitudinarianism, of which there are various evidences, was integrated into a deeper approach, and just as his practicality has this context of inwardness and has nothing superficial about it, so also the implications of doctrinal fundamentals for the practice of religion are brought out in his sermons on the Incarnation and the Passion. The characteristic practicality of Latitudinarianism and devotion in the traditional mode are combined within a theological framework and are expressed with feeling and directness. 'The consideration of our Lord's suffering in this manner is very useful in application to our practice',[4] he writes, sounding the authentic Latitudinarian note. But there is more than this, for if Barrow stresses that 'meditation on the cross'[5] has this outward context, so it has an inward and theological context also: 'it indeed may yield great joy and sprightly consolation to us, to contemplate our Lord upon the Cross, exercising his immense charity towards us, transacting all the work of our redemption'. With restraint he combines two central theological

1. *Twenty-two Sermons selected from the Works of the Rev. Isaac Barrow*, (*First Selection*, Vol. I, 1798), and (*Second Selection*, Vol. II, 1801), Vol. II, S. XV, p. 359.
2. *Ib.* S. XIV, p. 331.   4. *Ib.* Vol. II, S. III, p. 77.
3. *Ib.* S. XV, p. 358.   5. *Ib.*

interpretations of the Atonement,—'not only as a resolute sufferer but as a noble conqueror',—and there are far-heard echoes of Venantius Fortunatus,—'was ever tree adorned with trophies so pompous and splendid'.[1] 'How greatly we should be moved thereby',[2] he writes, for as it moves man to charity, humility and patience so 'that tragical cross . . . as in a glass' reflects man's loss and infirmity.[3] In all that he writes on the meaning of Christmas there is the same warmth, reflectiveness and realism, for because of it, 'joy is a duty'[4] and 'such as may not only minister a dry satisfaction to your reason, but sensibly touch your affections'.[5] It is not possible to describe Barrow as 'mens et praeterea nihil', for his emphasis on reason is neither exclusive nor unrelated to the total setting of personality.

Barrow's writing is plain and often vivid, conforming in this to the Latitudinarian pattern like that of Wilkins and to the simple style of the Royal Society to which both belonged. Like those of Tillotson and other Latitudinarians, his sermons are Scriptural, expository and practical, but there are frequent references to the Fathers who are described as 'wise instructors'[6] and to 'the Holy Scripture and ecclesiastical tradition interpreting it'.[7] Barrow, whose personal predilections inclined both to the new and to the old with regard to the new philosophy and to the writings of antiquity, after the manner depicted as characteristic of the new men of latitude by Simon Patrick, is firmly set within the theological method of Scripture, antiquity and reason. But it is his attitude to the latter which places him unequivocally in the tradition of the Cambridge Platonists and the Latitudinarians. He has that 'sense of our lives' frailty'[8] which is also expressed by Whichcote, and it momentarily lights with its transience the otherwise solid Latitudinarian feeling of being firmly set in a recognisable world of purpose and of responsibility. Barrow does not fall into the complacent error of making ratiocination the mark of humanity, but like Smith, he sees the human distinction in reflectiveness: 'it is a peculiar excellency of human nature which seemeth more to distinguish a man from any inferior rank of creatures than bare reason itself, that he can reflect on all that is done within him'. He makes

1. *Ib.* p. 81.
2. *Ib.* p. 86.
3. *Ib.* p. 83.
4. *Ib.* Vol. II, S. I, p. 1.

5. *Ib.* p. 3.
6. *Ib.* Vol. II, S. XXII, p. 545.
7. *Ib.* Vol. I, S. IV, p. 72.
8. *Ib.* Vol. I, S. XI, p. 224.

the same comment as Wilkins and Patrick that 'some shadows of other rational operations are discoverable in beasts; and it is not easy to convince them who from plausible experiments do affirm them sometimes to syllogise: but no good reason or experience can, I suppose, make it probable that they partake of this reflexive faculty'.[1] He is at one with More, Bentley and the new philosophy generally in the way in which he outlines the argument from design, 'from the manifold and manifest footsteps of admirable wisdom, skill and design apparent in the general order, and in the particular frame of creatures; the beautiful harmony of the whole and the artificial contrivance of each part of the world'.[2] This cannot be imagined as proceeding from chance or necessity, and it may be recalled that one of Barrow's closest friends was John Ray, author of *The Wisdom of God Manifested in the Works of Creation*, and that he himself had commended natural studies. In all this, Barrow's sympathy with and contribution to the new outlook is evident. Its effect is to be seen also in his general approach to those questions where differences in theological method were most apparent.

It is not simply that Barrow's choice of subjects is practical, but that his whole theological approach is orientated away from the thinking 'lately expressed by the professors of Leyden in their *Synopsis purioris Theologiae*'.[3] His position is expressed in the same terms as that of Wilkins, and if he does not make the same use of Aquinas as does the latter his ideas are cast in the same mould, for like Wilkins and Tillotson, he considers that 'the end of all religion is the bringing men to happiness'.[4] The Wisdom books feature largely in Barrow's work, and the characteristic nexus of ideas constitutes a significant element in his thought: 'as for wisdom, that may denote either sapience, a habit of knowing what is true; or prudence, a disposition of choosing what is good; we may here understand both, especially the latter, for as Tully saith of philosophy, the sum or whole of philosophy refers to living happily, so all divine wisdom doth respect good practice'.[5] Barrow's concern with the realities of the situation as he saw it determines his position in which, as in the case of Wilkins, these leading ideas are coupled with a strong emphasis on practical divinity: 'the study of

1. *Ib.* Vol. I, S. XVII, p. 345.   4. *Ib.* Vol. I, S. VIII, p. 154.
2. *Ib.* Vol. I, S. I, p. 4.   5. *Ib.* Vol. I, S. X, p. 196.
3. *Ib.* Vol. I, S. VII, p. 138.

moral philosophy, how exceedingly beneficial may it be to us, suggesting to us the dictates of reason concerning the nature and faculties of our soul, the chief good and end of our life, the way and means of attaining happiness, the best rules and method of practice'.[1]

It has been suggested earlier that Barrow's preoccupation with the practical was not dictated solely by the obvious needs of the times, but was a consequent part of his attitude to the wider questions under discussion in contemporary theology, an attitude combining something of the content of Cambridge Platonism with the form of Latitudinarianism. This is apparent in his reaction from the contemporary systematic deductions in dogmatic theology which he regards as being counter to the evidence of Scripture and antiquity. He charges the upholders of these views with basic misconceptions, maintaining that nature, providence and the Incarnation are progressive and cumulative evidence of 'the goodness and patience of God' who should not be thought of in terms inferior to these.[2] It follows that redemption is universal, 'not grounded upon any special love or any absolute decree concerning those persons who in event shall be saved . . . wherefore it proceedeth from God's natural goodness'.[3] It is not easy to see how 'any pretending reverence to Scripture should dare (upon consequences of their own devising) to question it'.[4] The nature, the practice and the liturgy of the Church from the beginning would be meaningless if it were not 'every baptised Christian' but only 'an uncertain and unknown part of the Church' which was involved.[5] Since this is evident from Scripture and antiquity the conclusion is that 'it is then a Catholic and true doctrine',[6] and it may be summarised by saying that all are 'salvabiles, capable of salvation, and salvandos, designed to salvation'.[7] For Barrow, the status of the individual member and the meaning of membership cannot be understood apart from these considerations which he regards as the plain meaning of Scripture and accepted as such during the first centuries: 'and it hath been the doctrine constantly with general consent delivered in and by the Catholic Church, that to all persons by the holy mystery of baptism duly initiated into

1. *Ib*. Vol. I, S. XVI, p. 334.
2. *Ib*. Vol. I, S. I and S. II, p. 25.
3. *Ib*. Vol. I, S. III, p. 56.
4. *Ib*. Vol. I, S. III, p. 39.
5. *Ib*. Vol. I, S. III, p. 55.
6. *Ib*. Vol. I, S. III, p. 56.
7. *Ib*. Vol. I, S. IV, p. 59.

Christianity, and admitted into the communion of Christ's body, the grace of the Holy Spirit is communicated, enabling them to perform the conditions of piety and virtue which they undertake'.[1]

The same considerations, namely the sense of Scripture and the opinion of early writers, are of weight in connection with the question of faith which Barrow defines as not only being firmly persuaded of truth but also that 'this persuasion of mind' is 'apt to produce . . . obedience'. He adds that 'this was the common and current notion of faith among the ancient Christians; neither do we . . . meet with any other in their writings; all of which things do abundantly confirm the truth thereof'.[2] There are other aspects also, for as well as the fact that 'the word faith is thus extended to comprehend . . . a purpose of obedience',[3] there is the question of that to which it relates. In Barrow's view, it 'doth relate only to propositions revealed by God (or at least deduced from principles of reason . . .) not unto other propositions concerning particular matter of fact, subject to private conscience or experience; nor to any conclusions depending on such propositions'.[4] He instances as a case in point the attitude which maintains that faith consists in 'being persuaded that . . . we stand possessed of his favour', and concludes that in Scripture, faith is regarded as a necessary prerequisite to 'especial . . . not general, benevolence'.[5] 'Much less', he continues, 'is that notion of faith right which defines faith to be a firm and certain knowledge of God's eternal good will towards us particularly'.[6] Barrow's reaction may be seen in the comment 'how many good people must this doctrine discourage and perplex'. He notes that theologically it is open to serious criticism in that it presupposes the idea that grace is indefectible, and that 'it inverts and confounds the order of things declared in Scripture',[7] the chief objection being that its conclusions are contrary to the general sense of Scripture.

It is against this general background that Barrow's practicality of outlook is expressed, and as in the case of Wilkins, there are very few of his sermons which are not in some way concerned with it. In view of the frequent references to the subject it might appear unnecessary to give instances, yet to omit illustrations altogether

1. *Ib*. Vol. I, S. V, p. 72.
2. *Ib*. Vol. I, S. VII, p. 124.
3. *Ib*. Vol. I, S. VII, p. 130.
4. *Ib*. Vol. I, S. VII, p. 132.
5. *Ib*. Vol. I, S. VII, p. 137.
6. *Ib*. p. 138.
7. *Ib*. p. 139.

might leave an impression that was less than adequate. Writing of how 'examples . . . direct practice', he observes that 'a system of precepts, though exquisitely compacted, is, in comparison, but a skeleton . . . exhibiting nothing of person, place, time, manner, degree, wherein chiefly the flesh and blood, the colours and graces, the life and soul of things do consist'.[1] Barrow's realistic approach has this quality of the seeing eye which prevents his writing from becoming pedestrian, and his depth of insight, so frequently in evidence when he analyses different qualities, has the same effect. Thus, he will point out as an analogy a mathematician giving life to his theorem by a diagram, or he will illustrate by comparison with a border dispute the region of difficult application and even of seeming self-contradiction between 'duty and miscarriage in practice: for although the extreme degrees, and even the middle regions of these things are very distant, yet the borders of them do lie very close together, and are in a manner contiguous; a certain ridge of separation running between them, which commonly . . . it is not easy to discern'.[2] He has the capacity of describing for example, gratitude or industry, in such a way as to relate them directly to experience. As has been indicated, the connection between obedience and faith sets this emphasis on practicality in a wider and deeper context than that of keeping rules. Yet Barrow betrays no sensitivity about laws and rules, and this was for many Puritans in his own day an evident token of his inability to grasp central truths. Barrow held that the reverse was the case, for just as faith is 'apt to produce obedience',[3] so both the setting and the goal of law is what he calls 'general charity', which leads to happiness. With Wilkins he quotes, 'Fear God, and keep his commandments, for this is the whole of man; (the whole duty, the whole design, the whole perfection, the sum of our wisdom and our happiness)'.[4] This is the background for the understanding of the numerous references to 'the observance of rules', to practice expressing itself in observing laws, to 'the truest and best rules of action'.[5] For Barrow, all law converges in charity and this is at once the purpose and the justification of rules: 'Scripture . . . often expressly declares charity to be the fulfilling of God's law, as the best expression of all our duty toward God, of faith in him, love and rever-

1. *Ib.* Vol. II, S. V, p. 125.
2. *Ib.* Vol. II, S. XVIII, p. 425.
3. *Ib.* Vol. I, S. VII, p. 124.
4. *Ib.* Vol. II, S. VII, p. 167.
5. *Ib.* S. X, p. 234., S. XI, p. 255.

ence of him, and as either formally containing, or naturally producing all our duty toward our neighbour'.[1] In fact, a clearer
exposition of the depth of Barrow's simple practicality could
scarcely be found. The similarity between Barrow's thought and
that of Wilkins is evident and it is further underlined by a shared
predilection for the Wisdom books and by the importance attached
to wisdom as prudence or practical reason.[2] Additional evidence of
Barrow's Latitudinarianism appears in the recurring theme of the
'innumerable advantages' of religion in that it regulates human
relationships in business and family affairs, in government and
friendship, and conduces to health, tranquillity and 'interior
content'.[3] Yet Barrow's whole approach is given another dimension not only by the theological context already mentioned but by
the insistence on the necessity of a vitalising source for that
practicality to which time and again he returns.[4]

Linking as he does in his person and in his work on mathematics and theology, the Cambridge Platonists, the Latitudinarians
and Wilkins with Ray the naturalist and Newton the mathematician, Barrow made his own contribution to theological method and
to the furtherance of mathematical studies, and in both respects
his work was of value.

1. *Ib*. S. XXII, p. 532.
2. *Ib*. S. XXI, p. 520, *ib*. Vol. I,
   S. IX, p. 173, S. X, p. 196.
3. *Ib*. Vol. II, S. XI, pp. 238–9, 261–2.
4. *Ib*. SS. XIV–XVII.

CHAPTER VII

THE NEW PHILOSOPHY AND THEOLOGICAL METHOD

As an exponent of the place and function of natural theology, as an upholder of reason and as an imaginative student of scientific matters, Wilkins left a varied impress on the period, but particularly in respect of the Latitudinarian movement and the new philosophy. While the former is hardly to be explained apart from the Cambridge Platonists, it now seems probable that sufficient account has not been taken of Wilkins's contribution. The terms in which Latitudinarianism expressed itself are in some measure due to the distinctive and individual element in this thought which had its effect on Tillotson and Stillingfleet.

His contact with the new philosophy was not simply by way of his participation in and promotion of it at Oxford, or of his connection with the Royal Society, but also by way of his influence on Ray. More and Cudworth had given much to Ray, and Wilkins's work on natural theology and his views on the place of the new philosophy had substantially helped in providing an integrated background of thought against which both could be seen to have the same bearing and direction. So Ray regarded his book, *The Wisdom of God manifested in the works of Creation*, as 'divinity',[1] not in spite of but because of its contents, for 'the enumeration and consideration of these works . . . justify the denominating such a discourse as this rather theological than philosophical'.[2] As to the method, fundamental truths have 'supernatural demonstrations . . . but not common to all persons or times, and so liable to . . . exception . . . but these proofs taken from effects, and operations, exposed to every man's view, not to be denied or questioned by any'[3] are such that cannot be ignored. The effect of the method of the new philosophy on theological method is clear in Ray's approach to the subject. It is the method outlined by More and followed by Bentley, and Wilkins played a part in its development.

1. *Ib*. Preface.
2. *Ib*. i.e. scientific.
3. *Ib*.

In his definitive biography of Ray, C. E. Raven accords a place of some importance to Wilkins in the thought of the period by reason of his influence on his contemporaries. Raven has in mind, of course, the effect of Wilkins on men like Ray, Boyle and Hooke, and the way in which he gathered together the group which was to be the nucleus of the Royal Society. But the same point may be made here in respect of Wilkins's contact with Tillotson, Stillingfleet and Patrick, for he transmitted to them a specific and recognisable element in their ideas. In fact, the significance of Wilkins grows clearer the more he is seen in relation to these *two* movements of thought, and his place in the development of theological method is found to be more deserving of note than has been supposed. Raven writes, 'Wilkins was one of those rather rare men who without specialised academic eminence by the range of their interests and quality of their personality exercise a creative influence upon history. He was not a great thinker or scholar, scientist or divine: he was not even a great organiser or administrator or leader: but judged by his effect upon his contemporaries and his achievement under circumstances of exceptional difficulty he was certainly a great man'.[1] He sees in Wilkins imagination and energy to accomplish and to stimulate hard work, and he comments on his industry, an example of which was the way in which Wilkins rewrote the *Essay towards a Real Character and Philosophical Language* when the original was destroyed in the Great Fire. Ray collaborated by providing tables of animals, birds, fishes and plants for the work the object of which was to evolve a universal and simplified speech to replace Latin which was going out of use.[2] The project was not a success but was typical of the imaginative side of Wilkins, and the demands which he made on Ray who finished his part of the task in three weeks were an indication of the relationship, for Ray professed a lifelong admiration for Wilkins.[3] The acquaintance began at Trinity, Cambridge, and 'was strengthened by Wilkins's friendship with Willughby',[4] and Ray frequently stayed with Wilkins. In both the *Wisdom* and the *Persuasive* he draws on the work of Wilkins, and in the latter acknowledges himself 'to have borrowed a good part'[5] of the material from Wilkins's book.

1. C. E. Raven, *John Ray*, p. 55.
2. *Ib.* p. 56.
3. *Ib.* 57.
4. *Ib.* p. 56.
5. Preface to the *Persuasive*.

John Ray, son of a blacksmith, was born at Black Notley in 1627, and the importance of his work for the development of theological method has already been touched upon. While it is of course as a naturalist and student of the new philosophy that Ray became known, he is far from being unimportant in the emergence of the new approach by which the design and purpose being revealed in the natural world and the real knowledge resulting from exact observation were being related to a theology in which experience was interpreted by reason. Like the Cambridge Platonists he saw knowledge as one, so that he could describe natural studies as 'part of the business of a Sabbath day'[1] and the study of physiology as 'a preparative to divinity'.[2] As a naturalist he was drawn to the idea of a plastic nature developed in Cudworth's *True Intellectual System*, and in the *Wisdom* he is indebted to More's *Antidote*, just as he in turn gave Butler the basis of the *Analogy* and Paley material for the *Natural Theology*. It was in fact a small world at the time, and community of ideas and contacts of individuals are a constantly recurring factor.

C. E. Raven's assessment of Ray takes account of this aspect of his work: 'We shall mistake the quality of his achievement if we misunderstand him here. He was not an anticipator of Darwin, even though he admits doubt of the fixity of species and records evidence of their transformation. He is not possessed of a clear and consistent philosophy foreshadowing the modern outlook, though there are abundant signs of a power to grasp the unity and inter-relationships of experience which lifts him high above most of his contemporaries. He is not a philosophic theologian, though his *Wisdom of God* supplied the basis for Butler's *Analogy* and is a greater book than Paley's *Natural Theology*. His greatness is that in a time of transition and universal turmoil he saw the need for precise and ordered knowledge, set himself to test the old and explore the new, and by dint of immense labour in the field and in the study laid the foundations of modern science in many branches of zoology and botany. He studied, corrected and collated the existing literature; he collected, identified, investigated, described and classified mammals, birds, reptiles, fishes and insects, cryptograms and all known plants; he contributed richly to the advance of geology and made observations in astronomy and physics; he was

1. *Widsom* (4th ed.), p. 199.
2. *Ib*. p. 204.

a pioneer in the study of language and first revealed the importance of dialect and folk-speech; he did as much as any man of his time to develop a new understanding and interpretation of religion; more perhaps than any man he enabled the transition from the medieval to the modern outlook'.[1]

Ray's many-sided ability extended to mathematics which he studied in company with Barrow: 'If Ray was fit to study alongside Barrow he must have had mathematical gifts of a high order'.[2] His work in the study of proverbs and dialect ranks him as pioneer in the subject,[3] and the fact that he used Latin for his writings on botany and zoology gave a world-wide currency to his work and helped to assure his place as 'the most eminent of contemporary naturalists'.[4] The fact that Ray's position was recognised by his contemporaries was due not simply to his ability but also, as Raven points out,[5] to his personality which made a uniform impression of modesty, of sociability, and of wide interests, on those who left an account of him and his work, and which is confirmed by his correspondence.

Admitted to Trinity College, Cambridge, in 1644, he went to Catharine Hall almost immediately owing to a scholarship being available there, and two years later he transferred to Trinity, where he was elected Fellow in 1649. He held various offices and appointments and in 1660 he was ordained in London by Sanderson. In 1662 he resigned his Fellowship under the Act of Uniformity which required a declaration on pain of forfeiture that the taking of the Covenant carried with it no obligation since it was in itself unlawful. Ray had not taken the Covenant but he could not agree that the Parliament had dispensing power, and since a declaration to this effect was required from all as a condition of remaining in their present places, he felt that he had no alternative but to resign. Raven points out that it was not a decision which he took lightly, but that his view of the situation was such that it would not permit him to see the matter in any other light. As to the ultimate effect of Ray's course of action, he maintains that although it cut him off from security and from the continued commerce of ideas which a University affords, it left him free to pursue his work in his chosen subject without the hindrance of other demands.[6]

1. *John Ray*, p. 11.
2. *Ib.* p. 35.
3. p. 33.
4. *Ib.* p. 30.
5. *Ib.* p. 67.
6. *Ib.* pp. 60–61

Inevitably, in view of his work Ray was an assiduous traveller, visiting Italy, Sicily, Switzerland, and France, studying anatomy, birds and fishes, as well as making journeys in England, Scotland and Wales, collecting material for his works on plants, ornithology and geology. This is not the place, even if one had the knowledge, to enlarge upon his work in these subjects, save to note that for Ray it was one with a religious interpretation of life which he considered to be strengthened by every fresh discovery in natural studies. Thus when he came to write the *Wisdom*, he utilised material from his observations and from those of others in these subjects to show the predominance in the created world of wisdom, order and design. The fact that in his preface he voices the feeling that he ought 'to write something in divinity, having written so much on other subjects' indicates the context in which he saw the researches which helped to lay the foundations of a new approach in these subjects. But he also convinced the traditionalists that this was a legitimate field for enquiry, and so commended the new philosophy that there developed as Raven points out[1] a type of theology capable of the task of interpretation in a period of changing ideas. His contribution therefore was not confined to his work as a naturalist, for its effects were felt in a wider area than that of specialised studies however far-reaching their implications. The influence of Whichcote, More, Cudworth and Wilkins, as Raven writes, gave him a theology in which reason, science, observation and exact knowledge had a function and a place.[2]

After resigning his Fellowship Ray returned to Essex, and between that time and the date of his death in 1705 he gave himself to travelling in the interests of his studies and to the production of his numerous works. From time to time he stayed with various friends, including Wilkins, of whom he had many in different professions, 'diverse in all else except their interest in nature'.[3] Among them were Willughby, who made several journeys with Ray and collaborated with him, Robinson, who 'kept in touch with scientists and was the chief link between them and Ray',[4] Sloane, Worthington and many others. In addition to his large output of published work, Ray maintained a correspondence extensive even for those days when such interchange of views took the place now supplied by learned journals, and many owed to him their interest

1. *Ib.* p. 478.   3. *Ib.* p. 66.
2. *Ib.* p. 37.   4. *Ib.* p. 208.

in natural history.[1] His personality which so impressed contemporaries was matched by an ability which subsequently ensured his recognition as one of the greatest naturalists.[2]

It is not however because of its relevance to the development of theological method that the aspect of Ray's work shown in *The Wisdom of God manifested in the Works of Creation* requires equal recognition, for as Raven indicates, it was 'certainly his most popular and influential achievement'.[3] Published in 1691, it was reprinted in the following year and reached a fourth edition by 1704. Its effect on other works has already been noted: 'more than any other single book it initiated the true adventure of modern science'.[4] It was also, in a way that More's *Antidote* was not, an essay in interpretation on the part of theology against a background of thought which was showing the beginnings of being scientific in a real sense. In fact Ray himself was one of those who made a contribution to the establishing of a frame of reference which was almost altogether lacking forty years earlier when More was at work on his book. One of the factors which was responsible for a good deal in this respect was the Royal Society, to which Ray had been admitted in 1667 and to which Willughby belonged and Wilkins, 'the chief mover and first secretary who had proposed him for election'.[5] Because of the quality of its membership it was saved from becoming just a clique of virtuosi or a gathering for the promotion of useful and interesting gadgets. By and large it became a forum for serious discussion and experiment which led to real advances and substantial achievements in mathematics, science, invention and natural studies. By these means it was possible to outline the preliminary sketch for a more settled picture of things as they are, and in 1652 nothing comparable had been available to More.

The book was dedicated to Lady Lettice Wendy, sister of Francis Willughby, Ray's friend and travelling-companion to whose liberality, as he wrote in the dedication, he owed the fact that he had the leisure to write.[6] Ray had done invaluable service by systematising, classifying and accurately describing, and so laying a real basis for natural studies. The results of this exact and discriminating observation are to be seen throughout *The*

1. *Ib.* p. 68.
2. *Ib.* p. 67.
3. *Ib.* p. 452.
4. *Ib.*
5. *Ib.* p. 145.
6. Dedication.

Wisdom of God manifested in the Works of Creation which contains countless instances of this first-hand observation and discussion of discoveries. But Ray did not confine himself to the work of identification and to sifting out elements of fiction and folk-lore and to accumulating a body of verified facts. In his book he concerns himself also with interpretation, with the meaning of the processes he has observed and with their relation to other processes within the whole: 'The novelty of the book consists in the fact that in it Ray turns from the preliminary task of identifying, describing and classifying to that of interpreting the significance of physical and physiological processes, studying the problems of form and function and of adaptation to environment, and observing behaviour and recording the achievements of instinct'.[1] He is attempting, as it were, to work out a general understanding in which the effect of each successive instance of observation is to be corroborative of design.

It is here that his specialised studies assume a wider context in that they become part of an understanding of the universe based on reason, and are productive of an attitude to theological questions which is conditioned by the method and findings of these studies. Ray merges the insights derived from Whichcote, Cudworth, More and Wilkins with the procedure and contents of the new philosophy, so that his book as well as being reckoned as having 'a primary place in the development of modern science'[2] can also be regarded as having a place in the development of theological method. Its effect was, as Ray intended, to show that the two were not only congruous but complementary, and that because of a common basis of reason there was a necessary connection between them.

In the preface Ray writes that he is aware that some may regard the book as superfluous since so much has been written on the same subject by Cudworth, Stillingfleet, More, Parker and Boyle. In spite of this he has thought it worth attempting since he has been able to put together material not easily available elsewhere, nor collected in one book.[3] Ray is supremely modest about his own achievements and their value.

The works of this visible world are divisible into celestial bodies such as the fixed stars, each with 'a chorus of planets moving about

1. *Ib.* p. 452.   3. Preface.
2. *Ib.* p. 457.

it,' and terrestial bodies.[1] These are either inanimate, 'the elements, meteors and fossils, of all sorts',[2] or animate, which includes animals, birds, fishes and insects.[3] All these visible works are indeed manifold, the stars being innumerable, the telescope having recently proved the conjecture that the Milky Way was made up of countless individual stars singly invisible to the eye: 'and it's likely that, had we more perfect telescopes, many thousands more might be discovered'.[4] It is not possible to make a guess at the number of inanimate terrrestial bodies, and Ray tentatively puts the number of animals at one hundred and fifty species as far as was known at present. Birds he estimated at five hundred species, and fish at more than six times that number, but it cannot be conjectured with any certainty how many species remain undiscovered.[5] As to insects, he quotes his friend Lister to the effect that there cannot be fewer than three thousand species, perhaps many more,[6] and he adds that in the summer of 1691 he found more species of butterflies in his own neighbourhood of Notley than he had previously assigned to the whole of England, and that there were many more as yet undiscovered.[7]

'What can we infer from all this?' he asks, but that the variety of creatures implies the 'unbounded capacity' of the wisdom that created them, as does the way in which they are adapted to their environments.[8] This is the second aspect of his theme, that these visible works 'are all very wisely contrived and adapted to ends both particular and general'.[9] Ray's work is a commentary on views such as those of Smith for whom all the creatures were 'so many glasses' reflecting the wisdom that made them.

This is the main part of the book, in which he makes full use of researches in natural studies concerning function, form, behaviour and adaptation, By way of a general introduction he examines first those systems which undertake to give an account of the universe on the basis of a 'mechanical hypothesis of matter, moved either uncertainly, or according to . . . laws, without the intervention . . . of any superior Agent'.[10]

Ray's analysis of these systems serves to delineate his own position in which the leading idea is that of purpose and design

1. *Wisdom*, p. 18. 6. *Ib.* p. 22.
2. *Ib.* p. 21. 7. *Ib.* p. 24.
3. *Ib.* p. 22. 8. *Ib.* p. 26.
4. *Ib.* p. 19. 9. *Ib.* p. 31.
5. *Ib.* p. 22. 10. *Ib.* p. 32.

confirmed by observation. The wide dissemination of his work must have greatly strengthened this idea, although he was aware of the difficulties inherent in it, as is clear from his adherence to the idea of a plastic nature which endeavours to avoid the dilemma entailed by the traditional teleology. In fairness to Ray his choice of the concept was in no way dictated by the fact that it seemed to provide a way out. Rather is it consistent with that vitalism passed on by More and Cudworth and which seemed to Ray to tally with his own observations: 'Why should each particular so observe its kind, as constantly to produce the same leaf for consistency, figure, division and edging; and bring forth the same kind of flower, and fruit, and seed, and that though you translate it into a soil which naturally puts forth no such kind of plant, so that it is some seminal form or virtue, which doth effect this or rather some intelligent plastic nature'.[1] Together with this plastic nature which regulates 'the whole economy of the plant', and combined with it, there is an inward vitality 'which appears in that a branch cut off of a plant will take root and grow and become a perfect plant itself'.[2]

Ray deals briefly with the view based on the eternity of matter and with the atomical hypothesis since, as he points out, the first has been fully treated by Tillotson and Wilkins,[3] and the second by Cudworth and Stillingfleet.[4] He devotes somewhat more space to an examination of the argument of Descartes because if accepted it 'evacuates' the argument from design, and in effect undermines what Ray sees as the fruitful contribution of the new philosophy to theological method.[5] In his criticism of mechanistic ideas, Ray with Cudworth frequently refers to a 'vital motion' and a 'vital principle' in which can be discerned the mutual impact on each other of the new philosophy and a theology in which immanence is emphasised, for they meet in a concept of nature in which the idea of omnipotence includes the notion of a plastic nature. It is fair to say that while Ray owes to the Cambridge Platonists something of the basic content of his thinking, he is indebted also to Wilkins for the form of its expression in terms of natural theology. The writings of the Cambridge Platonists show evidence of a

1. *Ib.* p. 116.
2. *Ib.* p. 118.
3. *Ib.* p. 33.
4. *Ib.* p. 38.
5. *Ib.* p. 42.

theology in which nature is taken account of, but those of Wilkins
and the Latitudinarians set themselves deliberately to construct a
natural theology. This is a different thing, something more formulated and simplified, and Ray shows its influence not only in
the simple form of his book but in an awareness, which he expresses, of the need for a clear and easily assimilated statement of
the position.[1] It is in fact significant in this connection that Ray
concludes his book with a summary by Wilkins.[2]

Ray notes Boyle's discussion of Descartes's exclusion of 'all
consideration of final causes from natural philosophy',[3] and
Cudworth's criticism of the 'hypothesis of matter so and so
divided and moved',[4] adding observations of his own. He finds
himself in disagreement with Boyle's *Free Enquiry into the Vulgar
Notion of Nature*, where it is stated that 'the great Author of
things did, when he first formed the universe and undistinguished
matter into the world, put its parts into various motions' and
'settled such laws or rules of local motion among the parts of
universal matter'.[5] However, on reading another work by the same
author, he finds that Boyle expresses himself as being dissatisfied
with the view that 'after the first formation of the universe all
things are brought to pass by the settled laws of nature' on the
grounds that inanimate bodies cannot understand what a law is and
what it enjoins: 'therefore the actions of inanimate bodies, which
cannot incite or moderate their own actions, are produced by real
power, not by laws'.[6] Ray's comment is 'so that we are in the main
agreed, differing chiefly about the Agent that executes those laws,
which he holds to be God himself immediately, we a plastic
nature'.[7] For Ray, two of the most convincing of the four arguments advanced by Cudworth in favour of a plastic nature, are
characteristically those based on observation, namely, 'the slow
and gradual process that is in the generation of things' and 'those
errors and bungles ... which argue the Agent not to be irresistible'.[8]

1. *Ib.* p. 44.
2. *Ib.* p. 463.
3. *Ib.* p. 43.
4. *Ib.* p. 45.
5. *Ib.* p. 53.
6. *Ib.* p. 56, *The Christian Virtuoso.*
7. *Ib.* p. 57. Cp. p. 55, 'there must, besides matter and law, be some efficient,
   and that either a quality or power inherent in the matter itself, which is hard
   to conceive, or some external intelligent Agent, either God himself immediately, or some plastic nature'.
8. *Ib.* p. 57.

After this digression in which the lines of general approach are laid down, Ray comes to take a view of the order, harmony, ends and uses, of the different divisions of the visible creation. He introduces the comparison between the works of nature and the works of art with the frequently-quoted passage from Wilkins's book on the way in which the microscope has revealed the minute delicacy and intricacy of the former.[1] He repeats the divisions of 'this material and visible world' into inanimate celestial bodies such as the sun, moon and stars, and inanimate terrestial bodies which are simple, like fire, water, earth and air, or imperfectly mixed as are meteors, or more perfectly mixed as stones, metals and minerals. There are also animate bodies which are graded from plants 'with a vegetative soul' through animals, birds, fishes and insects, which have 'a sensitive soul' to the human body with 'a rational soul'.[2] He is careful to stress that his recognition of this division is only by way of compliance with commonly-received opinion, and because it is easily understood and remembered: 'though I do not think it agreeable to philosphic verity and accuracy, but do rather incline to the atomic hypothesis'.[3]

The bodies called elements are not the only ingredients of mixed bodies, nor are they absolutely simple in themselves. He instances sea-water which contains salt, and both sea-water and fresh water are able to nourish fish, 'consequently containing the various parts of which their bodies are compounded'. Furthermore, certain metals, salts and some kinds of stones, generally referred to as mixed, are 'as simple as the elements themselves'.[4] Ray then goes on to enlarge on what he means by the atomic hypothesis: 'I should therefore with Dr Grew and others, rather attribute the various species of inanimate bodies to the divers figures of the minute particles of which they are made up'. The reason why no species of inanimate bodies disappear and no new ones are produced is because the number of atoms into which matter was at first divided is fixed. An additional reason given by Ray is that 'those minute parts are indivisible, not absolutely, but by any natural force; so that there neither is nor can be more or fewer of them: For were they divisible into small and diversely-figured parts by fire or any other natural agent, the species of nature must be confounded, some might be lost and destroyed, but new ones would certainly be produced'.[1]

Whether or no there can be discerned here some faint intimation of nuclear fission is less important than the fact that Ray's concept of matter makes an interesting comparison with that of Boyle. 'Boyle's view that all substances were composed of minute parts or atoms of a similar type, differing merely in their arrangement or motion, foreshadows modern concepts of the electrical structure of matter, but it also made transmutation seem likely'.[2] This idea of the transmutation of one metal into another was one that had been ardently pursued for centuries with the aim of transmuting baser metals into gold. Pilkington points out that Boyle mistakenly had thought that he had degraded gold into silver, and that such transmutations were possible on the basis of the uniformity of matter, the variety of its arrangement constituting the only difference between substances.[3]

Ray qualifies the view that substances were composed of atoms of a similar type, and does not consider 'these inanimate bodies to consist wholly of one sort of atoms, but that their bulk consists mainly or chiefly of one sort. But whereas it may be objected, that metals (which of all others seem to be most simple) may be transmuted one into another, and so the species doth not depend upon the being compounded of atoms of one figure; I answer, I am not fully satisfied of the matter of fact: but if any such transmutation be, possibly all metals may be of one species, and the diversity may proceed from the admixture of different bodies with the principles of the metal'.[4]

Boyle, the chief initiator of advance in chemistry, and Ray who occupies a similar position in natural studies, are moving in the same atmosphere of observation and deduction in their different subjects, and if in this particular instance Ray seems to be more questioning than the author of *The Sceptical Chymist*, they held to the same method of enquiry. They related the specific instances of their observation to the picture of the natural world as a whole seen within the framework of design, so that their work seemed to confirm and to illustrate in a totally new way the basic but more broadly-stated concepts of former times. Neither Ray nor Boyle were simply intellectualists, nor, on the other hand, were they

1. *Ib.* p. 68.
2. R. Pilkington, *Robert Boyle*, p. 141.
3. *Ib.*
4. loc. cit. p. 68.

simply maintaining the thesis of the unity of theology and the new philosophy. Rather, the fact seemed to emerge more and more clearly from their work that it is, in Ray's phrase, a 'preparative to divinity'.[1] Recurring in their work is what can best be described as a vein of poetry as they apprehend the prodigality of beauty and the intricacy of detail, and as they perceive that the subject is only beginning to be understood. 'Let us not think' wrote Ray, 'that the bounds of science are fixed like Hercules' Pillars, and inscribed with a ne plus ultra . . . the treasures of nature are inexhaustible'.[2]

Dealing with the heavenly bodies[3], Ray refers to their circular motion on their own axes, to gravity, to the relation of the sun and moon to the earth and to its natural processes. He is not prepared to attempt a definition of gravity, and while he holds it as reasonable to assume that this circular motion is as necessary to other planetary bodies as it is to the earth, he cannot understand the necessity of it, 'for want of understanding the nature of those bodies'.[4] This suspension of judgment combined with a confidence that further information would serve to confirm what present knowledge showed, namely, 'rule, order and constancy; the effects and arguments of wisdom',[5] is common to Ray, Boyle and others.

It is not difficult to see how this began to affect theology, for the patient tarrying on the emergence of new facts gave a calm, unhurried air, while the confidence that the new facts would be confirmatory resulted in a diffused optimism. Inevitably, it contributed to a decline of interest in a theology of election as the emphasis shifted from sovereignty to wisdom and away from a tendency to depreciate natural qualities. The full impact of natural theology outlined by More and Wilkins was felt once the writings of Ray and Boyle became known. It appeared to fit in with the vitalism of the Cambridge Platonists and with what they derived from Plotinus, Ficino and others, to encourage a habit of looking at things in terms of what may be loosely called immanentist ways of thinking. It combined with the idea of reason which the Latitudinarians took from sources already referred to, but was kept in position by their concern with practical questions. In consequence, the content of natural theology was never isolated from the experience of the human situation to become simply a hypothesis

1. *Ib.* p. 204.
2. *Ib.* p. 200.
3. *Ib.* p. 70.
4. *Ib.* p. 71.
5. *Ib.* p. 76.

guaranteeing the theological good intentions of those whose real interests lay elsewhere. This is clear in Wilkins's works, in Ray's *Persuasive*, and in the writings of Boyle. Implicit in the discussion of law in the *Ecclesiastical Polity*, natural theology fitted into a complementary position in the traditional nexus of Scripture, the Church and the use of the Book of Common Prayer, and remained a permanent element in theological method. The way in which it was used bears out the contention of A. E. Taylor that 'no living theology has ever arisen from mere intellectual curiosity' for it was only one element in the total theological outlook of the time, but was always present in some degree with its possibilities for effective contact with the scientific outlook.

It might be asserted that the emphasis on natural theology led to humanism, to an over-pragmatic approach and to a deficient sense of urgency. While this is an over-statement of the position, to deny that there is an element of truth in it would, in a sense, be to misunderstand the Cambridge Platonists, the Latitudinarians and the new philosophers. Either deliberately or incidentally, something of these tendencies is discernible, but they remain only part of the whole, an accepted consequence of what was an imperative need, that of asserting the existence of purpose and meaning.

Ray finds himself in agreement with Wilkins, whose writing on the subject he refers to, that there is probably life on the moon, but apart from this, its regulation of tides and its uses in connection with navigation and agriculture are enough to show it as a product of wisdom.[1]

He divides terrestrial bodies into inanimate and animate, the former being either simple or mixed.[2] The four elements, fire, water, earth and air are simple, but his use of the term element is only by way of compliance with commonly held opinion, for he does not regard them as the principles or components of all other bodies but rather as 'aggregates of bodies of the same species'.[3] Under all these headings, as throughout the book, the extent of Ray's observation and its discriminating character impart to the book its originality. On numerous occasions he quotes Harvey, Hulse, Robinson, Hook or Boyle, as confirming or illuminating something that he himself has observed. The book conveys an impression of being at first hand and must have been all the more

1. *Ib*. p. 76.   3. *Ib*. p. 79.
2. *Ib*. p. 78.

effective at the time by reason of the large number of observed and attested facts concerning different aspects of the natural world which Ray had collected.

The imperfectly mixed bodies are rain and wind, and the perfectly mixed inanimate bodies are stones, metals, minerals and salts.[1] Ray describes with accuracy and carefulness, yet his factual approach does not prevent the welling up of something deeper as he lingers for a moment over the beauty of precious stones—'the amethyst as it were tinctured with wine, the opal varying its colours like changeable taffeta'[2]—or the fact that 'there is a greater depth of art and skill in the structure of the meanest insect' than anyone can understand.[3] For him there was no need to force the thesis that natural studies had religious significance. He came to it, not as does the modern nature-lover, but by way of hard-won attestation and detailed observation leading to pure intellectual delight in the intricate varieties of form, and finally to wonder at the wisdom which 'shines forth as visibly in the structure of the minutest insect, as in that of a horse or elephant.'[4] For Ray, everything that he observed and understood pointed to the same conclusion, and in this, his attitude to nature was, if more scientific, close to that of the Cambridge Platonists.

From them, and in particular from Cudworth, he derived his use of the idea of plastic nature to which he refers in connection with different aspects of nature,[5] especially with regard to plants. These together with animals are the animate bodies, and Ray asks how the many varied species could maintain their separate identities, continue to show the same habit, such as climbing or creeping, and produce exactly the same seed and leaf and flower and fruit, unless through 'some intelligent plastic nature'.[6] It is not possible to account for 'the determination of the growth and magnitude of plants from mechanical principles, of matter moved without the presidency and guidance of some superior agent'.[7] He instances the fact that all species have a maximum size, and preserve their own structure as to leaves, flowers and seeds: 'that all this be done, and all these parts duly proportioned one to another, there seems to be necessary some intelligent plastic nature, which

1. *Ib*. pp. 101, 105.
2. *Ib*. p. 105.
3. *Ib*. p. 210.
4. *Ib*.
5. *Ib*. pp. 86, 88.
6. *Ib*. p. 117.
7. *Ib*. p. 117.

may understand and regulate the whole economy of the plant'.[1] In addition, if the separate parts of plants are considered it will be seen that roots, fibres, bark, leaves and buds, each have a particular purpose and use in respect of the development of the plant.[2] Ray does not neglect to add the further consideration of their beauty and symmetry,[3] quoting from More's *Antidote* which had helped to give shape to his own work.

Constantly, he is aware of design at a level of size where its intricacy is of the greatest interest, as in the case of most seeds which have in them 'a seminal plant perfectly formed' and whose 'elegant complication' is not only beautiful to examine but an indication that it could not have been 'so formed and folded up without wisdom and providence'.[4] Another example is 'the immense smallness of some seeds, not to be seen by the naked eye', of which a single plant may produce an enormous number and which is 'a convincing argument of the infinite understanding and art of the former of them'.[5] There is the 'lasting vitality' of seeds which ensures the continuance of the species, and the many instances of the perfect adaptation of plants to their conditions.[6] The idea of 'the signatures of plants, or the notes impressed upon them as indices of their virtues, though some lay great stress upon them, accounting them strong arguments to prove that some understanding principle is the highest original of the works of nature'[7] was not in accord with the facts. This was widely held by many, including More, but Ray regarded it as 'rather fancied by men, than designed by nature',[8] and that in any case more exact observation of the structure of plants offered a much more convincing proof of design. This and his refusal to accept the equally widely held view of the transmutation of metals are particular instances of his general attitude which resulted, as Raven emphasised, in a type of theological method adapted to a scientific age.

The final section of the first part of the book is a discussion of the form, physiology and instincts of animals, as these have bearing on the theme of the work. Ray sees the clear outlines of purpose in the way in which all things combine to assist in the maintenance of every species, not only the physical conformation

1. *Ib.* p. 118.
2. *Ib.* p. 119.
3. *Ib.* p. 121.
4. *Ib.* p. 126.

5. *Ib.* p. 127.
6. *Ib.* p. 128.
7. *Ib.* p. 131.
8. *Ib.*

of animals and birds but their habits, instincts, the fashion in which they utilise their environment, and the conditions of their growth.[1] On this subject of the conservation of the species, he notes Cudworth's point that the preserving of a due balance and proportion between the sexes 'doth necessarily infer a super-intending Providence',[2] and he adduces Boyle's observation that the various animals, insects and birds are produced at a time of year when their particular food is available.[3] To Boyle's examples Ray adds that of the wasp which does not usually appear until July although it might be expected that the earlier summer heat would promote its appearance, the governing factor being the ripening of the fruit which is its principal food.[4] A third instance pointing to the same conclusion as those of Cudworth and Boyle is Ray's own, that those insects which do not feed their young or prepare some provision for their maintenance, lay their eggs in places where the food is ready for the young when they are hatched.[5]

He considers that the various instincts of animals show that 'they are directed to ends unknown to them',[6] citing their instinct for self-preservation and the way in which weaker animals are provided with a variety of means of protecting themselves. Ray gives numerous illustrations, and refers to the migration of birds and of fish, concluding with Cudworth that animals are 'only passive to the instincts and impresses thereof upon them'.[7] He goes on to deal in detail with the exact suitability of the parts of the bodies of animals, birds and fishes, to their nature and manner of living. When he discusses the usefulness of the natural world to man, Ray makes it clear that this is but a 'subordinate usefulness',[8] but he adds that since man has the ability to use such materials, the fact that they can be of use 'is little less than a demonstration, that they were created intentionally, I do not say only, for those uses'.[9]

The first part of the book ends with some observations on the new philosophy, and in the second part he turns to a consideration, similar to that of More, of the earth and of the human frame.[10] He gives the reasons in favour of Copernicus as against the 'old

1. *Ib.* pp. 132–40.
2. *Ib.* p. 141.
3. *Ib.*
4. *Ib.* p. 142.
5. *Ib.*
6. *Ib.* p. 145.
7. *Ib.* p. 149.
8. *Ib.* p. 187.
9. *Ib.* p. 188.
10. *Ib.* p. 219.

hypothesis', and maintains that there is in Scripture the accepted usage of 'accommodation' in this connection.[1] As he enumerates some of the many kinds of trees and shrubs, dwelling on their usefulness and the way in which their number and variety underline the bountiful provision of the natural world, Ray is aware of 'the beauty, glory, and variety of this inferior world'.[2] There is something in his work which, if it did not turn to poetry as with More, is nevertheless the material of poetry as he considers the *Wisdom of God manifested in the Works of Creation*.

A detailed survey of the body leads to the conclusion that its form and parts are the effects of wisdom and design, and he advances eight general arguments showing how perfectly it is adapted to its functions. Towards the end of this part of the book Ray discusses spontaneous generation,[3] submitting the evidence against it, including the work of Malpighi and Redi and Wilkins's account of the repetition of the latter's experiments by the Royal Society.

The book concludes by drawing the inferences of thankfulness, obedience and service from the conclusions reached, conveying the same impression of practicality as does Wilkins's *Discourse*, references to which occur in this section. Ray writes 'the body is but the dark lanthorn, the soul or spirit is the candle of the Lord that burns in it',[4] and the customary 'partiality' to the one and 'neglect' of the other calls for the use of the 'means of grace' and the duties 'of worship and service'.[5]

The influence of Cudworth, More and Wilkins on Ray is supplemented by his wide reading, a constant reminder of which is the large number of works referred to, but he remains in the last resort independent of these, candid and original in the contribution which he made to the association of theological method with that of the new philosophy. The extent of his acquaintance with what was being done in the various spheres of study is indicated by the names which occur in the course of his book: Boyle, Nidd, Derham, Bentley, Sir Thomas Browne, Lister, Sloane, Robinson, Willis, Hooke, Molines, Malpighi, Redi, Bellini, Leeuwenhoek, Swammerdam, and many others. They serve to indicate the range of subjects in which he was interested, and the importance of his

1. *Ib*. p. 225.
2. *Ib*. p. 238.
3. *Ib*. p. 347.
4. *Ib*. p. 455.
5. *Ib*. p. 457.

own work for natural studies needs no emphasis. If one of the most important immediate results of Ray's book was the way in which its ideas were taken up and developed in Butler's *Analogy* which appeared in 1736, thirty years after Ray's death, the main permanent effect was the impetus it gave to the development of a theological method of which it was the most influential example.

It was natural theology with this difference, that there seemed to be a more direct and immediate involvement with the visible world than hitherto. Because a naturalist was in a position to provide so many instances and examples by way of illustration—'taken from effects and operations, exposed to every man's view', as Ray wrote—the sense of contact with the world of nature was reinforced because the inferences drawn were based on acual observation.

Ray's *Persuasive* was not one of his better-known books, and has not the same quality which is to be seen in the larger work. It is unoriginal, much of it being derived as he points out, from Wilkins, and although it is sincere, practical and restrained, its style adds little to the material. Its significance for theological method is to be found in the fact that its structure and contents place Ray with the Latitudinarians in that he shares in the characteristic aspects of their thinking. In the first place, he writes that he has borrowed a good part of the material from Wilkins, and in the second place, he describes it as 'practical divinity'.[1] Both factors make clear the nature of his treatment which is based on the idea of happiness, so that Ray follows the line of Wilkins, Tillotson and Stillingfleet.

The book appeared probably in 1700, at the instigation of his friend Edmund Elys, who had been a friend and correspondent of More, although little is known of the extent of his acquaintance with Ray, details of which might have shed some light on the latter's connection with the Cambridge Platonists. Ray had responded to the request as 'suitable to my profession and present condition', a reference, as he indicated, to his own ill-health. As to the book itself, it did 'not pretend to anything new', and might serve an an introduction.[2] The influence of Wilkins on Ray was not confined to the form and general outline of the book, for the

1. *A Persuasive to a Holy Life: From the Happiness which attends it Both in this World and in the World to come*, Preface (1719).
2. *Ib.*

central idea of the *Persuasive* is that of the happiness accompanying the practice of religion, a basic component in Wilkins's outlook. It is not usual to reckon Ray as a Latitudinarian, and while such a classification would be faulty and incomplete, the influence on him of certain ideas associated with the Latitudinarian point of view has hardly had due weight given to it. In particular, he shows the effect of the characteristically Latitudinarian ideas of happiness and of concern with practical divinity. He evinces the same moderateness of outlook and his whole work as a naturalist agreed with the Latitudinarian use of natural theology and contributed materially to its formation. Undoubtedly, his use of the concept of a plastic nature was due to the direct influence of the Cambridge Platonists, just as their work lay behind the changing attitude to the new philosophy as it had bearing on theological questions, and of which Ray's *Wisdom* was the outstanding example. But the closenesss of Ray's point of view to that of Wilkins and others not only in regard to natural theology generally, but in respect of other ideas characteristic of them, justifies drawing attention to the connection between him and the Latitudinarians which is clearly more than accidental.

The book begins by briefly noting that the object of happiness is not in riches, pleasure, honour or power, and that a life in which obedience to religion is effective is 'the only happy life'.[1] Accordingly, he considers the meaning of the terms 'holiness' and 'happiness', defining the former as 'perfect conformity . . . to the law and will of God', and adding that this 'is proper only to rational beings'.[2] Since such perfect obedience is not possible sincerity of obedience will be accepted instead, so that the definition means 'a sincere and constant desire and endeavour to obey'.[3] The emphasis, common to the Cambridge Platonists and to the Latitudinarians in this connection, on conformity and obedience, is the determining one for Ray, and is a constantly recurring factor from Hales to Simon Patrick. It belongs to a type of practicality which seems to be inherent in seventeenth-century Anglicanism, irrespective of differing views on other matters, occurring as much in the devotional books as in the general writing of the period.

As to happiness, it can be defined positively as the enjoyment of what is desirable, and negatively as the 'absence of whatever is

1. *Ib*. p. 2.   3. *Ib*. p. 5.
2. *Ib*. p. 4.

afflictive',[1] following two definitions from Boethius and Cicero. The objective happiness of man, writes Ray, using the familiar terms adopted by Wilkins, is God, 'his chief good, or last end', and 'his formal happiness is the enjoyment of this object, which consists in the knowledge and love of God'. This latter is the same as obedience, and Ray quotes Hammond to the effect that 'especially in the New Testament'[2] this is the case. Not only does he follow Wilkins in the discussion of the things in which happiness consists, but the approach is the same. Ray quotes the Wiseman, and shows the same concern with practical divinity, and while he once refers to Andrewes, his references, apart from the constant use of Wilkins's material, are more frequently to the Latitudinarians, who were close to his outlook. He mentions Patrick, Tillotson and Lloyd, and *The Whole Duty of Man*. Undoubtedly, the influence of the Cambridge Platonists counted for much in Ray's thinking, not simply in specific cases such as More's vitalism and Cudworth's ideas on a plastic nature, but in that they had to a large extent created the situation in which the work of the new philosophy was possible. The emphasis on immanence, as reflected in Smith's insistence that 'theology involves in its very nature the supposition of a power within . . . answering to a Power above',[3] or on the unity of reality and experience, and the view of reason, lay behind Ray's work. But Ray has also certain clear affinities with the Latitudinarians, and once the influence on the latter of Wilkins is noted, his association with Ray is seen to be the partial explanation of these elements in his friend's work.

But in the final assessment, it is what Ray himself did that is important, for the originality of his work not only ensured progress in natural studies but had its effect in a wider context, making a major contribution to the development of theological method in a significant time of transition.

Ray's background and the circumstances of his life could hardly provide a greater contrast than they did to those of Robert Boyle who was doubly fortunate in that, being born into a family of wealth and position, he was also a younger son and not obliged to be involved in public life and the management of affairs. His situation facilitated his work and provided the necessary conditions for it. Ray had achieved through a difficult decision a situa-

1. *Ib.* p. 7.   3. *Discourse* I.
2. *Ib.* p. 8.

tion in which his work was unhindered by claims on his time such as would have arisen had he continued to hold his post at Cambridge. Boyle was born to such a situation in which uninterrupted freedom was his from the start, and instead of going to the University he was sent abroad with a tutor. To this circumstance, as much as to any other single factor, was due in all probability the development of his interest in subjects which were not then seriously studied in the universities. Dissimilar as their situations were, Ray and Boyle resembled each other in many ways, and there are numerous references in Ray's work which show that he shared in the high contemporary estimate of Boyle.

This appreciation of Boyle was in no way due to his position, for his independence and integrity no less than the way in which his work caught the imagination of the times made an impression at once complex and simple. It was complex in that it was made up of recognition of Boyle's ability and application, and of awareness that the best-known of the new philosophers saw his dicoveries as being within the context of a general theological purpose. The author of the *Spring of the Air* was a writer on devotional subjects and a student of Oriental languages. The man who brought about the revision of the whole approach to chemistry and who shaped an entirely different view of the phenomena of the natural world was also for more than a quarter of a century a member of the society which inaugurated its work by missionary projects in New England. The impression was simple in that his disinterestedness and the way in which he declined such honours as a peerage conveyed clearly his singlemindedness and the retiring quality which he shared with Ray. Like Ray, he was one who gave himself unremittingly to work, and the output was matched by the demand which was not confined to specialists but originated with the growing desire of educated people to know more about the natural world, and which was typified by Samuel Pepys reading 'Mr Boyle's book of Colours' as he was rowed up the Thames. The fact that Pepys records his inability to understand it all is a further indication of the widespread interest taken by all kinds of people in the work done by the new philosophers. Pepys wrote, that the book was so technical 'that I can understand but little of it, but understand enough to see that he is a most excellent man'.[1] It was the general reaction of contemporaries who found the combination

1. Roger Pilkington, *Robert Boyle*, p. 139.

of new philosopher and practising member of the Church, of intellectual ability and sincere simplicity, a reassuring one. In this, both in temperament, in the context in which he saw his work and in the contribution which he made to the formation of a new outlook, he resembles Ray. Both had the same reluctance to go beyond the evidence and the same readiness to admit the absence of solutions to various problems. Both recognised the place of natural theology and it is not without significance in this connection that Boyle as well as Ray was associated with Wilkins in the beginnings of the Royal Society. Both saw the study of the works of the created world as revealing the wisdom and purpose which was differently and more fully revealed in Scripture. Again, both produced works without which advance in their respective subjects would have been delayed. If in a general estimate a larger part of Ray's work might be found to possess a higher quality of durability in his particular field of research, that of Boyle was equally important not only in terms of achievement but in that it accomplished the necessary preliminary steps which made advance possible. But in addition, Ray and Boyle by the cumulative effect of their studies in natural history and science as well as by specific books such as the *Wisdom* or the *Usefulness of Experimental Natural Philosophy* influenced the development of the new way of looking at theological questions. They differed in that Ray wrote much of his work in Latin, which helped in making his work available in other countries, while Boyle's experiments were described in English which helped in the popular diffusion of the new outlook. The conditions of their work too were dissimilar in that Boyle employed others such as Robert Hooke, while Ray worked more or less alone, save for the co-operation of friends like Willughby. This difference was however dictated more by the nature of the work involved than by any other considerations.

Robert Boyle was born at Lismore in 1626, the son of the Earl of Cork who from being a lawyer's assistant in London became one of the great magnates of the period. The future scientist was sent to Eton, and after four years to Stalbridge in Dorset, a newly-acquired property of his father. Here he was placed under a tutor named Marcombes with whom, in company with his brother Francis, he spent some years at Geneva. He was never to see his father again, for the Earl died in 1643 at the conclusion of the war in Ireland which had so adversely affected his property that

Robert Boyle on his return to England the following year found himself for the time being without resources and in debt to his friend and tutor Marcombes. His homecoming was made sombre by the loss of two of his brothers in the war, and by the bitter struggle between King and Parliament. Full of uncertainty as to his future, he learned on arrival in London that his sister Katharine, Viscountess Ranelagh, was living with her children in a house in St. James's. Despite her circumstances which at the time were less than satisfactory, she offered her brother a home and there began a long and intimate association of half a century. Katharine, the Sophronia of the *Reflections*, was a person of outstanding ability, and to Boyle who had never known his mother and who never married she gave the support he needed. An incidental benefit resulted from her sympathies with the Parliamentary side, as Roger Pilkington has pointed out, for the small estate at Stalbridge settled on Boyle by his father was secured to him, and 'at the end of the Civil War he obtained much more favourable treatment of his estates both at Stalbridge and in Ireland than he might otherwise have expected'.[1]

Here he settled for six years, during which he composed many of the *Occasional Reflections*, worked on an *Essay on the Scriptures*, wrote the story *The Martyrdom of Theodora and Didymus* which Dr Johnson regarded as 'the first religious romance ever to be written',[2] applied himself to the study of Oriental languages and began his interest in the new philosophy. This period of his life when he was in his early twenties shows the industry and application which remained a characteristic, but at this stage he was approaching something entirely new to him as far as scientific subjects were concerned. He was being drawn to it, as a letter to Katharine indicates,[3] and a letter of 1646 to Marcombes tells of his contact with those who called themselves the 'invisible or . . . the philosophical college'.[4] During his residence abroad his study had been in classics, theology and philosophy, and it was at Stalbridge that his natural capacity for observation turned in this direction. 'Little is known' writes his biographer 'of Boyle's early experiments at Stalbridge, though there is no doubt that they were along the traditional lines of the alchemists and were concerned with transmutation. Robert Boyle was born into an era when the alchemical

1. *Robert Boyle*, p. 71.   3. *Ib.* p. 73.
2. *Ib.* p. 113.   4. *Ib.* p. 76.

view of nature was currently accepted, and that he should have been an alchemist is as natural as that a student of the mid-twentieth century should subscribe to atomic physics'.[1] The remarkable thing is that with everything to find out Boyle was enabled to effect such substantial changes in the attitude of the time that he cleared the ground for further advance by his work and writings. For him the basic problem was that of matter, and around it, as Pilkington notes, were planned his researches. His discoveries were numerous and valuable, but were incidental to his scheme 'to formulate through experiment and observation a sound and all-embracing theory of the nature of things'.[2] For Boyle as for Ray there was always in the background the endeavour to interpret the world in scientific terms which corresponded with reality and to integrate this into the wider view of reality upon which theology could be brought to bear. This was the real context of 'serious and thorough inquiries into nature',[3] for by such investigation of 'this visible world' there was gained further insight into the power, the wisdom and goodness of its Creator. Boyle, like Ray, surveys the implications of the natural world, the variety of creatures, the beauty of trees, flowers and precious stones, the intricacy of design in the human body, the adaptation of animals 'to the perpetuation of their species, and the preservation of their lives'. In all this, wisdom is 'written in such large characters' that all may read: 'His power, His wisdom, and His goodness, in which the world, as well as the Bible, though in a differing, and in some points a darker way, is designed to instruct us'.

In the extent and variety of the natural world is seen power just as in close observation it is seen that 'the lineaments and traces of wisdom are so delicate and slender'. In the same way, goodness appears in the preservation of animals, 'the plentiful and easily attainable provision He makes according to the exigence of their several natures', and in the instincts and capacities which ensure their preservation. Boyle sees an especial goodness to man in 'God's liberality at once bestowing on him all those creatures, by endowing him with a reason enabling him to make use of them'. Probably because of the difference in their preoccupations he

1. *Ib.* p. 79.
2. *Ib.* p. 158.

3. Robert Boyle, *Some Considerations Touching The Usefulness of Experimental Natural Philosophy*, Pt. I, Essays II, III, IV, V.

makes more than Ray does of the idea of the usefulness of the rest of the creation to man: 'And it seems the grand business of restless nature so to constitute and manage his productions, as to furnish him with necessaries, accommodations, and pleasures'. Agreeing as he did with Ray in his attitude to the relation of the new philosophy to theology, Boyle sees this not only in terms of cross-fertilisation but in terms of a religious quality. Both Boyle and Ray have a depth of feeling and understanding through the contemplation of the works of the creation, which if it is not identical with that of More is akin to it. Boyle's religious experience abroad, the trend of his studies at Stalbridge when he turned to Oriental languages, his interest in the Corporation for the Spread of the Gospel in New England and in the provision of translations of the Scriptures, and his whole attitude as portrayed in the *Reflections*, were thus at one with his experiments and studies of the works of the creation. To these two sets of things Boyle gave himself: 'the things for which I think life valuable being the satisfaction that accrues from the improvement of knowledge, and the exercise of piety'.[1]

The first apparent contact between Boyle and those who were to form the Royal Society was in 1646. There were weekly meetings at Gresham College and at other places in London, although a group was formed at Oxford in consequence of some of the original members being appointed to posts there in 1648. These met first in the lodgings of Dr William Petty and subsequently in those of Wilkins who was then Warden of Wadham College. When Wilkins was appointed Master of Trinity, Cambridge, in the year before the Restoration, the meetings were then held in Boyle's lodgings, for he had taken up residence in Oxford in 1654, where he was to remain for fourteen years, gradually extending the area of his studies in chemistry and working with assistants such as Hooke in his laboratory on the experiments of which the first published result was the *Spring of the Air*.[2] Its appearance in 1660 placed Boyle in the forefront of the scientific movement, and on various grounds Roger Pilkington describes it as a landmark in the history of science.[3] Not only the material but the method of presentation

1. *Occasional Reflections upon Several Subjects* (2nd ed, 1669), p. 140.
2. *New Experiments Physico-mechanical, touching the Spring of the Air, and its Effects: Made for the most Part, in a New Pneumatical Engine.*
3. *Robert Boyle*, p. 144.

was new, and it was the first book of its kind in which the basis was inference from evidence and deduction from the results of experiments. But over and beyond this Boyle's experiments overthrew two traditional beliefs, namely, that 'air was an essential element . . . which was not a mixture with certain properties but of the very stuff of Nature herself'[1] and the idea that 'a vacuum was inconceivable'.[2] In a supplement to the second edition he formulated Boyle's Law, and in the following year he published *The Sceptical Chymist* which might be described as an attempt to discover a scientific method of enquiry.

The high regard felt by contemporaries for Boyle as an individual naturally tended to colour to some extent the estimate of him as a scientist. But when due allowance is made for this he is seen as one who accomplished essential preliminary work without which advance would not have been possible. Doubtless it was with Lavoisier a century later that real progress in chemistry was to begin, but without Boyle's work it would have been delayed.

Apart from his experiments with air, however, Boyle's achievements were considerable. 'He prepared the first chemical indicator in the form of a paper impregnated with syrup of violets, which would turn red in acid and green in alkaline fluids. He discovered various freezing mixtures and explained their working correctly, he used a form of refrigeration to preserve meat; he proved by experiment that although oils contracted when they solidified, water had the opposite tendency and expanded on freezing, and the bursting of the vessel was due to a tremendous expansive force and not to shrinkage of the fluid and the crushing of the vessels by Nature's alleged abhorrence of a vacuum, as was generally supposed. He demonstrated (but unfortunately did not follow up) the effect of temperature on the volume of air, and by use of his vacuum pump he increased the size of a bubble to 13,769 times the original volume. He experimented on odours and tastes and their perception and wrote the first book in the English language on electricity'. Boyle also succeeded in isolating phosphorus and nearly discovered carbon dioxide.[3]

The list is an extensive one and when it is added to Boyle's linguistic and Biblical studies and his various interests, it conveys an idea of the application which such a range of work required.

1. *Ib.* p. 145.   3. *Ib.* p. 156.
2. *Ib.* p. 147.

From the point of view of the effect of his work on the way in which theological questions were treated, however, the extent of his discoveries is less important than the general terms through which it found expression.

In 1652 Boyle paid a visit to Ireland to settle his affairs with the result that he had an assured income which made possible his residence and work in Oxford. He remained there until 1668 when he moved to his sister's house in London where he was to live for twenty-three years. 'Together they began each day with meditation and private devotions',[1] and Boyle continued his work, struggling against gradually increasing ill-health, and resorted to through the years by the members of the Royal Society, scholars and theological writers and others. In 1691 Boyle and his sister died within a week of each other. The steady flow of works on so many subjects, unified by the search for a comprehensive view of the nature of things and by the conviction of the complementary nature of science and theology, came to an end. But the memory of Boyle remained, for his candid and generous spirit was something upon which were unanimously agreed contemporaries like Ray and Pepys, Anthony à Wood and John Evelyn, the members of the Royal Society and the general mass of those who, if they lacked the knowledge to understand all he wrote, still saw what he was. His achievements in that field were of the first importance for the subject, but not the least valuable aspect of his work was the general and diffused influence exercised by his writings. The fact that they were so eagerly looked for and widely read helped to create a climate of opinion in which for many people it came to be assumed, as Boyle intended, that between science and religion there was no conflict. It was the object aimed at from different angles by Wilkins and Ray, and the cumulative effect of their writings on theological method was to emphasise the value of reason and to minimise the importance of authority. The immediate result of this, like the parallel work of the Latitudinarian writers, was to produce a favourable atmosphere in that it emphasised the alliance of the new philosophy and theology just when the growth of new knowledge produced a perplexing situation of transition. The overtones of order and of reasonableness in the new approach tallied also with the general reaction from the conditions and the presuppositions of thought of the decade before

1. *Ib.* p. 169.

the Restoration. By the end of the seventeenth century, the understanding of the natural world and its implications due in large
measure to the work of such as Boyle and Ray, had firmly established the position of natural theology. Part of the failure of the
succeeding period was its inability to keep natural theology in its
place, as the Cambridge Platonists and the naturalists and scientists had done, or to express it in adequate terms, as witness
Paley's work.

The scientists and naturalists regarded themselves as establishing reason and the deductive method against the non-rational
approach and the use of authorities, and in this they and the
Latitudinarians were following the whole trend of Whichcote's
writings. It was the misfortune of the period which followed that
it lost hold of the idea of the unity of things and of experience and
the element of inner understanding and poetical perception which
gave to Boyle and Ray a warmth and a religious quality as well as
the beginnings of a general theory of the nature of things. This
was something which in varying degrees they had shared with the
Cambridge Platonists, and the decreasing stress on it with the
corresponding increase of emphasis on reasonableness, was the
cause of the decline and of the unwelcome approval given to the
Latitudinarians on occasion by circles in which they did not seek it.
It was due in part also to the general trend as the eighteenth century advanced by which the category of rationality was, so to
speak, exalted at the expense of its proper context which was the
wholeness of life and experience. The easily explained distrust of
the post-Restoration period for any view of religion which appeared
to depend overmuch either on a subjective idea of assurance or on
an emotional response, was a natural reaction from the fiduciary
approach and from the atmosphere of the sect or gathered community. Much of this was grouped by Anglicans such as Patrick
under the heading of enthusiasm, but as time went on, and the
eighteenth century became the age of reason in a sense of the word
which would not have satisfied the Cambridge Platonists, so the
understandable distrust of enthusiasm became a distrust of feeling
and a marked tendency to discount any approach other than a
rather aridly reasonable one. But if theology lost opportunities
such as that of attempting a fuller statement which would take
account of these factors, it was not alone, for other branches of
study were similarly effected. 'With the development of the

mechanical in life and thought there came at first a deistic and then a virtually atheistic outlook'.[1] The progression from Locke through Lord Herbert of Cherbury and Matthew Tindal to Toland is one in which this devolution can be seen. Involved in it are the debasing of reason into ratiocination and the reduction of 'religion to an obedience to natural law'.[2] It is easy to be wise after the event and to discern where and at what point the work of the Latitudinarians and the scientists unwittingly contributed to this, but as has been suggested before their defence is that they did try to meet the new situation and they themselves kept insisting on the mutual and complementary relation of reason and revelation. The question should be asked as to what would have been the situation if they had not worked along such lines. Furthermore, it was a period of marked reaction, and there is a sense in which the position towards the close of the eighteenth century was the price paid for the seventeenth century's attempt to achieve a balance in theology. It meant that a great deal of the cultural and intellectual development in England and Europe moved apart from theology and from the Church, as writers like Bishop Butler noticed, and it meant also a period of loss of depth, a more or less stationary period, for theological method. And although the robust practicality of the Latitudinarians persisted and together with the Book of Common Prayer contrived to give substance and life to theological method, it can hardly be denied that the net result by the end of the eighteenth century was a theological method which needed to have the balance redressed in various important respects.

Neither Boyle nor Ray however had reached this stage. The Cambridge Platonists had begun to vindicate the place of reason in theological method, and the Latitudinarians were engaged in doing the same thing in a different way. The alliance with the new philosophy was prepared and it was the work of men like Boyle and Ray which made it effective by showing how it worked out in practice. The loss of depth which became apparent later is not a feature of their work which was part of that surge of creative originality moving through almost every subject from mathematics to classics in the seventeenth century, but which had spent itself by the middle of the following century.

1. C. E. Raven, *Natural Religion and Christian Theology* (First Series) p. 144.
2. *Ib.*

Boyle's *Occasional Reflections* are, as he himself emphasised, slight in content, and he refers to them as 'the following trifles',[1] noting that they were written for himself and not for publication. Some of them were composed when he was young and his 'unreadiness to publish these very long neglected papers'[2] was only overcome by his sister's request that they should be printed.

From the point of view of the present subject, the lengthy introductory preface is of interest in that it shows something of the place accorded to the study of nature, 'the contemplation of His works and the study of His word' being complementary.

The reflections give some side-lights on his life in the country, where as he writes to his sister, he is become 'so perfect a villager' that outside interests tend to disappear. If some of the reflections verge on the insipid, others have insight and there are occasional flashes of humour and the constant attempt 'to make the world both a library and an oratory',[3] a phrase which shows that Boyle's main preoccupation is never far from the centre. The way of 'moralising common incidents and common things' was not entirely new but was to be seen earlier in, for example, Bradford's works, as C. J. Stranks has pointed out.[4] The object was to encourage recollection and awareness of the further implications of the day to day events and situations, and Boyle indicates that for him this is one of the underlying ideas, so that the consideration of the 'most obvious works of nature, and the most familiar occurrences of human life' may afford a supply of 'instructors or remembrancers'.[5] The practice assists observation and discernment in the intellectual faculties, but he notes also that the will and affections are benefited and that this is a more important consideration 'in the present undertaking'.[6]

Boyle regards it as the object of the *Occasional Reflections* to 'make the world vocal' by using ordinary things in this way. His whole attitude is summed up in the view that the world is like a 'great book' and that 'the creatures are the true Egyptian hieroglyphics, that under the rude forms of birds and beasts conceal the mysterious secrets of knowledge and piety'.[7] Looked at in this way, the world would be seen to be 'what one of the Fathers loftily

1. *Occasional Reflections upon Several Subjects* (2nd ed. 1669), Introductory Preface.
2. *Ib.* Introductory Letter.
3. *Ib.* p. 78.
4. *Anglican Devotion*, p. 25.
5. Introductory Preface.
6. *Ib. Discourse*, Sect. IV, C. I.
7. *Ib.* Sect. III, C. VI.

styled it . . . a school for rational souls to learn the knowledge of God',[1] and 'every creature turn a preacher'.[2]

The book was widely read and perhaps the parodies of Swift and of Samuel Butler are indications of this, and it is generally accepted that the idea for *Gulliver's Travels* was suggested by it. Today its appeal would be limited for to many it would appear mannered and at times sententious, and at first sight it seems difficult to account for the interest taken by contemporaries which was not due simply to the acceptability of Boyle and his writings. Partly it was a matter of timing, for it coincides with the emergence of a new image, and helped to give substance to it. A new picture was beginning to take outline in the consciousness of the times, that of the thoughtful man who found not only sermons in stones but a clear demonstration of the workings of reason and design in the natural world. Eusebius, Philaretus and Lindamor in the *Occasional Reflections* conform to such a pattern, and if their style is sometimes stilted they are indicative of a new awareness of nature and of an awakening to a new area of reality into which men could gain entrance by reason and observation. It was not simply that analogies and intimations were suggested by the things of nature and by ordinary occurrences, for this was part of the author's design, but also that the practicality of treatment fitted in with what the Latitudinarians were saying and writing and with the new emphasis on the activity of educational and charitable projects. Boyle was not a Latitudinarian, but the conclusions of the first two Reflections, that 'though we cannot reach Heaven by our good works, we shall not obtain it without them' and that money spent on charitable objects is spent on happiness, accord with the general position of the Latitudinarians. It is not surprising to find in the *Occasional Reflections* references to the Wise man. Because of what science was revealing, Boyle, for the same reasons as Ray, has an aliveness to the mysterious beauty of things. It is not linked as closely to the influence of the Cambridge Platonists as is the same feeling in Ray, nor perhaps is it as frequently expressed, but it is there as in *The Usefulness of Experimental Natural Philosophy*, the same attitude which with Traherne expressed itself in the poetry of nature and with Boyle in the study of nature, and which was basically a religious evaluation of the world of sense. Again,

1. *Ib*. Sect. IV, C. I.
2. *Ib*. Sect. IV, C. V.

because of the habit of mind induced by the study of a subject in which the observation of facts in relation to causes played so large a part, the emphasis on the practical aspect of religion was as natural for Boyle as it was for Ray. Doubtless it coincided with the Latitudinarian viewpoint and was partly due to this, particularly in the case of Ray, but it was also part of a swing-over to a new way of thinking back from the visible and the observable. In this particular context, it is the form taken by what may be described as a basic quality of pragmatism which in one way or another makes itself felt during the period. If the word be dissociated from its modern philosophical associations and from the limited context of the material and physical, it is no inaccurate description of Anglican theological method in the seventeenth century. It is an attitude which relates in mutal authentication faith and fact, reason and revelation, history and dogma, grace and obligation, authority and freedom. At one end of the scale it is Hooker's theme in the *Ecclesiastical Polity* and at the other it is the painstaking practicality of the *Whole Duty of Man*. In between, it is the Cambridge Platonists endeavouring to catch the quicksilver of reason in its completeness, the practical divinity of Taylor and Sanderson, the Laudians looking to history, and the Latitudinarians confronting a situation of change. It is the centrality of the Scripture, the autonomy of reason, the vast and often undiscriminating knowledge in patristic studies. It is all these things and many men, the erudition of the hundreds whose names and work are known and the devotion of uncounted people whose number and names cannot be known, all encompassed in the day to day life of a Church in the ups and downs of history. It is something more easily recognised than defined and Boyle and his writings had a part in it.

The *Occasional Reflections* have a certain kinship with the attractively written *Religio Medici* of Sir Thomas Browne with its imaginative and sympathetic comments, its evocative prose and reflective style. But the relationship is one of matter rather than manner, for Browne's writing is elaborate as to form and suggestive rather than descriptive in its method. Though no scientist, his standpoint too is that of the thoughtful observer who sees beneath the surface of things, and finds 'as much divinity in Galen .. as in Suarez'.[1] It may be that there are in the *Religio Medici*

1 *Religio Medici* (Everyman's ed.), p. 16.

whispered echoes of the last enchantments of the Middle Ages, but Browne is at one with something quite different when he writes that where there is 'a joint silence' of Scripture and Church, he turns to 'the dictates of my reason'.[1] For him, 'the wisdom of bees, ants and spiders' is more to be remarked than the 'prodigious pieces of nature', and 'in these narrow engines there is more curious mathematics; and the civility of these little citizens more neatly sets forth the wisdom of their Maker'.[2] There is a glimpse here of Ray's theme, and in fact Ray was acquainted with Browne whose interest in natural studies was not simply literary and theoretical, for he was an amateur ornithologist. In this connection he sent details of different species to Ray when the latter was preparing his *Ornithology*, and Browne also produced a paper on Norfolk birds. In the *Catalogus Angliae* there are several references by Ray to plants shown to him by Browne.[3] These factual contacts are of interest in that they are a further indication of the extent of this combining of theological interests and natural studies in the seventeenth century. Browne's view is precisely that of Wilkins, Ray and Boyle: 'Thus there are two books from whence I collect my divinity; besides that written one of God, another of his servant nature, that universal and public manuscript, that lies expansed unto the eyes of all'.[4]

It seems probable that Boyle knew the *Religio Medici* in that although it was written about 1635 it was published in 1643 in consequence of a pirated edition having appeared the previous year. Certainly, the *Occasional Reflections* represent the same kind of thing, approached from a slightly different angle and treated in a rather different way. It must remain a matter for conjecture as to whether Boyle derived part of his inspiration for his *Reflections* from the following passage in the *Religio Medici* which is similar to the ideas in Boyle's preface, having a certain verbal resemblance. 'Surely the heathens knew better how to join and read these mystical letters (i.e. the ordinary effects of nature) than we Christians, who cast a more careless eye on these common hieroglyphics, and disdain to suck divinity from the flowers of nature'.[5] Possibly room should be left, especially at such a time, for the

1. *Ib.* p. 6.
2. *Ib.* p. 17.
3. C. E. Raven, *John Ray*, pp. 116, 319, 321, 337.

4. *Religio Medici*, p. 17.
5. *Ib.* p. 18 (v. p. 270 *supra*).

spontaneous combustion of ideas like these which were making their appearance in various guises and in different contexts. At any rate, the resemblance be it fortuitous or not is between Boyle's introductory material and certain aspects of the *Religio Medici*, and not between it and the *Occasional Reflections* themselves. As far as manner and presentation go, the latter are proper to the later period, its thinking and the style required by the Royal Society which was to be simple and unadorned. It would be possible on internal evidence alone to deduce that Latitudinarianism and the new philosophy had intervened. The real agreement is the more important one of basic outlook, and both helped to form the new image of the thoughtful man: 'We carry with us the wonders we seek without us: there is all Africa and her prodigies in us; we are that bold and adventurous piece of nature, which he that studies wisely learns in a compendium what others labour at in a divided piece and endless volume'.[1] Clear as he is about the place of reason and of the study of nature in relation to faith and the view of life as a whole, Browne is conscious of the fact that 'the whole creation is a mystery, and particularly that of man'.[2] There is a haunting quality as he writes 'thus we are men, and we know not how: there is something in us that can be without us, and will be after us; though it is strange that it hath no history what it was before us nor cannot tell how it entered in us'.[3]

There is depth and originality, reminiscences of earlier ways of thinking as well as evidence of the transitional nature of the times, for Browne believed in witches as Boyle accepted transmutation. But it is not hard to understand how Sir Kenelm Digby, sending out for a copy on its appearance, stayed up all night reading it. Like Boyle's *Occasional Reflections* it became a famous and a popular book at the time of its publication and a Latin edition made it available to other countries. But unlike Boyle's it was a book that never lost its charm across the intervening years when Boyle was remembered as a scientist and not as the author of the *Occasional Reflections* so popular in his own time.

Both books had a similar beginning for Browne records that he wrote 'for my private exercise and satisfaction' and the *Religio Medici* would never have been published had it not been for the importunity of friends on the occasion of the book's being

1. *Ib.* p. 17.   3. *Ib.* p. 42.
2. *Ib.* p. 40.

'surreptitiously published'.[1] As did Boyle, he regarded his book as a purely personal statement ('a private exercise directed to myself'), and urged that its contents should not be pressed too much, since a good deal of it was expressed 'in a soft and flexible sense'.[2] Like Boyle, he had experienced the thirst for discovery and had been a student of medicine and natural history in three Continental universities when Boyle was still but a small child. Described as an enthusiastic Anglican,[3] he had a tolerant and generous outlook at a time when such qualities were at a discount and were even a liability. While from the literary point of view the *Religio Medici* is an enduring book with that indescribable element of permanent contemporariness in it which is the gage and guarantee of lasting-ness, its author is obviously not a comparable figure with Boyle either in respect of the development of theological method or more obviously still with regard to natural studies and science. Never-theless he wrote a book which was aimed in the same general direction as that taken by the specialised studies of Boyle and Ray as these had impact on theology. It was an influential book which by its wide circulation helped in the formation of a new approach and in the evolving of a theological method which took account of it. If it be true, as is suggested, that the editor of the first collected edition of Browne's works was Tenison, this is understandable, for natural theology and sweet reasonableness notwithstanding, they are of one company.

As has been indicated, Boyle took the large view of his work as an attempt to interpret nature by means of experiment and observation in terms of creative purpose. It cannot be claimed that he arrived at a complete statement or that he formulated a theory which accounted for everything satisfactorily, for he held that the ideas to which he was most inclined did not provide all the explanations. Nevertheless it can be maintained that in respect of the impact of his writings on contemporaries and of the change wrought by them in the general understanding and assessment of the natural world and its implications, no scientist was to produce a more marked impression on the thinking of his times until the last decades of the nineteenth century when evolu-tion became the category of the age. Boyle was hardly in the same rank as Newton and his discoveries were not comparable with

1. *Ib*. Preface to the reader.
2. *Ib*.

3. *Religio Medici* (Everyman's ed.), Introduction, p. xii.

those of the latter, yet it can hardly be disputed that it was the work of Boyle which caught the imagination of the seventeenth century, and interpreting nature on a scientific basis, integrated this with the findings of theology. This is Boyle's real significance for theological method, and it places him in a more prominent position in this respect than Newton whose importance as a thinker was so much greater that he belongs in a sense to that small company whose work must ce viewed in a larger perspective than that of their own period. Simply because of his retiringness and the fact that he did not publish his work freely and in the easily intelligible form in which Boyle produced his researches, the immediate impact was at any rate delayed, and it was Boyle who played the leading part in the formation of a new outlook.

Boyle's attempt to evolve a comprehensive theory of the nature of things turns, as Pilkington has pointed out, on the problem of matter, for it is here in particular that science and theology make a mutual impact on each other not only in respect of purpose and design but also with regard to the manner of the control exercised in the working of the processes of nature. It must be asked then in what light Boyle viewed matter and what meaning he ascribed to the term nature.

In *The Sceptical Chymist*, published in 1661, Boyle clears the ground by outlining a scientific method based on experimental investigations. By his preference for the word element instead of the current term principle he goes a step nearer to grasping the concept of the scientific fact which Cassirer maintains eluded the Cambridge Platonists. In effect he is rejecting the older way of thinking which implies that there is an underlying essence in a thing, and he defines things in terms of component properties or elements.

The book is a discussion between an enquirer, a holder of the corpuscularian theory, an alchemist and an Aristotelian, and he examines the traditional four-element theory, that all mixed bodies are made up of earth, air, fire and water, and the three-principle view, which regarded salt, sulphur and mercury as the principles of things. He criticised them from the standpoint of the scientific method as being theoretical or intellectualist approaches to the problem of matter. For himself, Boyle favours the corpuscularian or atomic ideas, and he gives the reasons for this in a book published in 1674, *About the Excellency and Grounds of the Mechanical Hypothesis*.

He begins by dissociating the 'corpuscular or mechanical philosophy' from that of the 'Epicureans, that atoms, meeting together by chance in an infinite vacuum, are able of themselves to produce the world and all its phenomena'. Nor is it to be identified with that of 'some modern philosophers, that, supposing God to have put into the whole mass of matter such an invariable quantity of motion, He needed do no more to make the world, the material parts being able by their own unguided motions, to cast themselves into such a system (as we call by that name)'.[1] By mechanical philosophy he means 'such a philosophy, as reaches but to things purely corporeal, and distinguishing between the first original of things and the subsequent course of nature, teaches concerning the former, not only that God gave motion to matter, but that in the beginning He so guided the various motions of the parts of it as to contrive them into the world he designed (furnished with the seminal principles and structures or models of living creatures) and established those rules of motion and that order amongst things corporeal which we are wont to call the laws of nature. And having told this as to the former, it may be allowed as to the latter to teach, that the universe being once framed by God, and the laws of motion being settled and all upheld by His incessant concourse and general providence; the phenomena of the world thus constituted are physically produced by the mechanical affections of the parts of matter, and what they operate upon one another according to mechanical laws'.[2]

In other words, Boyle is saying with regard to 'the first original of things' that God gave motion to matter, for it does not belong to matter of itself. This motion differentiated matter into the variety of forms which it was designed to take and established the mechanical movement of things according to a settled order which is called the laws of nature. As to the subsequent course of nature, the world being so constituted, the phenomena are produced by secondary causes and by local motion governed by these laws which are mechanical in their functioning. Boyle was concerned not only with immediate causes, the sphere of scientific observation, but with ultimate causes, and in the study of the mechanism of the created order he saw the evidence of the wisdom of its Creator.

1. *About the Excellency and Grounds of the Mechanical Hypothesis*, p. 3.
2. *Ib.* p. 4.

THE SPIRIT OF ANGLICANISM

He proceeds then to give arguments in favour of the mechanical hypothesis, the first of which is the intelligibility and clarity of mechanical explanations.[1] 'Men do so easily understand one another's meaning when they talk of local motion, rest, bigness, shape, order, situation, and contexture of material substances; and these principles do afford such clear accounts of those things that are rightly deduced from them only' that even those who maintain other principles are quite satisfied to accept such explanations when they are available and to seek no further.[2] Furthermore, the mechanical philosophy is content with a minimum of basic principles, those of matter and motion,[3] than which there is no principle more 'primary'[4] or more simple in that neither of them can be resolved into anything else.[5]

Another argument is that of comprehensiveness, in that the corpuscular theory has no need to seek other explanations of the phenomena of nature, explanations which in fact add nothing to the knowledge of how the phenomenon is produced: 'they that to solve the phenomena of nature have recourse to agents which, though they involve no self-repugnancy in their very notions, as many of the judicious think "substantial forms" and "real qualities" to do; yet are such that we conceive not how they operate to bring effects to pass: these, I say, when they tell us of such indeterminate agents as "the soul of the world", "the universal spirit", "the plastic power" and the like; though they may in certain cases tell us some things, yet they tell us nothing that will satisfy the curiosity of an inquisitive person who seeks not so much to know what is the general agent that produces a phenomenon, as by what means and after what manner the phenomenon is produced'.[6]

In view of Boyle's statment that the idea of plastic nature is irrelevant as far as fact is concerned since it does not explain how a phenomenon is produced, it is as well to note that the grounds of Cudworth's approval of the 'atomical physiology of the ancients' were that 'it renders the corporeal world intelligible to us; since mechanism is a thing we can clearly understand'. The similarity to Boyle's viewpoint is increased by Cudworth's comment that 'to say that this or that is done by a form or quality, is nothing else

1. *Ib.* p. 5.
2. *Ib.* p. 6.
3. *Ib.* p. 8.
4. *Ib.* p. 8.
5. *Ib.* p. 9.
6. *Ib.* p. 16.

but to say that it is done we know not how'.[1] Cudworth fears
that the logical outcome of a purely mechanist view of phenomena
is 'a dead and wooden world . . . that hath nothing either vital
or magical at all in it. Whereas to those that are considerative, it
will plainly appear that there is a mixture of life or plastic nature
together with mechanism which runs through the whole corporeal
universe'.[2]

Both Boyle and Cudworth saw the whole process in religious as
well as in philosophical and scientific terms. The difference between their approach to the central problem of matter is not that
Cudworth disregards the importance of mechanism but that he
fights shy of a wholly mechanistic approach as leading at best to the
ideas of Descartes and at worst (and Boyle himself was aware of
this possibility) to materialism. Cudworth feels that allowance must
be made for what he calls the 'mixture of life . . . with mechanism',
and it is very significant in this connection that in his estimate of
Descartes's philosophy, while approving of 'the mechanic part of
it', he sees the 'acknowledging no other philosophical causes beside
material and mechanical'[3] as leading on to a position which neither
Descartes nor Boyle appeared to have visualised. They saw mechanism and teleology as complementary, as up to a point they were,
but they did not foresee that, stated as they were, their future
separation was a possibility. Ray followed Cudworth in accepting
the idea of a plastic nature and excluding such conclusions of
Descartes as that animals were automata so that his outlook is
organic rather than one which stresses mechanism. Such an
attitude was doubtless due in part to the nature of his subject just
as Boyle's studies gave rise to a preoccupation with 'by what
means and after what manner the phenomenon is produced'.
Boyle is looking by way of concentrating on mechanism for the
pragmatic concept which is necessary for progress in the subject
while Cudworth is entering a caveat that this must be part of a
more comprehensive view of the material world. He too wants to
know more about mechanism than that 'it is done we know not
how', but he is aware of the difficulty if the part is taken for the
whole. Then 'life and sense, reason and understanding, were really
nothing else but local motion' with the consequence that humanity

1. *The True Intellectual System of the*   2. *Ib.* C. III, xxvii.
   Universe, C.I. (xxxix).   3. *Ib.* C. III, xxxviii.

is 'but machines and automata . . . and that animals consisted of mere mechanism'.[1]

Boyle's research was an essential preliminary to further knowledge, and at a time when the fundamentals of belief were largely axiomatic, the position for which he worked seemed strengthened by it. But in fact the beginnings of separation between science and theology were already present, and the gulf widened according as mechanistic thinking came gradually to dominate the new philosophy. Whether this was inevitable as the possibilities of the new method came to be increasingly recognised, or whether the separation would have been so marked if the next century had produced theologians and biologists of the calibre of Cudworth and Ray, is difficult to say. Atmosphere is a powerful factor and it may be that the age of reason and the hypnotism of the machine would still have been too strong a combination. In all the circumstances of the time which seemed so favourable to his purpose of formulating an 'all-embracing theory of the nature of things', Boyle can hardly be held responsible for not foreseeing the way in which the situation would develop. It is well to note too that although Cudworth's insight was prophetic, it was developed within a frame of reference which did not take full account of the requirements of physical studies or of the extent of the pressure in this direction which the development of the subject exercised on the scientist.

Writing of the attempts to account for the phenomena of nature by 'the help of a determinate number of material ingredients', a reference to the theory that salt, sulphur and mercury, were the three basic components, or 'by introducing some general agents', Boyle maintains that an examination of these ideas 'as far as they have truth in them'[2] will bring the question back to mechanical principles.

As to the introduction of a general agent such as the *anima mundi*, or a plastic nature, or the *materia subtilis* of the Cartesians, 'though the Cartesians be mechanical philosophers', he asserts that if it is not intelligible and physical it can give no explanation of phenomena, and if it is then it is itself reducible to matter: 'the chief thing that inquisitive naturalists should look after in the explicating of difficult phenomena is not so much what the agent is or does, as what changes are made in the patient to

1. *Ib.* C. I, xli.
2. *About the Excellency and Grounds of the Mechanical Hypothesis*, p. 19.

bring it to exhibit the phenomena that are proposed; and by what means and after what manner those changes are effected. So that the mechanical philosopher being satisfied that one part of matter can act upon another but by virtue of local motion, he considers that as, if the proposed agent be not intelligible and physical, it can never physically explain the phenomena: so, if it be intelligible and physical it will be reducible to matter ... and, the indefinite divisibility of matter, the wonderful efficacy of motion, and the almost infinite variety of coalitions and structures that may be made of minute and insensible corpuscles, being duly weighed, I see not why a philosopher should think it impossible to make out by their help the mechanical possibility of any corporeal agent, how subtle or diffused or active soever it be, that can be solidly proved to be really existent in nature, by what name soever it be called or disguised'.[1]

Boyle enlarges on this as he considers the other hypothesis, pointing out that so long as the ingredients are treated 'but as quiescent things'[2] the material parts of bodies can only account for a fraction of the phenomena of nature. This necessitates supposing them to be active, and 'that things purely corporeal cannot be but by means of local motion, and the effects that may result from that, accompanying variously shaped, sized and aggregated parts of matter'.[3] This means that this view cannot avoid leaving the greater part of the phenomena of nature unexplained, 'without taking in the mechanical and more comprehensive affections of matter, especially local motion'.[4]

Until the traditional ideas of the past, the four element theory and the theory of the three hypostatic principles, and the new discipline of experiment and observation had been confronted with each other, progress in the subject could hardly be made. As far as attempting to understand the nature of the material world was concerned Boyle saw the mechanical hypothesis as he called it and corpuscularian ideas as providing a possible explanation. It is along these lines that he discusses the meaning of the word 'nature',[5] which in ordinary speech is used in such a way that nature is either personalised or has effects ascribed to it without any clear idea as to what is meant by this. There are those who regard it as the

---

1. *Ib.* p. 20.
2. *Ib.* p. 22.
3. *Ib.* p. 23.

4. *Ib.* p. 23.
5. *A Free Enquiry into the Vulgarly received Notion of Nature* (1685).

independent source of 'the phenomena of the universe', and those who think of it as a 'vice-gerent'. Boyle, who 'differs from both these parties', considers that a proper definition is needed, particularly 'with regard to religion'[1] to which the popular idea of nature is injurious in that it hinders the real investigation and true understanding of the phenomena of nature.[2]

In order to describe nature in general he distinguishes 'between the universal and the particular nature of things'. As to universal nature, 'that nature is the aggregate of the bodies that make up the world, framed as it is, considered as a principle, by virtue whereof they act and suffer according to the laws of motion prescribed by the Author of things'.[3] The particular nature of any individual body 'consists in the general nature applied to a distinct portion of the universe'. This means in effect that the particular nature of any body 'consists in a convention of the mechanical affections, such as bigness, figure, order, situation, contexture and local motion, of its parts . . . convenient and sufficient to constitute in or to entitle to its particular species or denominations, the particular body they make up, as the concourse of all these is considered as the principle of motion, rest and changes in that body'.[4]

General nature can be described as 'cosmical mechanism, that is, a comprisal of all the mechanical affections, figure, size, motion, that belong to the matter of the great system of the universe' and the nature of a particular body is 'the individual mechanism of that body'.[5] This is substantially the direction in which Newton was going and his *Principia*, published in 1686, established the mathematical and mechanistic outlook in an ever-widening area. C. E. Raven writes that 'Newton himself was constant in affirming the presence, energy and control of God as the ground and cause of all that is. But his followers, enthusiastic over the completeness of his demonstration—the first great integrative principle to be formulated by the New Philosophy—naturally regarded it as a vindication of a mechanistic outlook: and this was accentuated in the next century by the lack of worthy representatives of the biological sciences or of religion. In consequence Newton's own breadth of view and his interests other than mathematical were neglected, and he was made responsible for the

1. *Ib.* Preface.
2. *Ib.* p. 6.
3. *Ib.* p. 71.
4. *Ib.* p. 72.
5. *Ib.* p. 73.

conviction that the physical universe was a vast machine which men could understand, explain, manipulate and ultimately control'.[1]

In view of this it is of interest that the position maintained by Boyle in the *Free Enquiry* drew comment from Ray who quotes from it, that the 'Author of things . . . settled such laws or rules of local motion among the parts of the universal matter, that by his ordinary and preserving concourse, the several parts of the universe thus once completed should be able to maintain the great construction or system and economy of the mundane bodies, and propagate the species of living creatures'.[2] Ray could not fully acquiesce in this although he himself paid considerable attention to mechanism in nature, because he saw an over-emphasis on it as possibly leading to a view of the universe as self-moving mechanism. He was also of the opinion that it did not make sufficient allowance for the totality of observable facts. This is apparent in his remarks on the passage quoted from the enquiry into nature, where he notes that no matter how subtle the parts into which matter is divided and no matter how swiftly they be moved, matter is still 'senseless . . . and makes no nearer approach to sense, perception or vital energy than it had before'. As for external laws and rules of motion, matter is not capable of observing them, 'neither can those laws execute themselves: therefore there must besides matter and law be some efficient'. Because motion is a 'fluent thing' it does not follow that because a thing moves at this moment it will continue to do so the next, 'but it stands in as much need of an efficient to preserve and continue its motion as it did at first to produce it'.[3]

Ray foresaw the way in which mechanism could be made the basis of materialism, and he notes his satisfaction on reading *The Christian Virtuoso* at discovering that Boyle does not accept the deist view 'that after the first formation of the universe all things are brought to pass by the settled laws of nature', but that the actions of inanimate bodies are produced by power not by laws since such bodies are 'incapable of understanding what it is or what it enjoins'.[4] This means, as Ray indicates, that the two points of view are in agreement save as to the agent that executes

1. *Natural Religion and Christian Theology* (First Series), p. 134.
2. Ray, *Wisdom*, p. 54, reference to *Enquiry*, pp. 77-8.
3. Ray, *Wisdom*, p. 55.
4. Ray, *Wisdom*, p. 56.

the laws 'which he holds to be God himself immediately, we a plastic nature'.[1] But if Ray who valued Boyle's work as being one of the most important instruments in showing the unity of purpose in theology and the new philosophy, could discern its ambivalence in this respect, it is not surprising that the later trend of events should show a growing separation between them once the mechanical hypothesis was removed from this context. Boyle himself was aware of the possibilities but he saw no other explanation of the facts and he was satisfied that the mechanical hypothesis was the only method of approach to matters which, in his view, were of great importance to religion in connection with which it was his aim to consider them.[2]

In fact this is the unifying strain in Boyle's work but it is only part of his total approach for he saw natural religion as incomplete without revealed religion. This was no conventional acceptance but the reason for his extensive studies in Oriental languages that he might the better be able to see the process of revelation experienced through history in the Bible. The account of this process included miracle, and while Boyle laid stress on the regularity of law he regarded miracles as authenticating the authority of Christianity, as did the Latitudinarians, and like Stillingfleet he looked on its rapid spread as being a confirmation of the same nature. For him the wholeness of experience seemed naturally to include faith and scientific work, thought and practicality, and a quality of inwardness, of something not obtruded but which left an undivided impression, for Boyle was no shallow theorist aiming at an accommodation on minimal terms between religion and science.

The influence of his work on theological method, as far as its immediate effect was concerned, was to reinforce the conclusion that there was a basic agreement between the theologian and the scientist. This temporarily strengthened the position of religion at a time of transition, and because Boyle's works were so widely read by such a variety of people this was not confined to a limited area but helped to create a general feeling that whatever science might discover in the future would, like its present findings, be corroborative of fundamental truths. This was reinforced by the work of the Latitudinarians. The whole atmosphere of the new philosophy, being necessarily that of fact, deduction and experi-

1. *Ib.* p. 57.
2. *Ib.* Preface.

ment, merged with the more specifically theological reaction from the pre-Restoration situation to lay emphasis on the practical aspect and on the place of reason. This could be reckoned on the credit side, but because of this and by reason of the new philosophy's close link with natural theology, another result was a heavy overloading. Among the later consequences of this were a superficial reasonableness and a rather shallow matter-of-factness. Ultimately, the work of Boyle and of Newton may be regarded as having indirectly contributed to the situation in which the self-executing laws of nature were substituted for natural theology by those who concentrated on one feature of their work. But the irony of this does not touch their achievement from whatever aspect it is considered. It is an achievement the effects of which are not confined to progress in the knowledge of the material world and in the understanding of natural phenomena, for it helped to create in Anglican theological method a marked disposition to natural theology which has remained one of its most resistant components.

CHAPTER VIII

THE NEW PHILOSOPHY AND THEOLOGICAL METHOD (*continued*)

RICHARD BENTLEY was not a scientist although as Master of Trinity College, Cambridge, he founded a laboratory for Vigani, and corresponded with Newton. Nor was it in theology but in classical studies and criticism that he produced the work by which he is remembered as a scholar. Yet because of his appointment as the first lecturer under the terms of Boyle's will which made provision for a yearly course, and by the subsequent publication of his lectures, he contributed to the relating of theology to science along the line which had been developing from Glanvill and Wilkins to Ray and Boyle. His importance lies in the fact that he brought the process a stage further by showing that the traditional framework of theology was supported by the discoveries of Newton, and by interpreting the religious significance of Newtonian physics. As G. R. Cragg writes, 'If the Newtonian conception of the universe became within a generation a part of the outlook of educated men, it was not because they had read the *Principia*. The findings of the new physics had to be interpreted for the benefit of the ordinary person'.[1] He goes on to point out that Bentley was one of the first to undertake this task. The form and method of Bentley's Boyle lectures show that Wilkins, Ray and Boyle had initially succeeded in establishing as a working hypothesis that theological affirmations were strengthened by the latest developments of the new philosophy. Bentley maintains that those who regard themselves as 'disciples of mere natural reason' are not alone in their concern for its 'use and authority'. In a phrase that reflects the ideas and expressions of the Cambridge Platonists he writes that 'we look upon right reason as the native lamp of the soul, placed and kindled there by the Creator'. When he goes on to observe that 'even revelation itself is not shy nor unwilling to ascribe its own first credit and fundamental authority to the test and testimony of reason',[2] he is repeating Whichcote's assertion that what is not

1. G. R. Cragg, *From Puritanism to the Age of Reason*, p. 106.
2. From *A Sermon preached at the Public Commencement at Cambridge, 1696*, included in fifth ed. of the lectures (1724).

rational is not revealed. But he is going further towards the position of Latitudinarians such as Stillingfleet in whose *Origines Sacrae* revealed religion, reckoned as having its own authority, is also regarded as being in some measure validated by the fact that it can be shown to be credible because it is reasonable. This is a point of view not only to be expected in one of Bentley's generation but also because of his close and lasting association with Stillingfleet himself. In connection with his personal affiliations it is of interest that of those who were concerned officially with his nomination as Master of Trinity College, Cambridge, nearly all were prominent Latitudinarians. These were Tenison, Archbishop of Canterbury, Lloyd, Burnet and Patrick, the number being completed by Sharp, Archbishop of York. Like Bentley, Sharp was a Yorkshireman who had mathematical and scientific interests. He was also an admirer of Newton and he had known both More and Cudworth at Cambridge.

Bentley was born near Wakefield in 1662, and his father dying when Bentley was young, his grandfather decided that he should go to St. John's College, Cambridge, in 1676. He was appointed to Spalding School, Lincolnshire, in 1682, and after two years was chosen by Stillingfleet, then Dean of St. Paul's, as tutor to his son, a post in which he remained for six years during which he began the classical studies in which he was to inaugurate a new era.[1] In 1690 he was ordained and became chaplain to Stillingfleet and in the following year appeared his *Chronicle of Malelas* and *Letter to Mill*, the accuracy and learning of which made a marked impression on Continental scholars. In 1692 he was appointed to give the first series of the lectures founded under Boyle's will, and these too were widely noted and showed that the lecturer was as interested in the new discoveries in the phenomena of nature as he was in textual emendation and criticism. In the same year he was appointed to a prebendal stall at Worcester and in 1694 became keeper of the royal libraries and a fellow of the Royal Society. Hitherto he had resided with Stillingfleet but he now went to the lodgings at St. James's Palace which were allotted to him in his capacity as librarian, where he had weekly meetings with Wren, Evelyn, Locke, and Newton. The breadth of interest reflected here continued and when he became Master of Trinity he was in a position to help in the promotion of other branches of study, but he

1. Article in D.N.B.

himself turned more and more to his chosen subject. For nearly forty years from the time of his appointment as Master and as Vice-Chancellor of the University in 1700 he continued to produce works, such as the *Letters of Phalaris*, which placed him among those who in various countries helped to change the course of classical studies. It was with reference to Bentley's part in establishing method and critical standards in respect of textual emendation and historical evaluation that his greatest contribution was made: 'his genius is higher than any one of his books; his merit is larger than all of them together'.[1] Although this method was ultimately to have far-reaching effects in that it was not to confine itself to secular literature, it is Bentley's lectures which are influential in forming the new approach by way of evidence.

It has been suggested in an earlier chapter that he was developing something which had already found a firm footing in More's *Antidote* which first appeared in 1652 and which was the starting-point of Ray's *Wisdom* published in 1691. It is a basic element in the work of Boyle, Wilkins and the Latitudinarians, but Bentley performed the valuable service of incorporating Newton's findings into theological method in such a way that not only was the drift of these made intelligible to the ordinary reader but that they were seen to be confirmatory of the fundamental truths of religion. He set himself to study Newton's work, 'to whose most admirable sagacity and industry we shall frequently be obliged in this and the following discourse'.[2] He took care to ensure that he was accurately representing Newton's discoveries and corresponded with him in order to make sure that his conclusions and applications were consistent with these findings.

Newton's *Principia* made its appearance in 1686, and Bentley's lectures were given in 1692, the last three making use of Newton's work particularly in connection with the law of gravitation, and referring to the 'great serviceableness to religion'[3] of the mechanical philosophy as developed by Boyle. Reference has already been made to the similarity between Bentley's lectures and More's *Antidote* in form and in statment of method. It is probable that the publication of a collected edition of More's work in 1679 suggested to

1 Article in D.N.B.

2. *Eight Sermons preached at the Honourable Robert Boyle's Lectures in the first year, 1692*, 5th ed. 1724, p. 253.

3. *Ib.* p. 126.

Bentley the advisability of bringing this line of thought up to date in view of the effect which Newton's discoveries might be expected to have. Boyle himself had observed symptoms of religious decline as the new scientific outlook evolved and it was with this unwelcome development in view that he had founded the lectures. Bentley's subject accorded with this, and if his outline and method are the same as More's, he made a fresh contribution which the developing situation required. Bentley's treatment of design as seen in the nature of the faculties, the 'structure and origin of human bodies', and the 'origin and frame of the world', has been compared in another chapter with More's, and the deliberate exclusion from both books of any argument other than that arising from the study of the phenomena of nature has been seen to be a common feature in method.

In the second lecture, Bentley concentrates on what he calls the 'near and internal and convincing argument of the Being of God ... from human nature itself'.[1] His purpose will be to show that 'the very life and vital motion and the formal essence and nature of man'[2] constitute this argument in themselves. He maintains that it can be substantiated by showing the existence of 'an immaterial substance' in man, and 'that this spirit doth necessarily evince the existence of a supreme and spiritual Being'. In the same way, the argument is supported by the organical structure of human bodies 'whereby they are fitted to live and move and be vitally informed by the soul', and this is 'unquestionably the workmanship of a most wise and powerful and beneficent Maker'.[3]

As to the first of these points, there is something in human nature that 'thinks and apprehends and deliberates'[4] and these faculties and operations must proceed from some cause. If they are not inherent in matter as such, nor producible in matter by any motion or modification of it, it follows that 'they proceed from some cogitative substance'.[5] He goes on to show that 'no particular sort of matter, as the brain and animal spirits, hath any power of sense and perception' and that 'motion in general superadded to matter cannot produce any sense and perception'.[6] The notion of matter includes nothing but extension and bulk,[7] and that of body

1. *Ib*. p. 56.
2. *Ib*. p. 56.
3. *Ib*. p. 57.
4. *Ib*. p. 57.
5. *Ib*. p. 58.
6. *Ib*. p. 60.
7. *Ib*. p. 61.

'nothing but figure and site and a capacity of motion,' the latter
only causing a 'new order and contexture of parts'.[1] The result
of this is that the ideas of sensible qualities are seen not to be
something inherent in inanimate bodies, but are 'the effects of
their motion upon our nerves: and sympathetical and vital passions
produced within ourselves'.[2] Bentley then considered various
objections raised against this and concludes that sense and perception can never be the product of any kind of matter and motion,
but must necessarily proceed from 'incorporeal substance'.[3] This
is similar to More's treatment, as is Bentley's discussion of the
structure of human bodies, in which he shows that 'the usefulness
of the parts and the whole . . . arise from wisdom and design'.[4]
More says that 'the contrivance of the whole and every particular
is so evident an argument of exquisite skill in the Maker',[5] and
both he and Bentley go into great detail to show that, in the latter's
phrase, there is in this intricacy and adaptability 'an infallible token
of design and contrivance'.[6] Bentley's lectures have about them
a more modern and scientific air. More is aware of and notes the
impact on his subject of scientific and mathematical points, but
there is a felt difference between them. This is not due solely to
More's interest in psychic matters nor to his acceptance of such
concepts as those of the signatures of plants or spontaneous generation, and in fact More gives instances of first-hand observation
which Bentley does not. The difference is primarily one of atmosphere, for although their object and method is the same, More's
attitude to natural phenomena is mystical as well as enquiring. He
shares with Bentley the basic approach through reason but there is
another aspect of his outlook and temperament which has no
counterpart in Bentley's viewpoint. The latter is a theologian using
valuable material to support the fundamentals of belief; More is
this too but he approaches the question from within, from an
appreciation of the natural world which derives as much from his
philosophy as it does from his own observation. Bentley is at a
disadvantage by comparison in this respect for he is not a naturalist, so that More and Ray convey the same impression of being
within the subject while Bentley's whole attitude is more intellec-
tualised. This has an advantage from the point of view of what

1. *Ib*. p. 64.
2. *Ib*. p. 64.
3. *Ib*. p. 77.

4. *Ib*. p. 94.
5. *Antidote*, Bk. II, C. XII, I.
6. Bentley, op. cit. p. 184.

Bentley was setting out to do because he is in no danger of being unable to see the wood for the trees. Because he is approaching the matter from the angle of utilising the findings of the new philosophy he is better able to condense and to convey with clarity its implications. His own interests have been in a different type of study but he has seen clearly that people's thinking will be more and more conditioned by Boyle's and Newton's work so he sets himself to understand this and to show that it confirms the fundamentals of religion. He refers to Redi, and Malpighi to show that matter itself cannot produce life, and he mentions the work of others among the new philosophers but particularly that of Boyle and Newton. Of the former he says that the mechanical or corpuscular philosophy 'principally owes its re-establishment' to him in that he showed 'its great serviceableness to religion' and its superiority to a view of matter in terms of 'real qualities and substantial forms'.[1]

In the discussion of 'the origin and frame of the world' Bentley deals with the main natural phenomena as evidence of design in the light of Newton's discoveries, with particular reference to gravitation: 'The phenomena of the material world . . . its present frame and system and all the established laws of nature are constituted and preserved by gravitation alone'.[2] In the last three lectures he examines in detail the implications of Newton's work, and he writes 'I shall now proceed and build upon it as a truth solidly established'.[3] This is significant for the development of theological method, for it marks a decisive point in the evolution of something which, beginning with the Cambridge Platonists, took shape at first in the attempt of such as Glanvill and Wilkins to show that apprehension was needless since theology and the new philosophy were reconcileable. Through the steadily increasing emphasis on natural theology in Wilkins and the Latitudinarians, the tentatively accepted reconciliation developed into a firm position, as exemplified in Ray's *Wisdom* and Boyle's writings, a position in which this unity of direction was more and more illustrated by the discoveries of naturalists and scientists. With Bentley, this identity of interest is all but assumed and the object of theological method is to make use of these discoveries and to show that the implications of the new interpretations of the phenomena of nature,

1. *Ib*. p. 126.   3. *Ib*. p. 253.
2. *Ib*. p. 126.

far from favouring the views of mechanists and materialists, are confirmatory of the essential truths of religion. But Bentley, emphasising the place of natural theology, also maintains that there is 'a wide difference between what is contrary to reason and what is superior to it and out of its reach'.[1] It may be the case that what is 'inconsistent with natural reason'[2] can never in his view become part of the Church's essential credal affirmation, but this is not to say that reason decides the content, for 'reason may receive from revelation some further discoveries and new prospects of things and be fully convinced of the reality of them'.[3] Nevertheless this is closer to Tillotson at his most characteristic than it is to More, Ray and Boyle, and Bentley's associations with the Latitudinarians serve to strengthen the impression. He shares the aim of More, Ray and Boyle, but not the inward and meditative element which makes More see man as 'a priest in this magnificent temple of the universe',[4] a thought repeated by Boyle. Not being a naturalist or a scientist he does not enter in the same way into the appreciation of the natural world as it is evident from their work that they do. In the lectures, Bentley is writing as a theologian who sees a task and an opportunity and perhaps because of this restriction he is the more easily understood, and his exposition does not suffer from the side-issues incidental to the treatment of the same subject by a specialist in natural studies. His style is crisp and forceful and his lectures are easily read. A Latin version appeared in Berlin and a Dutch translation was published at Utrecht. Bentley's work was well done and performed a highly useful service at a time when Deism was beginning to develop and the idea was gaining ground that reason was really demonstration. Bentley foresaw how Newton's work could be pressed into service by this point of view and there can be no question of the value and of the timeliness of his contribution.

Isaac Newton is one of the outstanding figures not only of the period but of modern history by reason of the scope and importance of his work. To delay his entry into any discussion concerning the relations to each other of science and theology appears at first sight to play Hamlet without the Prince of Denmark until the last Act. Yet it is natural enough in view of the fact of dates for Newton was born in 1642 and did not go to Trinity College,

1. *Ib*. p. 351.
2. *Ib*. p. 351.
3. *Ib*. p. 352.
4. *Antidote*, Bk. II, C. XII, 17.

Cambridge, until the year after the founding of the Royal Society, and the *Philosophiae Naturalis Principia Mathematica* was not published until 1687. While he himself had achieved a place in scientific circles in his early thirties, the general diffusion of his discoveries did not begin to take place until the last ten years of the century and it is not for a considerable time after that that they came to be widely accepted and the system of Descartes remained in vogue until well on in the eighteenth century. In addition Newton was of a retiring disposition and often disinclined to continue his work. The full impact of his discoveries on the wider area of thought and general opinion was then delayed, so that Bentley's alertness to the value of an early and timely interpretation of Newton's discoveries can be appreciated. This did not escape Roger Cotes when he wrote the preface to the second edition of the *Principia* in 1713. He regarded Newton's 'distinguished work' as the 'safest protection' against attacks on religious truth and he writes 'This was felt long ago and first surprisingly demonstrated in learned English and Latin discourses by Richard Bentley . . . For many years an intimate friend of the celebrated author (since he aimed not only that the author should be esteemed by those who come after, but also that these uncommon writings should enjoy distinction among the literati of the world), he cared both for the reputation of his friend and for the advancement of the sciences'.[1] It appears from the preface that Bentley was responsible for the appearance of the edition and for Cotes's part, as professor of experimental philosophy, in writing the preface. Bentley is seen then not only as the friend of Newton and the interpreter of his work but as the active promoter in its dissemination. He appears in the light of theological entrepreneur to a great undertaking by means of which, as Cotes writes, 'the gates are now set open, and by the passage he has revealed we may freely enter into the knowledge of the hidden secrets and wonders of natural things'.[2] For Cotes, as for Bentley, Newton's work was not only the introduction to the real appreciation of 'the beauties of nature'[3] nor yet simply the best answer to those who held 'that all things are

1. *Sir Isaac Newton's Mathematical Principles of Natural Philosophy*, translated by Andrew Motte, edited by Florian Cajori (1934), Preface to Second Edition, p. xxxiii.
2. *Ib.* p. xxxii.
3. *Ib.*

governed by fate'.[1] It is both these things, but it is 'the best and most valuable fruit of philosophy' that it leads to reverence for and adoration of 'the great Maker' whose wisdom and goodness are everywhere apparent in 'the most wise and excellent contrivances of things'.[2]

Newton was born of country parentage at Woolsthorpe near Colsterworth in Lincolnshire, and he went to school at Grantham. During his schooldays he was very much interested in making mechanical things, but, as E. N. da C. Andrade writes, there was nothing 'to suggest exceptional genius'.[3] In 1661 he went to Trinity College, Cambridge, where he came into contact with Barrow, then professor of mathematics, who recognised Newton's ability in the subject and helped him to concentrate on it. He graduated in 1665, and the University closing in the same year because of the plague which had broken out in London, Newton returned to his home where he remained until 1667. This period was the time during which he turned to the subjects in which his work ensured such substantial progress in scientific and mathematical studies. He himself considered that his capacity for original work was higher then than at any other time, and he remarked that during those two years he 'minded mathematics and philosophy more than at any time since'.[4] He worked on many problems and although at the time he published none of the results of his work they were the basis of what he was to do later. Andrade writes that before he returned to Cambridge in 1667 he had 'mastered the basic laws of mechanics; convinced himself that they applied to heavenly as well as to earthly bodies and discovered the fundamental law of gravitational attraction: invented the methods of the infinitesimal calculus: and was well on the way to his great optical discoveries'.[5]

Shortly after his return to Cambridge he was made a Fellow and in the following year Barrow resigned his professorship of mathematics, arranging for Newton to succeed him. Newton began his work on optics about this time and made a reflecting telescope which he later sent to the Royal Society in answer to a request. The Society elected him a Fellow and asked for an account of the

1. *Ib.* p. xxxi.
2. *Ib.* p. xxxiii.
3. E. N. da C. Andrade, *Sir Isaac Newton*, p. 35.
4. *Ib.* p. 41.
5. *Ib.* p. 56.

invention. His reply, in which he discusses the discovery which had led to the construction of the telescope, that white light is a mixture of differently 'refrangible' rays, was his first publication in 1672. Its importance was at once apparent, although it marked the beginning of a series of disagreements on various points with Hooke. In this connection, Newton's disinclination to become involved in dispute is noticeable. He has been judged to be sensitive and the facts seem to bear this out. He was also disinclined to publish his work, and that this was partly due to his distaste for the disputations into which it drew him is confirmed by the fact that during the four years which followed he refrained from giving his discoveries to the learned world. But it may also be due to the periods during which, as he himself observed, his interest in the subject waned, and it is the case that for the last twenty years of his life he produced little of importance. A further consideration may well be that Newton had the casualness which sometimes accompanies genius. An instance of this may be seen in the circumstances which, as it were by chance, induced Halley the astronomer to suggest to Newton that he should make available an account of his discoveries. The question of the planetary motions was under discussion and Halley enquiring from Newton found that he had already calculated proofs of the elliptic orbit, but had not published his findings. Newton sent his work to Halley and later sent him an account of the principles of mechanics. Halley saw the importance of this and determined that Newton should be prevailed upon to publish a detailed statement of his discoveries. In this he had the support of the Royal Society and it was to the Society that Newton eventually sent the *Principia*, one of the most notable scientific books ever to be written.

The connection with the Royal Society explains the appearance of Pepys's name on the title page of the first edition for he held the office of President in 1686. But the fact that it was produced is due not only to Halley's success in interesting Newton but also to his financial backing of the project and to his supervision of the printing. In the same way, the publication of the second edition in 1713 was due to the care and interest of Cotes and Bentley. Newton's dislike of becoming involved in discussion and argument goes a long way to explain his reluctance to publish for he had found by experience that the one was the beginning of the other, and the experience was to be repeated. But two other factors account for it also, namely, the way in which he lost interest in a thing once he had satisfied himself as to a solution, and the desire not to be burdened with explanations, as he himself pointed out, to those of limited mathematical learning. Newton had his share of that aloneness which sometimes accompanies outstanding ability, the source of which is not a sense of superiority but an oppressive awareness of the limited number of those trained to understand his discoveries and a feeling that almost inevitably much of his work will be misunderstood. This explains his sensitivity and it is underlined by his arrangement of the *Principia* in such a form as 'to prevent the disputes which might be raised upon such accounts'.[1]

The unique nature of the book was recognised by those who were competent to make an assessment although years were to pass before Newton's views became generally accepted. When the book had been completed Newton again seemed to lose interest in science. His health at this time was not very good and he was also looking for a change of occupation. This came about some years afterwards through the help of his friend Montagu, and Newton was appointed Warden of the Mint in 1696 and became Master of the Mint three years later. He soon showed his practicality and administrative ability, and he took an active part in the affairs of the Royal Society which chose him as President in 1703. In the following year he produced his *Opticks* but it is likely that most of the work had been done before he came to London. By this time his place in the evolution of scientific studies was assured and he was knighted in 1705 for his work.

During the remaining twenty-two years of his life Newton was occupied with his duties and with the affairs of the Royal Society. He did not produce much new work, but printed work which he had done earlier and published new editions of his former work. Newton could be caustic at times and he was not of an easy temperament. His relations with Flamsteed were uneven and the protracted disagreements with Leibniz were a source of trouble over a period of years. Yet he was generous in his treatment of such as Cotes and Pemberton and appreciative of their abilities. He was liberal too with money but he lived simply and left a large fortune when he died in 1727 at the age of eighty-five, a national figure with an international reputation and this almost in spite

1. *Ib.* Bk. III, p. 397.

of himself, for he consistently shrank, as Andrade has observed, from intimacy with the outside world.[1] He commanded respect but he had not, like Boyle and Ray, the warmth of attractiveness, and the detachment which showed itself in his reluctance to publish and in his dislike of any kind of involvement appears also in the form of a reticence in personal contacts although he mixed freely with different kinds of people.

There can be no doubt as to the extent of Newton's interest in religious and theological matters nor of his close study of the Fathers of which his library contained a large selection. He was a Biblical student and interested in prophecy and the interpretation of the Apocalypse, as is clear from the annotations he made in the copy of Henry More's *On the Prophet Daniel and the Apocalypse* presented to him by the author. He corresponded with Locke on the same subject and there was published posthumously a work of Newton's, *Observations on the Prophecies of Daniel and the Apocalypse of St. John,* in which the attempt is made to connect subsequent history with prophecy. There is more than a suggestion in certain of his works that Newton inclined to Arian views, but if he was less orthodox than Boyle and Ray he was no less sincere. That he felt some uncertainty may seem to be confirmed by the fact that he never published these views during his lifetime, but there was no uncertainty in his conviction that there was common ground in science and religion. His central purpose in the *Principia* is described in a letter written to Bentley when the latter was preparing his lectures: 'when I wrote my treatise about our system, I had an eye on such principles as might work with considering men for the belief of a Deity; and nothing can rejoice me more than to find it useful for that purpose'.[2] It was through his scientific work, through the method used in the *Principia* and through the general import of his discoveries, and not through other works, that Newton's contribution to the support of the theological position in his time was made. Its effects are seen less in its influence on his friend John Craig, a prebendary of Salisbury who produced a *Theologiae Christianae Principia Mathematica*, the plan of which was suggested by Newton's book, than in the solid impact of his work through Bentley's lectures. Craig's book attempted

1. *Sir Isaac Newton,* p. 132.

2. *Sir Isaac Newton's Mathematical Principles of Natural Philosophy,* ed. Cajori, p. 669.

amongst other things to make a statement in mathematical terms of the ratio between present and future happiness, combining the new interest in mathematics with the familiar Latitudinarian approach! Although the idea itself hardly avoids the absurd it is indicative of the impression made by the new concept of mathematical certainty and of the mistaken expectation, in spite of earlier warnings such as those of Tenison, that it could be used in a theological context to demonstrate what was not, by its nature, demonstrable in such a way.

Newton's *Mathematical Principles of Natural Philosophy* was not an easy book even for mathematicians and it argues great versatility in Bentley that he mastered it sufficiently to work out its implications, although he had the advantage of meetings and correspondence with Newton. At the beginning of the book which deals with the system of the world Newton advises the reader who is not a mathematician that 'it is enough if one carefully reads the definitions, the laws of motion, and the first three sections of the first book. He may then pass on to this book, and consult such of the remaining propositions of the first two books, as the references in this, and his occasions, shall require'.[1]

In the preface to the first edition Newton lays it down that modern methods reject substantial forms and occult qualities in the investigation of natural phenomena, and that his purpose in this treatise is to 'cultivate' mathematics as far as it relates to science, 'to subject the phenomena of nature to the laws of mathematics'. He is writing about certain natural powers or forces of nature, and considers chiefly those things which relate to gravity, levity, elastic force and the resistance of fluids. Accordingly, his procedure will be to 'offer this work as the mathematical principles of philosophy, for the whole burden of philosophy seems to consist in this, from the phenomena of motions to investigate the forces of nature, and then from these forces to demonstrate the other phenomena; and to this end the general propositions in the first and second books are directed. In the third book, I give an example of this in the explication of the system of the world; for by the propositions mathematically demonstrated in the former books, in the third I derive from the celestial phenomena the forces of gravity with which bodies tend to the sun and the several planets. Then from these forces, by other propositions which are also mathematical, I

1. *Ib.* p. 397.

deduce the motions of the planets, the comets, the moon and the sea. I wish we could derive the rest of the phenomena of nature by the same kind of reasoning from mechanical principles, for I am induced by many reasons to suspect that they will all depend upon certain forces by which the particles of bodies, by some causes hitherto unknown, are either mutually impelled towards one another, and cohere in regular figures, or are repelled and recede from one another. These forces being unknown, philosophers have hitherto attempted the search of nature in vain; but I hope the principles here laid down will afford some light either to this or some truer method of philosophy'.[1]

The relevance of this to what was to happen in that area of thought where theology and science met in the investigation of the phenomena of nature and the implications of this for a view of the universe and of experience which would be consistent with new discoveries is apparent. For it is the outcome of what began with the Cambridge Platonists and Glanvill but it is different in that the controlling element is now the mathematics of science. The Cambridge Platonists had reacted from Descartes's treatment of the phenomena of nature by the new method of mathematical analysis, and while this was to be replaced by Newton's work the difference between it and the outlook of the Cambridge Platonists was just as marked. 'I offer this work as the mathematical principles of philosophy', wrote Newton, and both he and to a lesser degree Boyle are not working within the framework of organic thinking as were the Cambridge Platonists and Ray. The whole pull of their work was inevitably in the direction of what Newton called 'reasoning from mechanical principles', while the Cambridge Platonists were trying to understand nature from within in terms of its vital principle. For Boyle the question as to how phenomena were produced was the most important so that he saw nature primarily as mechanical while to the Cambridge Platonists it was plastic. But Newton went further in that he set out to explain the phenomena of nature in terms of 'the laws of mathematics'. The Cambridge Platonists were looking for a wider interpretation of experience which would be inclusive of the findings of science. The change brought about by turning away from the authoritarian theological method of their day made its main and controversial impact at the point where the concepts of theology were

1. Preface to first edition.

subjected to reason by admitting the autonomy of the latter and by asserting the unity of reality and experience. The rapid emergence of a fuller statement of natural theology was a response to a need, and the work of Wilkins and the Latitudinarians developed this aspect of the Cambridge Platonists' position in a particular way. But with Newton a new certainty about the phenomena of nature appeared with the development of the new physics, and the general effect of this on theology was initially to strengthen its position but ultimately to weaken its content. The unavoidable consequence of reasoning from mechanical principles was that the universe came more and more to be regarded as a machine operating in accordance with fixed laws. The effect of this on theology was to limit its concept of the Divine function to that of remote control, but this was to come about later and while the seeds of it were in Newton's work the fruit was not of his cultivation. Unconsciously, and contrary to his avowed intention, the thread of Newton's discoveries ran in the direction of a parting of the ways for science and theology, but this was not visualised when Cotes wrote the preface to the *Principia* at the beginning of the eighteenth century. Indeed the preface makes it clear that the views it contains are not yet accepted in any general sense, for its primary object, as Cajori noted, was to combat Descartes's theory of vortices.[1]

Writing to Newton about the preface, Cotes considers that something should be said as to the difference in 'the manner of philosophising made use of and wherein it differs from that of Descartes and others'. He also thinks it necessary to make clear 'the principle it employs ... by a short deduction of the principle of gravity from the phenomena of nature in a popular way that it may be understood by ordinary readers'.[2] Roger Cotes was a Fellow of Trinity College, Cambridge, and professor of experimental philosophy, and the purpose of his preface was to give an exposition of Newton's position and to examine the objections of Leibniz and the views of Descartes. Like Bentley he saw the implications of the new method, although both of them had mistakenly attributed to Newton the view that gravity was an inherent property of matter. Newton contradicted this in letters to Boyle and Bentley which were not published until later, but he clarified his position in the second edition.

1. *Ib.* p. 629.
2. *Ib.*

Cotes's preface testifies to the nature of the new method of
philosophy not only by his exposition of the Newtonian physics
but by his frequent use of such phrases as 'for it is mathematically
demonstrated'. There are, he maintains, three ways of treating
natural philosophy, the first of which was that of Aristotle. Those
who held this view 'affirm that the several effects of bodies arise
from the particular natures of those bodies, but whence it is that
bodies derive these natures they don't tell us; and therefore they
tell us nothing. And being entirely employed in giving names to
things, and not in searching into things themselves, they have
invented, we may say, a philosophical way of speaking, but they
have not made known to us true philosophy'.[1]

There is another class whose approach is more in accord with
the nature of the subject but who invalidate their method by
assuming hypotheses as the first principles of their speculations,
and 'although they afterwards proceed with the greatest accuracy
from those principles, may indeed form an ingenious romance, but
a romance it will still be'.[2] He is referring to those who assume
that matter is homogeneous and that the variety of forms arises
from the 'relations of the component particles'. He considers that
'they certainly proceed right' in respect of their method, 'but when
they take a liberty of imagining at pleasure unknown figures and
magnitudes, and uncertain situations and motions of the parts,
and moreover of supposing occult fluids, freely pervading the pores
of bodies, endued with an all-performing subtility, and agitated
with occult motions, they run out into dreams and chimeras, and
neglect the true constitution of things, which certainly is not to be
derived from fallacious conjectures, when we can scarce reach it
by the most certain observations'.[3]

There is then the third class, 'which possess experimental
philosophy. These indeed derive the causes of all things from the
most simple principles possible; but then they assume nothing as
a principle, that is not proved by phenomena. They frame no
hypothesis, nor receive them into philosophy otherwise than as
questions whose truth may be disputed. They proceed therefore
in a twofold method, synthetical and analytical. From some select
phenomena they deduce by analysis the forces of Nature and the
more simple laws of forces; and from thence by synthesis show the

1. *Ib.* p. xx.
2. *Ib.* p. xx.
3. *Ib.* p. xx.

constitution of the rest. This is that incomparably best way of philosophizing, which our renowned author most justly embraced in preference to the rest. Of this he has given us a most illustrious example, by the explication of the system of the world, most happily deduced from the theory of gravity'.[1]

Cotes's analysis of the changing method of the new philosophy shows clearly the emergence of the concept of the scientific fact. Forms and qualities, the vestiges of the alchemical idea of matter, the *anima mundi*, the *materia subtilis*, and the plastic nature are discarded in favour of the unadorned scientific fact. It is the emergence of what may be called the modern scientific outlook, and it is a significant stage in the journey begun a century before.

Its effect on theology can only be assessed by differentiating between its immediate influence and the long term result. As to the one, Newton's own purpose and Bentley's and Cotes's interpretation of his work were in accord. Newton, like Boyle, saw no opposition between mechanism and teleology, for 'blind metaphysical necessity, which is certainly the same always and everywhere, could produce no variety of things. All that diversity of natural things which we find suited to different times and places could arise from nothing but the ideas and will of a Being necessarily existing'.[2] Newton's work was regarded as substantiating the basis of theology and as answering those determinists who, in Cotes's words, saw all things as governed by fate.

As to the ultimate effect on theology, Newton would not have accepted the conclusions which some would later draw from his work. But it can hardly be gainsaid that the climate of thought created by the increasing emphasis on the scientific fact and on mechanism had an adverse effect on theological method which is more easily felt than defined. As the eighteenth century progressed there was no lack of books defending orthodoxy and the Anglican position. Rather was it as if the basis of theological method had become in some way narrowed down by the influence of the new discipline. The new physics had shown the basis of certainty about the nature of phenomena to be mathematical, and this had imperceptibly influenced the view of reality as a whole for theology as well as for the new philosophy. There was inevitably more emphasis on measurement, calculation and proof, so that the idea of

1. p. xxi.
2. *Ib.* p. 546.

reason with which theological method was working was unable to escape being affected in some degree by the current stress on ratiocination and demonstration. Added to this was the praiseworthy determination of theologians to reply to the Deists' claim that they alone upheld the claims of reason. But in endeavouring to show that the Deists had no monopoly of reason on their side, the theologians indirectly contributed to this limiting of the idea of reason. The desire to keep in step with the new intellectual developments when taken together with their concurrent mistrust of enthusiasm resulted in an inadequate assessment of the place of the affective side of personality in the evaluation of experience. This repercussed on the content of the idea of reason which was moving further and further away from that of the harmonious operation of the whole personality advocated by the works of the Cambridge Platonists. The Latitudinarians and their eighteenth-century successors had strenuously endeavoured to keep the contact between theology and science, and they were sturdily practical, but with few exceptions they were deficient in their understanding of the affective element in religion, and this was reflected in theological method during the later period. The enormous popularity of *The Whole Duty of Man* throughout the eighteenth century is an illuminating comment on the trend of things. For although it appeared in 1657, it exactly fitted in with the situation as it evolved during the following century. It displayed all the characteristics of the Latitudinarian outlook, with its practicality, its emphasis on reasonableness, happiness and prudence. 'It is all as plain and work-a-day as can be', writes C. J. Stranks, but he adds that behind it 'lies a well-considered theology'.[1] That theology was found by the eighteenth century to be in agreement with the climate of thought which had by then developed. The explanation of the popularity of the book lies in the fact that it presents the kind of Churchman's religion which the eighteenth century visualised, and its basis was in accord with what the period had been learning.

One of the consequences of the effect of the new science on theological method was a decreasing emphasis on faith regarded in terms of response. This emphasis had been a noticeable feature in the writings of More and Smith. Nor had More's attention to the evidential value of the unity of reality any counterpart in the later

1. C. J. Stranks, *Anglican Devotion*, p. 130.

period. Both Newton and Cotes show something of the sense of wonder which is found in the works of Boyle and Ray, but it is beginning to become less distinct and Cudworth's magical world is giving place to one which men regarded more or less as a vast machine. The stress on mechanism resulted in the exclusion as less than respectable of any element of mystery (in the sense of reality uncomprehended and unexplained). The idea of demonstration so proper to the nature of the physical sciences was becoming almost a category of the period, so that what was not in a narrow sense demonstrable was hardly relevant. While the emphasis on demonstration and analysis was a necessary stage in the development of science, it had a more general effect. The result for theological method was a kind of process of refrigeration by which form and shape were preserved and various elements were kept in a state of suspended animation to be used later, while other elements were lost or were temporarily in abeyance.

That this is not fanciful may be seen in Locke's *Reasonableness of Christianity* and Toland's *Christianity Not Mysterious*, both of which appeared in 1695 and influenced the course of things in the period which followed. For Locke and Toland reason was demonstration and it was a faculty carrying with it its own authentication. This was the point where the view of reason finally parted company with that of the Cambridge Platonists and the outlines of the eighteenth-century situation come into sight. Locke sought to express the evidence for the existence of God in terms of a demonstration which would be the equivalent of mathematical certainty, and Toland maintained that the idea of the mysterious was incompatible with what was reasonable. Despite the positive aspect of their work they contributed to the naive and complacent intellectualism which while it is associated chiefly with their eighteenth-century opponents was not confined to a limited area. The idea of reason which Locke and Toland upheld was conceived in terms which were impersonal and mathematical. Combined with an inadequate estimate of the significance of the totality of human experience, the result was an impoverishment of theological method and a coldly inhibited approach to religious practice, against which the works of William Law were perhaps the first reaction. The form of his work is that of his own time, but his interest in Behmen shows him as reaching back for that balance of reason and mysticism which such as More had looked for, and his influence on Wesley and on the Evangelicals was indicative of the pendulum-swing which would take place at the beginning of the nineteenth century.

The effect of Locke's writings on theological method is parallel to that of Newton's work, and in fact Locke was the philosophical counterpart of Newton, and like Newton the full impression on theological method of what he wrote was not seen until later in the eighteenth century when the work of both was to be used in a way that was unforeseen by the originators. Cotes's preface indicates that this was not regarded as a serious possibility in 1713, for he considers Newton's work as the great support of theological method, and the contents of the preface also show that even at that stage, twenty-six years after the publication of the *Principia*, it had not yet displaced Descartes.

It is clear then that, as far as the seventeenth century is concerned, it is the immediate rather than the ultimate effect of Newton's work on theological method which is to be seen, and this coincides with Newton's own estimate and that of Bentley and Cotes for whom Newton's discoveries occupied the same position with regard to theology as the new philosophy had for Wilkins and the Latitudinarians.

Having made an extensive examination of the celestial bodies and having given a mathematical explanation of their system with particular reference to gravity as 'the force which retains the celestial bodies in their orbits',[1] Newton writes that 'this most beautiful system of the sun, planets, and comets, could only proceed from the counsel and dominion of an intelligent and powerful Being'.[2] In view of later developments, it is worthy of note that Newton thinks of God in terms of power as well as of wisdom, of dominion rather than of remote control, as present Ruler rather than as absentee Creator. He continues, 'this Being governs all things, not as the soul of the world, but as Lord over all', adding that it is dominion 'which constitutes a God'.[3] Amplifying this he writes, 'we know him only by his most wise and excellent contrivances of things, and final causes; we admire him for his perfections; but we reverence and adore him on account of his dominion: for we adore him as his servants; and a god

1. *Mathematical Principles of Natural Philosophy*, ed. Cajori, p. 410.
2. *Ib.* p. 544.
3. *Ib.* p. 544.

without dominion, providence, and final causes, is nothing else but fate and nature'.[1] Those who afterwards laid emphasis solely on the mathematical and mechanistic aspects of his work ignored its basis and its breadth. There is an aspect which they found it more convenient to take no notice of, and while earlier critics such as Berkeley had only the first edition in which Newton had not enlarged on this, the inclusion of an addition on the subject in the 1713 edition at the request of Cotes left no question as to the position. In this addition, Newton made it clear that, like Boyle and Ray, he considered that the accord between science and theology was such that understanding of natural phenomena was an introduction to knowledge about the Creator of them 'to discourse of whom from the appearance of things, does certainly belong to natural philosophy'.[2] There is a passage in the *Opticks* where Newton writes that 'if natural philosophy in all its parts, by pursuing this method, shall at length be perfected, the bounds of moral philosophy will be also enlarged. For so far as we can know by natural philosophy what is the first cause, what power he has over us, and what benefits we receive from him, so far our duty towards him, as well as that towards one another, will appear to us by the light of nature'.[3] This is a full statement of the nature of the basic agreement between theology and science as Newton saw it, and it is significant for the understanding of his work that for him the effects of this agreement were not confined to the aspect of knowledge. In this he is at one with the period.

Newton's conviction that there was no opposition between theology and science, reinforced by those who like Bentley and Cotes interpreted his work to the period from 1687 to 1727, was a major contribution to the strengthening of the position of religion at a time when many intellectuals were being gradually estranged, and it materially influenced theological method. Yet the beginnings of separation were near and the subsequent story is one of an ever-widening gap with increasingly sporadic efforts to bridge it until the position was reached where classical nineteenth-century science and theology were out of contact. The process by which a balance was restored in theological method at the end of that period marked a resumption of the dialogue which had been broken off so long before. If the efforts at reconciliation were partial,

1. *Ib.* p. 546.
2. *Ib.* p. 546.

3. Sir Isaac Newton's *Opticks*, ed. E. T. Whittaker, p. 405.

tentative and frequently one-sided, at least the possibility of
contact was again envisaged.

Newton's other works being published much later exercised no
direct influence on theological method during the period. There
are certain elements however in his *Observations upon the Prophecies
of Daniel and the Apocalypse of St. John*, published in 1743, which
are relevant to later developments. First of these is his sharing in
the seventeenth-century interest in the Fathers in which his
reading is wide. But his use of the Fathers is historical rather than
as a theological frame of reference. He uses them not by way of the
appeal to antiquity but as sources for the verification of facts, such
as that 'the Apocalypse was received and studied in the first ages'.[1]
That he had a sense of history is clear from the book and that he
saw the importance of history is equally clear from his book *The
Chronology of the Ancient Kingdoms Amended* which he prepared
for publication and which appeared in the year after his death. The
fact that he was often incorrect in his estimate does not detract
from his prophetic insight into the importance of historicity and
of historical evidences. It is not claimed that Newton anticipated
the modern historical consciousness, but he did see the necessity
of having a trustworthy historical framework, and if he used much
of his historical knowledge in connection with his ideas of the
working out of prophecy, he also saw its indirect connection with
the critical evaluation of the books of the Old Testament with
regard to dates, authorship and composition.

This is another element in the book which, like his concern
with history, deserves recognition in that it looks ahead to what
would later become tremendously important, namely, the textual
analysis and criticism of the Bible. While it is the basis of the
book that 'the authority of the prophets is divine', Newton considers on historical grounds that the book of Genesis 'was not
written entirely in the form now extant, before the reign of Saul'.
He regards Samuel as the probable compiler into their present
form of the Pentateuch, Joshua and Judges, Moses and Joshua
being the first composers of them. He dates other books by historical events and he thinks that Ezra was the compiler of the
historical books and that he collected together 'the prophecies of
Isaiah, written at several times'. He sees Daniel as 'a collection of

1. *Observations upon the Prophecies of Daniel and the Apocalypse of St. John*,
Pt. II, Chap. I.

papers written at several times', and here again Ezra may have collected them as he may also have done with the psalms, some of which are 'as late as the Babylonian captivity'.[1] He is also aware that Zechariah is not a unity, 'part of the prophecies of Isaiah, or some other prophet, have been added to the end of the prophecies of Zechariah',[2] a piece of criticism which must have been reached by considering the contents on historical grounds. The last five chapters of Zechariah are now generally judged to be post-exilic and the prophecies of the so-called Trito-Isaiah are reckoned to date from the century which followed the return. Newton's conjectures on these subjects are sometimes correct and sometimes not, but what is of interest is his method of assessment and his introduction of a historical basis of criticism.

The same awareness of history appears in his idea of prophecy which he sees in terms of history and not of vaticination: 'The folly of interpreters has been, to foretell times and things by this prophecy . . . The design of God was much otherwise. He gave this and the prophecies of the Old Testament, not to gratify men's curiosities by enabling them to foreknow things, but that after they were fulfilled they might be interpreted by the event . . . For the event of things predicted many ages before will then be a convincing argument that the world is governed by providence'.[3]

Occupying a unique place by reason of his scientific discoveries which influenced theological method, his awareness of history is also significant in view of future developments which distantly and in outline he seemed to anticipate.

There may seem to be a great distance between the advanced discoveries of the *Principia* and the *Catalogue and Description of the Natural and Artificial Rarities belonging to the Royal Society*,[4] which Grew published in 1681, and in one sense so there is. Newton was endeavouring to explain by the new method the system of the world. The Society was cataloguing specimens of quadrupeds and birds, including a leopard's skin and 'the great red and blue parrot', and listing plants and minerals of which it had examples. The catalogue includes an air-pump given by Boyle, a weather-clock the gift of Sir Christopher Wren, an ear-trumpet

1. *Ib.* Pt. I, C. I.
2. *Ib.* Pt. I, C. I.
3. *Ib.* Pt. II, C. I.

4. *Museum Regalis Societatis: or a Catalogue and Description of the Natural and Artificial Rarities belonging to the Royal Society.* Nehemiah Grew.

and a microscope presented by Wilkins, and things which are frankly curiosities such as an Indian bracelet, a snow-shoe from Greenland and many other articles of a similar kind.

But in another sense the distance is not so great, for the salient fact is that things are listed in virtue of having been seen, measured and examined. The things listed are as much evidence of the emergence of the new and analytical curiosity as they are curiosities. They are the trophies of the new method, small gages of modernity.

The difficulty in recapitulation is the avoidance of unnecessary repetition of what has gone before. Nevertheless this is sometimes necessary in order to see the general outline clearly. What then are the characteristics of theological method which emerge and what sort of over-all impression do they convey?

First of all, the place and authority of Scripture does not vary throughout the seventeenth century. It is over and through all the writing of the period. In the *Ecclesiastical Polity* it is placed within the wider framework of law of which it is one of the primary expressions, differing in that it is revealed and not discovered by reason. But because all law is apprehended by reason and a law is that 'which pertaineth to reason', Scripture does not quench the light of natural reason but perfects it. Scripture is perfect for the purpose for which it was intended, and it is set within a liberal method of theology.

With Hales, an upholder of liberality, Scripture is yet the interpreter of its interpreters, and its spirit is more important than the letter. Literalism in one degree or another obtained throughout the period, but it endeavoured to accommodate new facts. So Stillingfleet, upholding the inerrancy of the Scripture narrative, endeavours to reconcile it with new discoveries about the universe. The Cambridge Platonists, though they are not afraid despite severe criticism to see some light in the pagan writers of antiquity and although More may raise questions about the first chapter of Genesis, take the same view. For the Latitudinarians it is central to their practical and expository preaching, and Patrick limits tradition by it and this was consistently the Anglican view. Scientists like Boyle gave time to its linguistic study and to devotional writing on it, and Newton's interest in its study was in no way excluded by the extent of his scientific work.

For the seventeenth century it is the criterion in all writing on doctrine, ecclesiastical origins and polity, and the deciding factor in all disputed questions, appealed to by and equally cogent for moderates, Puritans and Laudians. It is the rule of faith, and Beveridge speaks for all when he writes, 'what is here written we are bound to believe because it is written; and what is not here written we are not bound to believe because it is not written'.[1] It stands by an authority greater than reason, but it does not exclude the force of reason. Whichcote might be thought to be giving a partial view when he writes that Scripture in its method always proceeds 'by evidence of reason and argument'.[2] But Laud maintaining that the books of the Bible are 'infallible verity to the least point of them' and that the ultimate certainty of this is 'by faith', holds that nothing can prevent the Scriptures from being weighed 'at the balance of reason'. This is legitimate in itself for the Scriptures 'refuse not to be weighed by reason', but the mistake is in using this alone. Reason can show the superiority of the Christian religion 'which rest upon the authority of this book' to any other, but certainty as to the authority of Scripture itself depends upon 'no compelling or demonstrative ratiocination, but relies upon the strength of faith more than any other principle whatsoever'.[3]

This emphasis on reason was an enduring element in theological method and it was involved not only with the question of the authority of Scripture but with the question of the nature of authority itself and with the relationship between reason and faith. The treatment of the latter fluctuated according as the idea of reason varied from Hooker, through the Cambridge Platonists and the reasonableness of the Latitudinarians to the later equating of it with proof or demonstration. But it produced a consistent reaction against the identification of faith with assurance and an equally consistent reaction against systems and syllogisms. Throughout the century Anglican theological method stressed the position of reason in the scheme of things and the period has no writer who maintained the contrary.

The question as to the nature of authority and its source was raised in pressing form by the trend of events in Hooker's time, and the answer of the *Ecclesiastical Polity* was law. The importance of this for the subsequent development of theological method was

---

1. William Beveridge, *Ecclesia Anglicana Ecclesia Catholica*, *Works* L.A.C.T. ed. Vol. VII, p. 191.

2. Whichcote's *Aphorisms*, 117.

3. *Conference*, Section XVI.

two-fold. In the first place, it showed Scripture to be a primary part of law but not the whole of it. In the second place, Hooker, in the rationalist tradition of law inherited from Aquinas, reminded men not only that law is an implanted directive whereby all things tend to their own proper perfection, but that it is reason governing the universe. The law of nature is the law of reason, for voluntary agents partake of it by reason. The insistence on the autonomy of reason lay behind the liberality of method which Hooker sought to establish and which persisted in one form or another. It was the basis of the distinction betwen fundamentals and non-essentials which constituted an equally permanent element in the Anglican approach to theological questions.

Two further results of this emphasis on reason were the determination on the part of the theologians to relate theology to the thought of the times, particularly to scientific thought, and the constantly recurring element of practical divinity in seventeenth-century theology.

In the relationship of theology with science the emphasis was on natural reason, and, combining with and modifying the older expressions of the idea of natural law, it made natural theology a fixture in Anglican theological method. A secondary consequence was the awareness of the visible world which was in the background of Anglicanism in the seventeenth century, taking different forms from the mysticism through nature of More and Traherne to the reverent delight of Boyle and Ray, but having the same basis. Similarly, the idea of reason was basic to moral theology not only by way of the concept of natural law, but also through that of practical reason. This was connected up with faith in terms of response and obedience, of 'faith working through love' as some writers were wont to point out. Anglican theological method was never theoretical or intellectualist like the theology which Hales met at Dort or in which Sanderson was brought up. The reasons for this are complex but among them is the tendency to adhere to Scripture as a whole and to its sense. This is noticeable in many writers and it is a factor which militated against the idea of theological systems which frequently interpreted the whole or sense of Scripture by some particular part. The extreme predestinarian views current in some circles during the period were a case in point and Anglican theological method reacted vigorously from this. Another factor was the element of moral theology which concerned itself not only with questions of practice and obedience, but with the theological implications of social questions, such as usury, the duties of magistrates or the practice of enclosure. It is not that Anglican theologians of the period were anti-intellectual or did not like ideas when they met them—they were in fact highly esteemed for their learning—but they had firmly grasped the truth that reason was the human characteristic and that its sphere was not simply speculation but the whole range of human activities. That this from time to time produced what variously appeared as a kind of pragmatism or an affinity with Renaissance humanism or a pedestrian desire to be reasonable at all costs is true. But it is also true to say that right to the close of the eighteenth century Anglican theological method did not lose sight of the need for practicality or relevance, whatever it gained or lost in the process.

No assessment of the theological method of the seventeenth century can neglect to note also that for one reason or another a strain of immanentist ways of thinking made itself felt, generally in reaction from extremist views of faith or indefectible grace or arbitrary will. Here again the solvent acting on such ideas has usually been a combination of the appeal to Scripture in its total sense and the conviction such as that voiced by Whichcote when he wrote that 'we must have a reason for that which we believe above our reason'.[1]

The history of the seventeenth century is one of religious controversy and theological dispute, and it reveals Anglicanism as standing apart from Roman Catholicism, from Calvinism after an initial period of rapprochement, and from Puritanism and the various religious bodies in the latter half of the century. That there were many reasons, historical, doctrinal and political, for the situation is obvious, but beneath the surface was the feeling for the *via media* which was not in its essence compromise or an intellectual expedient but a quality of thinking, an approach in which elements usually regarded as mutually exclusive were seen to be in fact complementary. These things were held in a living tension, not in order to walk the tight-rope of compromise, but because they were seen to be mutually illuminating and to fertilise each other. There was the centrality of Scripture and the freedom of reason, the relation of revelation to reason and that of reason and

1. *Whichcote's Aphorisms*, 771.

faith, credal orthodoxy and liberty in non-essentials, the appeal to antiquity and the welcome to new knowledge, the historic continuity of the Church and the freedom of national Churches. Behind it all lies the healthy tension of freedom and authority, accepting neither authoritarianism nor uncontrolled liberty. This very quality by which it stood apart from these Churches on either side may yet be the means by which it can in the future deepen its contacts with those from whom it was then separated, and may be an instrument for reconciliation. An over-all characteristic of Anglican theological method is then this polarity or quality of living tension, which goes far towards explaining how the element of reason did not for the most part become over-weighted during the seventeenth century since it never existed in a vacuum, theologically speaking, but operated in conjunction with other elements such as the appeal to Scripture and to antiquity.

There are however other reasons, deeper and wider in extent, why Anglican theological method was prevented from becoming merely intellectual or predominantly and coldly rational, in spite of the pressure exercised in that direction by the developments and discoveries at the end of the seventeenth century. These reasons form an amalgam and their total effect was considerable.

First among them was the basic orthodoxy of Anglicanism in that just as its appeal to Scripture was a primary element in its theological method, so the substance of its preaching and teaching was the content of Scripture, the Creation, the Incarnation, the Atonement, the work of the Spirit, the Church and what More called 'the divine life in human life'. There was no concentrating on specific doctrines or particular parts of Scripture and no special pleading from history. Connected with this was the cumulative effect on theological method of the unceasing use of a liturgy and of the recitation of creeds, linking up the Church's present with the Church's past so that the appeal to antiquity was seen in the light of a living continuity. The effect can hardly be overestimated and it helps to explain the balance which for the most part the century maintained. Not least in importance in this connection was the fact that the theological method of the period took the fact of the Church into account, its continuity, its givenness, and its visible corporateness, as the extent of seventeenth-century writing on the Church testifies. The effect of this was more or less undesignedly to hold together Scripture, law and reason, within the life of the Church which for many was a living embodiment of that primitive antiquity which was sought in the writings of the first five centuries.

Nor can any estimate of the way in which the element of reason was kept in balance with other elements to their mutual benefit omit to take notice of the great output of devotional works during the century. They were many and varied and they contributed to the formation of an atmosphere in which it was hardly possible for theological method to become merely intellectual. Boyle the scientist writing his devotional works is a sufficient illustration of the point. Mention has been made of the similar effect of the widespread concern with moral theology, and similarly the parallel effect of the many catechetical books should not be forgotten. The extent to which the period made use of Aquinas is perhaps only now being realised, and it is well to recall that he too was a man of synthesis.

Such a summary, by condensation and omission, may defeat its own ends, but it serves to indicate the basic outlines of what is recognisably a coherent theological method which attempted to meet many different situations from the rise of Calvinism to the development of the new philosophy, and which for the most part learned by its attempts. Hampered by many difficulties including the transitional nature of the times and the unsettling political events which included civil war, the change from a monarchy to a commonwealth, persecution and the downfall of a dynasty, the proscription of the Church and the effects on it of power, there was one factor which helped. This was the fact that England was a small country whose population throughout the century never seems to have exceeded a figure of about five millions. Although poor communications may be set against this to some extent, yet they did not, for example, prevent Ray's lengthy tours. The result was that learned circles were small and people engaged on similar work were likely to be known to one another. Centres of learning were few, and the unique position of Oxford and Cambridge made the transmission and communication of ideas more easy. London was later to become a clearing-house for ideas and thus served the same purpose. The effect of this on theological method has been noted in the number of personal contacts between various writers, the Cambridge Platonists and the Latitudinarians, Burnet and both groups, Barrow and Newton, Barrow and Ray, Ray and

Wilkins, Wilkins and Boyle, Taylor and More, Hales and More, amongst others. This made for coherence and exchange of ideas and is a factor to be reckoned with in the understanding of the period.

The theological method of Anglicanism, unlike theological movements whose emphasis is chiefly on the transcendental, will always take account of natural theology. It will have, for want of a better word, a certain quality of humanism, for no human experience or field of enquiry can be alien to an outlook in which concern with the Creation and the Incarnation are to the fore. It will hold that theology owes to men a rational consideration of their problems, and its method will be one of liberality rather than of liberalism. It will have a historical consciousness in respect of doctrinal content and of the meaning of continuity. It will have an element of practical divinity which it will integrate into its concept of the spiritual life.

Within the corporate life of the visible Church this liberal orthodoxy will continually strive to help contemporaries to see what John Hales called 'the truth of things'. Conceding nothing from what is given, it will always be aware of the pressing need for making intellectual contact with the questioner, and for being concerned with interpreting what concerns contemporaries. It will recognise the obligation of being meaningful and it will remain sensitive to what is going on in philosophy and science, preserving its ability to criticise as well as to interpret. As free, yet not using its liberty as a cloak for a devitalising scepticism, it will see its freedom in terms of the truth which creates it.

CHAPTER IX

THE APPEAL TO ANTIQUITY

It is clear from what has gone before that the appeal to antiquity is so much an element in the theological method of Anglicanism in the seventeenth century that any attempt to evaluate it must necessarily be selective. Such an attempt shows that while the appeal to antiquity was not the creation of the seventeenth century, it was during that period that it evolved as a positive element and as an integral part of the Anglican approach to theological questions. The evolution was not without checks or halts and there were modifications. The validity of the method was questioned by some who held that the assured results were not commensurate with the effort. This was the view of the members of the Tew circle who felt that Daillé's *Traicté de l'employ des saincts pères* which appeared in 1631 confirmed the inconclusiveness of the method. Nor did it play much part in the thinking of the Cambridge Platonists, for although some of them refer to patristic writings and are obviously acquainted with them,[1] their concern was with other subjects. Nevertheless the appeal to antiquity during the period was in general so much a part of theological method that it was regarded as an accepted Anglican characteristic.

The appeal to antiquity was not simply to the Fathers as guarantors of some specific teaching or practice, although Andrewes, Bellarmine and du Moulin and their supporters quarried in their works for material to support their respective views. Rather was it the attempt, in addition to establishing identity of doctrine with the early period, to discover what the Church of the first centuries was like and to show the resemblance between it and the contemporary Church. Inevitably therefore the appeal to antiquity was involved in the controversies of the seventeenth century as to what were the teaching and the ecclesiastical polity of the Primitive Church. Of course, many among the English Puritans disallowed the appeal altogether, and as the *Admonitions*

1. There are, naturally enough in view of a certain sympathy of outlook, various references to Origen and to Clement of Alexandria.

and the work of Hooker indicate, they sought to erect an ecclesiastical system which they regarded as based on Scripture.
Others among the Reformed Churches, such as John Owen
or Andrewes's correspondent du Moulin, being more historically
minded, endeavoured, as did the Anglicans, to support their
position from the history of the first centuries. Discussing
'whether there be any Church state of divine institution' and
concluding that originally ecclesiastical polity was on a congrega-
tional basis, it is of note that Owen regards 'the continuation of a
successive ministry' as 'a dead image'.[1] For Anglicans however
the idea of continuity was a living one, and the appeal to antiquity had as its object to establish this continuity between the
teaching and order of the contemporary Church and those of the
early Church. The argument of the Counter-Reformation during
the period was to depend on the magisterial function of the present
Church, and to use the appeal to antiquity as a secondary or supporting consideration. This tended to give to Anglican theological
method a vested interest, so to speak, in the first four or five centuries, with the strengths and weaknesses that this entailed, as B. H.
G. Wormald has pointed out. He writes 'Accordingly, in all matters of doctrine, government and practice, both disciplinary and
liturgical, resort was to be had to this golden period as to a tribunal
without appeal'. But he also notes that the significant aspect of
the Anglican appeal to antiquity is, that Anglican theological
method being based on 'the primacy of Scripture', men like
'Andrewes and Laud were less burdened in their enquiry' than
others.[2] Their endeavour was not so much to establish an equation
between later teachings and the ideas of the patristic period,
though clearly this was an incidental part of the process. They did
not begin with the present situation and work back to the Fathers,
but took as their starting-point the primacy of Scripture. This,
they maintained, was best understood and interpreted in the
first centuries and therefore the writers of that period nearest to
Scripture revealed the teaching and practice of the Church at the
beginning, and this should be the pattern for subsequent ages.
'This Book chiefly' writes Andrewes, 'but in a good part also, by

1. John Owen, *An Enquiry into the Original Order and Communion of Evangelical*
   Churches, Preface, p.2 and p.165. Published in 1681 with an answer to
   Stillingfleet's *Unreasonableness of Separation*.
2. *Clarendon*, pp. 253–4.

the books of the ancient Fathers and lights of the Church, in whom the scent of this ointment was fresh'.[1] Laud, noting that 'the ancient Fathers relied upon the Scriptures'[2] and that they made 'the creed the rule of faith',[3] maintains that this is the standpoint of the Church of England and that therefore the appeal to antiquity supplied evidence of agreement with the early Church.[4]

In order to see the appeal to antiquity in its proper context it has to be remembered that for most seventeenth-century writers it was not an academic or antiquarian frame of reference nor was it primarily a method of doctrinal equation. Inevitably, the various controversies of the period encouraged a tendency to point-scoring by both sides, but in its positive aspect the context of the appeal to antiquity was continuity, as Laud observed, with the first four or five centuries 'when the Church was at the best'.[5] Furthermore, just as the appeal to antiquity was linked with, and derived the purpose of its use from the scriptural basis and its credal summaries, so it was not separated from the freedom of reason and liberality of method which are seen as much in Andrewes, Laud and Hammond as in Hales, Falkland and Chillingworth, though the approach differs in either case.

The appeal to antiquity meant therefore that, while the place of Scripture was central, Anglicans did not regard it as existing in a vacuum apart from the life of the Church within which it was formed in the first place. Due consideration should accordingly be given to its interpretation in those centuries nearest to its composition, to councils held during the same time, to the life-setting and practice of the primitive Church as illustrative of this. They did not however view the writings of the Fathers as a kind of second canon which was above criticism, and the place occupied by the patristic writings, the decisions of councils and the history of the patristic period, was a secondary one. On the other hand, the central place of Scripture limited the function of the Church in doctrinal matters, as Andrewes indicated to Bellarmine, and he held that this was in fact supported by Vincent of Lérins when he maintained that 'what always and everywhere and by all was believed'[6] constituted a test which could not be effectively com-

1. Andrewes, *Sermons*, p. 702.
2. *Conference* (3rd ed. 1673), p. 49.
3. *Ib.* p. 27.
4. *Ib.* p. 34.
5. *Ib.*
6. Andrewes, *Responsio* (L.A.C.T. ed.), p. 25.

plied with on any other basis. This continuity was then not only external and historical but internal and of agreement, and its consequence for theological method in the seventeenth century was important. In the first place, it anchored Anglican theological method to the fact of Church, and in the second place it kept theological method aware of history and sensitive to its implications. The results in both cases were lasting and were not without significance in the 1890's. The concern with the historical fact has never been absent for long from Anglican theology, and this was due in part to the way in which the appeal to antiquity was regarded as an essential element in method.

It has been said recently that 'the times call urgently for the Anglican witness to Scripture, tradition and reason' in respect of three kinds of situations now existing, namely, those centring on the problems which Biblical theology is creating, those involved in the questions of the reintegration of the Church, and finally the complex situations arising from the attempt to present the faith in terms relevant to contemporary man.[1] These are situations which in the past Anglicanism has encountered individually and separately during the seventeenth century. Has it the vigour and capacity now to confront them collectively and by a new effort of synthesis along the line of its own fusion of these three elements to make a contribution towards resolving these problems in the twentieth century? At all events, the combination of these three elements in the past produced a flexible, balanced and realistic theological method able to resist pressure and capable of assimilating new knowledge. Separately, these three elements are not the prerogative of any period or of any ecclesiastical interest. It is the way in which they are held together to constitute a theological method that is distinctive and which constitutes the Anglican approach in theology.

This method of synthesis is the method adopted by Hooker in dealing with Puritan objections in respect of 'the exercise of public duties in religion, or the functions of persons authorized thereunto'. In the fifth book of the *Ecclesiastical Polity* he justifies the existing order and rites of the Church of England by the three-fold test of 'intrinsic reasonableness', by 'the judgment of antiquity, and by the long continued practice of the whole Church;

1. A. M. Ramsey, *From Gore to Temple*, p. ix.

from which unnecessarily to swerve, experience hath never as yet found it safe', and by the 'authority of the Church itself'.[1] Hooker's use of the appeal to antiquity is part of his liberal method, and in his book the patristic writings are used in just such a way as has been outlined.

But the appeal to antiquity did not originate with Hooker, for Jewel, to whose early interest Hooker was indebted, writes 'we are come, as near as we possibly could, to the church of the apostles and of the old catholic bishops and fathers'.[2] Cranmer also looked to the Scripture, the Church 'from the beginning' and the Fathers.[3] But it was Andrewes who, in P. A. Welsby's words, made this 'the norm of Anglican apologetic'.[4]

This was not however the limit of the impression made by his work on seventeenth-century theological method. In a real sense Andrewes gave expression to what may be looked on as the classical Anglican approach summarised in his own phrase 'one canon . . . two testaments, three creeds, four general councils, five centuries, and the series of Fathers in that period . . . determine the boundary of our faith'.[5] But he clothed that framework in such a way as to make it a living form. To some extent, his work was as significant as Hooker's for the subsequent course of things and they supplemented each other in various ways, having more in common than is apparent at first sight. It was Andrewes's misfortune that circumstances did not contrive that his work was cast in some such permanent form as that of the *Ecclesiastical Polity*, but in spite of this handicap it had an effect which was lasting.

Andrewes was born in 1555 and in 1571 he entered Pembroke Hall, Cambridge, of which he became a Fellow four years later and Master in 1589. Then and later he maintained the habit of study, as his biographer Henry Isaacson records, and he had a marked ability in the study of languages. Just after the turn of the century Andrewes was appointed Dean of Westminster and when the work on the translation of the Bible was begun in 1604 he was naturally chosen as Chairman of one of the committees because of

1. *Ecclesiastical Polity*, Bk. V, Chapters VI, VII, VIII. 'Laws touching matter of order are changeable, by the power of the Church; articles concerning doctrine not so', *ib.* Chap. VIII, 2.
2. *Defence of the Apology* (1567), *Works* (Parker Society), Pt. III, p. 100.
3. *Remains* (ed. Jenkins), Vol. IV, p. 126.
4. *Lancelot Andrewes*, P. A. Welsby, p. 156.
5. *Opuscula*, p. 91 (L.A.C.T. ed.).

his knowledge of Hebrew in which of course he was not alone as others had made this and kindred studies their particular interest at this period. The following year he became bishop of Chichester and subsequently of Ely and of Winchester. Both Isaacson and Buckeridge have left a picture of Andrewes as devout and studious, charitable and practical. The continuing popularity of his *Preces Privatae* which went through many editions and reprints from the time of its first appearance in 1675 reinforced the opinions of contemporaries. Andrewes never seems to have been in danger of being forgotten but rather to have succeeded in catching the imagination of later times. But his real significance is due to his contribution to theological method which was of a formative nature. It was something which he inherited in part from such as Jewel whose work he valued.[1] It was something which he shared in part with Hooker, the preservation of the remainder of whose work, as C. J. Sisson has shown, was due to Andrewes.[2] What he inherited and shared he also enriched and it passed into the theology of the century, its origin often unrealised.

Anglicanism produced theologians far more than theologians produced Anglicanism, and indeed the absence from Anglicanism of any theologian who created a system or distinctive body of teaching is essentially a condition of the existence of its theological method. In few cases is this better illustrated than in the work of Andrewes, the whole theme of which was that Anglicanism had no specific teaching other than that of Scripture interpreted by the Primitive Church with which it had a continuity historical and doctrinal. Andrewes gave to this position held by previous writers and by the Book of Homilies a positive orientation, and brought it into association with the distinction between what was and was not fundamental, and with freedom in matters not defined, for his Catholicism was liberal and his sympathies wide. There is more than a hint of the Renaissance in the background of his thought, for he had an extensive knowledge of the classics as well as of patristic writings and history. The very breadth of his scholarship and knowledge of languages had about it a spaciousness which must have commended itself to his friend Bacon. The friendship and the fact that Bacon consulted with Andrewes about his own works seem to presuppose in the latter

1. *Opuscula*, p. 91.
2. C. J. Sisson, *The Judicious Marriage of Mr Hooker*, pp. 79–108.

an interest in the philosophical, observational and humanist approach which the *Essays* reveal. The reaction of Andrewes to Calvinist ideas, and the liberal view of the human situation in the *Judgment of the Lambeth Articles*, point in the same direction.

It is tolerably clear also that Andrewes inclined to the general position of the Arminians, although he refrained from committing himself mainly on the grounds that the Remonstrants, in reaction from the dogmatism of the Calvinists, tended themselves to become dogmatic on points which were not fundamental and therefore should be left open. This was the line taken in the *Judgment of the Lambeth Articles* in which however the similarity between the views of Andrewes and of the Remonstrants can be noted. Inevitably the liberality of such as Episcopius which made a deep impression on Hales at the Synod of Dort would strike an answering note in Andrewes for whom the distinction between things fundamental and questions of opinion was integral to his whole approach. Andrewes's attitude to the Remonstrants was also complicated by other factors, the first of which was the declared opposition to Arminianism of King James who had sent representatives to the Synod of Dort. His known views did not help to popularise the Arminian position in England. The second complication arose out of the visit to England in 1613 of Grotius, a leading Dutch Arminian, whose aim was to acquire sympathy for his views, and Calvinists in both countries were alarmed at the possibility of his influencing the King.[1] Matters were not simplified by the fact that the conflict had acquired political overtones in Holland.

On the occasion of Grotius's visit Casaubon had brought him to see Andrewes, and according to a letter written by Abbot, the Archbishop of Canterbury, the visitor had dominated the conversation and had seriously compromised Andrewes later by informing the King that the Bishop of Ely held the same views as himself. Andrewes denied this, and although Abbot regarded him as having at any rate inclined to that opinion, it should be borne in mind that Abbot was a Calvinist and Andrewes was not. A letter from John Chamberlain to Sir Dudley Carleton (to whom Hales had written his account of the proceedings at Dort) gave

1. Andrewes, *Minor Works*, pp. lxxxvii–iii (L.A.C.T. ed.).

further evidence of the way in which Grotius had jumped to conclusions about Andrewes's views and disseminated the idea which remained current for some time in Holland that Andrewes supported the Arminian position.[1]

Certainly Andrewes was influenced by the King's opposition, but then so was everyone else, as the Bishop of Llandaff noted on his return from the Synod of Dort. Nevertheless it is fair to say that Andrewes had recorded his view in the *Judgment of the Lambeth Articles* that the system which the Arminians opposed was based on what was speculative. But there is no indication that he was in agreement with the position of the Arminians, for his interest was in other matters. If he had never heard of the Arminians his own view of the need for reserve in dealing with such questions which he had expressed in the *Judgment of the Lambeth Articles* would have led him to the same conclusion. Grotius was known to have a favourable opinion of the Church of England which he had described in a letter as being congruous in many ways with the Church of the early centuries,[2] but there is no confirmation that Andrewes knew this. He was however aware of it in the case of Casaubon who had introduced Grotius to him. Isaac Casaubon, who came to England in 1610, had studied patristic writings and 'he was glad to avail himself of the opportunity afforded him . . . of gaining a closer knowledge of the English Church, of whose peculiar character he had hitherto been acquainted only by hearsay, and which seemed likely to furnish a solution of the doubts and difficulties which he felt, and which could not be satisfied by the claims of either of the religious communions in his own country'.[3] The letters and diary of Casaubon show that he and Andrewes were in frequent contact and that the acquaintance developed. Andrewes was naturally drawn to one who had independently come to the same conclusions as himself on the continuity of the Church of England, and he must have regarded Casaubon's agreement as a welcome and unsought confirmation of the position by one who had studied the Fathers unprejudiced by inherited allegiance or chosen affiliation.

Andrewes's thought is not speculative but meditative, which is very different, and there is in his work an element of realism and

1. P. A. Welsby, *Lancelot Andrewes*, p. 167.
2. Quoted in the preface to Thomas Comber's *Companion* (2nd ed. 1676).
3. Andrewes, *Minor Works*, Appendix C, p. lxxviii (L.A.C.T. ed).

a sense of the demands of practicality and of the historic fact. Negatively this appears in his reaction to the main points of contemporary Calvinism, and positively in his concern with the test of historicity and the fact of continuity. That this element appeared in his sermons is indicated by the large numbers who came to hear them as well as by the sermons themselves. No matter how much he may dissect a phrase his thought can be forcefully and directly expressed. As he relates the implications of the themes, for example, of the major festivals to the realities of circumstances and the practice of religion, it is clear that for Andrewes theology is concerned with life. In various forms this emphasis on practicality recurs, as when he writes 'Christianity is a meeting; and to this meeting go pia dogmata as well as bona opera . . . take one from the rest, and it is as much as the whole is worth'.[1]

As usual in the seventeenth century, practicality is connected with practical divinity and it would be no surprise to learn from Isaacson of Andrewes's interest in the subject even if his *Pattern of Catechistical Doctrine* did not happen to be published posthumously in 1630.[2] It was perhaps the first of these expositions based on the catechism, a number of which appeared during the seventeenth century and exercised a considerable influence. They were known as 'sums of divinity', and in addition to sections on the creed, prayer and the sacraments, they contained explanations of the decalogue and the duties. Almost two-thirds of Andrewes's book deals with various aspects of moral theology and despite the form in which it is presented the *Pattern* shows the devotional quality and the insight which later generations learned to associate with Andrewes. It would be difficult to overestimate the cumulative effect of these books in the building up of Anglicanism, and it is noteworthy that three of the best-known of them were published during the Commonwealth period. These were William Nicholson's *Plain and Full Exposition of the Catechism* (1655), Henry Hammond's *Practical Catechism* (1644), and Richard Sherlock's *The Catechism of the Church of England Explained* (1656).[3] The need for them was felt when the practice of catechising had more or less ceased, when as Nicholson put it, 'sermonising hath

---

1. *Sermons*, p. 106, and cp. pp. 161, 587.
2. *Life*, p. vii (L.A.C.T. ed).

3. For details of these books see *The Structure of Caroline Moral Theology*, pp. 168–71.

justled out this necessary instruction'.[1] Few single influences can have done more in bringing about the solidly practical outlook to which *The Whole Duty of Man* gave expression in a form which owed something to the catechetical books.[2] There were others, including Thomas Ken's *Exposition of the Church Catechism* (1685) and William Beveridge's *The Church Catechism Explained* (1704), and they took the general scheme of the catechism, in which the sections on creed, sacraments and duties are related to each other, and helped to make it part of a basic assumption. It was not accidental that the catechism dealt only with fundamentals and with practice, for its pedestrian and matter-of-fact approach is a deliberate expression of something which was reflected at various levels in the seventeenth century. It appeared in the Anglican attitude to the whole complex of questions concerning faith, works, justification and the decrees, and it might be summed up by saying that theology in its method and in its findings must take account of reason and experience. It was by no means a refusal to consider abstruse questions, as witness Sanderson's *Pacific Discourse* and Hammond's letters on the subject, but a strong disinclination to allow a disproportionate place to speculation in the manner, and with the results, which Hales observed at Dort. Chiefly, the catechetical books mirror an attitude which is part of Anglican theological method, but they also helped to give this attitude currency at the non-theological level by building up an assumption that theology must be realistic.

Thus the basic presuppositions of Anglican theological method created a situation which in turn affected theological method. The widespread if unformulated demand on the part of people generally for meaning and practicality is proved by the great popularity of *The Whole Duty of Man* and other similar works. The reaction of Sanderson to the book by Twiss is typical of one who was conversant with the questions raised, but who, having studied the *Ecclesiastical Polity* and because of his own concern with practical divinity, saw the need for maintaining the

1. Epistle dedicatory, *Plain and Full Exposition of the Catechism of the Church of England.*
2. As for example in the division of the three-fold duties to parallel the 'piously, soberly, justly' of Titus 2, v.12, the general scheme under which Andrewes treats faith, hope, love, humility, worship. This outline is followed in the two opening sections of *The Whole Duty of Man* and its general treatment resembles that of the other books.

balance. Anglican theology in the seventeenth century had a more
or less permanent context of practicality and liturgy, the latter in
the broad sense of the continued use of a Prayer Book in the
vernacular with all that this implies in the way of unconscious
absorption of credal content. This, almost as much as its combination of Scripture, tradition and reason, helped to keep Anglican
theology reasonably free from theorising. Heylyn's expressed
dislike of a system which makes use of syllogisms and Smith's
criticism of the knowledge 'got by mere speculation, which is
ushered in by syllogisms and demonstrations' have their counterpart in Andrewes. He observes that 'it is not without danger' to
suppose that religion is simply a matter of 'certain theses to be held,
dogmatical points, matters of opinion. And true it is, such points
there be; but they be not all'.[1]

The expositions of the catechism were part of this trend
which influenced theological method, just as they were in another
sense products of that method, and Andrewes was among the
first to see the usefulness of this kind of book. It was however the
situation before and after the Restoration which produced them
in more popular form, for if they had not existed it would have
been necessary to invent them. The catechetical books reflect
also the catechism's combination of practicality and devotion,
so that while they discuss all sorts of practical problems, they do
so in the context of the individual's participation in the liturgical
and sacramental life of the Church. This practical approach in no
way acted as a damper on the warmth and feeling of many of the
devotional writings of the period. Taylor was much occupied with
practical divinity, yet in *The Rules and Exercises of Holy Living*
(1649) under the three-fold heading used in the catechetical
books,[2] he produced a manual in which this solid, detailed, practical
divinity combines with spiritual depth and insight, the practical
sections being matched by those in which prayers and meditations
are arranged suitable to the subject. The same is true of William

---

1. *Sermons*, p. 161, cp. pp. 106, 587. In the latter sermon, Andrewes stresses
that this balance must be preserved, 'it is not safe to do otherwise, nor to
serve God by synechdoche'.
1. *The Rules and Exercises of Holy Living*, Chap. II, I, where he writes that the
Christian religion 'according to the apostle's arithmetic, hath but these
three parts of it; i. sobriety, ii. justice, iii. religion,' referring to Titus 2,
vv.11–13.

Law, for while he and Taylor use the phrase 'live by rule',[1] the
writings of both show that they regard this as but the necessary
framework for what More and Scougal call 'the divine life'. In
fact, the devotional works of the period display a remarkable
unanimity of method in combining moral theology, prayer, meditation and sacraments, in such a way that devotional practice and
practical divinity are seen to be two aspects of the same thing. In
this they are parallel to the general disposition of theological
method and faithfully reflect the characteristics of theology in the
seventeenth century.

Andrewes's *Preces Privatae*, which has had an influence on
later generations comparable to that of his sermons on his own,
is based, as H. B. Swete noted, on the devotional handling of the
creeds, and he describes its theology as being for the 'most part
an interpretation of the Apostles' and Nicene Creeds read in the
light of the experience of life'. He draws attention to the way in
which 'certain chief elements of devotion, such as commemoration,
petition, intercession' are combined with 'minuteness of detail',
and remarks on the unobtrusive way in which use is made of
extracts from liturgies.[2] This liturgical quality was remarked on by
Dean Church who described it as bringing the spirit of the
Prayer Book 'from the Church to the closet'.[3] Swete comments that
'the whole tone of the *Preces Privatae* is akin to that of the Greek
liturgies',[4] and Andrewes's interest in liturgy is closely connected
with the treatment commonly accorded in the seventeenth
century to antiquity as a general frame of reference. The interest
in the subject during the period was considerable, and it was usual
for writers such as Taylor, Thorndike, Hammond, L'Estrange,
Cosin and others to point to a continuity of liturgical outline as
between the main features of the primitive liturgies and the
Book of Common Prayer. Andrewes shared in this interest, and
Swete's comment on the kinship of the *Preces Privatae* is borne
out by references in the sermons such as, 'to very good purpose it
was, that the ancient Fathers of the Greek Church in their liturgy
. . .'[5] or by extracts and quotations. Andrewes's observations on

1. Taylor, *ib.* Chap. I, and Law, *Serious Call*, Chap. VIII.
2. Introduction to *Preces Privatae* (1920).
3. *Masters in English Theology* (ed. Barry), p. 105.
4. Loc. cit.
5. *Sermons*, p. 354.

the use of psalm 85 illustrates typically the wish to underline liturgical continuity, when he writes that this is 'one of the psalms selected of old by the Primitive Church, and so still retained by ours, as part of our office, or service of this day'.[1] His practical interest in the subject is shown in his *Notes on the Book of Common Prayer*, his *Form of Consecration of a Church and Churchyard*, and his *Form for Consecrating Church Plate*.

What may be called the aspect of liberality in Andrewes's writings, the distinction between what is plainly to be received and what is a matter of opinion, and his acceptance of the need for critical assessment, together with his *Preces Privatae* and his interest in moral theology and liturgical matters, are however secondary to his main concern. W. H. Ness writes, 'What he desired was to provide a standard within the history of the Church itself, by which the development of doctrine and institutions might be tested'.[2] P. A. Welsby notes that 'that standard or norm of faith for the Church, he reasoned, was exhibited in its purest form in the New Testament and in the first five centuries of Church history'. He points out that although Andrewes's knowledge of the Fathers was very extensive 'nevertheless he was not purely antiquarian for he does not imply that all subsequent developments are to be condemned, provided that they are not held to be de fide, nor does he contemplate a return to the precise conditions of the Primitive Church'.[3]

It is however in the sermons rather than in the *Responsio* or the *Tortura Torti* that the key to the appreciation of Andrewes's method of handling the appeal to antiquity is to be sought, for here the depth and range of his knowledge of the patristic period is seen in a way that is all the more impressive because it is incidental. In the other works he is speaking to a brief and although his mastery of the Fathers is equally clear and his deductions candid, as also in the letters to du Moulin, the writing is naturally more deliberate and sustained as he discusses the evidence for the type of standard which emerges from the history of the first five centuries. It is an uncomplicated appeal to 'Scriptures, Creeds, Councils and Fathers'[4] and the approach is through history and the writings of the patristic period. But in the sermons

1. *Sermons*, p. 96.
2. Quoted in P. A. Welsby, *Lancelot Andrewes*, p. 156.
3. *Ib.*
4. *Responsio*, p. 208 (L.A.C.T. ed.).

it is not the variety of the references and quotations numerous as they are, nor their appositeness, which is most noticeable, but rather the way in which they flow naturally out of the theme, seeming to illustrate it without effort. They convey an impression of knowledge at depth rather than of a writer producing relevant passages from material with which he is well-acquainted. There is no element of decorativeness or artificiality but rather of spontaneity, for Andrewes seems to think with the Fathers rather than merely to furnish extracts out of their writings. He is steeped in the atmosphere of the first 'five centuries, and the series of the Fathers in that period',[1] and in the sermons the effect of the long hours of study which Isaacson noted is seen in the ease with which the patristic comments on different subjects spring almost unbidden into use, to be merged illustratively with the theme.

Some examples may show Andrewes's natural and easy use of the writings of the Fathers. 'But let me also tell you a saying: it is St Basil's, and well worth your remembering'; 'I had rather you heard St Augustine than myself...'; 'The Fathers aptly resemble their case, that were the ante-nati before Christ, and ours that came after, to the two men that carried the great cluster of grapes, upon a staff between them. Both carried, but he that came behind saw that he carried: so did not he that went before'; Of fasting (on Matt.6,16) 'Which of the Fathers have not homilies yet extant in the praise of it? ... either we must cancel all antiquity, or we must acknowledge the constant use and observation of it ...;' On the reason for there being forty days in Lent, 'Ignatius hath said it before me: I dare say it after him'; On Christmas, 'As the very day whereon He was first seen, first showed to the world ... sure I am the Fathers fix it all upon one day, and upon this day by name. So Irenaeus, Augustine, Cyril set it down that this day it was'; 'And this rule, and the steps of the Fathers proceeding by this rule, are to me a warrant to expound and apply this verse, as they have done before, to the present occasion of this time'; Comments on verses, 'It is Irenaeus' own words', 'Gregory saith well', 'St Augustine hath long since defined it', 'The rule of the Fathers is (Hierome and Cyril have it) ...', 'It is but a grammar note (that of Hierome's)...' 'St Jerome saith of Job...';

1. *Opuscula*, p. 91 (L.A.C.T. ed.).

'Chrysostom, Oecumenius, the interpreters all weigh it:'[1] He has the facility for making his knowledge of the patristic period appear incidental, for he wears his learning lightly. If the style is the man, the knowledge of and manner of utilising sources is the scholar.

One of the sermons however provides an illustration of the method of the appeal to antiquity.[2] In it Andrewes deals with the appeal to antiquity as applied to the custom of keeping Easter and the time of it. He seems to hint that the question itself may not at the time have been altogether theoretical, but he is in fact endeavouring to discover the nature and authority of ecclesiastical custom, whether and under what conditions it exists, and this was always topical in the seventeenth century. It affords an example, in considerable detail, of how Andrewes regarded the appeal to antiquity as applicable in practice.

He begins by showing from the text that 'the Church hath her customs',[3] but that the mere existence of custom does not guarantee its worth. Nor is it enough if 'some one Church had it, but the rest never had any such', for this passage requires that the custom be 'apostolic . . . and . . . catholic' and another passage gives the authority for the custom of keeping Easter from the beginning.[4] But it is not necessary in this matter to go further than the fact that 'the Church's custom is clear enough' and 'the right base of this I take to be custom'.[5] Customs are not the same as traditions, the one being concerned with agenda and the other with credenda, and 'no custom . . . against Scripture' is to be observed.[6] The existence of custom from the beginning of the history of the Church is indicated by this passage, and he gives an instance of the respect for customs recommended by the first Nicene Council.[7] Andrewes goes on to show that every Church is free to establish customs so long as they do not conflict with general custom, and he concludes that the test of any custom is that it must be general and ancient.[8] Having shown that 'customs so qualified are to be kept', he turns to examine the custom of keeping Easter, pointing out that discussion arose as to the time of keeping it and not in respect of the

1. *Sermons*, pp. 641, 216, 356, 131, 217, 224, 64, 350, 161, 371, 392, 611, 612, 424, 614.
2. *Sermons*, p. 517 (I Cor.XI:16 is the passage).
3. *Ib*. p. 518.
4. I Cor. V: 7, 8, is the passage referred to.
5. *Ib*. p. 518.
6. *Ib*. p. 521.
7. *Ib*. p. 521.
8. *Ib*. p. 522.

custom itself which was everywhere observed.[1] The universality of the custom was underlined by the very differences themselves arising as to when Easter should be kept, and it seems from Andrewes's remark about the question never having been raised except by Aerius 'till now in our days' that opposition to the practice was known to exist in some extremist section of contemporary opinion.[2]

The period of investigation he delimits as the first five centuries, and having referred to the beginning of differences on the matter as recorded by Tertullian and Irenaeus, he cites the evidence of the 'cycli paschales or calendars made of purpose for the just keeping it, at the very time'.[3] In addition there were the 'paschales epistolae' sent out yearly from Alexandria 'to give notice of it in due time to other Churches'.[4]

The next and the most important material to be considered is the writings of the Fathers, of whom there is 'a full jury, Greek and Latin of them; and that of the most chief and eminent among them, St Basil, Nazianzen, Chrysostom, Nyssen, Theophilus, Alexandrinus, Cyril, Chrysologus, Leo'.[5] The material may be divided into four parts, discourses for the day, hymns for the festival, other writings such as commentaries, and instances of recorded practice,[6] and he gives examples of all four, so that the custom is verified by 'all these ways, by singing, by saying, by writing, by doing'.[7] Next he writes 'from the Fathers, I pass to the Councils, and plead it by all four', and he adds that 'before all these . . . by a dozen years at least was the Council of Arles, and in it, this custom proclaimed'.[8] Andrewes notes that its particular interest lies in the fact that Restitutus, bishop of London, was present, which indicated not only the antiquity of the custom but the geographical extent of its observance. He concludes with references to other writings of the patristic period, and the whole sermon serves as an illustration of the application of the appeal to antiquity.

The same method is the basis of the *Tortura*, the *Responsio* and the *Two Answers* (to du Perron),[9] and while these are to some

1. *Ib*. p. 523.
2. *Ib*. p. 524.
3. *Ib*. p. 524.
4. *Ib*. p. 525.
5. *Ib*. p. 525.
6. *Ib*. p. 525.
7. *Ib*. p. 526.
8. *Ib*. p. 527.
9. *Tortura Torti* (1609), *Responsio ad Apologiam Cardinalis Bellarmini* (1610), *Two Answers* (1629, posthumous).

extent deficient in arrangement due to being cast in the form of a reply, they are nevertheless as Welsby points out 'a positive statement'.[1] The importance of his work derives rather from the position it affirms than from any of his writings in particular, for although they were the outcome of a controversial situation as was Hooker's work, they were not produced in a durable form like that of the *Ecclesiastical Polity*. In this respect circumstances were not helpful to Andrewes in that he wrote in Latin and in the unsystematic form of a reply while Hooker wrote in the context of a general situation. Further, Andrewes's work was something in the nature of a command performance and therefore did not have the spontaneity and natural development of the *Ecclesiastical Polity*. But if the form of their work was dissimilar, Andrewes and Hooker resembled each other in purpose and temperament. Both became involved in controversy for which they had little inclination as their contemporaries noted. Chamberlain wrote to Carleton that Andrewes was 'appointed to answer Bellarmine about the oath of allegiance, which task I doubt how he will undertake and perform, being so contrary to his disposition',[2] and Hooker, in a letter concerning his debate with Travers which was 'the more unpleasant' to him because of his regard for the latter, felt that he was not intended for 'contentions'. In the same letter he records that he has begun a treatise in which his 'meaning is not to provoke any' but to provide an answer which will give satisfaction to those who really look for a solution of the question.[3]

Neither Hooker nor Andrewes refused to meet the situations in which their times placed them, for both produced able expositions of the basis of their position in Scripture, reason and antiquity, and both saw the need to establish and vindicate it. Circumstances demanded that they should take part in the controversies of their day, but it was circumstances and not inclination which involved them in disputation which they reluctantly recognised as inevitable in the existing situation. While the views of Hooker and Andrewes were essentially large, they naturally brought all the weight of their learning to combat the views of both Travers and Bellarmine, and to show the advantage of the Anglican position in terms of Scripture, reason and antiquity. Hooker was particularly successful in imparting a positive emphasis to his

1. P. A. Welsby, *Lancelot Andrewes*, p. 151.

2. *Life* (L.A.C.T. ed.), p. ix.

3. Walton's *Life* of Hooker.

work, but it has been remarked by Welsby that Andrewes in the *Tortura* tends to yield to the spirit of debate so that the work is of less permanent value than its successor the *Responsio*.[1] This he describes as the nearest approach to a positive statement of Andrewes's views on the use of antiquity as a criterion.[2] Part of the reason for this was that in the *Tortura* Andrewes was writing an official reply, 'unwillingly hastened on by the King'[3] who made suggestions and changes. These two books appeared as a result of the King's publication of his *Triplici Nodo*,[4] but what is of interest here is the place accorded to the early period. King James made use of Andrewes's knowledge of the writings of the Fathers, and his remarks on Hooker's 'clear manifestation of reason, and that backed with the authority of Scripture, the fathers and schoolmen, and with all law'[5] show that these elements were seen by contemporaries to be in the closest theological association from the beginning of the seventeenth century. While Hooker clarified the function of reason and placed the idea of law in perspective, Andrewes enlarged upon the standard existing in the history of the early centuries but neither did so in terms of one to the exclusion of the others although each laid the main emphasis on a different element in theological method in accordance with the circumstances in which he was writing.

To summarise the course of events which ultimately involved King James and Andrewes, Bellarmine, du Perron and Casaubon, is not relevant to the present subject, nor is it necessary to follow in detail the development of the ensuing argument. It had arisen out of the matter of the oath of allegiance, and when Andrewes in the *Tortura* had turned to the question of the supremacy the subjects quickly resolved themselves in effect into general statements of position on either side. Both Bellarmine and Andrewes, the one in the *Apologia* and the other in the *Responsio*, then moved on to the wider question of Catholicity, the former asserting that this depended on certain specific doctrines and the latter maintaining that these doctrines could not constitute such a test since they were not known during the first thousand years.[6] What is relevant to the development of theological method in the

1. P. A. Welsby, *Lancelot Andrewes*, p. 149.
2. *Ib.* p. 151.
3. *Ib.* p. 146.
4. *Ib.* pp. 144–46.
5. Walton's *Life* of Hooker.
6. *Responsio*, p. 72.

records of this debate is the way in which Andrewes based the vindication of his position on the historical and theological testimony of antiquity. If opinions are new, he writes, 'they are not ours. We appeal to antiquity, and to the most extreme antiquity', and again, 'we do not innovate; it may be we renovate what was customary among the ancients'.[1] For Andrewes the Catholicity of the Church was not dependent on propositions such as those advanced by Bellarmine, nor was it, as some Puritans held, an attribute of the invisible Church. It emerged from continuity with the Primitive Church, and the establishing of that continuity by reference to the standard evolving within the first five centuries was for Andrewes and his successors the reason for the emphasis on antiquity and the explanation of the continuing preoccupation with historicity in Anglican theological method. Referring to the definition of Vincent of Lérins, Andrewes writes: 'Let that be reckoned Catholic which always obtained everywhere among all, and which always and everywhere and by all was believed.'[2] Examining in the light of this definition three of the doctrines urged by Bellarmine as essential to Catholicity, namely the papal supremacy, transubstantiation and invocation of saints, and discussing a wide selection of relevant patristic references,[3] he writes that 'there is no principal dogma in which we do not agree with the Fathers and they with us'.[4]

Elsewhere he sums up the position, observing that it is sufficient 'if one should believe the canonical Scriptures, freely affirm the three Creeds, respect the first four Councils, and allow the unanimous consent of the Fathers, in anything necessary to salvation'.[5] Andrewes elaborates on this in considerable detail,[6] and his method of handling the subject is with reference to history and the teaching of the Primitive Church as seen in the writings of the Fathers. In this connection he points out that the reason why such names as Bede, Gregory, Bonaventure, Thomas Aquinas and Anselm are not included is their distance from the Apostles' time. As a river differs from its source being affected by the kind of country through which it passes, so they are not unaffected by the passage of time and by the times in which they lived. In other matters their testimony is of value, but for this

1. *Tortura*, p. 96.   4. *Ib.* p. 70.
2. *Responsio*, p. 25.   5. *Ib.* p. 208.
3. *Ib.* Chap. I, Chap. VIII. 6. *Ib.* pp. 208–33.

purpose they are not suited.[1] Whatever arguments are advanced
against the appeal to antiquity as made by Andrewes and those
who came after, it has to be borne in mind that the fixing of the
limits at the close of the first five centuries was not arbitrary or
merely convenient. Rather is this delimiting of dates controlled
by the reference back to Scripture and to the period after the
apostles. This is the justification of the appeal to antiquity, which
is really the appeal to antiquity interpreting Scripture, and therefore the centuries nearest to it bid fair to interpret it best, being
the centuries of the creeds, the four councils and the outstanding
patristic writers, and being also the period during which the canon
of Scripture itself was being established. As to later writers,
Andrewes uses the *Summa Theologica*, copies of which were in his
library as were some of the works of Cajetan whom he quotes.[2]
In fact the contents of his library and the many references in his
writings confirm that his reading was very far from being confined
to the patristic period. For him the importance of the early writers
was that they reflected the mind of the Church in the first centuries,
and it was this that gave meaning to the idea of continuity. This
was no mechanical concept for Andrewes but the transmission of
certain living qualities of faith and order the possession of which
linked the present Church with the primitive Church, being at
once the assurance and the norm of Catholicity.

The *Two Answers* covers much the same ground as the *Responsio*,
using the same method of appeal to the Fathers to substantiate the
position and practice of the Church of England, and it appears
also in the replies to the three letters of du Moulin.[3]

Andrewes's extensive knowledge of the patristic period enabled
him to present the appeal to antiquity in a positive form. Moreover the very breadth of the outline discerned in the first five
centuries merged with the liberality of outlook which led Andrewes
to mistrust the narrower formulations of later times and to differentiate between essentials and non-essentials. There is an element
of humanism in Andrewes, as Dean Church noted, and in one
sense he is a theologian of the Renaissance. Indeed there is an
affinity between them, for Hooker and Andrewes, Church and the

1. *Ib*, p. 233.
2. Andrewes, *Minor Works* (L.A.C.T. ed.), p. cxv.
3. *Two Answers to Cardinal Perron, Minor Works* (L.A.C.T. ed), *Responsiones
ad Petri Molinaei Epistolas, Opuscula* (L.A.C.T. ed.).

writers of *Lux Mundi*, have something basic in common which is
not shared in full by Pusey and Liddon, however marked the
superficial resemblance maybe. Both thought in terms of Scripture,
Catholicism and continuity, but there the resemblance ended.
The Tractarian leaders expressed their thought in a form that
was rigorous and unyieldingly conservative, while for the others,
credal affirmations did not exclude the influences of humanism
or the use of criticism. Side by side through their thought from
Hooker to *Lux Mundi* ran this vivid sense of the present reality of
continuity with the past, and the sense of the necessity of the
freedom of reason to differentiate and to assess, a combination
which came to be known later as liberal Catholicism but which
for the seventeenth century was the accepted theological method
of Anglicanism. To this the contribution of Andrewes was
important and its effect was lasting. Laud described him as 'the
great light of the Christian world'[1] in his diary, referring to the
death of Andrewes in 1626, and they had been in frequent contact.
Their views were similar but Laud was a practical man intent on
applying his ideas. When King James died, Laud found himself
in company with a king who shared his views, and who was
himself prepared to put into action the ideas of kingship which his
predecessor had held. Thus Laud's situation matched his inclination, and both contributed not a little to the tragic outcome.

Laud's attempts to secure uniformity are part of the history
of the period, and historians have judged them variously and not
infrequently from standpoints other than that of the setting of the
events. The immediate result appeared to be the destruction of his
design and the demolition of the whole structure within which it
evolved, but the design emerged again in the pattern of events at
the time of the Restoration when it might be said that the Laudian
party achieved for it a distinct measure of success. But it should
be recalled that the general position affirmed by such as Hammond,
Bramhall and Thorndike between 1645 and 1660 was not a party
position at all in respect of theological method. What gave them
cohesion as a group was their determination that the Restoration
would mean the return of the Church, which was by no means
certain at the time. Their policy has been described by Dr R. S.
Bosher as 'simple and traditional, the complete identification of

1. *Diary, Works* (ed. W. Scott and J. Bliss), p. 196.

the Anglican and Royalist causes'.[1] In his account of those who maintained this position it is clear that they were and acted as a party, for 'a study of Hammond's correspondence in the Harleian collection reveals how close-knit was the association of these men; their steady collaboration and clear-cut policy prepared the way for the Laudian triumph in the future settlement'.[2] What Bosher refers to as the 'total victory for Laud's followers within a generation of his overthrow'[3] was achieved by this policy which was political, theological and strategic. It was political in that they had succeeded in convincing Clarendon that 'the Church must be restored with the monarchy and without compromising concessions'. It was theological in that there was a great output of literary work in which Hammond was a leading figure. These writings, whether learned works or books intended for the general reader were essential since, as Duppa wrote to Farindon, 'there was never more need of the press, than when the pulpits . . . are shut up'.[4] It was also strategic in that many of the proscribed clergy, acting as tutors and private chaplains, ensured that 'a generation of young English squires absorbed the principles of "a proscribed and persecuted Church" '.[5] The result of this, as Bosher points out, was that the gentry who in 1640 were opposed to the bishops, gradually found a new alignment so that 'friendship and mutual sympathy accomplished the work which Laud's discipline had signally failed to do'.[6] It was this silent revolution accomplished by the Laudian clergy[7] which ensured the success of Laudian policy, for it explains a phenomenon noted with surprise in the Parliament of 1660, a solid block of young men, who supported it.[8]

Accordingly, what gave the Laudians cohesion as a party was policy not party theology in the later sense of the words. The theological method of Hammond, Bramhall and others, is with varying emphasis that of Scripture, reason and tradition, and in this respect they are close to Laud, the form of whose writings was influenced by the work of Hooker and Andrewes.

Laud was not primarily a theologian but he was theologically

1. R. S. Bosher, *The Making of the Restoration Settlement*, p. 30.
2. *Ib.* p. 30.
3. *Ib.* p. 2.
4. *Ib.* p. 37.
5. *Ib.* p. 39.
6. *Ib.* p. 40.
7. *Ib.* p. 200.
8. *Ib.* p. 40.

learned, with a wide knowledge of the Fathers as his writings indicate. Like most of his generation he had been accustomed to the scholastic writers, and in particular to Aquinas. References to the *Summa Theologica* and quotations from it are of frequent occurrence in the *Conference*. The many and diverse instances of the influence of Aquinas on seventeenth-century writing should be taken account of in connection with the more or less continuous inclination on the part of Anglican theological method towards effecting some sort of synthesis of faith and reason. The *Summa Theologica* can be seen as part of the background and it combined with other factors already noted to create a permanent pull in this direction. Laud was not exempt from this general tendency so that for him the three elements merge in a natural unity. Because of the degree of his involvement in the events of the times it is not always remembered that he was more than an ecclesiastical statesman and administrator, as may be seen from the posthumously published *Summarie of Devotions*,[1] from his *Diary* and from the competent learning of his theological writing.

Because he was chiefly concerned with procuring uniformity in accordance with his policy it is natural that one of the main factors in his outlook is the visible Church, visible in its continuity, 'one and the same Church still'.[2] Laud had caught a glimpse of the Church moving through the upheavals of history and like Andrewes he saw the significance of the first five centuries for later times, and he concluded that 'the Church of England is nearest of any Church now in being to the Primitive Church'.[3] It was his misfortune that he lacked the capacity to commend his vision to his opponents in terms that might have been acceptable to them. Doubtless this capacity, rare in any age, was hardly natural to the partisan temper of the times. But Laud's judgment seems to have been at fault also in that he underestimated both the vitality of Puritanism and the extent of the opposition within the Church to his policy. In the dedicatory preface to the *Conference* he justifies his attempts to ensure uniformity by pointing out the injurious and unsettling effects of 'the want of uniform and decent order in too many churches of the kingdom'. There can

1. Published in 1667 and arranged for the days of the week with prayers from various sources and for different occasions.
2. *A Relation of the Conference* (Between Laud and Fisher), 3rd ed. dedicatory preface.
3. *Ib.* p. 245.

be no doubt, he writes, that without 'inward worship' there can
be no reality, but 'external worship' is 'the great witness' to it.
This is the reason for endeavouring to secure 'decency and an
orderly settlement of the external worship of God in the Church.
For of that which is inward there can be no witness among men.
Now no external action in the world can be uniform without some
ceremonies. And these in religion, the ancienter they be, the better,
so they may fit time and place'. It is a mistake in his view to think
because some ceremonies are unnecessary none are needed, for
ceremonies are 'the hedge that fence the substance of religion'.[1]

In the preface he describes the Church as occupying a position
between that of Roman Catholics and that of Puritans, the one
opposing what is regarded as 'novelty in doctrine' in the Church
of England and the other refusing to accept the form of 'church-
government'. But in his view this *via media* is not deliberately
chosen as such but is incidental to the fact that 'she professes the
ancient Catholic Faith'. Laud maintains that there is in fact no
innovation but a return to the reaching of Scripture and the
Fathers, and that 'she practices church-government as it hath
been in use in all ages and all places'.[2] It is clear that like Andrewes
he sees the criterion of antiquity in relation to continuity and
Catholicity which is not in a 'narrow conclave', and his purpose
in the book is 'to lay open those wider gates of the Catholic Church,
confined to no age, time or place; nor knowing any bounds but
that faith which was once (and but once for all) delivered to the
saints'.[3]

As this last extract suggests, the appeal to antiquity depends
for Laud as for Andrewes on the centrality of Scripture: 'For that
all the positive articles of the present Church of England are
grounded upon Scripture, we are content to be judged by the joint
and constant belief of the Fathers, which lived within the first
four or five hundred years after Christ, when the Church was at
the best; and by the Councils held within those times.' That
Scripture contains all fundamentals is not only held by the
Church of England, but was the opinion of the Fathers, and it
does not exclude genuine, universal traditions: 'The Fathers are
plain, the Schoolmen not strangers in it. And have not we reason

1. *Conference*, preface, and compare   2. *Ib.*
   the original preface to the Book of   3. *Ib.* Preface.
   Common Prayer.

then to account it, as it is, the foundation of our faith? . . . and if the Scripture be the foundation to which we are to go for witness, if there be doubt about the faith, and in which we are to find the thing that is to be believed, as necessary in the faith; we never did, nor never will refuse any tradition that is universal and apostolic for the better exposition of the Scripture; nor any definition of the Church in which she goes to the Scripture for what she teaches; and thrusts nothing as fundamental in the faith upon the world, but what the Scripture fundamentally makes "materiam credendorum", the substance of that which is so to be believed, whether immediately and expressly in words, or more remotely, where a clear and full deduction draws it out'.[1] In his view some traditions are 'true and firm, and of great, both authority and use in the Church, as being apostolical, but yet not fundamental in the faith'.[2] The distinction between what is fundamental and non-fundamental turns on the fact that all necessary fundamentals are in Scripture and in the creed, so that the Fathers 'make the creed the rule of faith'.[3]

It is of considerable interest that a recent work of research into the nature and authority of tradition, R. P. C. Hanson's *Tradition in the Early Church*, affords support to the position of seventeenth-century writers in this connection. It is true that Hanson, in common with others today, finds it impossible to identify 'that enigmatic phenomenon . . . the rule of faith' with the baptismal creed, an identification assumed three centuries ago and upheld until recent times.[4] He gives reasons for supposing however that it did in fact develop into the declaratory creed, which was 'avowedly and unmistakably based upon the Scriptures and an interpretation of them'.[5] But what is of particular relevance for the seventeenth-century appeal to antiquity is the evidence adduced to show that the Fathers proved the rule of faith from Scripture,[6] thus disposing of the suggestion that tradition was treated as an independent authority in early times: 'the idea of the rule of faith as supplementing or complementing, or indeed adding anything whatever to, the Bible, is wholly absent from their

1. *Ib.* p. 34.
2. *Ib.* p. 28.
3. *Ib.* p. 27.

4. R. P. C. Hanson, *Tradition in the Early Church* (1962), p. 74, and cp. p. 65.
5. *Ib.* p. 127.
6. *Ib.* p. 108.

thoughts'.[1] He concludes that 'it is at any rate certain that all the Fathers believed that the rule of faith was in its contents identical with the contents of the Bible, and that they all regarded the rule as open to being proved from the Bible, but, with two doubtful exceptions, none of them regarded the Bible as open to being supported in its authority by the rule'.[2] Hanson's careful examination of patristic writings on this subject, apart from its own value, is valuable in respect of the confirmation it affords for the general position taken by the seventeenth-century writers which they maintained to be consonant with that of the early Church.

What has been referred to as the standard which emerged within the history of the first four or five hundred years is consequently not an end in itself from the point of view of seventeenth-century theological method, but its place is secondary to that of Scripture. It was derivative and interpretative and Laud summarises the position as being based 'upon the Scripture, and upon the Primitive Church expounding it'. This prevented the seventeenth century from regarding antiquity as an arbitrary criterion in itself or as a pattern to be artificially reproduced and reimposed, so that generally speaking its context was mainly expository. Nevertheless while Laud would not allow to tradition an independent authority, neither would he accept the position that Scripture was independent of the Church, for apart from interpretation, they were mutually dependent: 'the Scripture where 'tis plain should guide the Church; and the Church where there's doubt or difficulty should expound the Scripture; yet so as neither the Scripture should be forced, nor the Church so bound up, as that upon just and farther evidence, she may not revise that which in any case hath slipt by her'.[3] Laud's treatment of this relationship, which is another aspect of the constantly recurring question of the nature of authority, shows how the theological method has had effect. The question which arises is, how is 'Scripture known to be Scripture', or on what grounds is it to be accepted as authoritative? There are four possible answers, and according to his view 'no one of these doth it alone'. Firstly,

1. *Ib.* p. 126.   2. *Ib.* p. 125.
3. loc cit. preface, and cp. *ib.* p. 63, 'though they do materially, yet they do not equally confine the authority either of other. For Scripture doth infallibly confirm the authority of Church traditions truly so called: but tradition doth but morally and probably confirm the authority of the Scripture'.

there is 'the testimony and witness of the Church, and her tradition'. Secondly, there is 'the testimony which the Scripture gives to itself'. Thirdly, there is the inward testimony which by its nature is subjective 'so that hence can be drawn no proof to others'. Fourthly, there is natural reason.[1]

Taken together, on the analogy of the combination of Scripture, tradition and reason in the accepted theological method, they may constitute an effective approach to this fundamental problem, but individually none of them can furnish a satisfactory solution. Laud examines each answer separately, and referring to the fourth he points out that 'grace is never placed but in a reasonable creature' and while grace and faith are in a different category 'man . . . is still apt to search and seek for a reason why he will believe'.[2] Nothing can prevent him from weighing this matter 'at the balance of reason' and 'to the same weights he brings the tradition of the Church, the inward motives in Scripture itself'. He adds that 'the ancient Fathers relied upon the Scriptures' and they used arguments from natural reason to convince philosophers 'that they had sufficient warrant to rely, so much as they did, upon Scripture'. In his view faith is above reason, its 'proper place', but it does not contradict reason.[3]

Considering his active temperament and the constant demands of his position, the extent of Laud's reading is surprising, and considering the fact that he had no opportunity for systematic writing, the thought-out quality of what he produced is notable. Laud's outline is the outline of a balanced theology, a middle way, and this position he regards as being due not to a conscious effort to assess the arguments on either side, but to the undifferentiated nature of its sources in Scripture and antiquity. In view of his use of Hooker and references to him, it is not unexpected to find something of the element of liberality in his writings, and like Andrewes he wishes to keep fundamentals to the minimum and to allow liberty of opinion in secondary matters. His comment on the Articles points in the same direction when he denies that 'the book of Articles only was the continent of the Church of England's public doctrine: she is not so narrow, nor hath she purpose to exclude anything which she acknowledges hers, nor doth she wittingly permit any crossing of her public declarations; yet she

1. *Ib* p. 39.   3. *Ib.* p. 49.
2. *Ib.* p. 48.

is not such a shrew to her children, as to deny her blessing or denounce an anathema against them, if some peaceably dissent in some particulars remoter from the foundation'.[1] For Laud the appeal to antiquity was a practical matter and like Andrewes his traditionalism was a liberal conservatism.

The most sustained domestic criticism of the appeal to antiquity came from those who were associated with Lord Falkland, but in order to visualise the situation as it impinged on the development of theological method during the seventeenth century, it is necessary to note that there was no innate sense of opposition or of lines of party demarcation involved. Hammond defended the views of Falkland and Chillingworth, and Chillingworth approved Laudian practice in the preface to his book. Hales was Laud's friend and chaplain and Chillingworth was his godson. It is true that there was much of the Renaissance humanism of Erasmus in the members of the Tew group, but traces of something not altogether dissimilar are seen not only in Andrewes and Laud but also in Hammond who wrote in support of Grotius. Whether it came by way of Erasmus or Episcopius is in this connection hardly material, but what is significant is the intersection of the two groups not only in respect of association but of ideas.

Nevertheless at the time that Laud was commending the use of the criterion of antiquity, Falkland and his associates were concerned with what seemed to them to be a necessary radical simplification. In their view, not only the Counter-Reformation but the Reformation had raised superstructures on the original edifice. They had done so in pursuance of their several efforts to find an authoritative basis for what could be used as a valid doctrinal criterion. The Counter-Reformation had opted for the inerrant tradition of the present Church declaring Scripture, and the Reformation had adhered to Scripture as the self-declaring authority and criterion. The Church of England however while firmly maintaining the centrality of Scripture saw the criterion as Scripture interpreted by antiquity and refused to part with the fact of continuity and to adopt an attitude which virtually excluded historical considerations from theology. It was at this point that the members of the Tew circle diverged, for their attitude to the fundamental dilemma as to what was the authority in matters of doctrine was in effect to deny that such an authority could or

1. *Ib.* p. 32.

should be found. They held that the only necessary or possible criterion was that part of the Bible which was plain to and agreed upon by all. This had a convincing air which was by no means altogether superficial or specious, but it must be admitted that as a solution it was in practice more facile than effective. Nor was it in effect as candid as it appeared for its optimistic rationalism left some important questions unanswered and indeed unasked. On the credit side must be set their praiseworthy impatience with the unreal aspects of the seventeenth-century scene and their desire for a more practical approach. They reacted from what they regarded as the tedious tracing of ecclesiastical pedigrees and entailing of opinions, but while they gave expression to something that was genuine they greatly oversimplified the position. They held that the appeal to antiquity had not helped to provide the looked-for criterion but by reason of the complex nature of the material, had rather succeeded in adding further complications. This if it could be sustained was a serious blow to the traditional Anglican approach, and the publication of Daillé's book provided Falkland and his associates with material to support their position. As a Huguenot, Daillé had been concerned with showing by evidence from the patristic period that doctrinal corruptions had set in so early and differences of opinion among patristic writers had in the same way appeared so soon that antiquity could provide no settled criterion, and that this was provided by Scripture only. The members of the Tew group accompanied Daillé as far as this, agreeing in his estimate of antiquity, but they parted company in that for Daillé the sufficiency of Scripture as a criterion was not the same as it was for Chillingworth.

It should be added also that the difference between certain members of the Tew circle on the subject of antiquity as compared with the views of Andrewes or Laud needs qualification. Chillingworth for example does not dispense with it entirely nor is Andrewes's or Laud's use of patristic sources uncritical. Where it is used the appeal to antiquity is always to a consent of antiquity, and it is always secondary to the primary place of Scripture. It is considerations such as these which ultimately explain why the appeal to antiquity was never abandoned by Anglicans, for its function being largely confirmatory, its usefulness was less impaired at this stage by Daillé's work or later in the century by the writings of Petavius than might have been supposed.

It is in fact difficult to see how the historical criterion could be dispensed with, for some appeal to the facts of history is from time to time essential in any doctrinal assessment. When too much is built on it there results an artificial preoccupation with antiquity, as if agreement with it were in some way an end in itself. When it is undervalued there remains no objective check by which opinions or practice may be shown to be in accord with those of early times.

There is no evidence that Andrewes and Laud held any but a balanced view of the use of antiquity by which it filled such a supporting rôle. Andrewes regarded the appeal to antiquity as showing that 'there is no principal dogma in which we do not agree with the Fathers and they with us'. It was along these broad lines that the writers of the seventeenth century considered that their general position could be seen as consonant with that of the first centuries. It is also the fact that they did invest antiquity with a kind of subsidiary authority which derived from the stated view that the nearer a writer was in point of time to the period of the composition of the Scriptures, the more likely he was to interpret them correctly. It is here that the difference between this point of view and that of the members of the Tew group, as exemplified by writers like Hyde, becomes apparent. The critical attitude of the Tew circle had undoubtedly received an impetus from Daillé's book which is reflected, for example, in Chillingworth's observations concerning patristic disagreement on various points. But it is to be questioned whether the general position as to the substantial agreement between the contemporary Church and the Church of the first five centuries on what constituted fundamentals was in fact seriously impaired, for it was this and not an imagined unanimity in all matters that provided the *raison d'être* of the use of antiquity as a criterion. The real difference of viewpoint lay in the fact that the Tew circle queried the usefulness of such an appeal by maintaining that there was no inherent value in antiquity as such, and that what Andrewes referred to as nearness to or distance 'from the Apostles' time' was in fact irrelevant. Hales wrote that 'the circumstance ... of time ... is merely impertinent',[1] and this was the real point of divergence. The appeal to antiquity was regarded by its exponents as the appeal to antiquity interpreting Scripture, the nearness of the one to the

1. Quoted in B. H. G. Wormald, *Clarendon*, p. 254.

other guaranteeing the accuracy and essential congruity of the interpretation. This the writers of Tew did not accept, and they considered that Daillé's work had helped to show that differences and mistakes in interpretation appeared at an early stage. B. H. G. Wormald has pointed out that Falkland and his friends were not concerned with proving what Daillé was attempting to prove, namely, that 'the Reformers were incomparably more reliable than the Fathers' [1] In fact, they had no particular interest in any century, and their refusal of the presuppositions of the historical theology of Andrewes and Laud stemmed primarily from the fact that they were turning in the direction of a general restatement similar in some respects to that which occupied the Cambridge Platonists. Superficially there is a resemblance, but circumstances were against the Tew group, the members of which were soon claimed by war or exile, and to whom time did not give the opportunity of developing more fully what had been begun.

As far as the idea of antiquity as a standard within the history of the first five centuries is concerned, it would be fair to say that they partially removed it from the context in which its exponents used it, and they transferred it into the context of an ancients against moderns discussion. This is particularly true of Hyde, whose view it was that the only use of antiquity was to consult it in order to discover 'matter of fact'.[2] This is the purely historical use of antiquity as opposed to the historical theology of Andrewes and Laud. For them the facts so discovered had an interpretative value in direct ratio to their antiquity, whereas for Hyde they were seen simply in relation to a process of historical verification, and reference has already been made to Newton's rather similar point of view.

B. H. G. Wormald's discussion of two of Hyde's works shows the persisting influence of Tew, for they were written in 1670, the date of the essay *Of the reverence due to Antiquity*, and in 1673, when the *Animadversions* was published.[3] The related questions of a possible change in Hyde's opinions and of the degree in which he shared Falkland's views do not arise here. But what is of interest is the way in which for this circle of thinkers a distinct modification of the accepted combination of elements in

1. *Ib.* p. 253.
2. *Essays*, II, quoted in *Clarendon*, p. 274.
3. *Ib.* pp. 264–75.

theological method was coming about through their attitude in the matter of antiquity and as a result of the complex of ideas which earned for them the name of rational theologians. They were however more than this, and the ideas which Falkland shared with Erasmus whom he often quotes, and which Hales had in common with Episcopius, constitute an outlook which was compounded of humanism, the freedom of reason and a reaction from systems in the direction of simplicity combined with the conviction that only that which was so evident that all agreed upon it was of fundamental importance.

The Tew circle was not of the same calibre as the Cambridge Platonists whose work left a permanent mark on theological method and to whom circumstances were kinder, but they were moving in a somewhat similar direction. This modification which might be more accurately described as a redistribution of emphasis is noticeable in both groups in respect of the question of antiquity. The Cambridge Platonists clearly had a wide knowledge of ancient literature and history, as may be seen from the works of Cudworth and Whichcote, and Smith and More knew and used patristic writings, but they approached the past from the point of view of reason and philosophy, and not as a criterion within the history of the early centuries after the fashion of Andrewes and Laud. They were not drawn to historical theology because they were concerned with aspects of things unaffected by the particularity of history, and the content of their work did not call for such an appraisal. The members of the Tew circle, however, looked for some modification or revision by means of which the idea of antiquity would be divested of any but a merely factual significance.

It is perhaps worth noting that, with the exception of the Cambridge Platonists, no group at this stage in the seventeenth century ignores any of the three elements traditionally combined in Anglican theological method. Chillingworth, Hyde and Falkland, however they criticise the use and purpose of the appeal to antiquity retain some aspect of it or preserve it in some attenuated form. Within the broad outlines of theological method during the century, as theology comes into contact with other influences such as that of Descartes or the new philosophy or of systems such as Calvinism, various shifts of emphasis, perceptible modifications or heightened stresses occur in respect of these three different components. This movement and awareness of the implications of changing situations is seen as much in Hooker and Andrewes as it is in Chillingworth and Whichcote or in Pearson and Stillingfleet. It is however movement from stability, from a more or less common position, for there is in the writings of the seventeenth century despite varieties of situation and approach, a unity which has nothing contrived about it and which meets divergent requirements with the same method but distributing the emphasis differently. To put it another way, there is no essential difference in the views of Hooker, Taylor, Sanderson, Hammond, Wilkins, Boyle, Stillingfleet and Patrick. Each responds to his own situation by putting the main stress on the element or elements of theological method which answer to it, and this gives the work of each a distinctive colour and individuality.

Among the various groups in the seventeenth century the Latitudinarians, unexpectedly in view of developments in the following century, preserve the balance of theological method in respect of the use of antiquity as a criterion within the history of the first centuries. Joseph Glanvill regarded the position as based on 'the grounds of Scripture, right reason and the best and purest antiquity',[1] and Tenison's views on the subject and Simon Patrick's full treatment of tradition and the way in which he keeps the elements of theological method in balance have already been referred to. Mention has also been made of his *Brief Account* in which he describes the Latitudinarians as combining Scripture, 'in interpreting whereof they carefully attend to the sense of the ancient Church', with reason, and he holds that 'the same conclusions do naturally flow from all these several principles'. Stillingfleet's treatment of the subject of antiquity will be examined later, and a case can be made for regarding the Latitudinarians as one of the stabilising influences in preserving proportion between the different elements of theological method during the seventeenth century. In the following century, however, Middleton, Hoadly and Watson refused, as Sykes points out, to grant the confirming and supporting function of antiquity, although he instances two books by Waterland in which it is maintained that 'Scripture and antiquity (under the conduct of right reason) are what we ought to abide by' as eighteenth-century examples of the accepted method.[2] Waterland's *Review of the Doctrine of the Eucharist* might also be listed, in the introduction of which he

1. N. Sykes, *From Sheldon to Secker*, p. 149.   2. *Ib.* p. 167.

indicates that the same method is followed and that 'great regard
. . . ought to be paid to the known sense and judgment of the
apostolical Fathers'. But in spite of this the signs of change are
there and there is an increasing tendency from the middle of the
eighteenth century for theological method to lose perspective once
the inner relationship of check and stimulus between its components was disturbed. An illustration of this can be seen in the
extracts given by Sykes[1] from the writings of Middleton, Hoadly
and Watson, where the denying of any vitality to the concept of
referring to the opinions of the patristic period or of councils not
only leaves an unexplained gap, but results in an aggressively one-
sided approach.

Reference has been made to B. H. G. Wormald's discussion of
Hyde's views and it is evident that the readjustments common to
the members of the Tew circle stem from the fact that their whole
approach differed from that of the majority of their contemporaries. Their distinctive outlook arose from the impact of what
Wormald calls their critical humanism on the disturbed and
controversial situation of the time: 'it was a view which was not
only critical in regard to the consequences of controversy, but
deeply sceptical in regard to the factors which produced it'.[2] It
was a liberality of outlook tolerant of differences and sensitive to
the claims of reason, having at its centre the opinion that the only
effective criterion was that part of Scripture upon which all were
agreed. Chillingworth writes that as to 'plain places, and in such
all things necessary are contained, we are sufficiently certain of
the meaning of them, neither need they any interpreter. If of
obscure and difficult places, we confess we are uncertain of the
sense of many of them. But then we say there is no necessity we
should be certain'.[3]

Wormald has pointed out the influence of Chillingworth on
Hyde's views that 'essential principles' in Scripture are clear and
written 'with that plainness in what is necessary, that there
remains no difficulty',[4] and that 'reason shall contribute more'
in the matter of obedience to authority than does 'resignation
to . . . authority'.[5] It is basically this line of thought which results

1. *Ib.* pp. 168–9.
2. *Ib.* p. 247.
3. Chillingworth, *The Religion of Protestants* (4th ed. 1674), p. 64.

4. *Animadversions*, pp. 148–9, quoted
in *Clarendon*, p. 266.
5. *Animadversions*, p. 205.

in the attitude of the Tew circle to antiquity, for while Hyde
maintains the respect of the Church of England for tradition, it is
'where the tradition is as universal or as manifest as it is in that
of the Scripture'.[1] He adds that it is impossible to 'concur in all
that the Fathers have taught, who were never all of one mind, and
therefore may very lawfully have their reasons examined by the
reasons of other men'.[2] Indicating the similarities between the
Animadversions and two of the *Essays*, Wormald shows how in the
first essay the idea expressed was the characteristic one that the
real cause of controversy was failure to distinguish essentials.[3]
In the second essay, on the subject *Of the reverence due to Antiquity*,
he remarks on Hyde's reiteration of the view of Scripture that
'whatsoever is too hard for us there to understand, is in no degree
necessary for us to know'.[4] Hyde held that in view of this many
subjects under dispute could not be decided from Scripture, and
the fact that there had been such disputes from the beginning
raised the question of the value of the appeal to antiquity. 'The
concurrent testimony and consent of those times'[5] was hard to
ascertain, and the antiquity of an opinion was not, as events
showed a necessary guarantee in that it could be mistaken or
defective. An indication of this was the disagreement of the
Fathers on different matters, although where there was agreement
it should be accepted. Hyde distinguishes between what he regards
as resignation to antiquity and reverence for the past, but he was
aware that his position was different from those who endeavoured
to find a doctrinal support in it. This is clear from his method of
approach to history as a whole in which he attempts to show the
superiority of later learning, and in which he suggests that the
past should be looked at critically and to discover 'matter of
fact'.[6] In practice, as Wormald notes, 'Hyde's contention was
that the appeal to antiquity should be discontinued',[7] and it
seems as if the reason for this was not only the background of
critical humanism but also the notion of an irreducible minimum
basis which was unaffected by the criterion of the first five
centuries.

1. *Ib.* p. 174.
2. *Ib.* p. 189.
3. *Clarendon*, p. 269. *Against the multi-
plying controversies by insisting upon
particulars that are not necessary to
the point in debate.*
4. *Ib.* p. 270.
5. *Ib.* p. 271.
6. *Ib.* p. 274.
7. *Ib.* p. 271.

The same position is found in Falkland's *Discourse* in which it is maintained that those who follow reason 'in the interpretation of the Scriptures, and search for tradition' will be helped to find the solution or forgiven 'if they miss it'.[1] Falkland writes that he doubts 'whether Councils be fit deciders of questions; for such they cannot be, if they beget more, and men have cause to be in greater doubts afterwards (none of the former being diminished) than they were at first'.[2] Accepting the conclusions of Daillé, he finds a similar inconclusiveness in the use of the Fathers, 'that nothing is wholly proveable by sufficient testimonies of the first ages, to have had primary and general tradition'[3] except the books of Scripture and what is so plainly derived from them as not to be subject of debate. Whether there is at bottom such a great difference between this and the position of Andrewes is open to question, but it can hardly be questioned that Falkland's general attitude to the patristic period is different from the positive approach of Andrewes and Laud. He writes of the Fathers that 'many are lost, many not lost not to be gotten, many uncertain whether Fathers or no Fathers, and these, which we have, and know, being too many for almost any industry to read over'. For Falkland the writings of the patristic period are a source of references rather than a standard of reference, and he holds that their extent and diversity make any other use of them impracticable. His approach to the question may be gathered from the comment that it is not possible to 'know what they thought at all times, from what they were moved to say at some one time by some collateral consideration'.[4] To what extent this was the point at issue, and how far this and the general position of Tew affected the presuppositions of the accepted appeal to the criterion of antiquity which was largely confirmatory in form, is another question.

Here a point of some difficulty arises in connection with an accurate assessment of the views of the Tew group. They are usually regarded as opposing the appeal to antiquity, and this is clearly correct as far as it goes, but it may be asked whether in fact they themselves really understood what a subordinate rôle it occupied for its exponents. It is difficult to avoid the impression

1. Falkland's *Discourse of Infallibility* and *Reply*, included in Vol. II of Hammond's *Works* (2nd ed. 1684), *Discourse*, Sect. xi. p. 562.

2. *Ib.* sect. 17.
3. *Reply*, p. 684.
4. *Discourse*, p. 564.

that the members of the Tew circle put up a man of straw in that
they are constantly emphasising the impossibility of obtaining
anything like unanimity from the writings of the first five
centuries. It is possible in this connection that being impressed
by the work of Daillé, to whom Falkland refers with approval,[1]
and seeing in it a confirmation of their approach by way of reason
and an agreed basis to end controversy, their application of its
findings to the appeal to antiquity was partly beside the point.
Daillé had furnished evidence of the early appearance of divergences and disagreements in the patristic period and this seemed
to the Tew writers to indicate that antiquity could not provide
such a unanimity as would put points under debate beyond
controversy. The application of this to the appeal to antiquity
however is not as telling as might appear, for in its accepted form
this was not to the supposed unanimity of antiquity, but to
antiquity as confirmatory of Scripture and as showing that the
general consent of antiquity on fundamentals was dependent on
and conditioned by the centrality of Scripture. There is a suggestion of being at cross-purposes here in that the writings of
Hyde and Falkland seem to indicate that their reaction against
antiquity was not occasioned by refusal of considerations such as
these. The chief reason would appear to be a consequence of
their general position to which freedom of reason and the superiority of modern learning were integral, and with neither of which
resignation to antiquity was consistent. Similar misunderstandings
as to the use of the criterion of antiquity in the middle of the
eighteenth century are to be seen in Middleton and Watson,
arising out of the fact that they evidently did not understand that
its function was supplementary. If however they missed something of the point, the work of the Tew group contributed to the
emergence of some kind of historical criticism of the past which
served as a check to prevent, in Hyde's words, respect for antiquity
becoming resignation to antiquity.

The views of Hales have been dealt with in some detail, and it is
enough to add that although he often quotes from patristic
writings his whole approach to antiquity as providing a criterion
is similar to that of the other members of the circle. He considers
that it is not 'knowledge of antiquity . . . nor authority of councils'
that resolves questions but 'the plain uncontroversable' part of

1. *Reply*, p. 684.

Scripture, and he regards many of the discussions of other matters as unnecessary.[1]

Reference has also been made to Chillingworth, and in this connection he draws attention to the early appearance of differences, concluding that antiquity cannot therefore provide a definite criterion 'unless it be absolute and primitive'.[2] By conformity with antiquity he means conformity with 'the primitive and apostolic'.[3] This is the same as Hyde's view when he wrote that tradition was acceptable 'where the tradition is as universal or as manifest as it is in that of Scripture'. Commenting on the influence of Chillingworth on Hyde, Wormald remarks that Hyde 'is saying that Scripture, its existence and its authority, is precisely the only certain part of tradition'.[4] Hyde referred to the difficulty of uncertainty, and for Chillingworth also this was the consideration which required a modification of the accepted form of the appeal to antiquity. He wrote that there are 'councils against councils, some Fathers against others, the same Fathers against themselves, a consent of Fathers of one age against a consent of Fathers of another age, ... in a word, there is no sufficient certainty but of Scripture only'.[5] This emphasis is central for Chillingworth and constitutes the nub of the question of antiquity. It is not so much a matter of the value of the patristic writings or even of a qualified use of them as it is a question of the difficulties attendant on using them as a certain standard of reference. In regard to this it might be maintained that Chillingworth expects more from the appeal to antiquity than do those who advocate it. This seems to be borne out by his explicit agreement that Anglican teaching and practice can be shown to be consonant with antiquity,[6] and Andrewes and Laud said no more than this. In fact he appears to make more use of patristic sources than do others associated with Falkland's circle, and he states that while everything from St Augustine's writings is not authoritative, he agrees that 'considering the nearness of his time to the apostles

---

1. *Golden Remains of the Ever-memorable Mr John Hales* (1688), p. 31. He shared Hyde's views of the advantages of modern learning as compared with that of antiquity, instancing 'the skill in the original languages' of modern commentators, adding that this was not 'to discountenance antiquity' but to give all 'their due'. *Ib.* p. 27.

2. *Religion of Protestants*, p. 225.

3. *Ib.* p. 73.

4. *Clarendon*, p. 265.

5. Loc. cit. p. 290.

6. *Ib.* pp. 224-5.

I think it a good probable way, and therefore am apt enough to follow it, when I see no reason to the contrary'.[1] This, although he qualifies it, is one of the accepted supports of the appeal to antiquity.

A further instance of his moderate treatment of the subject is seen in the assessment of the historical situation in the first five centuries and its consequences for theology. Some held, he maintains, that signs of change and disagreement were evident in the period after the apostolic times, and therefore they aimed at restoring 'an exact conformity with the apostolic times', and took their standard of reference 'only from Scripture'. Others regarding the Church of the early centuries as having maintained unchanged what it had received, wished to 'reduce the Church to the condition of the fourth and fifth ages' using as a criterion 'the writings of Fathers, and the decrees of councils of the first five ages'. But in his view 'they did best that followed Scripture interpreted by Catholic written tradition'.[2]

This extract would lead to the supposition that what was under criticism here was not so much the accepted form of the appeal to antiquity, as antiquity considered in relation to something different, for the members of the Tew circle were looking at the matter from the point of view of their own attitude to the problem of authority. Andrewes and Laud approached it from the point of view of continuity and agreement on fundamentals between the Church of the first five centuries and the contemporary Church. They attached greater importance to the interpretative aspect of patristic writings and to what Hales called 'the circumstance of time' than did Falkland and his associates. In one sense, particularly in the case of Chillingworth, the difference between the two groups was less in practice than is usually supposed. But considered in terms of general outlook, the difference is there, for they were looking for different things with a different end in view.

What has taken place in the outlook of the Tew circle is a readjustment between the component elements of the traditional theological method. The use of antiquity continues in an attenuated form but emptied of the idea of a standard of reference by

1. *Ib.* p. 116.
2. *Ib.* p. 221. He also wrote that he agreed that 'the judgment of a Council, though not infallible, is yet so far directive, and obliging, that without apparent reason to the contrary' it ought not be refused. *Ib.* loc. cit. p. 154.

means of a new kind of historical criticism being brought to bear on historical theology. Scripture retains its centrality for the Tew writers, but here too there is a different emphasis in consequence of their general position. This position, to which critical humanism had made a marked contribution, produced a reaction against dogmatism and systems which was notable in Hales but characteristic of them all. In its effect on their idea of reason it placed their work within a wider movement the affiliations of which ran in different directions, to the Arminians, to Episcopius and to the Cambridge Platonists.

CHAPTER X

THE APPEAL TO ANTIQUITY (*continued*)

THE connections between various groups and individuals in the seventeenth century have been noted as a factor making for the interchange of ideas. A further result of these contacts was to emphasise an existing measure of agreement which cut across differences of outlook, and this has been seen to be the case with regard to the members of the Tew group and the Laudians, for 'the circles of Laud and Falkland intersected'.[1] Hyde, Hales, Chillingworth and Sheldon were friends both of Laud and Falkland, Chillingworth being Laud's godson and Hales his chaplain. The latter had discussed one of his publications with Laud, and Chillingworth's book, in the preface of which Laud's policy was defended, had appeared with Laud's approval. Gilbert Sheldon, later to be Archbiship of Canterbury, became with Hammond a leader of the Laudian party, and Hammond in his writings supported Chillingworth and Falkland. The biographer of Hales was the Laudian Pearson, and Jeremy Taylor who had been associated with the Laudians had been acquainted with Chillingworth and More, and there are affinities with the outlook of both groups in his work. This interlocking of groups and individuals is worth re-emphasising, for there does not seem to be any feeling of a divided mind or of a sense of strain such as would arise from a self-conscious effort at reconciling opposite or divergent trends of opinion. The explanation lies in the fact that in the seventeenth century there was general agreement on the basis, and a more or less common attitude. The variety of approach resulting from different outlook and temperament and from the needs of different

1. G. Every, *The High Church Party 1688–1718*, p. 2. For the sake of reference, the Tew circle composed of Falkland, Hyde, Francis Wenman, Sidney Godolphin, Edmund Waller, Gilbert Sheldon, George Morley, John Earle, John Hales, William Chillingworth (*Clarendon*, p. 244). Among the Laudians Bosher lists, John Bramhall, Brian Walton, Herbert Thorndike, Henry Hammond, John Pearson, Jeremy Taylor, Peter Heylyn, Thomas Pierce, Henry Ferne, Richard Sterne, John Fell, John Dolben, William Sancroft, Peter Gunning, Bruno Ryves, Humphrey Henchman, Anthony Sparrow, George Wilde, Richard Allestree, John Barwick (*The Making of the Restoration Settlement*, pp. 29–30).

situations was allowed for by the use of a theological method which was firmly centred but adaptable. Within its components there existed the possibility of contact with a variety of subjects and situations, and also a capacity for readjusting emphasis in order to cope with new ideas. This more than anything else is the basis of that general agreement subsisting between individuals and groups which a later age with some justification would assign to different and more or less opposing schools. It is in this general agreement that Hooker and Andrewes, Taylor and Chillingworth, Hammond and Sheldon, are at one. It might be described as the spirit of Anglicanism, including as it does the centrality of Scripture and the visibility and continuity of the Church, both confirmed by antiquity, and illuminated by the freedom of reason and liberality of view-point. It constitutes the shared attitude of the seventeenth century, and although one group may lay the main emphasis on one aspect and another may criticise it, the awareness of a common ground of agreement was a fact until the appearance of parties as a result of events in the closing years of the century. From the point of view of emphasis on certain doctrinal aspects, however, the beginnings of this lay further back in the years of the Commonwealth. While it was their policy which gave the cohesion of a party to the Laudians, circumstances during this period were combining to give a specific orientation to the labours and writings of men like Hammond at home and Bramhall in exile. Increasing stringency on the part of the authorities in applying the laws against the Church of England brought home the need for showing, as Hammond wrote, that 'the Church of England is not invisible; it is still preserved in bishops and presbyters rightly ordained, and multitudes rightly baptised'.[1] The situation required the stressing of the visibility and continuity of the Church, and the Laudians under the leadership of Hammond set themselves to show this in a large number of works on various subjects. One of the results was a considerable growth of emphasis on the appeal to antiquity in relation to the form of Church-government. While Hammond and others preserved the traditional balance of theological method, the beginnings of a distinctive approach can be seen, which, carried a stage further by Bull, Pearson, Dodwell and Beveridge, combined with the events of the Revolution of 1689 to produce an alignment so that High

1. Henry Hammond, *Works* (1774), Vol. I, p. 369, *Of Schism*, Chap. XI.

Church and Latitudinarian became descriptions of parties in a way that would have had little or no meaning earlier.

Hammond's part during this period has already been referred to, and for a time his position was so unfavourable that a reward was offered for him.[1] Yet in his unwavering attitude he was no aggressive propagandist, and the 'sweetness of carriage' which, according to Fell, was remembered by his contemporaries from his schooldays, made the same impression on Baxter. Although the latter regarded 'Dr Hammond's new way'[2] as the original source of the Laudian party's uncompromising position, he looked on Hammond's death as 'a very great loss', holding that if he had lived, 'much of the violence which after followed' might have been avoided.[3]

Hammond was born in 1605, the son of a physician, and at school he showed an aptitude for classical studies. He went to Magdalen College, Oxford, becoming a Fellow, and his work at the University was marked by an application which not even the events of the Civil War or the uncertainties of his situation curtailed. For more than ten years before his death in 1660 he lived privately at Westwood, Worcestershire, and during that period published a large number of works. Fell recounts that after obtaining his degree he 'bought a system of divinity' intending to begin its study but instead he returned to classical studies for a while. It is significant for the form which his work was to take that 'when he resumed his purpose for theology, he took a quite different course of reading from the other too much usual, beginning that science at the upper end, as conceiving it most reasonable to search for primitive truth in the primitive writers'.[4] Hammond became rector of Penshurst in Kent in 1633, and ten years later was obliged to leave because of his political sympathies. He twice attended the King during his imprisonment and was himself under restraint for a while. After leaving Penshurst he spent some time at Oxford before going to Worcestershire, and while at Oxford he published the *Practical Catechism*. Fell writes of his 'industry and diligence'[5] in continuing his writing in unfavourable circumstances, and refers to his practical charitableness, his daily services and catechising when he was at

1. *Life*, John Fell, *Works*, Vol. I, p. 9. 3. *Ib.* p. 29.
2. R. S. Bosher, *The Making of the* 4. *Works*, Vol. I, p. 4.
   Restoration Settlement, p. 16. 5. *Ib.* p. 25.

Penshurst.[1] He describes him as interested in music[2] and with a wide knowledge of classical and modern writings, as well as being 'learned in School-divinity, and a master in Church-antiquity, perfect and ready in the sense of the Fathers, Councils, ecclesiastical historians and liturgies'.[3] Hammond never married and died in the year of the Restoration, and there can be no doubt that the work he accomplished in the preceding years was important in itself and in its results.

Hammond differs from the Tew writers and resembles Andrewes in his general approach, and, like Andrewes, he is interested in antiquity, history, Biblical versions and translations, and liturgical matters. Referring to the *Paraphrase and Annotations*, R. L. Colie writes, 'Henry Hammond, whose annotations upon the Bible were to stand for his church in the place of the Genevan annotations, still influential in England, was strongly Arminian'.[4] Certainly, the same strain which caused Andrewes to be regarded as Arminian by some of his contemporaries was present also in Hammond's work and was recognised in his own time. Le Clerc, who had left the Calvinist camp for that of the Remonstrants, translated Hammond's annotations.[5] Le Clerc's position may be gauged from the fact that he had an interest in natural studies and corresponded with the Latitudinarians and had contact with Bentley. As he also produced an edition of one of Grotius's works, it may be presumed that he saw a congenial quality in Hammond's writings. In fact, Hammond himself defended Grotius from the imputation that he favoured Socinianism, and he refers to Grotius's opinion of the Church of England that 'of all Churches in the world, it was the most careful observer, and transcriber of primitive antiquity'.[6] In Hammond's *Pacific Discourse*, in what Fell called the rational quality of his discourses, there can be seen the complex of ideas which includes the autonomy of reason, a reaction from systems and a differentiation between what is fundamental and what is speculative or secondary. It was not so much Arminianism proper as that liberality of outlook of which Arminianism was a particular manifestation. There is a

1. *Ib.* p. 5.
2. *Ib.* p. 22.
3. *Ib.* p. 24.
4. R. L. Colie, *Light and Enlightenment: A Study of the Cambridge Platonists and the Dutch Arminians*, p. 21.
5. *Ib.* p. 34.
6. *Works*, Vol. II, p. 93, *A Continuation of the Defence of Hugo Grotius* (1656).

basic kinship with a whole section of thought from Hooker to the Latitudinarians in Hammond's view that while right reason and the law of nature need to be supplemented, what has been in this respect 'super-added to the law of nature, right reason will of its own accord commend as best'.[1]

Hammond has been regarded so much as a Laudian *pur sang* that in the interest of emphasising the underlying agreement of the period attention should be drawn to the apparently unnoticed and curious similarity in his writings with certain points of view usually looked on as being distinctively Latitudinarian. The title *Of the Reasonableness of Christian Religion* seems to foreshadow Tillotson, but even more striking is the resemblance in the treatment of the subject which differs very little from that of Wilkins. The method of the book is to show first the validity of the testimony or affirmation on which the Christian religion is based, and then to show its advantages. Hammond writes that 'the first will render the belief rational . . . the second will render the belief gainful',[2] and this is the same as the Latitudinarian approach. As to the first point, the affirmation rests on the authority of the records of the Old and New Testaments, and, like Stillingfleet, he refers to miracles and to 'the success which attended it'.[3] Apart from the records of witnesses 'there is no rational evidence imaginable for those that lived not in that age', nor can there be any more authentic proof 'of matter of fact'.[4] Having discussed the question of historical evidence in relation to the New Testament and its content and some points raised against it, he concludes that because of the nature of the testimony on which it is based, and the means by which it is conveyed, it may 'be concluded a rational ground of belief'.[5] While he points out in considerable detail how reason is limited by the authority of this testimony, there is a suggestion of the later attitude which is heightened when he writes 'that which is really the most advantageous is always most rational, most prudent for man to choose'.[6] This sounds the true note of Latitudinarianism, and he goes on to develop this in precisely the same way as did Wilkins, dividing the advantages into outward and inward. Among the

1. *Works*, Vol. I, p. 192, *Of the Reasona bleness of Christian Religion*.
2. *Works*, Vol. I, p. 182. *Of the Reasonableness of Christian Religion* (1650).
3. *Ib.* p. 189.
4. *Ib.* p. 187.
5. *Ib.* p. 191.
6. *Ib.* p. 195.

former are peace and plenty which are public advantages arising from 'industry and diligence', and 'comfortableness and cheerfulness' which are individual outward advantages. Inward advantages are such pleasures as friendship, 'relieving those in want', obedience and contentment, and behind them are the advantages of grace, faith and hope. He regards present and future advantages as 'evidence of the rationalness of religion'.[1] Like Wilkins he includes health and other outward benefits among external advantages, and like Wilkins he looks at the matter in the context of practical divinity.

This is one of these agreements which are unexpected only if the fact of basic and underlying agreement in the seventeenth century is ignored. Whether the work had any direct influence on Stillingfleet or on Wilkins is not known, although the date of its publication makes this a possibility, but in itself it is an indication of the way in which this line of thought was not confined to any group but was making itself generally felt in the middle of the century.

Hammond's interest in practical divinity, another common factor, is seen in the *Practical Catechism* and other writings in which the variety of subjects included shows the importance he attached to it.[2] The *Paraphrase and Annotations* has been referred to, and Hammond stresses 'the use of ordinary means' in the study and interpretation of Scripture: 'the use of learning, study, meditation, rational inference, collation of places, consulting of the original languages, and ancient copies, and expositions of the Fathers of the Church'.[3] He regards subjective individualism in this connection as leading to the superseding of the 'written . . . Canon',[4] and his own method is to concentrate on the text and translation, and in the paraphrase and annotations to avoid 'doctrinal conclusions and deductions' and analogies and to make use only of the 'literal sense of each place'.[5] In the Commonwealth

1. *Ib.* pp. 197–200.
2. Among these publications are, *Of Conscience* (1644), *Of Sins of Weakness and Wilfulness* (1645), and *Of a Late or Death-bed Repentance* (1645).
3. *Works*, Vol. IV, *A Paraphrase and Annotations upon all the books of the New Testament*, Postscript to preface.
4. *Ib.*
5. *Ib.* Preface. With regard to 'the original text', Hammond notes that 'many learned men' have worked on this and their findings are available, and he himself adds some readings from three manuscripts. As to the translation, he prepared 'a new one' and used it marginally where it might seem to help in some point.

period there appeared in many quarters a tendency,[1] the beginnings of which Hooker had noted earlier, in which an introspective illuminism took precedence of the literal meaning. Writers such as Hammond saw that to make the individualism of inward enlightenment the criterion undermined not only the basis of historicity and reason, but also, by its implications the visible Church. The book was not only an instance of Hammond's thoroughness and ability but was a typical and useful product of the position which was his by temperament as well as by circumstances.[2]

His interest in liturgical matters, noted by Fell, was not simply a by-product of his acquaintance with the writings of the patristic period, but had a practical significance in that it was part of the general statement of the Anglican position at a time when the 'abolition of the liturgy'[3] appeared to mark a final stage in a process of systematic obliteration. Hammond saw the theological function of liturgy: 'this indeed is a prerogative of the liturgy which hath always been used as an hedge to keep out errors' and cannot belong to any form 'which hath neither creed nor catechism.'[4] He maintains that there were early signs of the appearance of a liturgy, and he refers to the liturgies of St James, St Basil and St Chrysostom, to 'the compiler of the Apostles' Constitutions' and to 'the liturgic writers',[5] to show the continuance in the Prayer Book liturgy of various elements contained in them. Quoting other patristic sources as evidence of similarity between primitive and present practice, he notes that the comparison shows the same 'general form exactly continued'.[6] The removal of later features from the liturgy 'argues our compliance with the ancient Church', and he observes that it was 'the care of antiquity'[7] which was the grounds of Casaubon's approval of the Church of England. Hammond's interest was more than a general one, and

1. The views of James Nayler are a case in point; he refers to those 'who trade in the letter, and are ignorant of the mystery' as being unable to 'understand the Scriptures', *James Nayler, The Rebel Saint*, Emilia Fogelklou, p. 111.
2. Hammond's writings were extensive and Fell refers to the amount of his correspondence, commenting that he was to some degree facilitated by ease in composition and creative capacity.
3. *A View of the Directory* (1645), preface, *Works*, Vol. I.
4. *Ib.* Vol. I, p. 178, and cp. Laud, *Conference*, preface.
5. *A Copy of Some Papers, Works*, Vol. I, pp. 213, 221.
6. *Ib.* Vol. I, p. 261, and cp. *A View of the Directory, Works*, Vol. I, pp. 141, 158.
7. *Ib.* Vol. I, p. 169.

his understanding of the subject may be seen in comments such as that 'for the order of the offertory, it must first be observed, that in the Primitive Apostolic Church, the offertory was a considerable part of the action'.[1]

For Hammond, antiquity as a criterion in history is part of the wider dependence on 'antiquity, or Scripture, or rational deductions from either'[2] which constitutes the whole Anglican theological approach. Behind it or involved with it are two related factors, the elements of liberality or humanism, and the matter of fundamentals. It is impossible to separate completely these strands in his work, for they are the constituent parts of his outlook, distinguishable certainly but so inter-related as to form a whole. The way in which these elements combine in Hammond's thought can be seen in *Of Fundamentals*, the conclusions of which agree with Laud and Chillingworth that the foundation is contained in Scripture or in 'the creeds or confessions of the universal Church'.[3] He quotes from the Fathers to show that, in Theophylact's words 'the faith is . . . the foundation', adding from St Augustine 'this is the faith which being comprised in few words is in the creed delivered'.[4] The New Testament indicates that 'there was in the apostles' times such a foundation laid' which was variously referred to as 'the foundation', 'the deposit', 'the faith once for all delivered', or 'the form of sound words'.[5] That this was passed on to their successors is agreed by the patristic writers, and Hammond, quoting St Paul that 'other foundation can no man lay than that is laid, which is Jesus Christ', points out at length that the foundation was in effect the content of the credal summary.[6] His conclusion therefore which he considers to be supported by the writings of antiquity is 'that creed which is delivered down to us by the ancient Churches (I mean those of the first three hundred years) and by them entitled to the name "the Apostles", and expounded in the homilies of the Fathers . . . is in all reason to be deemed the sum of that foundation'.[7] Laud had made the same point about fundamentals and the fact that the patristic writers 'make the creed the rule of faith',[8] and Chillingworth also stressed that 'the creed contains all necessary

1. *Ib*. Vol. I, p. 153.
2. *Of Fundamentals* (1654), *Works*, Vol. I, p. 300.
3. *Ib*. Vol. I, p. 280.
4. *Ib*. Vol. I, p. 277.
5. *Ib*. Vol. I, p. 278.
6. *Ib*. Vol. I, p. 280.
7. *Ib*. Vol. p. 287.
8. *Conference*, p. 28.

points of belief', noting that it was so regarded 'upon the authority of the ancient Church, and written tradition, which . . . gave
this constant testimony unto it'.[1] It is this basic agreement which
is behind similarity of approach and coincidence of ideas in
questions nearer the surface, and it is an agreement formed by
the free interplay and action upon each other of the elements of
a shared method. This method is in turn the outcome and active
expression of a deep-seated conviction as to what constitutes
fundamentals.

On the foundation is based what Hammond pictures as the
superstructure of obedience which may be regarded as a new
'edition of the old codex', a general law for the explanation and
improvement of laws but which does not invalidate any substantial precept of natural law or of the old dispensation.[2] In fact, its
purpose is not conceived in terms of a digest of law but of 'the
production of an entire new creature'. Since it deals with rational
and voluntary agents, this is 'by way of persuasion' for liberty
is something real and not illusory.[3] Hammond, like all other
Anglican writers of the time, is acutely aware of the fact that the
point of separation for theology in the contemporary situation is
the point at which the reality of freedom and rationality makes its
impact on dogmatic formulations. If in addition such formulations
are not of the foundation but essentially speculative there is no
question as to which must go. This stubborn realism is deeply
embedded in seventeenth-century Anglican writing and it is the
rock upon which the impressive imported system, its valuable
emphasis on transcendence impaired by an increasing preoccupation with the speculative, ultimately foundered. Whether this is
described as rationalism or humanism is immaterial for this is
simply to view the matter from the standpoint of language. If it
is pragmatism to decline the imposition of theory on the observed
nature of personality and the facts of experience, then for Anglicans
the period shows a marked quality of pragmatism. But at the root
of this attitude lies the Anglican assertion that only the foundation
is authoritative. This is brought out in connection with
Hammond's view that solifidian and fiduciary ideas hinder[4] the
implementation of the design of the superstructure, when he

1. *Religion of Protestants* (1674 ed.),   3. *Ib.*
    Chap. IV, p. 152.   4. *Ib.* p. 300.
2. Loc. cit. p. 296.

observes that the Articles purposely avoid 'the mention of any decree of reprobation'. He draws a contrast between this and those 'that enter into farther speculations herein'.[1] As in the case of Heylyn and others, his contention is that absolute predestination evacuates (to use his own term) the force of fundamentals and removes the motive for energy and effort. He makes it clear however that what is in question is not the preordering of 'all things that come to pass', the decreeing that things will be disposed and ordered in a particular way. What he is referring to is the predetermining of the means as well as the ends—the 'influence or causality in the production of them'.[2] In other words, it is the predetermination of the acts of men's wills which is involved.[3] The essence of an action is its voluntary nature and if the expression of this is predetermined, the 'honour and dignity' of human nature is no longer there and men become 'necessary not rational agents'. Hammond writes that this is 'destructive to all that is established among men, to all that is most precious to human nature', for it eliminates any real function of will or understanding and these are the faculties which are characteristic of man and which essentially denominate him as human.[4] Here, as from Hooker onwards, it is the admixture of that understanding of human acts in their voluntariness and rationality which is integral to practical divinity, that acts as an anchor to theological method and checks any tendency to swing into the current of speculation which had been running so strongly a generation before.

Hammond describes as the necessary means for the building up of the superstructure of obedience, the sacraments, catechising, confirmation, the use of liturgy and preaching, which have been 'the universal practice of the Church'.[5]

In his *Paraenesis* Hammond turns to the way in which the foundation is transmitted, namely, by means of 'apostolical traditions . . . as well as by apostolical writings'.[6] This brings him to the practical application of the appeal to antiquity in respect of establishing what is authentic tradition and always recognised as such: 'so the way of trial of any tradition, pretended to be

1. *Ib.* p. 307.
2. *Ib.* p. 309.
3. *Ib.* p. 310: 'I say not the doctrine of God's predetermining his own will, but his predetermining the acts of our will.'
4. *Ib.* p. 312.
5. *Ib.* p. 322.
6. *A Paraenesis: or Seasonable Exhortatory, Works*, Vol. I, p. 387.

apostolical, whether it be such or no, is by devolving it to those same, or the like Fathers, and Councils.' As to the qualifications of such testimonies, 'the resolution will be unquestionable', if it be confined to the terms, universality, antiquity and consent, as laid down by Vincent of Lérins. With regard to universality of time, Hammond considers that it must be 'cautiously understood' bearing in mind that the application is chiefly to the 'first and purest ages'.[1] In his summary of the position it is noticeable that the ultimate authenticating factor is the consonance of the testimony of antiquity with the evidence of Scripture: 'the universal consent of the doctors of the first ages, bearing testimony that such a doctrine was from the apostles' preachings delivered to all churches by them planted, or their general conform testimony herein, without any considerable dissenters producible, is, I acknowledge . . . authentic or worthy of belief, and so hath been made use of by the orthodox of all times as sufficient for the rejecting of any new doctrine'.[2] This is basically the position of Andrewes and Laud, and Hammond goes on to indicate that general councils also provide, through their conclusions, a further means of establishing such qualifications.[3] As to the proposition that a general council cannot or shall not err, his view is not so very different from Falkland's opinion that there is 'no better expounder to follow them than reason'.[4] Hammond distinguishes 'between theological verity and Catholic faith', the former including things which are believed to be true but are not a necessary part of fundamentals and which 'are offered to belief upon grounds of reason'. It is to this class of things 'which . . . carry great weight of probability with them' that he refers the question.[5] Nevertheless, in Hammond's writings as compared with Falkland's, the emphasis favours the appeal to antiquity, and the latter could not maintain that 'the sure way of judging aright in any particular debate, must be by appealing to the fountains, apostolical, original doctrine, and tradition, and for that, to those that are competent testifiers in the matter, to councils universally received, or to such other testimony as is truly universal'.[6]

Hammond's very wide acquaintance with patristic studies, which in fact lie behind most of his work, appears not only in the use made

1. *Ib.* p. 388.
2. *Ib.* p. 390.
3. *Ib.* p. 390.
4. *Discourse.*
5. Hammond, *Works*, Vol. I, p. 403.
6. *Ib.* p. 406.

of such sources but in the form of his treatment of them, for there is in his approach to the subject a close connection between the appeal to antiquity and the fact of the visibility of the Church. As he wrote of a saying of Ignatius concerning episcopacy, 'whatsoever is thought of it, it is the voice of the first antiquity'.[1] The concern to show in his writings the agreement on matters of teaching and church-government as between the Anglican Church (his own term)[2] and the Church of the first centuries, was matched by his practical concern for 'the securing a succession to the Church, thereby to preserve its future being'.[3] This was the practical expression of the connection which he saw between the appeal to antiquity as a historical method in theology and the fact of the historical continuity of the Church. This found a fuller statement in the four *Dissertations*,[4] the substance of which is to show that the traditional form of church-government is supported by Scripture and antiquity.

Hammond's work reveals a balanced theological method by which, building on a clear-cut understanding as to what may legitimately be regarded as constituting fundamentals, Scripture and antiquity are held in such a relationship with reason that the claims of authority and freedom hardly trench upon each other. Such a relationship was more viable during most of the seventeenth century than at a later date since it had behind it the backing of an almost universally agreed attitude to Scripture which was felt to have an air of separateness which carried with it its own authority. Furthermore, the period was capable of exercising freedom in one sphere and of accepting authority in another with a lack of concern which was quite unconscious and which a later age would be unlikely to find congenial, much less possible. But essentially this relationship was not the product of a momentary situation, although it was in some degree aided by the conditions of the time, for it went deeper and the nature of its contribution to theological method can hardly be in doubt.

Hammond is in the tradition of Hooker as well as of Andrewes. Not only do his works proclaim the kinship, for it might have been Hooker who wrote 'as the affirmation is, such is the belief',[5] but

1. *Ib.* p. 215.
2. *Ib.* p. 230.
3. Fell's *Life, ib.* p. 19.
4. *Dissertationes Quatuor, quibus episcopatus jura ex S. Scripturis et*

primaeva antiquitate adstruuntur (1638). *Works*, Vol. I, cp. p. 742.
5. *Ib.* p. 182 (*Of the Reasonableness of Christian Religion*, Chap. I).

he expresses himself in the same kind of terms to which Hooker had introduced so many. Instances of the immediate influence of Hooker on various seventeenth-century writers are of course numerous, but the diffused influence is greater, for the work of Hooker cast the mould in which the shape of theological method was formed. Hammond refers on more than one occasion to it,[1] but his own writings without losing individuality or discounting the effect of changed circumstances are illustrative of the extent to which the *Ecclesiastical Polity* made itself felt in the thinking of a century.

He had passed through the situation which Hooker had foreseen, but it did not succeed in extinguishing hope for the future which persists in his books, some of which were written when the grounds for hope seemed to have disappeared. Through the calamities of the time and the deprivation which put an end to his public work, he courageously gave his energy especially by means of his writings to building for a future which must have appeared more than problematical to many and which he himself was only destined to glimpse. Not only did he set himself to meeting the pressing need for books of every kind, but he encouraged others like Sheldon and Sanderson to do the same. There was an indomitable quality about his application which stimulated others, and in one of his letters to Sheldon he puts forward an idea suggested by the conclusion of one of Bramhall's books, that they should 'endeavour to raise £600 per annum . . . for seven years to maintain a society of twenty exiled scholars',[2] and if it could be done, to obtain names from Bramhall. The latter, having escaped from Ireland narrowly evading capture by Parliamentary frigates, had spent twelve years from 1648 in exile on the Continent and was one of the leading figures during that period when more or less the only outward expression of the Church's existence was to be found abroad in the English ambassadors' chapels.

John Bramhall was born at Pontefract in Yorkshire in 1594, and went to Sidney Sussex College, Cambridge, in 1608, where the Master was Samuel Ward. Ward had been one of the representatives at Dort in 1621, but his position may be gauged from the fact that, in a letter to Ussher, he referred to Hooker who 'in mine opinion doth truly explicate the nature of sacraments',[3] and

1. E.g. in the Preface to *A View of the New Directory* (1645).
2. R. S. Bosher, *The Making of the Restoration Settlement*, p. 36.
3. Parr, *Life of James Ussher*, p. 438.

from his influence on Bramhall. The latter wrote, 'When I was a young student in theology, Dr Ward declared his mind to me, to this purpose, that it was impossible that the present controversies of the Church should be rightly determined or reconciled, without a deep insight into the doctrine of the primitive Fathers, and a competent skill in school theology. The former affordeth us a right pattern, and the second smootheth it over, and planeth away the knots'.[1] Once again the same influences are making themselves felt, and Bramhall's work is seen to have behind it not only the Fathers, but Hooker and Aquinas, for although he does not mention Hooker by name there is a similarity of approach and both he and Bramhall are influenced by Aquinas at much the same points, such as the nature of human acts. This diffused effect of Aquinas extends, of course at varying levels of intensity, from Hooker to the Latitudinarians. Although many felt with Glanvill that 'Thomas is but Aristotle sainted',[2] the *Summa Theologica* left a mark faint at times but sometimes clear as in discussions of law, acts and reason, on seventeenth-century theology and its method. Bramhall acknowledges it as do Laud, Andrewes, Sanderson and Hammond, and its effect on Wilkins and others has been noted. Baxter made a close study of Aquinas and other scholastic writers, and has left on record not only his sense of temperamental affinity with them, but an awareness of their influence on the form of his own work. His interest in, and study of practical divinity, fits in with this, and furnishes yet another illustration of the impact of this line of thinking on the writings of the seventeenth century, and of the close connection felt to exist between the two.[3]

Bramhall held posts at York where he was engaged in parochial work and was made use of by Archbishop Matthew, and at Ripon where he showed administrative ability and also characteristic courage: 'He showed his exceeding great love to his flock, in staying among them in the time of a most contagious and destructive pestilence.'[4] This courage led him to give up his work in England where he was one of Charles I's High Commissioners and to accept the invitation of Strafford to come to Ireland.

1. Bramhall, *Works* (1676 ed.), p. 636.
2. Joseph Glanvill, *Vanity of Dogmatizing*, p. 152.
3. *Reliquiae Baxterianae* (1696, ed. Sylvester), Bk. I, Pt. I, 5.
4. *Life*, by Bishop Vesey, prefaced to the edition of 1676.

Appointed Lord Deputy of Ireland in 1633, it was part of Strafford's purpose to bring about certain church reforms in the country, a project in which he was supported by a friend of Bramhall's, Sir Christopher Wandesford. To him Strafford had written to persuade Bramhall to undertake the work. They were anxious to secure the help of one who was not only an able administrator, for Strafford's intention was not simply to set affairs in order but to implement Laud's policy of bringing the Church of Ireland and the Church of England into line in the matter of the Articles which had been accepted by the Irish Convocation in 1615. The nub of the matter was that the Irish Articles as well as agreeing with the English Articles incorporated also the content of the nine Lambeth Articles of 1595. The details of the matter are not relevant in this connection, but the upshot was that Bramhall, working with Strafford and Laud, obtained the removal of the Irish Articles despite the opposition of the Primate, Ussher, although this did not affect the relations between them, for when Strafford fell and an attempt was made to impeach Bramhall, Ussher spoke on his behalf. Accused of treason by those who had resented his part in the changes inaugurated by Strafford, Bramhall's courage had not failed him and he had attended Parliament in Dublin where he was committed to prison. Ussher did what he could for him, but it was the record of his own disinterestedness in recovering alienated Church property which made it clear during the proceedings that what was in fact at issue was not the alleged treason of the defendant but the opposition of the plaintiffs to the policy which he had followed since becoming Bishop of Derry in 1634. By direction of the King, Bramhall was liberated but by this time events were gathering momentum. A petition had appeared for abolishing episcopacy in Ireland and soon the rebellion began, and Bramhall was advised to leave. Arrived in England he gave his active support to the Royalist cause, and in 1643 he published anonymously the *Serpent Salve*, a reply to the anonymous *Observations upon some of his Majesty's late Answers* which had made its appearance the previous year. This book advocated parliamentarianism and independency against royalism and episcopacy and in the latter connection Bramhall shows himself to be misinformed as to the sigificance and ecclesiastical status of superintendents in Germany.

The battle of Marston Moor in 1644 virtually extinguished royalist hopes, and with others, Bramhall escaped from England. His work in Ireland and the publication of the *Serpent Salve* made it impossible for him to remain, and for the next four years he was mainly at Brussels in the company of the ambassador, Sir Henry de Vic, occupying himself with his writing and providing the services of the Church for the exiles. In 1648 he returned to Ireland in spite of the danger of capture, for he had two narrow escapes while there, and his biographer records that Cromwell was seeking his arrest. From that year until the changed course of events twelve years later, Bramhall's circumstances were straitened and impoverished and he had at times the greatest difficulty in obtaining a livelihood. What is remarkable is that in such conditions, deprived of books and leisure, he published during his years on the continent all his writings with the exception of the first.[1] That he was not only a man of mettle but a man of parts is clear from his books which show the extent of his learning and the quality of his scholarship. In an atmosphere of controversy, poverty and political uncertainty, amid the unrealities of an exiled Court which existed more or less on sufferance and a calculated charity and which was exposed to the strain and frustration of its situation, Bramhall, like Hammond in England, wrote in support of the Church's position when to the outward eye the future held little promise. In John Evelyn's phrase, it was then customary to argue the visibility and existence of the Church from the chapel of the ambassador, Sir Richard Brown, whose house in Paris was a centre for the exiles during those years.[2] Unlike Hammond, Bramhall had no library, as he notes more than once, and his leisure was scanty by reason of the pressure of events and the necessity of making a living. Nevertheless, in spite of this and notwithstanding the impermanent form in which circumstances required that nearly all his work was to be cast, there is in Bramhall's writings a positive and constructive basis.

As the years of exile drew to a close, it was evident that they

---

1. *A Fair Warning to take heed of the Scottish Discipline* (1649); *Answer to de la Milletière* (1653); *A Just Vindication of the Church of England* (1654); *A Replication to the Survey* (1656); *Schism Guarded* (1658); *The Consecration of Protestants Bishops vindicated* (1658); *The Catching of Leviathan* (1658).
2. *Diary of John Evelyn*, February 12, 1683. It was this chapel which the wife of Grotius attended on the recommendation of her husband.

had taken their toll of one who in his own words did not 'serve the times'. He had been ill in 1659, and he had been concerned with Hyde and Nicholas about the succession, a matter which was becoming more pressing as the number of the surviving bishops dwindled. When he returned to England in the summer of 1660 after his long absence, he plunged once more into affairs, concerning himself with the filling of the vacant sees. Being nominated Archbishop of Armagh, he was himself to be the instrument of renewal and in January 1661 Bramhall, ill and with only two more years of his life remaining, consecrated nearly the whole Irish episcopate in Dublin. He had chosen Jeremy Taylor as the preacher for the occasion, and the sermon on the apostolic succession was printed at Bramhall's request. During the next two years he devoted himself to affairs, and the practical ability developed long before at Ripon was again put to use, and he died at work in 1663. Forthright and not always judicious, he combined in an unusual degree the characteristics of the scholar, the man of action and the administrator. By him and by others of his generation the Church was generously served in adversity.

As far as his writings were concerned Bramhall, like Andrewes, was another who was the victim of the circumstances of his times. The situation demanded that his books should be in the form of replies and answers, and the vigour of his prose and the genuine learning displayed both serve to indicate the kind of work he would have produced had he the time and the occasion to present his material in a more permanent and suitable shape. But perhaps he is not to be commiserated with so much as Andrewes was for Bramhall was a willing controversialist in that he readily stepped into a gap when both Andrewes and Hooker had a positive disinclination to do so. Yet there is more of candour than of combativeness in his writings as was fitting in one who was a scholar. The folio edition of 1676 brings out the nature of his work, dividing it into three sections, and it is noticeable that all are responses or vindications. They include his *Just Vindication of the Church of England*, *An Answer to de la Milletière*, *A Replication to the Bishop of Chalcedon's Survey*, *Schism Guarded* and *The Consecration of Protestant Bishops Vindicated* in one group. The second section comprises *A Fair Warning to take heed of the Scottish Discipline*, *The Serpent Salve* and a discussion of one of

Baxter's works, while the third deals with the writings of Hobbes. The division illustrates the three-fold presentation of Bramhall's material, but in spite of the fact that his work is framed in this way the impression is far from negative. Bramhall was too learned and his views were too thought-out for him to be merely a natural debater of points raised by others, and it is evident that he is not simply meeting issues as they are raised but rather confronting them from a stable and coherent stand-point. His approach is a positive and contructive application of Scripture, antiquity and reason. He has a strong sense of history and considerable historical knowledge, and on the other hand his treatment of Hobbes's views on freedom and necessity shows that he is aware of the implications of the new determinism and alive to what it means for religion.

Among those nearer his own time whose works influenced Bramhall's writings were Andrewes and Hammond and particularly Richard Field whose book *Of the Church* is often referred to by Bramhall. Field belonged to an earlier generation and was Dean of Gloucester from 1610 until his death six years later, and his book was published in 1606.[1] The reason for Bramhall's use of Field's work is not merely that there is a certain natural affinity between them. In Bramhall's time the appeal to antiquity was acutely topical in its application. At home, others were thinking in terms of gathered membership and the invisible Church, and abroad, the continuity which Andrewes and others had stressed was being called in question. The application of the appeal to antiquity derived urgency and point from the contemporary plight of the Church so suppressed outwardly in England that Hammond had to emphasise its essential visibility and continuity in its clergy and laity. Field handled the basis of these pressing questions in a way that commended itself to Bramhall. He answers the question 'who are the Church?' by saying that membership consists of 'divers sorts', some who accept the deposit of truth but not entirely, some who accept it but not in unity, some who hold it not in sincerity and some who accept it in unity and sincerity. To speak as some do of the elect as being 'of the Church' does not mean 'that others are not at all, nor in any sort of the Church',[2]

---

1. Field was born in 1561. The work consists of five books, four of which were published in 1606 and the fifth in 1610.
2. *Of the Church*, Bk. I, Chap. VII.

and his conclusion is that some are in the Church in one degree or another, while others are of the Church.[1] He writes 'Hence it cometh that we say there is a visible and an invisible Church, not meaning to make two distinct Churches . . . but to distinguish the divers considerations of the same Church'. This Church, Field maintains, is visible in respect of its credal profession, the use of sacraments and the ministry. Those who so participate are 'discernable' but the elect are not known to men, and in respect of them the Church may be called invisible, but it cannot be regarded as invisible in respect of credal profession and practice. 'The persons, then, of them of whom the Church consisteth are visible . . . and in this sort the Church cannot be invisible, neither did any of our men teach that it is or may be'.[2] He repudiates the idea that 'perfection amongst men on earth' can be expected in respect of membership.[3] The society of the Church includes people of all sorts and at different stages of development.

There are three permanent notes which distinguish the Church, 'the entire profession of faith', 'the use of the ceremonies and sacraments' appointed, and 'an union or connexion of men in this profession and use of these sacraments, under lawful pastors.'[4] With regard to the latter this is 'absolutely and essentially necessary to the being of a Church',[5] and in the fifth book he deals in detail, with the subject of the three orders of ministry. He emphasises the succession, but questions whether in certain circumstances, and considered absolutely, it is necessary to the being of a Church.[6] It is clear from what he writes elsewhere, however, that the circumstances he envisages are strictly limited, for 'none may ordain but they only, unless it be in cases of extreme necessity, as when all bishops are extinguished by death, or fallen into heresy'.[7] He notes that 'a continued succession of bishops' is not enough in the sense of a 'bare personal succession' and that it must also include holding 'the faith their predecessors did'. It was in this way that the Fathers approached the matter, 'by showing affirmatively the faith they defended to have been received by all those bishops, whose succession they urged against their adversaries'.[8] Field was widely versed in the writings and history of the early

1. *Ib*. Chap. IX.
2. *Ib*. Chap. X.
3. *Ib*. Chap. XVIII.
4. Bk. II, Chap. II.

5. *Ib*. Chap. VI.
6. *Ib*.
7. Bk. V, Chap. XXVII.
8. *Ib*. Bk. III, Chap. XL.

period, as is apparent for example in his treatment of Councils which is full and detailed.[1] In connection with what has been noted before of the attitude of various writers of the period to this aspect of the appeal to antiquity, his conclusions are of interest. While it may not be affirmed with complete certainty that the pronouncements of a General Council are undoubtedly true, the presumption is so strong that they are to be accepted 'unless we do most certainly know the contrary'. It is permissible to entertain a private doubt so long as there is a genuine attempt to resolve it, and it is not necessary 'expressly to believe whatsoever the Council hath concluded, though it be true, unless by some other means it appear unto us to be true, and we be convinced of it in some other sort than by the bare determination of the Council only'. It is sufficient to believe it implicitly and to be ready to believe it expressly. Notwithstanding, Field holds that in view of the subjects they deal with, the time and manner of their proceedings, 'they are and ever were expressly to be believed by all such as perfectly understand the meaning of their determination'.

Like his friend Hooker, Field was a man of one book and it proved to be an influential one. He himself hoped that it would be a definitive work, and it certainly was used by later writers such as Bramhall who, if they did not agree with everything in it, found its material comprehensive and its treatment balanced. Field's lucid style helped to commend his learning, and the book left its impress on Bramhall in connection with the interpretation of Scripture as well as in respect of the appeal to antiquity and of the idea of continuity as these affected his views on the Church.

Bramhall's position appears in a positive and simple form throughout his writings, and as with Laud, Andrewes, Hammond and others, it finds its criterion in the early centuries, and its motivating force in the idea of continuity. He writes that the 'ground for unity of faith is the creed; and for unity of government, the same form of discipline, which was used in the Primitive Church, and is derived from them to us'.[2] In another connection, he makes the point that the basis is 'the authority of the Primitive Fathers and the General Councils, which are the Representative Body of the Universal Church'.[3] The undifferentiated nature of

1. *Ib.* Bk. V, Chaps. XLVIII–LII.   3. *Ib.* p. 625.
2. *Works* (1676), p. 407.

this basis is emphasised, 'the old faith of the whole Christian world, that is the creed of the apostles, explicated by the Nicene, Constantinopolitan, Ephesine, and Chalcedonian Fathers'.[1] Conversely, this is brought out by the fact that the chief causes of separation are innovations and the disrupting of continuity.[2] Despite the form of his writings, this positive quality is the main aspect and it is forcefully and constantly reiterated, so that the main elements are continuity as a realised fact and agreement with the first centuries as to fundamentals. 'Our religion is the same it was, our Church the same it was, our Holy Orders the same they were', he writes, pointing out that it is for this reason that the Church of England adopts what seems to some a negative attitude in respect of 'new articles of faith', as he terms them, or the equating of 'opinions with fundamental truths'. Those who regard this as a negative attitude miss the point that it is in fact the consequence of this position which is based on a central positive affirmation, 'not considering that our positive articles are those general truths . . . our negation is only of human controverted additions'.[3] The simplicity of this position is its strength, in Bramhall's view, since it requires no special pleading, and its criterion is 'the infallible rule of faith, that is, the Holy Scriptures, interpreted by the Catholic Church'.[4]

To those who considered that Anglicans had forsaken tradition, he replied that by tradition two things could be meant, either the tradition of a particular Church which might be contradicted by that of another, or the tradition which was received always, everywhere and by all.[5] This was basic to his whole outlook, and it was the abandoning of this view of tradition which was in a large measure responsible for later disruptions and disunity. It is 'separation from the pure primitive Church which produced the second separation',[6] i.e. the Reformation. It is this interplay of the

1. *Ib.* p. 349.
2. *Ib.* p. 61: as in the case of 'whosoever doth limit the Catholic Church unto his own sect, excluding all the rest of the Christian world, by new doctrines', or (p. 62) in the case of 'whosoever doth wilfully break the line of apostolical succession, which is the very nerves and sinews of ecclesiastical unity and communion, both with the present Church, and with the Catholic symbolical Church of all successive ages'.
3. *Ib.* p. 101.
4. *Ib.* p. 141.
5. *Ib.* p. 290.
6. *Ib.* p. 156.

idea of continuity with that of the finality of fundamentals which is one of the characteristic aspects of the spirit of Anglicanism. When Bramhall wrote that 'the generation of new articles is the corruption of the old creed',[1] he was the representative of a whole facet of Anglican thought which insisted on the permanent and unchanging quality of fundamentals, and which looked back to the Primitive Church not simply because it had the cachet of antiquity, but because the writings of the period revealed that the creed was the foundation from the beginning. In the return to this position—'if the creed or necessary points of faith were reduced to what they were in the time of the four first oecumenical councils, according to the decree of the third general council'— Bramhall sees the possibility of unity, for who, he asks, would say that 'the faith of the primitive fathers was insufficient'.[2]

This fusing of continuity and fundamentals bears upon Bramhall's analysis of Catholicity. 'The communion of the Christian Catholic Church,' he writes, 'is partly internal, partly external.' The former consists chiefly in acceptance of 'the same entire substance of saving necessary truth revealed by the apostles', in judgments of mutual charity, in the desire to achieve external communion, and in refusal to exclude those 'which profess the ancient faith of the apostles and primitive fathers, established in the first general councils, and comprehended in the Apostolic, Nicene and Athanasian creeds'. External communion consists in having the same creeds, sacraments, liturgy, and in accepting the same 'authority, that is, episcopacy or a general council'. Internal communion is a mutual obligation for all, even in the case of those with whom external communion, for one reason or another, is not possible.

It follows that Catholicity implies acceptance of the authority of the 'Universal Church, and its representative a general council', the maintaining of internal communion with all and external communion where that is possible, and the approving of no changes which are not made by lawful authority on sufficient grounds and with due moderation. It derives also 'by the uninterrupted line of apostolical succession', and depends on acceptance of the contents of 'Scripture . . . that infallible rule' and on the acceptance of the unanimous and universal practice of the Church. Similarly, it precludes 'censuring others of different

1. *Ib.* p. 151.   2. *Ib.* p. 137.

judgment . . . in inferior questions', and 'obtruding opinions upon others as articles of faith'.[1] This emphasis on continuity and on fundamentals as opposed to opinions is strongly marked. His writings have a developed sense of history, not only in respect of the early period but also of later times, and his knowledge of the subject shows acquaintance with a wide range of sources. Combined with this is the frequently reiterated assertion that 'men may vary in their judgments'[2] so long as they accept fundamentals. This is central for the seventeenth-century writers, and for none more than for Bramhall. His favourable view of the Eastern Churches was based on the fact that 'they exact of no man . . . any other creed',[3] and he saw it as the explanation of the agreement of the first centuries that 'no Church exacted more in point of faith than the primitive creed'.[4] His work is an example of the application of that nexus of ideas, fundamentals and continuity, the appeal to Scripture and the appeal to antiquity, which was characteristic of Anglicanism. Nevertheless, his reading of the Fathers themselves shows signs of that equally characteristic historical sense which is basically historical criticism. He writes 'we receive the Fathers as competent witnesses of the faith, and practice and tradition of the Church in their respective ages . . . but in those things which they had upon the credit of a suppositious author, the conclusion always follows the weaker part'.[5]

As with Andrewes, Hammond and others, the corollary of this attitude to fundamentals was a liberality of outlook in secondary questions, and in a significant phrase he objects to the view 'which will admit no latitude in religion, but makes each nicety a fundamental'.[6] The expression of this liberality varies, as in his preference for the writings of Grotius and others. While he makes it clear that his attitude is not uncritical, what appeals to Bramhall about these writings is, first of all, what he calls their 'charitable way' of dealing with debated points, and he refers also to the 'clearer judgments' by which they penetrated beneath the surface of these matters. Although he does not accept everything maintained in them, he stresses that what impresses him about those who produced them is their independence of mind and 'free spirits'. His feeling for Grotius indicates his own outlook, for he

1. *Ib.* pp. 57–61.
2. *Ib.* p. 137.
3. *Ib.* p. 160.
4. *Ib.* p. 171.
5. *Ib.* p. 205.
6. *Ib.* p. 494.

writes of him that 'he was in affection a friend, and in desire a true son of the Church of England'.[1] There is a further indication of this in his treatment of Baxter's criticism of Grotius, when he notes that times have changed since he and others like him were regarded as Pelagians for maintaining 'some old innocent truths' which the Church had always maintained 'before Arminius was born'.[2] In other words, he is making the point, equally clear in other writings of the period, that this general approach preceded both Arminius and Calvin. In another connection, he lays emphasis on the fact that 'justification by special faith' was never accounted an article either by the English Church or by its leading theologians, although some individuals brought it forward as a 'private opinion'.[3] The same general outlook appears also in his attitude to the Articles, maintained by others too, regarding them as 'theological verities' and not as definitive and obligatory, and their function as a domestic one 'for the preservation of unity'.[4] His view is that no one is obliged to accept them but only to refrain from calling them in question. Bramhall's writings furnish an instance of the combination of the appeal to Scripture and the appeal to antiquity with the liberal approach to other matters, an approach which stems as much from an attitude to reason and the reality of freedom as it does from the conviction that only fundamentals are authoritative.

This is seen in his answer to Hobbes's views on liberty and necessity where his main purpose is to establish the reality of freedom, and in which the influence of the *Summa Theologica* in respect of the element of rationality is evident. 'Reason is ... the original of true liberty',[5] Bramhill writes and he regards the determinism of Hobbes as depriving human nature of its essential characteristic: 'it destroys liberty, and dishonours the nature of man. It makes the second causes and outward objects to be the rackets, and men to be but the tennis-balls of destiny'.[6] Liberty consists in 'the elective power of the rational will', and liberty from necessity may be defined as 'an universal immunity from all inevitability and determination'.[7]

Hobbes's work illustrates one of the directions in which the

1. *Ib.* p. 611.
2. *Ib.* p. 608.
3. *Ib.* p. 226.
4. *Ib.* pp. 248, 345.

5. *Ib.* p. 651.
6. *Ib.* p. 667.
7. *Ib.* p. 654.

new philosophy turned in the seventeenth century in that it led some to accept naturalism as an explanation. Like most of the new philosophers Hobbes regarded scholasticism as a system of terminology corresponding to nothing real in nature. Carried over into the sphere of personality and psychology, this meant the rejection of that picture of man in which the basic elements of personality are rationality and freedom. For Aquinas 'those acts are properly called human, which are voluntary, because the will is the rational appetite, which is proper to man'.[1] Free will, in the accepted sense of the term, has no meaning for Hobbes. Acted upon by the mechanical naturalism then beginning to make itself felt, he opts in effect for a kind of determinism. The will is part of a complex of inter-related elements, of unsuspected compulsions and responses to stimuli, and is therefore in no real sense free. This determinism, which he did not apply in his work on political theory, is the main element in the writings of Hobbes, and Bramhall saw its dangerous implications.

In the seventeenth century, as the work of the new philosophers got under way, there was a steady moving away from scholastic and Aristotelian ideas in respect of the explanation of the natural world. In fact, the chief criticism of these ideas was that they did not explain at all. But with regard to questions of the nature of personality and the voluntariness of actions, the influence of the *Summa Theologica* persisted, leaving the same impress on Bramhall and Sanderson as it had on Hooker. Nor were the Latitudinarians exempt from its influence in this connection although they had a general relationship with the new philosophy. This continuing influence was due to several contributory factors in the situation. The widespread interest among Anglican writers in practical divinity made for the use of that section of the *Summa Theologica* which dealt with human acts and the nature of personality, and it was this part of Aquinas's work which had always made its impact in the seventeenth century. Also, there was a natural inclination towards a theology of synthesis, and this was a characteristic of the *Summa Theologica*. Moreover, the situation in the earlier part of the century had shown the need for an approach to basic problems in which reason was active and free, and this made the same part of the *Summa Theologica*, with its emphasis on reason, congenial. Bound up with this was the view

1. *Summa Theologica* (Pt. II, 1st Pt.), Q. 6.

common to Aquinas and to the seventeenth-century writers that reason was the human characteristic, and this, as has been seen, affected the whole idea of 'happiness as man's proper good'[1] which the Latitudinarians took from the *Summa Theologica*, as well as the understanding of those acts by which it was to be attained.

The tendency on the part of the Anglican writers had been to follow the lead of Aquinas and to adopt the clear-cut and traditional approach to questions of personality. This was a simplified faculty psychology of will, intellect and feelings, with reason as director. Bramhall was in full accord with the position of Aquinas that rationality required and implied free-will: 'reason is . . . the original of true liberty which judgeth and representeth to the will, whether this or that be convenient, whether this or that be more convenient'.[2] This brought him into conflict with the views put forward by Hobbes, who did not see the picture in such clearly-defined outline. Bramhall maintained that 'the formal reason of liberty is election. The necessary requisite to election is deliberation. Deliberation implieth the actual use of reason'.[3] It seemed to be primarily on the understanding of what deliberation signified that the opposition between the older rationalism and the new determinism turned. For Hobbes, the process of deliberation was not simply rational but included the interplay of unconscious influences which preceded the act of choosing, so that while the ultimate act of the will, its choice, was voluntary, yet the will was not really autonomous having been determined beforehand in some measure by other conditioning influences. Bramhall, on the other hand, accepted the view of the *Summa Theologica* that 'man acts from judgment' and that this judgment proceeds from 'some act of comparison in the reason, therefore he acts from free judgment'.[4] The older view did not recognise the complicated nature of choice and response and did not allow for the action of submerged factors. Its departmentalised understanding of personality made for an over-simplification of the process. Hobbes took account of this, but his understanding of it was so coloured by current mechanistic and naturalistic ideas that he almost entirely excluded

1. Cp. *Summa Theologica*, Pt. I, Q. 83, Art. I.
2. *Ib.* p. 651. Cp. *Summa Theologica*, Pt. I, Q. 83, Art. I: 'and forasmuch as man is rational it is necessary that man have free-will'.
3. *Ib.* p. 661.
4. *Summa Theologica*, Pt. I, Q. 83, Art. I.

reason in its proper function and so qualified the element of voluntariness as to make it virtually non-existent. That Bramhall saw this appears from his comment that this meant 'that all human wills . . . and each propension of our wills, even during our deliberation, are as much necessitated as anything else whatsoever'.[1]

The extent of Bramhall's closeness to Aquinas in this connection may be seen by making a comparison of his work with the relevant section of the *Summa Theologica*.[2] Not only is the substance the same, but also the form in which it is expressed, and Bramhall takes over the examples as well as the terms used. Attention has been drawn to the fact that he is not alone in this, but his referring back of the subject to its treatment by the scholastics is more deliberate than that of any other writer of the period, including Sanderson, although by reason of the specialised nature of his writings the latter made a wider use of the same source. So Bramhall writes 'to know what spontaneity is, let us consult a while with the Schools about the distinct order of voluntary, or involuntary actions'.[3] 'The competent skill in school theology' which Ward had recommended to him years ago because of its usefulness for clarification had been acquired. Its legacy for Bramhall was a conviction that reason in its free action could never be discounted, together with a sharpness of outline in his thinking which occasionally gave a shallowness to his treatment of subjects such as this which required depth as well as clarity if their full proportions were to be made evident.

Following the *Summa Theologica*, he distinguishes the extrinsic and intrinsic principles of actions, borrowing the illustrations as well. Instances of the first, which are violent acts, are the throwing of a stone upwards or the dragging of a person by force. An example of the second would be the falling of a stone downwards 'without any manner of knowledge of the end', and these are natural acts. Voluntary acts are those that proceed from an internal principle, 'with an imperfect knowledge of the end'. These are sometimes called spontaneous acts, and examples of them are the actions of people of unsound mind, children, animals and 'the

1. *Ib.* p. 667.
2. Pt. II, 1st i.e. Pt., Q. 6, Artt. 1–8: although he does not specifically mention the *Summa Theologica* nor give references to it to indicate his sources.
3. *Ib.* p. 661.

inconsiderate acts of men of judgment'. Finally, free actions are such as proceed from an intrinsic cause, 'with a more perfect knowledge of the end, which are elected upon deliberation'. He distinguishes between the last two types of action by defining a free act as 'only that which proceeds from the free election of the rational will after deliberation; but every act that proceeds from the sensitive appetite of man or beast, without deliberation, is truly voluntary'. Circumstances, however, can change the one into the other, as when a man throws his cargo into the sea to save his life. This is not only a voluntary but a free act, and apart from the circumstances, such an act would not be done willingly or spontaneously. The illustration again is from the *Summa Theologica*, as is that of the man who shoots at a stag in the undergrowth and kills his friend, an example designed to show that knowledge is a necessary condition of voluntariness.[1] While free actions are those only 'which proceed merely from election without any outward necessitation', Bramhall notes that there are mixed actions, resulting from 'the concurrence of free and natural agents', as when a man walking through the streets of set purpose is accidentally struck by a falling tile. The injury was not necessary since he freely chose to go that way, and neither was it free because 'he did not deliberate of that accident'. It was contingent, and therefore there are contingent acts which are not free.

His conclusion is that the will can only be necessitated in a limited sense. There is in the will a two-fold action, 'the one more remote, called "imperatus", that is, in truth, the act of some inferior faculty, subject to the command of the will: as to open and shut one's eyes'. Without doubt these actions may be compelled. But the elicit act of the will, while it may be 'hindered by the intervening impediment of the understanding', may not be compelled.

All this is derived from, and is to be paralleled in, the *Summa Theologica*, from which in this connection Bramhall takes the expression and the substance of his views. No picture of the

---

1. With regard to this illustration, Bramhall develops it from two slightly different illustrations in the *Summa Theologica*. In one of these, a man wishing to kill his enemy, does so in ignorance, thinking to kill a stag. Ignorance in this case causes non-voluntariness, since what is unknown cannot be actually willed. In the other, a man, after taking precautions, shoots an arrow and kills a passer-by. Such ignorance causes involuntariness. (*Ib.* Q. 6, Art. 8.)

development of theological method in the seventeenth century
which hopes to achieve a degree of verisimilitude can fail to take
account of the influence of the *Summa Theologica*. Nor can it
fail to note that the point of entry of its influence is mainly though
not entirely in connection with the function of reason and in
connection with matters involving certain clearly defined aspects
of practical divinity, such as law, acts and happiness considered
as the ultimate good. The influence of the *Summa Theologica*
preceded and reinforced the quest for a reasonable theology as
this went on in other directions, impelled by other influences and
evoked by varying situations. It strengthened the search, in
circumstances different to those of its own origins, for that which
it was itself designed to be, a theology of synthesis in which the
claims of faith and reason were not mutually exclusive.

Despite the frequent hard words of the seventeenth century, and
the rejection of its philosophical background by the new philosophers, its influence persisted for the greater part of the period
until the changing century with its fresh interpretation of the
human situation turned to other problems. Bramhall, however,
who was little if at all influenced by the new philosophy, was
firmly set in the earlier succession of writers from Hooker to
Wilkins whose work showed in some degree or another their
knowledge of it. Bramhall makes his approval of it clearer than do
any of his contemporaries, emphasising its usefulness from the
point of view of method: 'it may be the Schoolmen have started
many superfluous questions, and some of dangerous consequence,
but yet I say the weightier ecclesiastical controversies will never
be understood and stated succinctly, without the help of their
necessary distinctions'.[1] This was plainly put, and doubtless it
indicates something of a natural affinity, for Bramhall's capable
and vigorous lucidity probably found something akin in the con-
densed clarity of the *Summa Theologica*. A capacity for this type
of clear and close reasoning appears in his protracted discussion
with Hobbes, and the effect of the *Summa Theologica* on Bramhall's
writing on this subject is seen not only in the material but in the
total impression conveyed.

The work of Bramhall illustrates the cohesion of the three
elements in the theological method which Andrewes did so much
to establish in the seventeenth century. Central to it is the appeal

1. *Ib.* p. 734.

to Scripture, and the appeal to antiquity depends on this and is used to underline not only historical continuity but agreement on fundamentals in the first centuries. Linked with the question of fundamentals is that of liberty in matters that are not essential, with a consequent emphasis on reason. The concern with continuity and the visibility of the Church is to the fore in Bramhall's writings. He refuses to accept Baxter's inference that the consequence of the stress on succession is to unchurch others, and he draws a distinction between the nature and the integrity of a Church.[1] Nor will he agree that Baxter's differentiation between 'old . . . and new episcopal divines' in this connection corresponds to the facts: 'we are old episcopal divines, one and all'.[2]

What emerges from a survey of the century is that this theological method, mainly in virtue of the place accorded to reason from Hooker onwards, is by its nature committed to being involved in a variety of matters, from natural theology to the questions raised by determinism. It is also clear that it is not a vague approach, capable of being moulded out of recognition by the impact on itself of those subjects which it endeavours to put into perspective, for it is resistant as well as flexible. The most that can be said on this side is that different situations have brought into play one constituent element of the method more than the others. But the varying situations, from the Anglican-Puritan tension to the arrival of the new philosophy, have not created the particular element in theological method. Rather have they evoked or given a more prominent place to what was always part of it. Its adaptability does not conceal the fact that this theological method derived outline and definiteness from its concern with the finality of fundamentals and with the historical.

For these reasons, and because it was actively associated with liturgy which imparted a quality of life and contact to its self-expression, it was never in danger of degenerating into an attitude fashioned by changing contemporary developments. Being firmly based, it was not dominated by change but was ready to assimilate. This solidity was due in part, as has been suggested, to the emphasis on the historical in the form taken by the appeal to antiquity. The criterion of the first centuries was not regarded only in terms of the verification of fundamentals, but as a factual

1. *Ib.* p. 614.   2. *Ib.* p. 616.

contact of present and past history in the continuity of the Church. The inevitability of the link between the appeal to antiquity and questions of the Church in respect of visibility and continuity is reflected in the number of books on the subject during the period, from Bilson's work in 1593 to that of Beveridge, Burscough and Hume at the beginning of the eighteenth century, in almost all of which the standard of reference is sought within the history of the first centuries.[1] Bilson writes of 'the general consent of all antiquity', and his purpose is 'that by comparing it might appear, which side came nearest' to the Scriptures and the 'ancient Church'.[2] Bancroft, whose book appeared in the same year,[3] treats the subject in the same way, as did writers as dissimilar in their general view-point as Davenant and Taylor, Pearson, who defended Hammond's work on the epistles of Ignatius, and Thorndike, who co-operated with them both in the years preceding 1660. The appeal to antiquity was so much a part of theological method in the seventeenth century that it can only be treated selectively and with reference to its salient features. That it did not escape criticism from such as Hales, Hyde and Falkland, and that it was more or less ignored by the Cambridge Platonists, did not in the aggregate detract very much from the importance accorded to it. Although it was again a subject of debate in the later part of the century, its assertion by Bull and Dodwell was as vigorous as ever.

Bull and also Patrick had come to seek episcopal ordination during the Commonwealth primarily as a result of Herbert Thorndike's writings showing the force of the criterion of early history and patristic works in the matter of Orders. In *Just Weights and Measures* (1662), for example, he maintains that the standard of the primitive Church is that by which all change must be measured, and it is the 'visible unity' which is central to his theme.[4] Thorndike's work, particularly his *Epilogue* (1659), was part of that remarkable output which Hammond did so much to promote during the decade from 1650 to 1660, as was also Pearson's *Exposition of the Creed* which appeared in the same year. Widely learned in patristic studies, Pearson shows this aspect of

1. Egg. Beveridge, *Sermons on the Office of the Priesthood* (1708); Burscough, *Discourse of the Unity of the Church* (1699); Hume, *The Sacred Succession* (1710).
2. *The Perpetual Government of Christ's Church*, preface.
3. *A Survey of the pretended Holy Discipline.*　　　4. Cp. Chap. I, III.

theological method at its most typical. In the dedication he writes that 'in Christianity there can be no concerning truth which is not ancient; and whatsoever is truly new, is certainly false'.[1] The modern desire for novelty is nowhere more misplaced than in such a context, where the object is 'the first faith' to which there is not 'a more probable guide than the Creed, received in all ages of the Church' and which in turn 'leads ... to the Scriptures, from whence it was at first deduced'.[2]

Pearson visualises two kinds of readers 'which though they may agree in judgment, yet must differ in their capacities',[3] and so the book itself is plainly written, without quotations in other languages in the text, the margin being reserved for patristic and historical references. His method is to show the creed as being 'a brief comprehension' or summary of what is more fully contained in Scripture, and the text is devoted to this while the confirming and illustrating records of early writings and conciliar decrees are marginally noted. This plan of procedure, coupled with simplicity of expression, ensured permanency for the book which passed through many editions.

Here again the underlying unity of outlook in seventeenth-century Anglicanism is tacitly assumed, and there is no need of a reminder that Pearson was the biographer of Hales, for he deliberately adheres to a theological method in which the three elements are fused. He writes 'I proceed upon such principles as they themselves allow, that is, upon the Word of God delivered in the Old and New Testament, alleged according to the true sense, and applied by right reason; not urging the authority of the Church which they reject, but only giving in the margin the sense of the primitive fathers'.[4] This agreed basis made itself felt throughout the period, sometimes in unexpected ways. That writers such as Andrewes, Bramhall and Pearson, should set store by the criterion of antiquity was an inevitable consequence of their position and circumstances. But it seems to have been forgotten that Stillingfleet, writing from a specifically Latitudinarian view-point, similarly made use of the appeal to antiquity, though in a rather more subtle way which bears the impress of the characteristic reasonableness of the Latitudinarians. The *Rational Account*

1. *An Exposition of the Creed* (1659),   3. *Ib.* Preface.
   dedication.   4. *Ib.*
2. *Ib.*

(1664) is in fact a vindication of Laud's *Conference*, but with the changed overtones of forty years later. Once again a circle is completed and Stillingfleet supports Laud's general position just as the Laudian Hammond sympathised with certain aspects of the writings of Falkland and Grotius, and expresses himself in terms which may have helped in the formulation of Latitudinarian ideas and which, at the very least, coincided with them in all respects.

The form of Stillingfleet's book was created by the earlier work, and he deals with much the same subjects as did Laud, but his book is larger not only because of amplification but because of the particular way in which he develops the theme within the context of new facts and situations. These have brought about a changed attitude which has distributed the emphasis differently, but the theme remains unchanged and Stillingfleet's object is to modernise its application, for he regards himself as being in general agreement with the older book. As to 'the style and way of writing', he favours that popularised by the Royal Society, 'to join clearness of expression with evidence of reason'.[1] The book shows the range of his reading in the literature of the early period and further illustrates some aspects of the historical interest evident in *Origines Sacrae*. The changed climate of opinion is apparent from the expressed intention to give what is termed 'a rational account'[2] of the subject, but the invariable aspects of Anglican theological method make an early appearance also. 'The apostolical creed' is a condensing of fundamentals, and 'the creed must suppose the Scripture'.[3] The three elements of 'Scripture, reason, or the consent of the Primitive Church'[4] are the standard of assay. Authorities have proportionate value, but the basic Latitudinarian independence of such considerations appears in Stillingfleet's assertion that 'all these would not one jot persuade us contrary to commonsense, and the large experience of the world'.[5] There is none of the brash confidence of Watson or Middleton however in Stillingfleet's attitude and he specifically notes that 'the practice of the Church from apostolical times is a great confirmation'.[6] When he deals with the whole question of authority, reason and faith, he

1. *A Rational Account* (1681 ed.), preface.
2. *Ib.* Preface.
3. *Ib.* Chap. IV, p. 91.
4. *Ib.* Chap. II, p. 41.
5. *Ib.* p. 42.
6. *Ib.* Chap. IV, p. 101.

writes 'but still as the assent is, so the evidence must be'.[1] This is another of those half-heard echoes of the *Ecclesiastical Polity* which more than any direct quotation testify to the abiding impression of Hooker on a century.

There is a great deal of reference to patristic writings in the book which shows the extent to which Stillingfleet is at home in such surroundings, but the individuality of the work appears in the more subtle way in which the subject is approached. He is aware of the existence of differences among the Fathers on various questions, and he notes that 'nothing ought to be looked on as an article of faith among the Fathers but what they declare that they believe on account of Divine revelation'.[2] He adds that it is not 'enough to prove that one or two Fathers did speak something tending to it, but that all who had occasion to mention it, did speak of it as the doctrine of the Church'.[3] If any of them base any specific teaching on 'the sense of doubtful places of Scripture' there is no more obligation or reason to accept this than there is to accept that such in fact is the meaning of those places. The matter then resolves itself into a question not of 'the judgment of the Fathers' but of 'the sense of Scripture which they and we both rely upon'.[4] In effect, Stillingfleet has recourse to the Fathers not so much as to a dictionary of antiquity as to a handbook of the first centuries in order that he may discover their method. What he is anxious to do is to establish that, in their own times and situation, they also proceeded by way of rational inference and by the use of Scripture as definitive in the matter of fundamentals. The difference as compared with Laud's treatment of the appeal to antiquity is one of degree rather than of kind. Both regarded it as a means of demonstrating that antiquity held the same view with regard to the relationship of Scripture to fundamentals. But the period intervening between the publication of the two books had given a new urgency to the whole question of method, that is, of the mutual relationship of authority and reason. Accordingly, as a Latitudinarian, Stillingfleet is interested in showing that the Fathers did not disregard rational evidence for faith, nor consider it incompatible with revelation, in their method. He writes, for example, of Clement of Alexandria, that 'we see that he insists on rational evidence as the great and

1. *Ib*. Chap. V, p. 129.   3. *Ib*. p. 596.
2. *Ib*. p. 595.   4. *Ib*. p. 597.

sufficient testimony into which our faith is resolved as to the being
of a Divine revelation'.[1] The difference, while palpable, is mainly
one of direction of emphasis, and it reveals the impact of the
new situation on the tried method of the appeal to antiquity,
which Stillingfleet is not prepared to give up although he thinks
it has been frequently misused and has certain limitations. It is a
variation of the appeal to antiquity, not altogether dissimilar in
some points to that of Chillingworth, but more constructive
and more integrated into the accepted theological method.

The main difference, as compared with Laud's work, arises
from the way in which Stillingfleet relates the assessment of
method in the writings of the patristic period to the investigation
of what he calls 'the question of the resolution of faith'.[2] He is
endeavouring to come to grips with a basic and practical question,
made more pressing for his contemporaries because of the unsettling effects of new discoveries, namely, how can it be known what
revelation is, 'or what those things are which are immediately revealed'.[3] Various solutions had been offered by different Christian
traditions, such as that of the infallible book or the testimony
of the present Church. But for Stillingfleet, to say 'that the resolution of faith is into God's infallible testimony, without showing
on what account this testimony is to be believed, is to tell us that
which no one doubts of, and to escape that which is the main
question'.[4] It is the question asked by Laud in the *Conference* as
to how Scripture can be known to be what it claims to be, and
Stillingfleet later on puts it in the same form.[5] Stillingfleet is
clear that no solution is effective which discounts the element of
reason: 'when we speak thereof of the resolving of faith, we mean,
what are the rational inducements to believe, or what evidence
there is in the object propounded to make us firmly assent to it'.
He is not afraid to stress the element of rational assent because he
holds that there is an essential confusion which has befogged the
issue. This confusion is between the way in which 'saving faith
is wrought in us' and the 'rational inducements which do incline
the mind to a firm assent', between the 'efficient cause' and the
'grounds of faith'.[6] Any discussion of the resolution of faith
implies that in that context faith means 'a rational and discursive

1. *Ib.* p. 255.   4. *Ib.*
2. *Ib.* p. 189.   5. *Ib.* p. 189.
3. *Ib.* p. 188.   6. *Ib.*

act of the mind'. Because it is 'an assent upon evidence', it must
be a rational and discursive act of which an intelligible account
may be given: 'and this account which men are able to give why
they do believe, or on what ground they do it, is that which we
call resolving faith.'[1]

Stillingfleet's discussion of this is of interest from the point of
view of theological method, for it gives clear indication of how
ways of thinking coloured by fiduciary ideas which have moulded
the general acceptance of what the term faith implies are being
set aside. Instead, there is being recommended a clear recognition
of the intellectual element in faith, such as would be effective in
a new situation where the major problem was the reconciliation
of reason and faith, of religion and the new philosophy. In this,
he is reiterating the affirmation of the *Summa Theologica*, that
faith, as it is the principle of the act of believing, must necessarily
reside in the intellect.[2] Stillingfleet is not questioning the origin
or infusing of faith, but rather, endeavouring to separate what he
calls 'the operation of the spirit whereby saving faith is wrought
in us' from the aspect of assent, of faith as 'a persuasion of the
mind'. This is largely the position outlined in the *Summa Theologica*, for although there is no specific connection in respect of
the subject, the approach to it is along the same lines.[3] This is
more or less inevitable since both were attempting to do more or
less the same thing. Stillingfleet is resisting the semi-mystical
idea of faith which had obtained such currency in the contemporary English scene, and this is clear not only from his insistence
on the rational element, but also in his obvious wariness of the
subjective element. For example, he writes of 'its efficient cause,
which some improperly call the testimony of the spirit'.[4] He
attempts to provide some clarification of the subject by distinguishing between the way in which 'faith is wrought . . . by way
of efficiency' and the 'grounds of faith', the 'reason causing the
mind to assent to what is propounded to it'. 'Our question' he
writes, 'is not then concerning the necessity of infused habits
of grace, but of those rational inducements which do incline the
mind to a firm assent'. He considers that without this, faith would
be 'an unaccountable thing', and the Latitudinarian inheritance
from the Cambridge Platonists appears in the statement that,

1. *Ib.*
2. Pt. II (Second Pt.), Q. 4, A.2.
3. Cp. Q. 6, A.1.
4. *Ib.* p. 189.

without this, 'the spirit of revelation would not be the spirit of wisdom'. The Latitudinarian urge to explain in terms acceptable to the age is evident in the contention that if no other account of faith can be given than that it is so 'wrought', then 'religion would be exposed to the contempt of all unbelievers'.[1]

This leads up to the central question already referred to, which had been discussed by Laud, namely, how it can be known in what the content of revelation consists. 'There are then in the question of the resolution of faith, these three questions to be resolved: First, why I believe those things to be true which are contained in the book called Scripture? 2. Why I believe the doctrine contained in that book to be divine? 3. Why I believe the books themselves to be of divine revelation?'[2] Stillingfleet's conclusion is that moral certainty is a sufficient foundation for faith and that 'the nature of certainty is not so much to be taken from the matters themselves, as from the grounds inducing the assent'.[3]

He then endeavours to establish the judgment of antiquity in the matter so as to show that the early writers concurred in this 'way of resolving faith'.[4] He writes that it is no small confirmation to him of this method that it should be 'so exactly concurring . . . to the unanimous consent of antiquity'. This is a variation on what was always implicit in the Anglican appeal to antiquity, namely, that the patristic period was governed by the same presuppositions as to faith, reason and fundamentals. It is an appeal to the method of antiquity as much as to history, and therefore to call it historical theology is only a partial description. Stillingfleet's method is that combination of elements which is the bedrock of seventeenth-century theology, 'and next to Scripture and reason, I attribute so much to the sense of the Christian Church in the ages next succeeding the apostles'.[5]

Stillingfleet maintains that, while it is possible to take passages out of their context in the writings of antiquity, a consideration of 'the scope and design of their writings' supports his position.[6] Having quoted from the work of Justin Martyr, he writes 'so that here we have most evidently all those things concurring . . . in the resolution of faith: moral inducement preparing the mind,

1. *Ib.*
2. *Ib.* p. 190.
3. *Ib.* p. 191.
4. *Ib.* p. 243.
5. *Ib.* p. 243.
6. *Ib.* p. 244.

rational evidence from the thing into which faith is resolved, and divine grace requisite in the nature of an efficient cause'.[1] He has chosen Justin Martyr not only because he was a philosopher who became a Christian, but because he lived so near to the times of the apostles, and he 'resolved his faith . . . into the evidence of the doctrine of Christianity, and not into the infallibility of any Church'.[2] Irenaeus was always regarded as favouring tradition, but Stillingfleet concludes that 'his appeal was only to tradition in a matter of fact'.[3] His purpose was to ascertain 'whether the apostles left any oral traditions in the Churches which should be the rule to interpret Scriptures by, or no? And the whole design of Irenaeus is to prove the contrary'.[4] Stillingfleet's reference to Clement of Alexandria has already been noted, and he refers to other patristic writers as well. There is a passage in the book which deserves quotation because it shows the relation of the 'resolving of faith' to the writings of the Fathers and illustrates the form taken by the appeal to antiquity in a Latitudinarian context.

Stillingfleet writes 'it were easy to continue an account of the same grounds of faith, through the succeeding writers of the Christian Church, who have designedly writ on that subject, in vindication of Christian religion, which they unanimously prove to be divine, chiefly by these arguments; from the undoubted miracles which were wrought by Christ and His apostles, from the exact fulfilling of prophecies, and the admirable propagation of the Christian doctrine; all which are particularly insisted on by Origen against Celsus; by Tertullian, in his Apologetic, . . . and elsewhere; by Minucius Felix, Arnobius, and Lactantius; not to mention Eusebius in his books of preparation and demonstration evangelical; Cyril's Answer to Julian and others . . . Only that which is most pertinent to our present purpose, I shall here add, whether is it credible that these persons who fully understood the doctrine of Christianity, who were themselves rational and inquisitive men . . . should so unanimously agree in insisting on the evidence of matter of fact, for the truth of the thing declared in Scripture, and the fore-mentioned arguments for the divinity of

1. *Ib*. p. 246.
2. *Ib*. p. 248.
3. p. 249, and 'where he speaks most concerning tradition, he makes the resolution of faith to be wholly and entirely to the Scripture'. (ib.)
4. *Ib*. p. 251.

the doctrine therein delivered, had it not been the judgment of the Church they lived in that the resolution of faith was into those grounds on which they insisted?'[1]

It is worthy of note that those aspects of apologetic which also appeared in *Origines Sacrae*, and which were so frequently regarded as characteristic of Stillingfleet, and typical of Latutidinarianism, namely, the appeal to miracles, to prophecy and to the success of the spread of Christianity, are by him referred back to the writings of the Fathers. In fact, Stillingfleet's use of patristic sources is greater than has been supposed, and Simon Patrick's statement that the Latitudinarians made considerable use of the Fathers may be recalled. The fact is that men like Stillingfleet and Patrick were far more substantially and solidly Anglican in the full sense than they have been represented as being. Their theological method, while they strained every nerve to meet the demand for reasonableness, was by no means as poor a thing as some critics would like to maintain.

The Latitudinarians have had a bad press, chiefly, one suspects, because their critics have fastened on one aspect of their writings, without a clear understanding of the origins of this, and without apparently troubling to understand them as a whole. If it were firmly grasped that seventeenth-century theological method is dialectic, a truer image of the period in general and of the Latitudinarians in particular would have resulted. Doubtless they were themselves partly to blame, as was suggested earlier, but those who followed them succeeded in obliterating the way in which they adhered with modifications to the common basis of theological method in the appeal to Scripture, to antiquity and to reason. Their own over-emphasis helped, but they were ill-served by their imitators and immediate successors. Tillotson made a vast impression on a century, but part of the penalty of wide and indiscriminate imitation was that there was passed on what was easily caricatured and quickly displaced from its proper perspective. In the same way, their successors, Middleton, Hoadly and Watson, debased the coinage and completely rejected patristic studies, thus disrupting the proportion of that theological method which, because of its dialectic nature, had hitherto held together Scripture, antiquity and reason. This had been a relationship of mutual support and of mutual check, and the Latitudinarians

1. *Ib.* p. 257.

were part of it, just as were Andrewes or Hammond, though with the stress applied at a different point to meet a different situation. In respect of the appeal to antiquity, Hyde, Hales and Falkland dissented in a way which was not the case with the Latitudinarians. Chillingworth was closer to them, and it is not fanciful to see in him less of the spirit of critical humanism which actuated the writers of the Tew circle, and more of what was later to be regarded as Latitudinarianism. But as far as holding the appeal to antiquity in conjunction with Scripture and reason was concerned, Stillingfleet's work fitted into the ambit of the accepted theological method. That he was prepared to use the appeal to antiquity in such a way as to relate it to the needs of the situation as he saw it was in the best tradition of that method.

As already mentioned William Lloyd was another Latitudinarian whose views on episcopacy did not match with those of Wilkins in respect of the proposals for an accommodation which had been put forward in 1668–9 by the latter and by Sir Matthew Hale. Lloyd's friendship with Wilkins was balanced theologically by his equally close friendship with Henry Dodwell, in whose company he visited Holland in 1677. Both had a mutual friendship with Pearson, for whom, after his death, Dodwell performed the same office which Pearson had done for Hales in editing his work. It is necessary to bring out the numerous instances of this constant inter-relationship during the period, as between Laudians and Latitudinarians, for it is the best commentary on the fact that, in spite of varying views on different questions, parties had not yet emerged. The beginnings of the High Church party and of the later type of Latitudinarianism were already visible, and the later writings of Dodwell and Bull's works contributed to this, but until then there continued a constant attempt to hold together in a liberal orthodoxy the appeal to Scripture, to antiquity and to reason. There was a common basis, either explicitly stated or tacitly accepted, and by and large, a common theological method by means of which, although with differing emphases on antiquity or reason, the many questions of the century from church government to the impact of the new philosophy were approached. The emergence of parties was an inevitable outcome of the march of events in the post-Restoration period. The various non-theological factors which made for differences becoming set and fixed along party lines, as between conformist and non-conformist, High

Church and Latitudinarian, helped also to produce what was later to become party theology. It is Every's contention that the High Church Party was an expression not used until the closing years of the seventeenth century because the party so described had no individual or separate existence before 1689.[1] His analysis of the period up to this date[2] has bearing on the fortunes of the appeal to antiquity and the way in which it was applied, and it helps to show how the appeal to antiquity came to focus increasingly on questions of ecclesiastical polity.

In the seventeenth century, investigation of early Church history had brought into prominence the primitive diocese, small in area, in which the rôle of the bishop was that of pastoral administration in conjunction with the presbyters. Various deductions were made from this state of affairs by Independents, Presbyterians and the upholders of episcopacy. Laud himself did not seek any reform of episcopacy on this primitive pattern, nor did he seem to think that antiquity provided a complete system of Church polity, for his concern was with the practical application of episcopacy as a working system. Among his critics, however, Ussher and Williams of Lincoln wished to reduce episcopacy and presbyterianism to a common primitive pattern. In Every's view, the result of this was that 'primitive episcopacy entered into competition with presbyterianism and independency for the right to be called the only true and original Church polity'. Ussher himself was sympathetic to the non-episcopal Reformed Churches but his adaptation to the defence of episcopacy of a type of argument used to assert the exclusive claims of presbytery opened the way for others later to take exactly the same line to show the contrary.[3] (In fact, this is borne out by many Anglican books at the end of the century and the beginning of the next, in which this point of view is rigorously maintained.)

Every points out that Thorndike had followed up Ussher's 'reduction of episcopacy', and that reform along these lines would have been acceptable to Baxter and others, but when Charles II and Clarendon gave indications of moving in this direction in the Royal Declaration of October 1660, a Bill on these lines was rejected in Parliament by a 'significant combination of

1. *The High Church Party*, 1688–1718, George Every, preface, p. xiii.

2. *Ib.* Chap. I.

3. *Ib.* p. 6.

Independents and Cavaliers'.[1] The Latitudinarians were prepared to make concessions, but as Every notes,[2] their latitude extended to discipline as well, and it was on this matter that the accommodation proposals proceeding from them on two separate occasions foundered, for Baxter was not prepared to accept them for this reason. Thus, not only the proposal of Wilkins and Hale, but that of Tillotson and Stillingfleet in 1674, which had a far wider support in the Church, came to nothing. 'On the other hand' writes Every, 'the patristic scholars who followed in Thorndike's footsteps, though obstinate about ordination and often about liturgical issues, were more constructive in the matter of discipline. The exploration of primitive episcopacy was pursued, not by Stillingfleet ... but by Pearson in his *Vindiciae Ignatianae*, Beveridge in his collection of Greek canons, and Henry Dodwell in his *Two Letters of Advice to Theological Students*. All these books were published in 1672'.[3] Dodwell's views became increasingly exclusive, but the general movement of the students of the patristic writings was in this direction. Dodwell's friend, John Fell, produced most of his better-known editions of the Fathers between 1677 and 1684, and the cumulative effect of works such as these was considerable, particularly when the appeal to antiquity was coming under fire once more.

The significance of all this for the appeal to antiquity, from the point of view of theological method, was that slowly it was beginning to become a party matter. Imperceptibly, it was being gradually isolated from the element of reason and from the ambit of liberality, and its sphere of application was often, though not always, narrowed down. Something of this process can be discerned in the writings of George Bull who had been ordained in 1655 by the ejected Bishop of Oxford. Six years previously Bull had left Oxford, having refused to accept the Commonwealth, and he held successively various West Country parishes before becoming Archdeacon of Llandaff in 1686 and Bishop of Laud's old diocese of St David's in 1705. In his books the appeal to antiquity is the chief element, and his expert and extensive knowledge of the patristic period is evident in the *Defence of the Nicene Faith* (1685), which replied to Petavius; in the *Judgment of the Catholic Church* (1694), which was officially commended in France, and in the *Primitive*

1. *Ib*. p. 9.   3. *Ib*.
2. *Ib*. p. 10.

and Apostolic Tradition which was published in 1710, the year of his death.

Bull's concentration on this aspect of theology, however, should not obscure the fact that his first work, the *Harmonia Apostolica* which appeared in 1670, was on the subject of justification. In it he shows himself to hold a view of justification which refuses to depreciate good works and which carries with it the same emphasis on obedience common to the Cambridge Platonists to Andrewes, Laud, Hammond and Bramhall. Bull criticises the Lutheran doctrine of justification, and he was reckoned by many as a Socinian and an Arminian in consequence. The absurdity of the first accusation needed little comment and was adequately disposed of by the publication of the *Defensio*. Nor was it accurate to call him an Arminian, for that admiration for Episcopius and for Grotius which was shared by so convinced a Laudian as Hammond, so scholastic a writer as Bramhall as well as by the Latitudinarians, found no place in his writings. On the contrary, he writes against them for he regarded Episcopius and Grotius as undermining the authority and the necessary function of the Fathers, and he comments adversely on the influence of the Remonstrant writers on such as Laud and Sheldon. He joins issue with the Latitudinarians of his own time, and it is clear that an alignment is gradually taking place within seventeenth-century Anglican theology, with the active upholders of patristic theology beginning to become compact and coherent. It is in fact the first outlines of the High Church party which are taking shape. Bull shares the views on justification of those who, from Andrewes onwards, have been reckoned as Arminian by outsiders. He agrees with their anti-Calvinism, but what may be loosely described as their liberality is not paralleled in his outlook. It is not that his attitude is illiberal, but rather that this whole side of things does not seem to interest him, for his thinking is cast in the mould of the appeal to the criterion of the early centuries. It would not be accurate to depict the habit of his mind as authoritative, for his approach to the patristic writings is that of the period. Rather is it that he sees the theological situation in his day as becoming an ancients versus moderns situation, and he assembles all his evidence to show that the Arian and Unitarian tendencies of his own time stood condemned by the judgment of antiquity. The line runs from Bull to Pusey and the Tractarians rather than to Gore and the *Lux Mundi* writers, in respect of the place accorded to the criterion of antiquity. Nevertheless, for Bull there is nothing of the dead hand about the appeal to antiquity. Rather do his researches in the ante-Nicene writings convince him not only of their agreement with the Council but of their value in confirming the agreement of the first centuries as to the nature of fundamentals. This is brought out in the *Defensio* where he questions the findings of Petavius who alleged that the writings of the earlier period do not coincide in certain important respects with the Council. The line taken by Petavius was that this could be explained by the idea of development. Bull endeavoured to demonstrate the inaccuracy of the deductions and the inadmissability of any idea which implied that fundamentals were not final and were not so held from the beginning.

In spite of the massive marshalling of the evidence by Bull, the suspicion continued to gain ground as the eighteenth century advanced that if antiquity could be made to speak with the accent of Petavius as well as with the words of Bull, it was at best an uncertain voice. There were not a few who, like Waterland in his *Vindication* and in his *Critical History of the Athanasian Creed*, opposed the trend of the times by the three-fold test of 'Scripture, and antiquity, under the conduct of right reason',[1] making full use of patristic writings as interpretative of Scripture. But the rejection of the standard of antiquity by Hoadly, Middleton and Watson, helped on the process of discrediting, and the self-conscious simplicity with which they disclaimed the need of any such support, even if it were effective support, carried weight. The disrupting of the proportion of theological method was coming about and the eventual emergence of parties was assured.

Although patristic studies occupied the main place in Bull's work, his first book which involved him in controversy was the *Harmonia Apostolica* and it dealt with the subject of justification in much the same way as had More and Smith, Fowler and Hammond. The design of the work, which Bull describes as an antidote to solifidianism,[2] is to explain the teaching of the Epistle of St James on justification by works, and to show the agreement between St Paul and St James. As stated earlier in this chapter, he refuses to accept any idea of justification which excludes good

1. N. Sykes, *From Sheldon to Secker*, p. 167.
2. *Harmonia Apostolica*, (1703 ed.), To the Reader.

works. In the manner made familiar by a large body of seventeenth-century writing, Bull claims that the burden of the Old and New Testaments is that the first requisite is obedience, the religious response of the individual which includes good works.[1] He examines the use of the term 'to justify'[2] and he maintains that the faith to which St Paul attributes justification is not a solitary thing but that 'it denotes the entire condition of the evangelical covenant, and embraces all the works of Christian piety'.[3] If in this connection he expounded the characteristic attitude of the majority of seventeenth-century Anglicans, he soon turned however to the practical application of the past to the present. Another situation was then developing, and the works of Sandius, with their Arian tendencies, as he himself notes, 'were everywhere in the hands of our young students in divinity and others',[4] so he set about confronting this trend in theology with what the study of antiquity revealed concerning the faith and judgment of the Church in the first three centuries. This was the origin of the *Defensio*, of which Waterland said that 'the main substance of it is not to be confuted', and which found no publisher for five years until it was recommended by Dr Jane, Regius Professor of Divinity at Oxford, to Fell then Bishop of Oxford who published it, writes Bull, 'at his charge'.[5]

Bull discerned a growing partiality in the times to the ideas of those whom he regarded as modern Arians[6] and Unitarians,[7] and he held that the earlier works of Episcopius and Petavius had contributed to this. It was therefore the theme of his subsequent writing to show the substantial agreement of the ante-Nicene writers with the Nicene faith. Although the connection of the appeal to antiquity with questions of ecclesiastical polity obviously mattered to Bull since Thorndike's work on the subject had led him to seek episcopal ordination, it is not this aspect of the question which appears in his own work. He sees the appeal to antiquity not only as authenticating the final and unchanging character of

1. *Ib.* Chap. II.
2. *Ib.* Chap. I.
3. *Ib.* Chap. IV, §. 4, and cp. Chap. XVIII, §. 6.
4. *A Defence of the Nicene Faith* (1730 ed.), To the Reader.
5. *Ib.*
6. *The Judgment of the Catholic Church of the three first centuries* (1730 ed.), Chap. III, p. 158.
7. *The Primitive and Apostolical Tradition* (1730 ed.), p. 286.

fundamentals, but as the basis of the answer to the minimising trend of the time. Something of this is brought out by his translator, Holland, who found the application equally of value and the need even more pressing by 1725, when he produced an English version of the *Defensio*. He had been impelled to undertake it by the development of the situation which required a full treatment of the subject in English, a point proved by the fact that Nelson and Waterland who had commended Bull's policy of writing in Latin for scholars found themselves constrained to support 'the same principles, he did, in their mother tongue. The successors of Sandius, Episcopius and Zuicker, men as well skilled in languages as they, have discovered a nearer way to their end than mature consideration, and a separate address to the proper judges'. He goes on to point out that 'they have filled all places with their vain boasts of the ancients', and have relied more on popular appeal than on the judgment of those competent to give it, adding 'we have no occasion to cross the seas for men of this mould'.[1]

Holland justifies Bull's practice of extensive quotation by the nature of the subject and because those who take the opposite view make use of a similar method. 'It is pretended by Dr Clarke, Dr Whitby etc. that the Fathers of the three first centuries are on their side', and they quote freely and refer to manuscripts and conjecture about readings. It is therefore necessary, writes Holland, to make clear the meaning and context of passages, and to show how their content agrees with Scripture 'from the apostolical age to that period in which the present creed was declared'.[2] While he grants that there is a certain heaviness in such a procedure, he holds that in such a subject there can be no substitute for a thorough use of sources.

The translator's introduction is of interest from the point of view of theological method because he sets himself 'to give some account of this way in writing, of appeals to antiquity'.[3] The terms in which he develops the subject have a distinct flavour of the eighteenth century and of the later Latitudinarian outlook, which adds piquancy to his approval of the appeal to antiquity. There is something more significant however about it, for Holland represents that solid Anglicanism of the times in that he grasps, as does

1. *The Works of George Bull* (Translated by F. Holland, 1730 ed.). Translator's preface.

2. *Ib.*
3. *Ib.*

Waterland, the importance of the relationship between the three elements for theological method. Awareness of this essential proportion of theology persisted through the eighteenth century in spite of the growth of the partisan approach and in fact it never really disappeared. When the Evangelical and Tractarian movements had made their responses to the needs of the times, it was gradually called into action again and began to clothe itself once more with life and with relevance as the increasing complexity of the human scene made ever-growing demands for a faith 'that was not afraid to reason nor ashamed to adore'. Firmly based on the primacy of Scripture and on the finality of fundamentals, reaching back to antiquity as to a living source of continuity of faith and order, it had and has a creed to offer and a liberality of outlook and a freedom of movement for the human spirit which is not only its attraction but its truth. The two great movements of the nineteenth century contributed much that was invaluable to Anglicanism, and it is probably the case that those contributions could not have been made effectively, after the deadness of the late eighteenth century, without the aid of what may be called in rough terms party theology. But it also seems to be the case that in difficult times during the seventeenth century the spirit of Anglicanism was coping with a variety of equally pressing problems and situations from a more stable centre when it held the three elements of theological method in proportion. Later history from the time of *Lux Mundi* onwards suggests that this is indeed its vocation, for nothing less answers the whole need or goes to meet the situation in anything like its entirety.

Some inkling of what was to follow lies behind the attitude of Holland to the use of antiquity and the kind of reasons he gives for his approval of it. That approval is coloured by the thinking of the times but it shows a capacity for insight into the theological situation and for the evaluation of the various elements. This way of writing, Holland maintains, is not in essence argumentative or authoritative but depends on demonstration: 'it does not formally dispute, where the sentiment is never so argumentative; nor only count names in producing so many persons of the same opinion. It lays down the evidence in its full strength, and then asks, whether it is conclusive or not'. It is clear from this that Holland sees and appreciates the historical and factual quality of the appeal to antiquity, and in this connection he evidently shares the view of

Andrewes and others concerning the factor of time since he regards the early writers as having 'far greater opportunities of knowing the truth'. He agrees also as to the secondary nature of its function, that 'it will adjust the sense of difficult Scriptures, and give us a rational account of the authority of our Bible'. He returns to this point again in connection with the main contention of Bull's work which 'is reduced to the proof of this fact, that the Nicene Fathers did not define or declare anything as an article of faith which was not so from the beginning'. He maintains that 'it is not written in opposition to, or as a supplement of the Scripture doctrine, but as a strong probability that the doctrine said to be contained therein by the orthodox, is the true sense of Scripture'. He adds that 'it claims not upon infallibility and strict certainty, but upon this rational foundation', that it is scarcely possible that the Fathers should not have understood the first principles involved.[1]

The appeal to antiquity for Holland is knit together with Scripture and reason, deriving its *raison d'être* from the one and its authentication from the other. Added point is lent to this example of the vigorous continuance of a proportionate theological method in the eighteenth century by the distinctively Latitudinarian approval of 'this way of writing'. He considers that the general consensus of different writers, languages and designs, 'comes greatly recommended to every modest and sensible man'. It answers to 'the good sense and mature judgment of all men' that such a method should be used, and he regards the appeal to antiquity as being 'really an appeal to the sense of mankind upon the most sacred doctrine of the Church'. These are the authentic accents of Latitudinarian moderation, and it is particularly pointed that he should remark on Chillingworth's attitude to antiquity that no one could 'pay a greater deference to it than he does'. But Latitudinarianism is only incidental to Holland's balanced view of the place and function of the appeal to antiquity in theological method. He had a clear idea of what it sets out to do: 'there is in it no controversy about words, but from the collation of an author with himself, or those of the same age, or others with whom he either plainly professed, or might reasonably be supposed to agree in sentiment; no depreciating Holy Scripture, nor advancing the tradition of the truly Catholic Church; but such a

1. Translator's preface.

temperate procedure, as allows the one to be what it truly is, the greatest authority, and the other the soundest explication'.

He obviously has in mind the position of writers of the type of Middleton, Watson and Hoadly, when he criticises those who claim that the primacy of Scripture is in some way opposed to the use of antiquity, and who make a cult of an artificial simplicity. Under the first heading, Holland accuses those who with 'artful harangue . . . recommend the authority of Holy Scripture, as though it was determined by their adversaries to lay aside that divine book for human and fallible writings. Who would think that after all, no more was intended than to use the best means of understanding the difficult parts of it?'[1] This really is the whole point about the misrepresentation of the appeal to antiquity then and now. There are others, he continues, who 'make it their business to cry down antiquity, not by showing that it is of no use', but by 'gravely proving' what was never in question, namely, that it is not on an equality with Scripture, or what was never denied, that the Fathers are fallible and 'have actually erred in many particulars'. This sort of argument is to put up a man of straw, and he states the traditional Anglican attitude in the matter when he asks 'though the Bible can receive no new force or strength from the Fathers; may it not receive from them some light and explication? Why then should we obstinately refuse our own advantage, and separate things, which may with the greatest benefit be joined together?' It is this supplementary and explanatory rôle which the appeal to antiquity has filled from Andrewes onwards, and for that matter, before his time.

As to those who 'insist upon the simplicity of the most ancient creeds, and decry all subsequent explications', Holland observes that creeds are after all but extracts of Scripture, and only obligatory in so far as they are in agreement with it. What reasonable exception can be taken to the Nicene creed by those who accept the Apostles' creed? If brevity and simplicity are synonymous and are a necessary part of ancient creeds, there is a still shorter and simpler one in the Acts of the Apostles, and 'which Episcopius admires', and will that be a sufficient standard? Explanation of difficulties, in his view, has always been allowed, and 'neither reason nor Scripture encourages us to believe that truth is always upon the surface' so that objections to metaphysical arguments

1. *Ib.*

and implications are beside the point and in any case are freely used by *both* parties to the discussion.[1]

Holland's introductory essay is a valuable indication of the way in which a scholarly country clergyman of 1725 thought about theological method. That there were many like him is sufficiently guaranteed by the later turn of events. Possibly he had a clearer picture of it in the round than had Bull, for the latter was presenting the appeal to antiquity as the counter to a definite line of thought and to its particular exponents. Thus his work is aimed at the writings of Episcopius, Petavius and others, and by this circumstance alone the appeal to antiquity acquired a potentially partisan context. Furthermore, the *Defensio* was written on a specific subject in a particular way in which the use of antiquity was narrowed down to show that Petavius and Sandius were wrong to hold that most of the ante-Nicene Fathers were of Arius's opinion.[2] The whole weight of the evidence of the early writings was focussed on establishing an identity of teaching as between them and the Nicene Fathers. This ancients-against-moderns situation which had been developing caused the whole area of patristic studies to become one of conflict which was far from academic in its implications. Bull's immense learning in this field, coupled with the sense of urgency which he felt at the wrong direction taken as he saw it by theology in his day tended to make eventually for a disproportionate emphasis on antiquity in the house of its friends. These factors combined more or less indirectly to upset the equilibrium of theological method. Although these effects were not disseminated everywhere in the century which followed, they led in the long run to a virtual separation and gradual diminution of the fruitful relationship between the three elements of theological method. That this, as much as any historical considerations and circumstances, lay behind the appearance of High, Low and Broad parties, is hardly open to question.

It is not necessary to follow Bull's treatment of the subject in which his design is to disprove from the original sources the allegation that there is a substantial and significant difference in teaching between the ante-Nicene and the Nicene Fathers. The practical upshot of this was something which reached in all directions, not only to the liberal views of Episcopius, to Petavius with his ideas of development, to Grotius, to Sandius, to Zuicker,

1. *Ib.*   2. *Ib.* Vol. I, p. 8, preamble.

and to the near-Unitarianism of Bull's time, but as he himself remarked, to Socinus. This was the crux for seventeenth-century orthodoxy and Bull saw no stronger support than that of antiquity by appealing to which it could be demonstrated that the alleged difference was a fiction. In the *Defensio*, as also in *The Judgment of the Catholic Church of the three first centuries*,[1] and in *The Primitive and Apostolic Tradition*, Bull set about showing that there was no truth in the suggestion that the Nicene differed from earlier credal affirmations, or in the contention that the ante-Nicene writers differed from the Nicene Fathers and 'were of Arius's opinion'.[2]

In the latter part of the seventeenth century this was far from being an academic question, for in many quarters at home and abroad nothing more or less than a reassessment of traditional Christology was making itself felt. Between the liberality of Episcopius and the radicalism of Socinus there was a wide gap, but to Bull who saw Sandius's works being disseminated and to Holland who saw the next stage developing, the gap did not seem so wide. To them, and to many who shared their feelings of apprehension, the best answer appeared to be that the orthodoxy which was being brought into question was no conciliar formulation but the apostolic tradition itself. This, Bull considered to be the verdict when appeal was made to the writings of the first centuries, 'that all the approved fathers and doctors of the Church to a man, who were before the Council of Nice, even from the days of the apostles, taught the very same thing . . . which the Nicene Fathers determined concerning the Son's divinity against Arius'.[3] To the investigation of the question Bull brought not only an unrivalled knowledge of the sources but an up-to-date patristic scholarship, for his work was not simply a compilation of extracts.

As far as theological method is concerned, Bull gives his views on the place of antiquity in relation to Scripture in clear terms: 'I am, and always shall be, afraid of interpreting Scripture contrary to the stream of antiquity, unless upon the most clear arguments against it, a case which I believe will never happen. The consentient judgment of primitive antiquity would surely outweigh a

1. He looks on this as 'the complement or finishing of the Defence of the Nicene Creed'. (*The Judgment of the Catholic Church*, Vol. II, 1730 ed. p. 105).
2. *Defense of the Nicene Faith*, preamble, (Vol. I, p. 8).
3. *Ib.* preface.

multitude of probabilities and plausible reasonings'.[1] It is evident that for Bull the function of antiquity is interpretative and confirmatory, but the importance attached to the evidence of the patristic writings as against any other kind of argument is significant. In effect, and although this is to some extent dictated by the nature of the subject, Bull's method is entirely historical. He writes that he has replied to Episcopius's position 'from the testimonies of the first fathers and ecclesiastical history'.[2]

At its best the function of the appeal to antiquity is to produce evidence, and the insistence on historical confirmation is its chief concern and its strength. Its weakness, however, in spite of what Holland emphasises to the contrary, is that in certain circumstances the appeal to antiquity can convey the impression of producing authorities rather than of adducing evidence. These circumstances were present in Bull's case where the whole form of his work was prescribed by the subject the elucidation of which called for an exclusive use of the appeal to antiquity. Certainly, he at no time separates it from its illustrative relationship with Scripture, but it is noticeable that he does not seem to connect it with reason or place it within the same theological perspective as Holland does. Bull's translator had a fuller picture of theological method, but it is true that the nature of the task which Bull set himself helped to heighten this impression. His problem was to deal with criticisms of the appeal to antiquity on the basis of the examination of the sources, and this inevitably brought it into prominence. Yet he regarded it as 'a study which next to the holy Scriptures, should be the foundation of all theology'.[3] In a sense, this is no more than Andrewes, Hammond or Bramhall maintained, but there is present in them something which is not found in Bull's writings. Possibly it ought not to be overstressed since they were all-round writers dealing with a variety of subjects and Bull was a specialist. Nevertheless, there is a difference, real but hard to define, as all questions of atmosphere must be. It comes to the surface for a moment in asides such as that on Origen 'who, if any of the ancients, was a free-thinker in divinity, a Latitudinarian father'.[4] It can be detected in a reference, doubtless

1. *Ib.* Vol. I, p. 17 (*Defensio*, Sect. I, Chap. I).
2. *Ib.* Vol. II, p. 103 (*Judgment*, preface).
3. *Ib.* Vol. I, p. 14 (*Defensio*, Sect. I, Chap. I).
4. *Ib.* Vol. II, p. 115 (*Judgment*, Chap. I).

to the Latitudinarians themselves, as a 'sort of men, as mediators, of a pacificatory genius, and an odd design, to bring together contraries'.[1]

The fact is that the clear outlines of Bull's thinking on the subject derive from a close and intensive study of the sources which left him convinced that in the ultimate analysis the position of Episcopius and others could not be substantiated. The evidence Bull assembled was weighty (Waterland held that it could not be answered) and his verdict on Episcopius's *Institutes* was the scholar's one that he was 'inconsiderate', in that he 'despised the ancients' and yet was ready to 'pronounce so boldly in a matter of such importance concerning the opinion of the Primitive Church, before he well knew it himself'. He quotes Episcopius's comment on the 'drudgery' of those 'who are pleased to spend all their time and pains in those wild researches of fathers and councils'.[2] Writing of the way in which Sandius attempts to base the claims of modern Arianism on the spurious letters of Ignatius, he notes that 'any one would believe he had never seen the editions of Ussher and Vossius'[3] or read Hammond and Pearson. His own work shows that he has read and weighed the modern works dealing with the subject from all points of view, and it is his awareness of what is being said and written by contemporaries, and of the implications of the whole subject, which preserves the work from being merely research and turns it into a practical apologia. Hitherto, the use of the appeal to antiquity in the seventeenth century was by and large to substantiate the general position taken by Anglican apologetic. It was used interpretatively in connection with Scripture, and to show that the same attitude to Scripture and the creeds in respect of fundamentals was shared by Anglicans and by the writers of the early centuries. It was used to emphasise the continuity of the present Church with the primitive Church. It was the appeal to a norm or standard within the history of the first five centuries, and to this extent it was historical theology in that it looked to the authenticating nature of evidence obtainable from a given period of history.

The distinctiveness of Bull's application of the appeal to antiquity lay in the fact that he used it to counter the contemporary

1. *Ib.* Vol. II, p. 103 (*Judgment*, preface).
2. *Ib.* Vol. II, pp. 103, 105.
3. *Ib.* Vol. I, p. 79 (*Defensio*, Sect. II, Chap. II).

minimising trends in respect of credal content and the terms in which this had been formulated. He and others saw orthodoxy endangered by a revival of Arian ideas and of the opinions of Socinus in the form of a modern Unitarianism, and he lumped them together as far as their effects were concerned, voicing his suspicions of any spirit of concession or accommodation. For Bull orthodoxy was not so much a primal dogmatic formulation as the original deposit which was safeguarded and preserved by the form taken in the affirmations of the creeds. This was the basis of his contention, and it goes far towards explaining the attitude of suspicion which was beginning to be displayed to modernity by the students of the patristic period. Bull and his fellows visualised the theological situation in their day in terms of ancients-against-moderns. The important point about this, however, was that the issue involved was not that 'the old is better', but that the tendency of certain moderns was to whittle down what Bull and those who agreed with him regarded as irreducible.

It is not therefore in any real sense informative to draw a comparison between the welcoming attitude to modernity of Bull's contemporaries, the Latitudinarians, and that of Bull himself. In fact, what was in question were two quite different manifestations of modernity, the one hostile and the other not apparently so. The one hinged on historical theology which was being called in question, and the other on reason which was being jubilantly heralded as the common ground of science and religion. In one case, a specifically theological situation had to be dealt with, while in the other, it was more a matter of initial adjustment and of preliminary soundings. One was a particular instance, with certain measureable consequences for the orthodoxy which Bull and his colleagues upheld. The other was a question of the diffused impact of a general atmosphere, with a certain amount of intellectual euphoria present as a result of the optimism with which many theologians and new philosophers regarded the rapprochement.

Hammond had earlier been able to combine quite naturally the active appeal to antiquity with the insights of an embryonic Latitudinarianism on some subjects. Bull, on the other hand, was tied to a specific situation, that of the defence of fundamentals in terms of the Nicene faith. As he saw it the situation admitted of no relaxation of the argument and he pressed home the conclusions

of his researches into the writings of the Fathers as much against
the moderate latitude of Episcopius as against the more radical
interpretations of the evidence by other writers. Undeviating in
his adherence to this line, Bull handles the opinions of others
honestly and critically but always paying tribute to genuine
learning wherever he meets it. His work remains an example of
that exact use of sources and thoroughness of investigation with
which theology can never afford to dispense. Not only his own
Church acknowledged a debt to a writer who described himself
as an exile from the commonwealth of letters but whose careful
scholarship informed his own judgment and set a standard for
the work of others.

As time passed, the earlier unity already noted gave place
gradually to a situation in which lines were drawn and the ultimate
result was to limit temporarily the area of effectiveness for theological method. But despite the varying estimates of its usefulness
consequent upon the different situations in which theology found
itself, the appeal to antiquity persisted as a characteristic of
Anglicanism, so that it can still be described today as 'going back
to a consciously patristic approach to Christian doctrine'.[1]

It will have been noted that throughout these pages one problem is of constant recurrence. The problem of authority appears
in differing guise and in a variety of settings, and both its presentation and the solutions offered are connected with each of the three
elements of theological method. Hooker would not grant that it
resided in an infallible book, nor Andrewes in an infallible tradition, nor the Cambridge Platonists in a self-authenticating rationalism. In fact, seventeenth-century Anglicanism, taking it by
and large, saw no solution to the problem of authority which did
not admit of the mutually illuminating relationship of Scripture,
antiquity and reason, and refused any solution which insulated
authority against the testing of history and the free action of
reason. It must be such an authority as can stand investigation and
command freely-given adherence. It must evoke rather than re-
press the response of the individual, and refuse to pronounce on
matters that are not essential. In so far as it was consciously
formulated, it is not an easy solution, but it was the contention
of the seventeenth-century writers that there was no easy solution
which was at the same time true.

1. Gerald Vann, *St Thomas Aquinas*, p. 161.

It has been already suggested in the course of these chapters that the end of the nineteenth century saw a revival of the proportion of theological method in circumstances very like those of the mid-seventeenth century in respect of the impact on theology of new knowledge and ideas in science and philosophy and history. The *Lux Mundi* writers were to the fore in this, and a fitting illustration of the point may be seen in Gore's comments on authority and antiquity in the Bampton Lectures for 1891. In the seventh lecture, analysing the nature and function of authority, he concudes that 'there is then an ideal of paternal authority, the authority which exists to develop sonship; and this is the authority of Christ. St Augustine describes well the character of authority as thus conceived, when he says, that "authority is prior to reason in order of time, but reason is prior to authority in essence". In other words, all legitimate authority represents the higher reason, educating the development of the lower'. Gore goes on to say that authority, as a higher sort of reason, 'stimulates . . . not conscience only . . . but also the faculty of reason and free judgment'. While developing reason it frees it and satisfies it on its own level, for it is above reason and not below it. With the authentic Anglican appeal to the historical fact and to the freedom of reason, Gore shows how these factors delimit authority but only to make it more durable and more real. 'Thus, so far as history enters into the things of faith', he writes, 'and with history the occasion for criticism and investigation, authority must be able to present its historical credentials in a shape which corresponds to the requirements of reason. Its historical supports must be as satisfactory as historical supports can be'. For this reason, and because it is education for sonship, it will not be too explicit on secondary matters for its function is to stimulate the higher faculties.[1]

It is Gore's contention that 'the mind of the Church of England' gives a fair expression to this ideal of authority. The resemblance to the typically seventeenth-century position is clear as he develops this, pointing out that the Catechism is 'a dogmatic basis for education, clear and distinct up to a certain point, but leaving a great deal for the individual churchman to do'. It contains 'the creed as a summary of theology, the Lord's prayer as the type of prayer, the ten commandments with their explanation as a rule of duty, the teaching about the sacraments as a law of church

1. *Ib.* pp. 181–3 (2nd ed.).

membership'. It is supplemented by the services, and the member of the Church grows 'into a clearer apprehension of what he has been taught by familiarity with the Scriptures; on points left doubtful in the explicit formulas he is to form his own judgment'. The end result aimed at is seen in terms of conviction and growth rather than of 'passive acceptance'.[1]

This attitude to authority, to reason and to freedom in things not defined, is parallel to seventeenth-century writing on the subject. The same is true also of Gore's approach to antiquity in this connection. He emphasises that this concept of authority corresponds to that of the New Testament 'in respect of that very thing which is often imputed to it as an objection; namely that it leaves so much for the individual to do for himself, and lays so much stress on historical verification, if not by every individual at least in the society as a whole. I may add that this ideal represents also the method of the early Church. Certainly, among Christians of the first four centuries, in the Church of Irenaeus and Origen, in the Church represented by the catechetical lectures of Cyril of Jerusalem or Gregory of Nyssa, there was a requirement made on the intelligence and patience of the individual at least as great as that made by the English Church even in its present condition. And it needs to be remembered, that in appealing across the ages to the Church of the first centuries we are not appealing merely to a Church which is primitive, but to one which existed under intellectual conditions comparatively like our own'.

This is essentially what Andrewes, Hammond and Stillingfleet maintained, and he agrees with the whole consensus of seventeenth-century writing when he notes that 'two instrumentalities, the Church and the Bible' outwardly represent authority.[2] He writes that 'This is commonly recognised as the Anglican view,— "the Church to teach, the Bible to prove",—and it is, I may say, unquestionably the view of the ancient Church',[3] and in a note to the lecture he draws attention to the way in which the Church of the first centuries made the Scriptures the basis of belief and the creed the rule of faith.[4]

So our investigation ends where it began, with the question of authority and its relation to theological method, but in between

1. *Ib*. pp. 183–4.   3. *Ib*. p. 188.
2. *Ib*. p. 187.   4. *Ib*. p. 252.

Hooker and Gore lies a vast amalgam of thought and event, the thinking and living of the Church through almost four centuries in the course of which something was evolved, tempered and strengthened, which is of permanent value. It is a method, the inward tension of which is neither an accident nor an embarrassment, but the natural expression of its life and purpose. This tension arises not from the attempt to do justice to all sides of the question, but from the attempt to encompass the question in its truth and reality. The dialectic nature of this theological method answers the deep need for catholicity and for freedom, and it holds by an idea of authority which is worthy of its origins, convinced that 'the truth shall make you free', and it is the expression of the spirit of Anglicanism.

In a book on Henry More, recently published, Aharon Lichtenstein refers to the complexity and transitional character of the seventeenth century in which questions of reason and authority constituted the central problems. He comments that, 'the keynote of the period—an Ariadne's thread which guides us through the labyrinthine mazes of seventeenth-century religious thought—is clearly the problem of reason. The rôle of reason, its nature, its realm, and its validity—this is the central axis around which the major religious issues of the period clearly revolve. In one form or another, virtually all the principal developments in the intellectual, religious, and theological life of the age are somehow bound up with this protean problem. It is the crucial factor in relation to the two questions with which English religious thought of the earlier seventeenth century was primarily concerned: the nature of religion—of God, man, and their relation; and the source and repository of religious authority, past and present. Finally, the various conceptions of reason provide a sensitive barometer which measures the significant and decisive changes which took place in English religious thought during the course of the century'.[1] Accordingly as the period is surveyed a pattern emerges which confirms the accuracy of this assessment of the situation during the seventeenth century.

What has been attempted in these pages is an analysis of those

---

1. Aharon Lichtenstein, *Henry More, The Rational Theology of a Cambridge Platonist* (1962), p. viii. This scholarly and detailed examination of More's thought unfortunately appeared too late to be used in connection with the Cambridge Platonists.

elements which theologically speaking constitute the spirit of Anglicanism. Yet those constituents were not evolved in a vacuum or by disembodied spirits. What is so striking is the consistency of this theological method throughout a troubled and significant century, passing as it did through many minds, through epoch-making changes of thought, through the impact of great events and political upheaval, and through the subtle influences of dawning modernity. In this sense it did not and could not escape being part of history and in fact it made use of history. In another sense it has a perennial quality which is altogether independent of considerations of personality and event.

BIBLIOGRAPHY

Chapter I

RICHARD HOOKER: *Of the Laws of Ecclesiastical Polity.* The first four books were printed apparently in 1592 or 1594 and the fifth in 1597, the sixth and eighth in 1648 and 1651 and the seventh first appeared in Gauden's edition of Hooker's works in 1662.

An Admonition to the Parliament and *A Second Admonition: Puritan Manifestoes*, ed. W. H. Frere and C. E. Douglas, 1954.

WILLIAM CHILLINGWORTH: *The Religion of Protestants, a Safe Way of Salvation* (1637.)

JOHN HALES: *The Golden Remains of the Ever Memorable Mr John Hales*, ed. John Pearson, 1659.

LUCIUS CARY, LORD FALKLAND: *The Discourse; The Answer* and *The Reply*, published in 1651 in one volume.

The Unity of the Church of England Asserted (Anon. 1710).

A Vindication of the Primitive Church and Diocesan Episcopacy (Anon. 1682).

Chapter II

PETER HEYLYN: *Historia Quinquarticularis* (1660).

LANCELOT ANDREWES: Collected edition (L.A.C.T.).

ROBERT SANDERSON: Collected edition (L.A.C.T.).

JEREMY TAYLOR: Collected edition, by R. Heber (1828).

Chapter III

BENJAMIN WHICHCOTE: the sermons were published in 1698 and the discourses in 1701 and a collected edition appeared in 1751. The aphorisms were printed two years later and there is an edition of these by W. R. Inge.

JOHN SMITH: the *Select Discourses* were first published in 1660 with a second edition in 1673.

GEORGE RUST: *Discourses* (ed. Joseph Glanvill, 1682).

HENRY MORE: *Philosophical Poems of Henry More*, ed. G. Bullough. A collected edition of his works was published during his lifetime, in 1679.

Chapter IV

RALPH CUDWORTH: *The True Intellectual System of the Universe* (1678); *Treatise concerning Eternal and Mutable Morality* (1731).

NATHANAEL CULVERWEL: *An Elegant and Learned Discourse of the Light of Nature* (1652).

JOHN WORTHINGTON: *Miscellanies* (1704).

CHAPTER V

JOHN TILLOTSON: *Works* in a collected edition (1752).

EDWARD STILLINGFLEET: *Irenicum* (1659); *Origines Sacrae* (1662); *A Rational Account* (1664); *The Unreasonableness of Separation* (1680). A collected edition appeared in 1710.

E. FOWLER: *The Principles and Practices of certain Moderate Divines of the Church of England, abusively called Latitudinarians* (1670).

JOSEPH GLANVILL: *The Vanity of Dogmatizing* (1661); *Scepsis Scientifica* (1665); *Philosophia Pia* (1671); *Essays on several important subjects in Philosophy and Religion* (1676).

T. SPRAT: *History of the Royal Society* (2nd ed. 1702).

G. BURNET: *History of His Own Time* (1734), and editions in 1823 and 1897.

CHAPTER VI

ISAAC BARROW: Collected edition by Tillotson (1683–9); *Theological Works* (Oxford, 1818); *Works*, by A. Napier (Cambridge, 1859); also *Twenty-two Sermons selected from the works of Isaac Barrow*, First Selection, Vol. I (1798), Second Selection, Vol. II (1801).

SIMON PATRICK: *A Friendly Debate between a Conformist and a Non-Conformist* (1668); *An Account of the New Sect of Latitude Men* (1662), probably by Patrick. A collected edition of his writings was edited by A. Taylor.

SETH WARD: *Six Sermons* (1672).

JOHN WILKINS: *Of the Principles and Duties of Natural Religion* (1675 ed.); *Sermons* (1682 ed.); *The Mathematical and Philosophical Works* (1802).

CHAPTER VII

JOHN RAY: *The Wisdom of God manifested in the Works of Creation* (1691); the *Persuasive* (1700).

ROBERT BOYLE: *Occasional Reflections upon Several Subjects* (2nd ed. 1669); *New Experiments Physico-Mechanical* (1660); *Some Considerations touching the Usefulness of Experimental Natural Philosophy* (1663); *The Sceptical Chymist* (1661); *The Excellency of Theology Compared with Natural Philosophy* (1673); *About the Excellency and Grounds of the Mechanical Hypothesis* (1674); *A Free Enquiry into the Vulgarly received Notion of Nature* (1685); *The Christian Virtuoso* (1690). A collected edition was published in 1744.

CHAPTER VIII

RICHARD BENTLEY: *Eight Sermons preached at the Honourable Robert Boyle's Lectures in the first year*, 1962 (1724 ed.).

ISAAC NEWTON: *Principia Mathematica* (1686); *Opticks* (1704).

JOHN LOCKE: *The Reasonableness of Christianity* (1695).

JOHN TOLAND: *Christianity Not Mysterious* (1695).

Chapter IX

John Owen: *An Enquiry into the Original Order and Communion of Evangelical Churches* (1681).

William Laud: *A Relation of the Conference* (1639). L.A.C.T. ed.

Chapter X

Henry Hammond: *Works* in a collected edition (L.A.C.T.).

John Bramhall: *Works* in a collected edition, 1676, and also L.A.C.T. ed.

Richard Field: *Of the Church* (1606, 1610).

Herbert Thorndike: *An Epilogue to the Tragedy of the Church of England* (1659); *Just Weights and Measures* (1662). Collected edition, L.A.C.T.

John Pearson: *An Exposition of the Creed* (1659).

George Bull: *Harmonia Apostolica* (1670); *Defensio Fidei Nicaenae* (1685); *Judicium Ecclesiae Catholicae* (1694); *Primitiva et Apostolica Traditio* (1710). *Works*, Holland's translated edition of 1730 and L.A.C.T. edition.

INDEX

Sprat, Bishop Thomas, 88, 158, 168, 169–70
Stapulensis, 79
Stillingfleet, Bishop Edward, vi, 74, 114, 158, 171, 172, 179–87, 188, 189, 190, 197, 200, 201, 203, 207, 209, 212, 220, 240, 241, 246, 248, 258, 284, 287, 309, 317, 348, 387–394, 397, 412
Stranks, C. J., 50, 51, 53, 66–67, 86, 270, 303
Suarez, 273
Swammerdam, 179, 257
Swete, H. B., 327
Swift, Jonathan, 170, 175, 271
Sydenham, Thomas, 156
Sykes, N., 171, 178–79, 348, 349

Taylor, A., 189
Taylor, A. E., 253
Taylor, Bishop Jeremy, 12, 38, 39, 49–80, 86, 147, 149, 150, 167, 197, 272, 315, 326, 327, 348, 356, 357, 372, 386
Tenison, Archbishop Thomas, 158, 172, 187, 190, 200, 287
Terence, 85
Tertullian, 183
Tew circle, members of the, 356
Theodoret, 79
Theologia Germanica, the, 101, 105
Thorndike, Herbert, 336, 386, 396, 397, 400
Tillotson, Archbishop John, 81, 114, 144, 158, 160, 163, 171–79, 182, 185, 186, 187, 188, 189, 190, 197, 200, 201, 203, 204, 207, 209, 212, 220, 231, 234, 235, 240, 241, 248, 258, 260, 292, 360, 394
Tindal, Matthew, 269
Toland, J., 269, 304
Tower, Richard, 156
Tractarian Movement, the, 198–200, 402
Traherne, Thomas, 116–18, 144, 271, 311
Travers, 332
Tuckney, Anthony, 17, 96–98, 140, 210
Tulloch, J., 98
Tully, 92, 97, 188, 210, 211, 217, 220, 223, 235
Twiss, 32, 325

Ussher (or Usher), Archbishop James, 145, 368, 370, 396, 408

Venantius, Fortunatus, 234
Vesey, Bishop John, 369
Vidler, A. R., 155
Vincent of Lérins, 318, 334, 366
Vossius, 408

Wade, G. I., 117
Wake, Archbishop William, 178
Wall, 149
Waller, Edmund, 12
Waller, 14
Wallis, 169
Walton, Izaak, 31, 32, 34, 332, 333
Ward, Bishop Seth, 167, 169, 200–3, 231
Wendy, Lady Lettice, 245
Wenman, Francis, 12
Wentworth, Earl of Strafford, 100, 370
Werenfels, Samuel, 178
Wesley, John, 305
Whichcote, Benjamin, 17, 18, 73, 81, 82, 83, 84, 85, 86–90, 91, 94, 96, 97, 98, 101, 112, 121, 124, 131, 139, 144, 145, 148, 149, 163, 187, 189, 191, 230, 234, 244, 246, 252, 268, 286, 310, 312, 347, 348
White, Gilbert, 113
Whitgift, Archbishop John, 10, 28, 30
Whittaker, E. T., 306
Wilcox, 3
Wilkins, Bishop John, 49, 114, 148, 169, 187, 201, 203–31, 232, 234, 235, 237, 238, 239, 240, 241, 244, 245, 248, 249, 257, 258, 259, 260, 265, 267, 273, 288, 300, 308, 315, 348, 360, 361, 369, 384, 395
Wilkins, Walter, 203
William of Orange, 158
Willis, 169
Willughby, Francis, 147, 151, 156, 199, 241, 244, 245
á Wood, Anthony, 267
Wood, T., 51
Woodward, John, 156
Wormald, B. H. G., 13, 14, 346, 349, 350, 353.
Worthington, John, 83, 94, 95, 144–152, 164, 167, 170, 187, 244
Wren, Sir Christopher, 169, 308

Zuicker, 401, 405
Zwingli, 5, 79